The Bible after Deleuze

The Bible after Deleuze

Affects, Assemblages, Bodies without Organs

STEPHEN D. MOORE

OXFORD
UNIVERSITY PRESS

Oxford University Press is a department of the University of Oxford. It furthers
the University's objective of excellence in research, scholarship, and education
by publishing worldwide. Oxford is a registered trade mark of Oxford University
Press in the UK and certain other countries.

Published in the United States of America by Oxford University Press
198 Madison Avenue, New York, NY 10016, United States of America.

© Oxford University Press 2023

All rights reserved. No part of this publication may be reproduced, stored in
a retrieval system, or transmitted, in any form or by any means, without the
prior permission in writing of Oxford University Press, or as expressly permitted
by law, by license, or under terms agreed with the appropriate reproduction
rights organization. Inquiries concerning reproduction outside the scope of the
above should be sent to the Rights Department, Oxford University Press, at the
address above.

You must not circulate this work in any other form
and you must impose this same condition on any acquirer.

CIP data is on file at the Library of Congress

ISBN 978–0–19–758125–4

DOI: 10.1093/oso/9780197581254.001.0001

1 3 5 7 9 8 6 4 2

Printed by Integrated Books International, United States of America

Contents

Acknowledgments	vii
Abbreviations	ix

INTRODELEUZE (who and why?)	1
Deleuze in Theory	3
The Box and the Machine	12
The Deleuze Affect	34
. . . and the Bible?	51

1. TEXT (the Bible without organs)	58
Part I: At the Bible Study with Foucault and Deleuze	58
What Is a Biblical Author?	58
Knowledge, Power, Desire	64
Part II: At the Bible Study with Deleuze and Guattari	72
In Flux, in Assemblage	73
The Book of Order-Words	77
A Bible That Expresses Everything While Communicating Nothing	85
How Do You Make Yourself a Bible without Organs?	98

2. BODY (why there are no bodies in the Bible, and how to read them anyway)	111
Part I: The Eclipse of the Ancient Body	112
Bodies Discoursed and Performed	112
Bodies in a Noumenal Night	116
Part II: The Ponderous Weight of the Incorporeal Synoptic Body	123
Nonrepresenting the Synoptic Body	123
What Is a Body When It Is Incorporeal?	127
The Mundane Miracle of Reading (Everywhere Enacted Daily)	140

3. SEX (a thousand tiny sexes, a trillion tiny Jesuses)	146
Part I: The Deleuzian Queer	147
Desiring and Naming	147
The Proletariat of Eros (Producing the Product Society Cannot Want)	150
Part II: Queer Mark	156
The Coming, and Becoming, of Christ	156
The Crucified Body without Organs	163
The Risen Body without Organs	169

vi CONTENTS

4. RACE (Jesus and the white faciality machine)   181
    Part I: The *Matter* of Race   182
    White Light   182
    Dark Matter, I   184
    Jesus in Jackboots   186
    Dark Matter, II   190
    Is Race Structured Like a Language?   195
    Part II: Race and Face   199
    Assembling Race   199
    Facing Race   208
    Defacing Race   219

5. POLITICS (beastly boasts, apocalyptic affects)   233
    Unmethodological Prelude   234
    Tweets from the Bottomless Abyss   243
    Larval Fascisms, Insect Apocalypses   253
    Horrible Hope   264
    Post-Beast Postscript   270

Index   285

Acknowledgments

This was an exhilarating book to write. It was not written in a vacuum (how could it have been? in space no one can hear you think aloud), but rather in the affective bloom-spaces, the cozily nested assemblages of Drew Theological School. I'm immensely grateful for the unstinting deanly support of Melanie Johnson-DeBaufre; the contagious collegial enthusiasm of Catherine Keller (who read and annotated the "Politics" chapter); the more muted, but still vital, encouragement of the colleagues and students who attended my "Sinking and Swimming While Reading My Bible with Deleuze and Guattari" presentation when the book was gestating; and, much later, the students in my cross-area "Poststructuralism and Since" doctoral seminar who gamely waded through draft versions of most of the main chapters. Since they had so little choice in the matter, yet so much of value to contribute, I dedicate this book to them: Gonzalo Alers, Deok Ryeol Bak, Yajenlemla Chang, Brigid Dwyer, Hunter Edwards, J. D. Mechelke, Isabella Novsima, Jane Okang, William Pitre, Beth Quick, Dan Siedell, and Keith Torregrossa.

Yajenlemla also assisted invaluably in the preparation of the book manuscript, and with the index. I'm extremely grateful to Yajen for her indefatigable efforts on behalf of the project. The "Race" and "Politics" chapters of the book owe more to my outstanding Black colleagues on the Drew Theological School faculty than they will ever know; special thanks to Kenneth Ngwa and Althea Spencer-Miller in particular, my biblical studies coworkers.

Deep gratitude is also due to George Aichele and Hannah Strømmen who provided incisive comments and essential guidance at the book's larval stage. Double thanks to Hannah who subsequently appraised the entire manuscript once it emerged from its cocoon.

Steve Wiggins, acquisitions editor for OUP, was a voice of encouragement from the start, and even after the book had been acquired, continued to dispense crucial advice. Project editor Brent Matheny, production editor Phillippa Clubbs, and copyeditor Bob Land were also outstanding.

Each of the book's main chapters was summoned into existence by an invitation. The book project itself, indeed, began to coalesce in consequence of a 2016 invitation by Clarissa Breu and Markus Öhler to participate in a

viii   ACKNOWLEDGMENTS

singular conference they had organized at the Universität Wien. The "Text" chapter would not exist had Jason Coker and Scott Elliott not called it forth for their collection, *The Bible and Theory* (Lanham, MD: Lexington Books / Fortress Academic, 2020). What I wrote for that volume, in accordance with Jason's and Scott's strict specifications, served as the seed for the "Text" chapter in the present book. The situation is similar with regard to the "Sex" chapter. A slimmer version of it appeared in a thematic issue of the *Journal for Interdisciplinary Biblical Studies* that Chris Greenough and Meredith Warren commissioned to celebrate the thirtieth anniversary of the coming out of queer theory. And the "Politics" chapter had its beginnings in an article John McDowell commissioned for a thematic issue of the journal *Religions* titled "Hope in Dark Times." Stephen Ahearne-Kroll and Wongi Park, meanwhile, set the "Body" chapter and the "Race" chapter in motion, respectively. I am grateful to all these friends and colleagues for their motivating invitations, and to the three publishers named above for permission to reprint material in revised and expanded form.

A special word of appreciation, finally, to Gregory Seigworth, affect theorist extraordinaire and authority on all things Deleuzian. His willingness to talk Deleuze with me and his interest in reading the manuscript meant a great deal to me. Thank you, Greg.

Abbreviations

Works by Gilles Deleuze

Bergsonism
Bergsonism, trans. Hugh Tomlinson and Barbara Habberjam (New York: Zone Books, 1991). ET of *Le Bergsonisme* (Paris: Presses Universitaires de France, 1966).

Coldness and Cruelty
Masochism: Gilles Deleuze, *Coldness and Cruelty*; Leopold von Sacher-Masoch, *Venus in Furs*, trans. Jean McNeil (New York: Zone Books, 1991). ET of *Présentation de Sacher-Masoch: Le Froid et le Cruel. Avec le texte intégral de La Vénus à la Fourrure* (Paris: Éditions de Minuit, 1967).

Cinema 1
Cinema 1: The Movement-Image, trans. Hugh Tomlinson and Barbara Habberjam (Minneapolis: University of Minnesota Press, 1986). ET of *Cinéma 1. L'image-mouvement* (Paris: Éditions de Minuit, 1983).

Cinema 2
Cinema 2: The Time-Image, trans. Hugh Tomlinson and Robert Galeta (Minneapolis: University of Minnesota Press, 1989). ET of *Cinéma 2. L'image-temps* (Paris: Éditions de Minuit, 1985).

Desert Islands
Desert Islands and Other Texts 1953–1974, trans. Michael Taormina (Los Angeles: Semiotext[e], 2004). ET of *L'île déserte. Textes et entretiens 1953–1974*, ed. David Lapoujade (Paris: Éditions de Minuit, 2002).

Difference and Repetition
Difference and Repetition, trans. Paul Patton (New York: Columbia University Press, 1994). ET of *Différence et répétition* (Paris: Presses Universitaires de France, 1968).

Essays Critical and Clinical
Essays Critical and Clinical, trans. Daniel W. Smith and Michael A. Greco (Minneapolis: University of Minnesota Press, 1997). ET of *Critique et Clinique* (Paris: Éditions de Minuit, 1993).

Expressionism in Philosophy
Expressionism in Philosophy: Spinoza, trans. Martin Joughin (New York: Zone Books, 1992). ET of *Spinoza et la problème de l'expression* (Paris: Éditions de Minuit, 1968).

X ABBREVIATIONS

The Fold
The Fold: Leibniz and the Baroque, trans. Tom Conley (Minneapolis: University of Minnesota Press, 1993). ET of *Le Pli. Leibniz et le baroque* (Paris: Éditions de Minuit, 1988).

Foucault
Foucault, trans. and ed. Seán Hand (Minneapolis: University of Minnesota Press, 1988). ET of *Foucault* (Paris: Éditions de Minuit, 1986).

Francis Bacon
Francis Bacon: The Logic of Sensation, trans. Daniel W. Smith (Minneapolis: University of Minnesota Press, 2003). ET of *Francis Bacon: Logique de la sensation*, 2 vols. (Paris: Éditions de la Différence, 1981).

"Leibniz"
The Deleuze Seminars: "Leibniz: Philosophy and the Creation of Concepts," Lectures 1 and 2, April 15–22, 1980 (transcript), trans. Charles J. Stivale: https://dele uze.cla.purdue.edu/seminars/leibniz-philosophy-and-creation-concepts/lecture-01.

Letters and Other Texts
Letters and Other Texts, trans. Ames Hodges (South Pasadena, CA: Semiotext[e], 2020). ET of *Lettres et autres textes*, ed. David Lapoujade (Paris: Éditions de Minuit, 2015).

The Logic of Sense
The Logic of Sense, trans. Mark Lester with Charles Stivale (New York: Columbia University Press, 1990). ET of *Logique du sens* (Paris: Éditions de Minuit, 1969).

Negotiations
Negotiations, 1972–1990 (New York: Columbia University Press, 1995). ET of *Pourparlers 1972–1990* (Paris: Éditions de Minuit, 1990).

Nietzsche and Philosophy
Nietzsche and Philosophy, trans. Hugh Tomlinson (New York: Columbia University Press, 2006). ET of *Nietzsche et la philosophie* (Paris: Presses Universitaires de France, 1962).

Practical Philosophy
Spinoza: Practical Philosophy, trans. Robert Hurley (San Francisco: City Lights Books, 1988). ET of *Spinoza: Philosophie pratique* (Paris: Éditions de Minuit, 1981, revised and expanded edition of 1970 original).

Proust and Signs
Proust and Signs: The Complete Text, trans. Richard Howard (Minneapolis: University of Minnesota Press, 2000). ET of *Proust et les signes*, 3rd ed. (Paris: Presses Universitaires de France, 1976; 1st ed. 1964).

Pure Immanence
Pure Immanence: Essays on a Life, trans. Anne Boyman (New York: Zone Books, 2001). ET of three separately published French essays.

ABBREVIATIONS   xi

Two Regimes of Madness	*Two Regimes of Madness: Texts and Interviews 1975–1995*, trans. Ames Hodges and Mike Taormina (New York: Semiotext[e], 2006). ET of *Deux régimes de fous. Textes et entretiens 1975–1995*, ed. David Lapoujade (Paris: Éditions de Minuit, 2003).
"Responses"	"Responses to a Series of Questions," 1981 interview by Arnaud Villani in *Collapse III*, ed. Robin Mackay (Falmouth, UK: Urbanomic, 2007), 39–43.
"Spinoza's Concept of *Affect*"	"Lecture Transcripts on Spinoza's Concept of *Affect*," January 24, 1978–March 24, 1981 (excerpted transcripts), trans. Émilie Deleuze and Julien Deleuze: https://www.gold.ac.uk/ media/images-by-section/departments/resea rch-centres-and-units/research-centres/cen tre-for-invention-and-social-process/deleuze _spinoza_affect.pdf.
"A Thousand Plateaus I, Lecture 4"	*The Deleuze Seminars*: "A Thousand Plateaus I: Deleuze at Paris 8," Lecture 4, December 9, 1975 (transcript), trans. Graeme Thomson and Silvia Maglioni: https://deleuze.cla.pur due.edu/seminars/thousand-plateaus-i-dele uze-paris-8-video-links/lecture-04.
"A Thousand Plateaus I, Lecture 6"	*The Deleuze Seminars*: "A Thousand Plateaus I: Deleuze at Paris 8," Lecture 6, January 6, 1976 (transcript), trans. Graeme Thomson and Silvia Maglioni: https://deleuze.cla.purdue. edu/seminars/thousand-plateaus-i-deleuze- paris-8-video-links/lecture-06.
"A Thousand Plateaus V, Lecture 6"	*The Deleuze Seminars*: "A Thousand Plateaus V: The State Apparatus and War-Machines II," Lecture 6, January 22, 1980 (transcript), trans. Charles J. Stivale: https://deleuze.cla.purdue. edu/seminars/thousand-plateaus-i-deleuze- paris-8-video-links/lecture-06.
"The Velocities of Thought"	*The Deleuze Seminars*: "Spinoza: The Velocities of Thought," January 1978–March 1981 (transcript), trans. Timothy S. Murphy and Charles J. Stivale: https://deleuze.cla.purdue. edu/seminars/spinoza-velocities-thought/lect ure-00.

xii ABBREVIATIONS

Works by Félix Guattari

The Anti-Oedipus Papers	*The Anti-Oedipus Papers*, ed. Stéphane Nadaud, trans. Kélina Gotman (New York: Semiotext[e], 2006). ET of previously unpublished writings.
Chaosmosis	*Chaosmosis: An Ethico-Aesthetic Paradigm*, trans. Paul Bains and Julian Pefanis (Bloomington: Indiana University Press, 1995). ET of *Chaosmose* (Paris: Éditions Galilée, 1992).
Chaosophy	*Chaosophy: Texts and Interviews 1972–1977*, ed. Sylvère Lotringer, trans. David L. Sweet, Jarred Becker, and Taylor Adkins (Los Angeles: Semiotext[e], 2009). ET of separately published essays and interviews.
"Existential Affects"	"Ritornellos and Existential Affects," trans. Juliana Schiesari and Georges Van Den Abbeele, in *The Guattari Reader*, ed. Gary Genosko (Oxford: Blackwell, 1996), 158–71. ET of "Ritournelles et affects existentiels," *Chimères* 7 (1989): 1–15.
"From Transference"	"From Transference to the Aesthetic Paradigm: A Conversation with Félix Guattari," in *A Shock to Thought: Expression after Deleuze and Guattari*, ed. Brian Massumi (New York: Routledge, 2002), 240–45.
The Machinic Unconscious	*The Machinic Unconscious: Essays in Schizoanalysis*, trans. Taylor Adkins (Los Angeles: Semiotext[e], 2011). ET of *L'inconscient machinique: Essais de schizo-analyse* (Paris: Éditions Recherche, 1979).
Molecular Revolution	*Molecular Revolution: Psychiatry and Politics*, trans. Rosemary Sheed (New York: Penguin Books, 1984). ET of *Psychanalyse et transversalité* (Paris: Maspero, 1972) with *La Révolution moléculaire* (Paris: Éditions Recherches, 1977).
Schizoanalytic Cartographies	*Schizoanalytic Cartographies*, trans. Andrew Goffey (New York: Bloomsbury Academic, 2013). ET of *Cartographies schizoanalytiques* (Paris: Éditions Galilée, 1989).
The Three Ecologies	*The Three Ecologies*, trans. Ian Pindar and Paul Sutton (London: The Athlone Press, 2000). ET of *Les trois écologies* (Paris: Éditions Galilée, 1989).

ABBREVIATIONS xiii

Works by Gilles Deleuze and Félix Guattari

Anti-Oedipus	*Anti-Oedipus: Capitalism and Schizophrenia*, trans. Robert Hurley, Mark Seem, and Helen R. Lane (New York: Viking Press, 1977). ET of *L'Anti-Oedipe. Capitalisme et schizophrénie* (Paris: Éditions de Minuit, 1972).
Kafka	*Kafka: Toward a Minor Literature*, trans. Dana Polan (Minneapolis: University of Minnesota Press, 1986). ET of *Kafka: Pour une littérature mineure* (Paris: Éditions de Minuit, 1975).
A Thousand Plateaus	*A Thousand Plateaus: Capitalism and Schizophrenia*, trans. Brian Massumi (Minneapolis: University of Minnesota Press, 1987). ET of *Mille plateaux. Capitalisme et schizophrénie* (Paris: Éditions de Minuit, 1980).
What Is Philosophy?	*What Is Philosophy?* trans. Hugh Tomlinson and Graham Burchell (New York: Columbia University Press, 1994). ET of *Qu'est-ce que la philosophie?* (Paris: Éditions de Minuit, 1991).

Works by Gilles Deleuze and Claire Parnet

L'Abécédaire	Transcript of *L'Abécédaire de Gilles Deleuze, avec Claire Parnet*, dir. Pierre-André Boutang (1996), ed. and trans. Charles J. Stivale: https://deleuze.cla.purdue.edu/sites/defa ult/files/pdf/lectures/en/ABCMsRevised-NotesComplete0 51120_1.pdf.
Dialogues	*Dialogues*, trans. Hugh Tomlinson and Barbara Habberjam (New York: Columbia University Press, 1987). ET of *Dialogues* (Paris: Flammarion, 1977).
Dialogues II	*Dialogues II*, trans. Hugh Tomlinson, Barbara Habberjam, Eliot Ross Albert, and Joseph Hughes (New York: Columbia University Press, 2007). ET of the original *Dialogues* plus two separately published essays.

INTRODELEUZE (who and why?)

Who was Deleuze? Who is Deleuze? And why read the Bible with him or them? After all, Deleuze is the thinker whose posttheistic definition of theology is "the science of non-existing entities" (*The Logic of Sense*, 281). Coming from Deleuze, however, this is not a tongue-in-cheek putdown of theology, a snide dismissal of its insatiable obsession with entities unseen and unseeable—which is what makes the remark interesting. Deleuze accorded more serious attention to the nonexisting—the incorporeal, the virtual, the transcendental—than any other atheistic philosopher one might name. An implacable materialist and thinker of immanence, Deleuze nevertheless styled himself "a pure metaphysician" ("Responses," 42).[1] This is not to imply that Deleuze can be assimilated to, say, Christianity, at least as most Christians conceive of it. He cannot. But neither can most of the Bible be assimilated to Christianity as generally practiced, and to that extent at least Deleuze and the Bible make a promising pair. The paradoxical non-places in between the empirical and the transcendental

> "Empiricism is a mysticism" (Deleuze, *Difference and Repetition*, xx).

and the rational and the irrational in which Deleuze maneuvered so comfortably make him relevant not only to the Bible, moreover, but also to scholarship on the Bible.

To begin with, Deleuze's memorable pronouncement on the disjunctive symbiosis of the rational and the irrational perfectly captures the ineluctable in-betweenness of critical biblical scholarship as an interstitial enterprise with one foot precariously balanced in the halls of academe and the other unsteadily balanced in houses of worship: "Theology: everything about it is quite rational if you accept sin, the immaculate conception, and the incarnation. Reason is always a region carved out of the irrational—not sheltered

---

[1] A metaphysician of immanence? Deleuze's metaphysical is, above all, the virtual, and Deleuze's virtual is enfolded in the actual (and vice versa), as we shall see.

The Bible after Deleuze. Stephen D. Moore, Oxford University Press. © Oxford University Press 2023.
DOI: 10.1093/oso/9780197581254.003.0001

2 THE BIBLE AFTER DELEUZE

from the irrational at all, but traversed by it and only defined by a particular kind of relationship among irrational factors. Underneath all reason lies delirium, and drift" (Deleuze, *Desert Islands*, 262). Underneath, too, lies desire, "investments of desire" that are not simply synonymous with "investments of interest" (263). In short, "the rational is always the rationality of an irrational" (262).

What delirium, what drift, what desire seethes chaotically beneath the unruffled, reasonable surface of a typical biblical-scholarly tome, technical article, or conference paper? Who can say? But the transaction taking place in these staid publications and sedate presentations is most often with wild-eyed prophets, ecstatic seers, mad martyrs, and other ancient proclaimers of "visions and revelations" (2 Cor 12:1). Deleuzian theory equips us to venture beneath and behind biblical-scholarly reason and explore the irrational out of which it is carved,

> **"When delirium falls back into the *clinical state*, words no longer open out onto anything, we no longer hear or see anything through them except a night whose history, colors, and songs have been lost" (Deleuze, *Essays Critical and Clinical*, lv).**

and by means other than the psychoanalytic, as we shall see.

But Deleuzian theory enables us to do much more than that, as this book attempts to demonstrate. One important facet of that additional capability is encapsulated in Deleuze's own most explicit pronouncement on what he takes the Bible to be, a pronouncement that, on the face of it, might seem more appropriate on the lips of a sixteenth-century Reformer than a twentieth-century postreligious (post-)poststructuralist: "For the end of Scripture is to subject us to models of life, to make us obey, and ground our obedience" (*Expressionism in Philosophy*, 56).[2] Appended from Deleuze's statement, however, dangling ponderously below it, is not a *sola scriptura* hermeneutic so much as the still-cocooned elements of a neopragmatic para-poststructuralist theory of language.

But we're getting ahead of ourselves. Once again, who was, who is, Deleuze, and what might it mean to read the Bible—or anything whatsoever: textual, contextual, or transtextual—with him or them?

---

[2] Admittedly, Deleuze is paraphrasing Spinoza here. But there is no reason to suppose that Deleuze himself saw the Bible differently.

Deleuze in Theory

From Not Quite Structuralism to . . . Not Exactly Poststructuralism

Gilles Deleuze, born into a middle-class Parisian family on January 18, 1925,

"Academics' lives are seldom interesting" (Deleuze, *Negotiations*, 137).

dead since November 4, 1995 (when he cast himself from the window of his third-floor Parisian apartment, having gradually been rendered incapable of speaking or even of writing by a suffocating respiratory illness) was a philosopher, preeminently. Personally, I find his philosophy fascinating and compelling. His philosophical magnum opus, however, *Difference and Repetition*, is among the least important of his books for the book I want to write since I am not a philosopher but a biblical scholar, a person paid to obsess about the Bible, to think and talk about it constantly, above all by *interpreting* it incessantly, which immediately puts me at odds with Deleuze, for whom the compulsion to interpret was, as we shall see, a deadly disease, a condition he dubbed *interpretosis* (Deleuze and Parnet, *Dialogues II*, 47; Deleuze and Guattari, *A Thousand Plateaus*, 114, 117). The disease has seeped so deeply into my bones that it may well be incurable. Still, if there are other ways to read the Bible, I will bare my arm trustingly for Dr. Deleuze's needle.

It is not Deleuze the philosopher, in any case, whom I will be reading, and reading with, but Deleuze the theorist, since the Bible and theory—reading the former with and through the latter—has long been my passion. What makes Deleuze a theorist in the specific sense in which that term is employed in my sector of the humanities? Deleuze's philosophy, catalyzed by his extraordinarily creative collaborations with (anti-)psychiatrist and activist Félix Guattari, exuberantly overflowed the conventional philosophy container, incorporating recurrent engagement with literature and the visual arts (even while resolutely refusing to interpret them) and extending into radical social analysis and iconoclastic cultural critique. In other words, Deleuze was a theorist in the classic French mode, not least in his style of writing that regularly leaned into the "literary" with frequent flashes of lyricism and quasi-poetic technical terms (*Body without Organs, dark precursor, line of flight, becoming-animal, becoming-intense, becoming-imperceptible*, and the like).

4 THE BIBLE AFTER DELEUZE

To put it yet another way, Deleuze was a transdisciplinary thinker whose thought still has the capacity to engender effects in disciplines far from his own, even one as distantly removed as biblical studies—which action-at-a-distance phenomenon accords, as it happens, with Deleuze's own conception of theory: "A theory is always local, related to a limited domain, though it can be applied to another domain that is more or less distant. The rule of application is never one of resemblance" (*Desert Islands*, 206). One might add that when a specific local theory comes to be applied in a multiplicity of other domains, some of them light-years away, that theory expands to become Theory, and Deleuzian Theory squeezes in comfortably (but also uncomfortably, as we shall see) beside Derridean Theory, Foucauldian Theory, Lacanian Theory, and other similarly outsized expressions of capital-T Theory (limiting ourselves only to the French varieties). So where exactly does Deleuze fit in Theory's tale?

Who Deleuze once was is not who Deleuze now is. Deleuze came of age intellectually with French structuralism in the 1950s and 1960s, but to the side of it. Which side and why are explained later. But first the symbiotic interarticulations.

It was not that Deleuze dismissed structuralism (initially, anyway) or declined to move in its orbit. His 1967 essay "How Do We Recognize Structuralism?" (*Desert Islands*, 170–92) is respectful even when critical—but before long it is indelibly Deleuzian, meaning that standard structuralist preoccupations are translated into emerging Deleuzian concepts.[3] Relatedly, Deleuze and Michel Foucault, the latter (unhappily) hailed as an arch-structuralist in 1960s Paris, constituted a singularly ardent mutual admiration club,[4] Foucault early announcing, "Perhaps one day, this century will be known as Deleuzian" (a compliment Deleuze would modestly pass off as a joke);[5] and Deleuze, much later, publishing his *Foucault*, a book that

---

[3] One example will have to suffice. "Perhaps the word virtuality would precisely designate the mode of the structure," Deleuze muses at one point (*Desert Islands*, 178), virtuality by then having become a persistent preoccupation of his own.

[4] At least until 1977 when they had a philosophical falling out.

[5] Michel Foucault, "Theatrum Philosophicum" (1970), in *Aesthetics, Method, and Epistemology*, ed. James D. Faubion, trans. Robert Hurley et al., Essential Works of Foucault, 1954–1984 (New York: New Press, 1998), vol. 2, 343; Deleuze, *Negotiations*, 4: "His little remark is a joke" (see also 88–89). Read in context, Foucault's words sound neither flippant nor sarcastic, but exceedingly few readers would have taken them seriously in 1970. As late as 1988, Seán Hand, the English translator of Deleuze's *Foucault*, could write, "Various reasons have been given as to why today there are still no 'Deleuzians'" (*Foucault*, xli). By now, there are probably more Deleuzians in the world than Belgians.

INTRODELEUZE (WHO AND WHY?)   5

translates Foucauldian thoughts into Deleuzian thoughts with suspiciously few rips or seams.[6]

And when the term "post-structuralist" (still hyphenated) is later coined (when and by whom is aptly unknown, given poststructuralism's disdain for origins, but its first tentative usages are trickling into print in the United States by the mid-1970s)[7] and begins to circulate in the anglophone world, and Foucault is "promoted" from (reluctant) structuralist

> **"I have never been a structuralist."[8]**

to (equally reluctant) poststructuralist,

> **"I . . . do not understand what kind of [philosophical] problem is common to the people we call 'postmodern' or 'post-structuralist.'"[9]**

Deleuze likewise has the poststructuralist sticker affixed to his forehead, being included in the first anthology of poststructuralist theory and criticism.[10]

Notable, too, in this context is the symbiotic relationship Jacques Derrida unexpectedly claimed to have had with Deleuze in his moving eulogy for him following his tragic death: "From the very beginning, all of his books . . . have been for me not only, of course, strong provocations to think but each time the flustering, really flustering, experience of a closeness or of a nearly total affinity. . . . Deleuze undoubtedly still remains, despite so many dissimilarities,

---

[6] Foucault had recently died as Deleuze penned the book, and in it Deleuze appears to be performing a postmortem reconciliation of Foucault's thought with his own.

[7] See, for example, Gerald Prince, "Narrative Signs and Tangents," *Diacritics* 4, no. 3 (1974): 4; Marie-Rose Logan, "Graphesis," *Yale French Studies* 52 (1975): 11.

[8] Michel Foucault, "Structuralism and Post-Structuralism" (1983), in *Aesthetics, Method, and Epistemology*, 437.

[9] Foucault, "Structuralism and Post-Structuralism," 448. In contrast, Deleuze's published writings contain no pronouncements either on poststructuralism or postmodernism per se—although he did comment briefly on deconstruction, as we shall see.

[10] Along with Foucault, Jacques Derrida, Roland Barthes, and Paul de Man, among others, all thinkers who, by then, were coming to be seen as seminal poststructuralists. See Josué V. Harari, ed., *Textual Strategies: Perspectives in Post-Structuralist Criticism* (Ithaca, NY: Cornell University Press, 1979). Neither Deleuze nor even Foucault resisted the poststructuralist moniker in this instance, apparently. Harari remarks in his preface: "I am grateful to Deleuze and Foucault for giving me a free hand to edit their [previously published] texts with an American readership in mind" (13).

6 THE BIBLE AFTER DELEUZE

the one among all those of my 'generation' to whom I have always considered myself closest."[11]

That would not have been my own sense at all, by which I simply mean that during the 1980s and 1990s when poststructuralism ruled the theoretical roost, most of all in North America, and increasing numbers of restless biblical scholars (a fidgety flock with which I myself ran) were reading the proliferating literature of, and on, poststructuralism with fervid fascination, seeking to apply one or other French thinker to this or that biblical text, I would have been incapable of slotting Deleuze neatly into my own minimetanarrative of how French structuralism mutated into French poststructuralism, a saga in which Derrida, of course, played a leading role. Deleuze didn't seem to fit neatly into any of the readymade pockets in such a saga.

But when the English translation of Deleuze and Guattari's *Mille Plateaux* began to appear on the "theory" shelves of academic bookstores in 1987,

> "*A Thousand Plateaus*, which . . . was our most ambitious, most immoderate and worst-received work" (Deleuze and Parnet, *Dialogues II*, ix).

I promptly purchased it. It was immediately clear—even from a brief, bemused inspection of its contents—that it ranked alongside Derrida's *Glas* as one of the most exotic blooms to date of the Parisian intellectual hothouse.[12] But it gathered dust on my bookshelf during the next two decades, only occasionally being picked up and peered into, while I busily applied the unambiguously poststructuralist French poststructuralists and their postcolonial and queer progeny to biblical texts.

Tall Tales of Theory Told around the Campfire

"High" poststructuralist theory, however, had lost so much air by the opening decade of the present century that the most notable theory-related development seemed to many of us in biblical studies to be the funereal "theory is dead" refrain echoing from numerous quarters—so much so that when

---

[11] Jacques Derrida, "I'm Going to Have to Wander All Alone" (1995), trans. Leonard Lawler, in Derrida, *The Work of Mourning*, ed. Pascale-Anne Brault and Michael Naas (Chicago: University of Chicago Press, 2001), 192–93.

[12] *Glas* has recently appeared in a second English translation (the first was in 1986): Jacques Derrida, *Clang*, trans. David Wills and Geoffrey Bennington, Posthumanities 62 (Minneapolis: University of Minnesota Press, [1974] 2020).

INTRODELEUZE (WHO AND WHY?) 7

Yvonne Sherwood and I began to write a book on the Bible and theory near the end of that decade, the theory-is-dead rumor seemed to be its logical point of departure.[13] The book ends by detailing what we saw as theory's unfinished business in biblical studies, but mainly by way of the "turn to religion" associated with such Continental philosopher-theorists as Alain Badiou, Giorgio Agamben, Slavoj Žižek, and "later" Derrida, which, simultaneously, was a (re)turn to what Sherwood and I termed big, flabby, old-fashioned words, "among them universalism, democracy, humanism, religion, faith, belief, Christianity, the messianic, Saint Paul, truth, justice, forgiveness, friendship, the kingdom, the neighbor, hospitality, and even, for God's sake, evil."[14]

I did not yet know all that *A Thousand Plateaus* was accomplishing, meanwhile, from its position of dusty neglect on my bookshelf. For still further "turns" were underway in theory, an affective turn, a nonrepresentational turn, an ontological turn, and a nonhuman turn, and Deleuzoguattarian thought was among the most powerful engines driving each of these lumbering transdisciplinary discourses around their respective bends. In a discipline as high-walled as biblical studies, one normally learns of the emergence of such discourses only when they begin to generate textbooks, anthologies, and other field-coalescing primers. One acquires *The Affect Theory Reader*, say, which a friend has enthusiastically recommended.[15] One trawls through "An Inventory of Shimmers," the collection's dazzling introduction (which one will soon be recommending in turn to interested students as "an important work of theory in its own right"), not yet properly aware that the thought-world into which the introduction's opening paragraphs plunge us is Deleuzian through and through, that Deleuze is being copiously channeled even without being named: "Affect arises in the midst of *in-between-ness*: in the capacities to act and be acted upon.... Affect is found in those intensities that pass body to body (human, nonhuman, part-body...).... Affect... is the name we give to those forces—visceral forces beneath, alongside, or generally

---

[13] Stephen D. Moore and Yvonne Sherwood, *The Invention of the Biblical Scholar: A Critical Manifesto* (Minneapolis: Fortress Press, 2011), 2–11. Our main interlocutor in these pages is Terry Eagleton, whose *After Theory* (New York: Basic Books, 2003) was the eponymous exemplar of the "after theory" discourse.

[14] Moore and Sherwood, *The Invention of the Biblical Scholar*, 127.

[15] Melissa Gregg and Gregory J. Seigworth, eds., *The Affect Theory Reader* (Durham, NC: Duke University Press, 2010).

8 THE BIBLE AFTER DELEUZE

other than conscious knowing . . . —that . . . drive us toward movement, toward thought," and so on.[16]

Deleuze's explicit cameo in "An Inventory of Shimmers" comes four pages later and in connection with what will turn out to be a repeatedly recited origin story for affect theory ("Undoubtedly the watershed moment for the most recent resurgence of interest and intrigue regarding affect and theories of affect . . . ").[17] It's a well-plotted, pleasingly symmetrical backstory. The year: 1995. The protagonists: Two essays, each in open revolt against post-structuralist dogma. One essay is a rumination by revered queer theorist Eve Sedgwick and accomplice Adam Frank on the psychobiological affect theory of Silvan Tomkins (as unlikely a catalyst as might possibly be imagined for a post-poststructuralist thought experiment).[18] The other essay is a reflection on affect by Deleuzoguattarian translator and expositor Brian Massumi that transmits and extends Deleuze's para-poststructuralist cogitations on that topic.[19] One dutifully dredges up and peruses both pieces, finding Massumi's "The Autonomy of Affect" in particular to be an extraordinarily original work of theory, an almost casual yet thoroughly forceful break with post-structuralist orthodoxy—specifically, with its particular brand of social constructivism, extending to its general fixation with (human) language and its corollary devaluation of the nonhuman.

Seigworth and Gregg's origin story of affect theory's genesis, then, turns out, when excavated, to yield a larger etiological saga of post-poststructuralism's emergence—or, better, of one of its many emergences, the one intimated associated with Deleuze. Such sagas are paths imaginatively cut through terrain that seemed to most of us who originally traversed it less a trackless waste than an already trail-dissected landscape. But it is a

---

[16] Seigworth and Gregg, "An Inventory of Shimmers," in Gregg and Seigworth, *The Affect Theory Reader*, 1. Deleuzian affect also permeates another field-consolidating text for affect theory, Patricia Ticineto Clough with Jean Halley, eds., *The Affective Turn: Theorizing the Social* (Durham, NC: Duke University Press, 2007)—and not just its introduction but the entire collection (as Clough herself makes explicit: "Introduction," 1).

[17] Seigworth and Gregg, "Inventory of Shimmers," 5.

[18] Eve Kosofsky Sedgwick and Adam Frank, "Shame in the Cybernetic Fold: Reading Silvan Tomkins," in *Shame and Its Sisters: A Silvan Tomkins Reader*, ed. Sedgwick and Frank (Durham, NC: Duke University Press, 1995), 1–28, reprinted in Eve Kosofsky Sedgwick, *Touching Feeling: Affect, Pedagogy, Performativity* (Durham, NC: Duke University Press, 2003), 93–121. The term "affect theory" first appears in Silvan Tomkins, *Affect, Imagery, Consciousness*; vol. 1: *The Positive Affects* (New York: Springer, 1962), 263. In recent decades, however, affect theory has become something altogether different from anything Tomkins might have anticipated or imagined.

[19] Brian Massumi, "The Autonomy of Affect," *Cultural Critique* 31 (1995): 83–109, reprinted in his *Parables for the Virtual: Movement, Affect, Sensation*, Post-Contemporary Interventions (Durham, NC: Duke University Press, 2002), 23–45. We return later to Massumi's relationship with Deleuze.

landscape always being disassembled and reassembled. The tales of auspicious birth, swift maturation, and slow or sudden demise that we tell each other around our disciplinary campfires constitute side trails dug off the main trails, all of them leading to vistas not visible when we first traveled through. We camp on those rises, tell more tales, and cut more trails.

Deleuze and ...

What is solid, then, in this tale of theory I have been trying to tell? What seems unquestionably to be the case is that an extraordinary number of books on Deleuze have flooded forth in recent decades, a deluge that at present shows no signs of subsiding. The "Deleuze and ..." industry has been in overdrive in the humanities and social sciences,

> **"The AND ... between the elements or between the sets. AND, AND, AND—stammering.... An AND between the two, which is neither the one nor the other, nor the one which becomes the other.... The line of flight which passes between the two terms.... This does not belong to the dialectic" (Deleuze and Parnet, *Dialogues II*, 34–35).**

careening from the entirely to-be-expected[20]—*Deleuze and Philosophy, Gilles Deleuze and Metaphysics, Deleuze and Ancient Greek Physics, Deleuze and Ethics, Deleuze and Pragmatism, Deleuze and the Problem of Affect, Deleuze and Becoming, Deleuze and History, Deleuze and the Genesis of Representation, Gilles Deleuze and the Ruin of Representation, Deleuze and Desire, Deleuze and the Body, Deleuze and Sex, Deleuze and Gender, Deleuze and Masculinity, Deleuze and Feminist Theory, Deleuze and Queer Theory, Deleuze and Race, Deleuze and the Postcolonial, Deleuze and the Unconscious, Deleuze and Psychology, Deleuze and Psychoanalysis, Deleuze and Children, Deleuze and the Sign, Deleuze and Language, Deleuze and Literature, Deleuze and Film, Deleuze and Art,[21] Deleuze and Music, Deleuze and Performance, Deleuze and the Humanities, Deleuze and Research Methodologies, Deleuze*

---

[20] What follows is merely a selection, and an anglophone selection at that, from a much larger body of books on "applied Deleuze" (many of whose titles do not follow the *Deleuze and ...* convention), not to mention the extensive *Deleuze, Guattari, and ...* subgenre. There have also, of course, been hundreds of times more articles and essays of this sort.

[21] As with *Deleuze and Philosophy, Deleuze and Literature, Deleuze and Film*, and *Deleuze and Art* may be singled out as stand-ins for many books on each of these topics.

10 THE BIBLE AFTER DELEUZE

and the Social, Deleuze and Marx, Deleuze and Political Activism, Deleuze and Anarchism, Deleuze and Fascism, Deleuze and Politics, Deleuze and World Politics, Deleuze and Geophilosophy, Deleuze and the Contemporary World, Deleuze and New Technology, Deleuze and Science, Deleuze and Space, Deleuze and the Three Syntheses of Time, Deleuze and Evolutionary Theory, Deleuze and the Animal, Deleuze and Ethology, Deleuze and the Non/Human, Deleuze and Environmental Damage, and (why not?) *Deleuze and the Meaning of Life*—to the rather less obvious—*Deleuze and Asia, Deleuze and the History of Mathematics, Deleuze and Architecture, Deleuze and the City, Deleuze and Design, Deleuze and Law, Deleuze and Education, Deleuze and the Physically Active Body, Deleuze and Lifelong Learning,* and on down another long list.[22] Academic theologians, meanwhile, and religion scholars more broadly, have not been slow to immerse themselves in the flow: *Deleuze and Religion, Deleuze and the Schizoanalysis of Religion, Deleuze and Buddhism, Deleuze and the Naming of God, Deleuze and Theology, Theology after Deleuze, Rethinking Philosophy and Theology with Deleuze, Iconoclastic Theology: Gilles Deleuze and the Secretion of Atheism, Mysticism as Revolt: Foucault, Deleuze and Theology beyond Representation,* and so on.[23]

---

[22] A list that immediately begins to sound staid if one strays off the bookish beaten path. Limiting oneself to the Deleuzian *terminus technicus* Body without Organs, for instance, one quickly encounters, "Becoming a Body without Organs through Tuba Performance"; "Deleuze's Bodies without Organs Explained to Children"; "How Do You Dress a Body without Organs? Affective Fashion and Nonhuman Becoming"; "Deleuze and the Body without Organs: Disreading the Fit Feminine Identity" (which is on Deleuze and Pilates); Body without Organs art works and art exhibitions; Body without Organs T-shirts, tote bags, mugs, and spiral notebooks; *Body without Organs,* an online literary journal for teen authors; the Colombian death metal band *Corps-san-Organes* (Body without Organs), whose albums include such titles as *The Deleuzian Century, Vol. 1* and *The Deleuzian Century, Vol. 2*; and the Swedish band BWO (formerly, Bodies without Organs), whose founding member is a Deleuzian philosopher and that has enjoyed considerable commercial success, twice being voted Sweden's most popular band.

[23] *Deleuze and the Bible*? At the time of writing, two books come closest to being full-length studies of this sort: George Aichele, *Simulating Jesus: Reality Effects in the Gospels,* BibleWorld (London: Equinox, 2011), and Brennan W. Breed, *Nomadic Text: A Theory of Biblical Reception History,* Indiana Studies in Biblical Literature (Bloomington: Indiana University Press, 2014). Bradley H. McLean, however, has long been the most prolific cross-reader of Deleuze and the Bible. Recent articles and essays in this vein include his "Deleuze's Interpretation of Job as Heroic Figure in the History of Rationality," *Religions* 10, no. 3 (2019): https://doi.org/10.3390/rel10030141; "What Does *A Thousand Plateaus* Contribute to the Study of Early Christianity?," *Deleuze and Guattari Studies* 14, no. 3 (2020): 533–53; and "The Deleuzoguattarian Body of Christ without Organs," in *Critical Theory and Early Christianity,* ed. Matthew G. Whitlock, Studies in Ancient Religion and Culture (Sheffield, UK: Equinox, 2022), 127—46, one of four essays in a section on Deleuze in this volume. Forthcoming as I write is McLean's *Deleuze, Guattari and the Machine in Early Christianity: Schizoanalysis, Affect and Multiplicity* (New York: Bloomsbury Academic). More than a dozen additional articles or book chapters by other biblical scholars that engage Deleuze or Deleuze and Guattari could also be listed (and several of them are referenced in the chapters that follow).

INTRODELEUZE (WHO AND WHY?)   11

Looming in the mist above the deluge, meanwhile, is a towering irony—namely, that the superstar theorist du jour has been dead since the year when the internet first went public and Bill Clinton met Monica Lewinsky, and the theoretical supertext du jour, *A Thousand Plateaus*, was penned when Iran still had a shah and the Bee Gees ruled the world of popular music. This disjunction inhabits a larger paradox. Aliveness and deadness, currency and irrelevance, electrifying immediacy and shrug-inducing remoteness commingle without combining, like oil and water, in the cauldron of contemporary theory generally. The students in my "Poststructuralism and Since" seminar are acutely aware of the dissonance. They encounter French theory as a series of museum exhibits, as, indeed, do I at this late stage of my life. We begin on what appears to be the ground floor: "Here's Derrida's 'Structure, Sign, and Play,' and there, of course, is his *Of Grammatology*. But wait, if we go down to the basement level, we'll see a lot of the same stuff on display in Lacan's 'The Instance of the Letter in the Unconscious,' even though it's so much earlier." And so it goes on, floor by floor (the postcolonial theory floor, the queer theory floor, the affect theory floor, the new materialism floor . . .), until we arrive at the final corridors on the final floors, all recently added, and with construction already underway on the post-post-poststructuralism annex.

An impressive set of displays all told, but the earlier ones are all dioramas replete with stuffed figures, reconstructed backdrops, and false perspectives. Long gone is the age when French theory was a project in process, when most of it had yet to be translated, when many of the major theorists were involved with the social movements of their day, when many traditionalists in many fields of the humanities felt the French wave, channeled by devotees in those fields, as a tidal force rushing in, threatening to erode the venerable foundations of their disciplines. And their fears were not always unwarranted. That's more or less what happened in literary studies, although not in biblical studies. What has mainly eroded the eighteenth- and nineteenth century foundations of biblical studies is not French theory but liberation hermeneutics, most extensively in much of the Majority World, in which a radical reconstruction of the European model of biblical studies has occurred during the past half century or so.[24]

---

[24] I have written elsewhere about this Global North–Global South divide in biblical studies, elaborating a tale of two disciplines that is also a tale of two worlds; see my "These Incommensurate Activities We Call 'Biblical Studies': A Future-Oriented History of Their Bifurcated Present," in *Present and Future of Biblical Studies*, ed. Tat-siong Benny Liew, Biblical Interpretation Series 161 (Leiden, The Netherlands: Brill, 2018), 274–96. Like many, I believe the long-term future of biblical

12   THE BIBLE AFTER DELEUZE

The Box and the Machine

Boxed In

In the Minority World, in contrast, the foundations of biblical scholarship have remained remarkably solid. These foundations amount to a sturdy set of hallowed assumptions about history and historiography, language and literature, communication and authorship, and representation and interpretation that Deleuze sought to demolish. What interests me more, however, than the monotonous swing of the wrecking ball is what Deleuzian thought equips us to build in the rubble—less another all but immobile edifice (even if that were possible) than an ultramobile machine busily connecting with innumerable other machines. And just as the centuries-old building, a factory for interpretation, produced box-books, the machine produces machine-books.

"There are, you see, two ways of reading a book," Deleuze explains (*Negotiations*, 7). A biblical book, even? Yes, even that. You may, if you wish, if you have been habituated by your training to do so, treat the book "as a box with something inside" (7). That something might be—almost always for biblical scholars has been—the *meaning* its author millennia ago is assumed to have delicately placed within the box. "And you treat the next book like a box contained in the first or containing it," continues Deleuze (7). You treat the Gospels of Matthew and Luke, say, like two elaborately carved boxes, reliquaries, that each contain the Gospel of Mark; and you treat the meanings of each of these larger, grander boxes as meticulous remodelings of the meaning each bigger box builder extracted from the Markan box. "And you annotate and interpret and question, and write a book about the book" (7–8). You place the biblical box-book within your own specially crafted box-book. The fragile, fossilized meaning contained within the biblical box now becomes the meaning expertly preserved and exhaustively labeled within your own more expansive box. You write a biblical commentary, in other words.

I have by now degenerated into caricature, needless to say—and about a methodology (the attempted revivification of ancient biblical meanings, approached as though embedded in amber) that is second nature to me

studies lies in the Majority World, which ever increasingly is the locus of lived Christianity and hence of active engagement with the Bible. Is it finally time, then, to throw in the towel on French critical theory? Not yet for me, I confess. Not while there are still assumption-jolting, exegetical-energy-pumping, ethically important things to say about the Bible and biblical studies that such theory equips us to say and that otherwise might never be said.

INTRODELEUZE (WHO AND WHY?) 13

professionally, that I employ reflexively in much of my teaching, and the exercise of which suffuses me with agreeable affects. But how else might a book be approached?

The Bottomless Circuit Board

You might instead treat the book as a "non-signifying machine," recommends Deleuze (*Negotiations*, 8). The only questions to be put to such a machine-book are not hermeneutic ones but pragmatic ones: "Does it work, and how does it work?" (8). Deleuze continues blithely: "There's nothing to explain, nothing to understand, nothing to interpret. It's like plugging into an electric circuit" (8).

A deceptively simple statement. What the machine-book plugs into *proximately* is more or less describable, as we shall see. But what the machine-book plugs into *ultimately* is so immense and so intricate as to beggar description, although describing that indescribably immense intricacy is the principal project of Deleuzian philosophy, which, more even than that of Derrida, is a philosophy of everything there is, was, and might yet be. The following sentence from A *Thousand Plateaus*, unscrewed from its immediate context, succinctly encapsulates that everything, which, however, is not a thing or other entity but a massive undulating movement, an all-enfolding process: "Everything ties together in an asymmetrical block of becomings, an instantaneous zigzag" (278).

Ultimately, the block of becomings is what Deleuze and Guattari name *the plane of immanence (plan d'immanence),*[25] the "unlimited One-All" (*What Is Philosophy?*, 35)

> "A single and same voice for the whole thousand-voiced multiple,
> a single and same Ocean for all the drops" (Deleuze, *Difference and Repetition*, 304).

---

[25] Its synonym is the *plane of consistency*, which is the term that predominates in A *Thousand Plateaus*. By the time we reach *What Is Philosophy?*, however, the plane of immanence has eclipsed the plane of consistency as the term of choice, and even become the title of a chapter of the book (35–60). Yet a further synonym for the plane of immanence in A *Thousand Plateaus* is the *plane of composition*, which, however, only crops up twice in it (258, 542 n. 52). In *What Is Philosophy?*, in contrast, the plane of composition features prominently and has evolved its own distinctive contours relative to the plane of immanence (see esp. 66–67, 216).

14   THE BIBLE AFTER DELEUZE

that is in perpetual motion, each of its infinite movements caught within, folded into, every other movement "so that the return of one instantaneously relaunches another," causing the plane of immanence to be ceaselessly woven "like a gigantic shuttle" (Deleuze and Guattari, *What Is Philosophy?*, 38).

All immensely abstruse-sounding, perhaps; but the plane of immanence does not float free of the mundane realm of the actual, which is to say the realm of the cultural, the social, the political, and much else besides—an incalculable quantity of much-elseness, indeed, only an infinitesimal fraction of which is human.

More precisely, the actual and the virtual constitute the twin engine of the plane of immanence, the actual endlessly unfolding from the virtual and the virtual in turn endlessly reenfolding within the actual.[26] This is not to say that the actual is where the transcendental air-filled rubber of the plane of immanence meets the material road of the real so much as to say that the rubber and the road coconstitute each other continually. As its name implies, the plane of immanence does all that it does (which is to say, everything) without ever once lifting off from the material. How could it, since it is, indeed, coextensive with "the material universe" (Deleuze, *Cinema 1*, 59). And why would it, since the plane of immanence is nothing other than "the plane of matter" itself (61)?

Ultimately, then, this is the bottomless circuit board into which Deleuze casually recommends in *Negotiations* (8) that the machine-book be plugged. What of the machine-Book of books which we biblical scholars have clutched so long to our chests, staggering under its stupendous weight, its unused power cord dangling limply below it, threatening to trip us up? What might be the potential payoff for plugging that cord into Deleuze's cosmic electronic circuit of unceasing interimplication and unbounded interimbrication?

History and Becoming

The payoff may be expressed in a word, or two words, that Deleuze himself seldom if ever used: *freedom, liberation*.[27] As emerged particularly in

---

[26] A process elaborated and illustrated periodically in this book; see, for example, pp. 129–130, 139–140, and 158–160.

[27] Which has not prevented certain theologians, most notably Kristien Justaert, from staging dialogues between Deleuzian thought and liberation theology; see especially her "Liberation Theology: Deleuze and Althaus-Reid," *SubStance* 39, no. 1 (2010): 154–64, together with her *Theology after Deleuze*, Deleuze Encounters (New York: Continuum, 2012), 119–30.

INTRODELEUZE (WHO AND WHY?)   15

his work with Guattari, he preferred words or phrases like *deterritorialization* or *line of flight*. In *A Thousand Plateaus*, indeed, these terms, together with their synonyms[28] (*becoming, rhizomatic, nomadic, smooth space, speeds, destratification, the molecular, the Body without Organs, probe-heads, the plane of consistency / the plane of immanence*, and others too numerous to name), their antonyms (*territorialization, reterritorialization, apparatus of capture, arboreal, sedentary, striated space, slownesses, stratification, the molar, the organism, faciality, the plane of organization*), and the synonyms of those antonyms, recur with such obsessive regularity as to form the basic vocabulary of "Deleuzoguattarese."

Deleuze and Guattari would likely have concurred with Foucault when he declares, "All my analyses are against the idea of universal necessities in human existence. They show the arbitrariness of institutions and show which space of freedom we can still enjoy and how many changes can still be made."[29] If anything, indeed, Deleuze and Guattari were yet more allergic to supposed universal necessities and entrenched institutions, but their avenue of approach to such assumptions and conventions was more insistently micropolitical and microhistorical

> "On the one hand, *masses or flows*, with their . . . quanta of deterritorialization . . . ; on the other hand, *classes or segments*, with their binary organization. . . . The difference between macrohistory and microhistory has nothing to do with . . . durations . . . , long or short" (*A Thousand Plateaus*, 221).

than that of Foucault. For all his acute sensitivity to the microphysics of power, Foucault arguably possessed a level of comfort with historiography in the metanarrative mode (most of his major books hinge on sweeping historical narratives) that was conspicuously lacking in Deleuze and Guattari.[30] The successive chapter titles alone of *A Thousand Plateaus* read like fragments of a noncumulative counter-metanarrative: "1914: One or Several Wolves?"; "10,000 B.C.: The Geology of Morals (Who Does the Earth Think It Is?")"; "November 20, 1923: Postulates of Linguistics"; "587 B.C.–A.D. 70: On

[28] More precisely, their nonsynonymous synonyms (to adapt a concept from Derrida).

[29] Michel Foucault, "Truth, Power, Self: An Interview," in *Technologies of the Self: A Seminar with Michel Foucault*, ed. Luther H. Martin, Huck Gutman, and Patrick H. Hutton (Amherst: University of Massachusetts Press, 1988), 11.

[30] So it seems to me, at any rate. Deleuze himself, however, lavished the benefit of the doubt on Foucault in this matter; see, for example, Deleuze, *Foucault*, 21–22, 116–17; *Negotiations*, 94–95.

16 THE BIBLE AFTER DELEUZE

Several Regimes of Signs"; "November 28, 1947: How Do You Make Yourself a Body without Organs"; "Year Zero: Faciality," and so on.[31]

In a dialogue with Marxist philosopher Antonio Negri, Deleuze reflected how, in the wake of May 1968—that momentous eruption in France of mass student demonstrations and occupations, trade union strikes, and general leftist activism that brought the authoritarian de Gaulle government to its knees and the economy to a grinding halt—he became ever more aware of the necessity "of distinguishing between becoming and history," of attending to the "nonhistorical cloud" that envelops every historical event (Deleuze, *Negotiations*, 170). "What history [as a discursive labor] grasps in an event is the way it's actualized in particular circumstances," but "the event's becoming is beyond the scope of history" (170). To begin to reassemble the becoming of a particular peasant revolt, say, what one first "needs to know is which peasants, in which areas of the south of France, stopped greeting the local landowners" (Deleuze and Guattari, *A Thousand Plateaus*, 216).

What of the peasant revolt of sorts that was the Jesus movement? How might the Deleuzian concept of becoming interface or interlace with proto-Christian historiography? Briefly stated, each of the New Testament Gospels, to a greater or lesser extent, present us with literary reassemblings of the lost originary events, installing their audiences in those events "as in a becoming" (Deleuze and Guattari, *What Is Philosophy?*, 111),[32] while modern scholars of earliest Christianity typically labor to translate those affective ephemera into History.

Consider Jesus's first appearance in the Gospel of John following the mythological fanfare of its prologue (1:1–18), a descent from heaven to earth so abrupt as to raise a cloud of dust. "Rabbi . . . , where are you staying [*pou meneis*]?," two of the Baptist's disciples ask the captivating stranger whose advent has elicited cryptic words from their teacher (1:29–36), and they receive a wink and a coy invitation in response: "Come and see!" (1:38–39a).[33] They take off after him, the story hurrying along behind to catch up with them, and the saga, the *history*, of earliest Christianity lumbering still farther behind,

---

[31] Deleuze and Guattari also specify that the chapters, or "plateaus," do not have to be read in any particular order (*A Thousand Plateaus*, xx).

[32] Deleuze and Guattari are not, however, reflecting on proto-Christian becomings. In addition to my own brief experiment with such reflection in what follows, see Dong Hyeon Jeong, "Jesus' 'Triumphal Entry' as Flash Mob Event: Molecular 'r'evolution in Mark 11:1-11," *The Bible and Critical Theory* 15, no. 2 (2019): 109-27.

[33] Throughout this book, when not venturing my own translations of the biblical material I quote, I use the New Revised Standard Version (as here).

> "All history does is to translate a coexistence of becomings into a succession" (Deleuze and Guattari, *A Thousand Plateaus*, 430).

almost immediately losing the trail altogether.

What is being narrated here, however, is as momentous as it is mundane. To put a grandiose spin on the quotidian encounter between the attractive stranger and his soon-to-be disciples (and again with words borrowed from Deleuze and Guattari), "it launches a people, an earth, like the arrow and discus of a new world that is neverending, that is always in the process of coming about" (*What Is Philosophy?*, 112). The ephemeral encounter marks the forever lost beginning of a singular social experiment, a beginning that, as such, unfolds in an "unhistorical vapor" (112). For "history is not experimentation, it is only the set of almost negative conditions that makes possible the experimentation of something that escapes history" (111).[34] The Johannine narrative plunges us into a becoming rather than a history,

> "Becoming begins in history and returns to it, but it is not of history. The opposite of history is not the eternal, but becoming" (Deleuze, *Two Regimes of Madness*, 377).

an affective ambience rather than an origin. The Johannine "call of the first disciples" is microhistorical no less than micropolitical. On reading it or hearing it read, we descend "into a world of microdeterminations, attractions, and desires" (Deleuze and Guattari, *A Thousand Plateaus*, 221), a flowing world too fine-grained for macrohistory's large-mesh net. With microhistory, in contrast, "there is a sense of history as possibility, the multiplicity of what is possible, the profusion of multiple possibilities at every moment" (Deleuze, *Two Regimes of Madness*, 200).

The "historian" among the evangelists, meanwhile, the author whom tradition named Luke, himself attempts to transform becoming into history in a manner that is instructive in its inelegance. A thoroughly pivotal, altogether elusive, and entirely vaporous event is encapsulated as follows by this author: "the word of God came [*egeneto rhēma theou*] to John son of Zechariah in the wilderness" (3:2b). But Luke attempts to seal the vapor within a monumental historical mausoleum, one richly engraved with despotic names,

---

[34] That is why "becomings are much more important than history in *A Thousand Plateaus*" (Deleuze, *Negotiations*, 30).

18 THE BIBLE AFTER DELEUZE

all assembled under the implicit inscription ROMAN HISTORY: "In the fifteenth year of the reign of Emperor Tiberius, when Pontius Pilate was governor of Judea, and Herod was tetrarch of Galilee, and his brother Philip tetrarch of the region of Iturea and Trachonitis, and Lysanias tetrarch of Abilene,[35] during the high-priesthood of Annas and Caiaphas, the word of God came to John . . ." (3:1–2). Luke thereby tries, and fails, to assimilate becoming to history, the vibrantly virtual to the repressively actual, the unknowably new to the all-too-well-known, the micropolitical to the macropolitical, the molecular to the molar.

Let us return to France and to May 1968, which, as it happens, exploded within the "imperial presidency" of Charles de Gaulle, as it is commonly called, and a concomitant "politics of grandeur" that a Roman emperor would not have found uncongenial. Deleuze and Guattari disassemble the molecular politics of the event as follows:

> From the viewpoint of micropolitics, a society is defined by its lines of flight, which are molecular. There is always something that flows or flees, that escapes the binary organizations, the resonance apparatus, and the overcoding machine. . . . May 1968 in France was molecular, making what led up to it all the more imperceptible from the viewpoint of macropolitics. . . . Those who evaluated things in macropolitical terms understood nothing of the event because something unaccountable was escaping. The politicians, the parties, the unions, many leftists, were utterly vexed. . . . It was as though they had been temporarily deprived of the entire dualism machine that made them valid spokespeople. . . . A molecular flow was escaping, miniscule at first, then swelling, without, however, ceasing to be unassignable. The reverse, however, is also true: molecular escapes and movements would be nothing if they did not return to the molar organizations to reshuffle their segments, their binary distributions of sexes, classes, and parties. (*A Thousand Plateaus*, 216–17)

This is as macropolitical as Deleuze and Guattari, or Deleuze solo, ever get.[36] There will likely never be a micropolitical party on any election ballot, and

---

[35] To imagine that we switch from "Roman History" to "Jewish History" after the mention of Pontius Pilate would be misleading, to the extent that Herod Antipas, his half-brother Philip, and Lysanias were each Roman client rulers, and the high priests Annas and his son-in-law Caiaphas were both Roman appointees.

[36] In their books, anyway. Interviews and position pieces do address macropolitics on occasion, such as several items in Deleuze's *Two Regimes of Madness*, not least his "The Gulf War: A Despicable War" (375–76).

one doesn't read Deleuze and/or Guattari for macropolitical manifestos. Yet their multifaceted micropolitical thought experiments do dovetail with many macropolitical liberation movements, if only to further radicalize the concepts of freedom that fuel such struggles

"The American Revolution failed long before the Soviet Revolution. Revolutionary situations and experiments are engendered by capitalism itself" (Deleuze, *Two Regimes of Madness*, 379).

or to name previously unacknowledged forms of oppression that also require resistance. In the "Year Zero: Faciality" chapter (or plateau) of *A Thousand Plateaus*, to name but one such instance (and one to which I devote a chapter of my own later), it is not only white-on-Black-or-brown racism that is in Deleuze and Guattari's analytic sights; their ultimate target is the "abstract machine" that produces faces of whatever kind, of whatever color; and they urge a dismantling of the face altogether and passage into a postfacial future.

Interpretosis: Symptoms and Treatment

But let us return to texts and the reading of texts. Like most biblical scholars, my body begins to twitch alarmingly if separated too long from the moldering stack of ancient literary texts that are our bread and butter and the addictive delight of devouring them by deciphering them. But deciphering was not the preferred Deleuzian strategy for reading literary texts, as we have already glimpsed. On the one hand, Deleuze did have an intense relationship with literature,

"One sometimes gets the impression that it's through literature more than ... philosophy that you inaugurate a new kind of thinking" (Parnet to Deleuze in *L'Abécédaire*, n.p.).

so much so that "literature is everywhere present in [his] work" (Deleuze, *Negotiations*, 142). On the other hand, Deleuze did not aspire to *interpret* literature, hence much of the interest of his interactions with literary texts—and the refreshing conundrum his reading practice poses for the interpretation-sodden field of biblical studies. For Deleuze did read literature, and even read it closely. But how does one read closely and critically without interpreting?

20 THE BIBLE AFTER DELEUZE

The question would likely induce a yawn in many denizens of literature departments whose academic titles might suggest to the uninitiated that the quest for ever improved interpretations of their specialist bodies of literature is precisely their professional raison d'être. One such professor is even laughing as he yawns. "At present I really can't imagine what a 'new interpretation' of *Robinson Crusoe* would look like," he chuckles. "So we're on to the myriad of other things you can do with texts, other than talking about their 'meaning.'"[37] Biblical scholars are less likely to be amused. For our part, we really can't imagine a professional world *without* periodic new interpretations of Genesis 1:28, Isaiah 53, Job 19:25–27, Mark 16:8, Romans 1:26–27, Revelation 17:9-11, or any of the myriad of other biblical passages, verses, or partial verses (Leviticus 16:21c, anyone?) that we find so utterly absorbing as to happily devote entire summers to coming up with yet further interpretations of them to add to the already teetering piles of past interpretations. But what else might we do with our texts during our summers or where else might we go with them? Deleuze again is our tour guide.

As a philosopher of pure immanence, pitilessly hostile to the transcendent[38] in all its guises,

"Transcendence, vertical Being, imperial State in the sky or on earth"
(Deleuze and Guattari, *What Is Philosophy?*, 43).

not least that of interiority (divine transcendence turned inside out and surreptitiously smuggled within the human),[39] Deleuze is unsurprisingly unsympathetic to any depth hermeneutic predicated upon an interiorized

[37] Jeffrey Nealon, "Jeffrey Nealon," in *The Rebirth of American Literary Theory and Criticism: Scholars Discuss Intellectual Origins and Turning Points*, ed. H. Aram Veeser (New York: Anthem Press, 2020), 231. Some years earlier, Nealon had detailed what he termed the "anti-hermeneutic" thrust in literary studies, and at the head of the long list of what he saw as its main catalysts were "critical theories invested in Deleuze and Guattari." Jeffrey T. Nealon, *Post-Postmodernism, or, the Cultural Logic of Just-in-Time Capitalism* (Stanford, CA: Stanford University Press, 2012), 126–45 (quotation from 132).

[38] Although not the *transcendental*, which Deleuze, following Kant, distinguishes from the *transcendent*. Deleuze conceives of the transcendental as fully immanent, hence *transcendental empiricism*, his paradoxical name for his philosophical project (*Difference and Repetition*, 56–57, 143–44). In Deleuze's final essay, "Immanence: A Life," "the transcendental field" becomes (another) synonym for the plane of immanence (*Pure Immanence*, 26).

[39] Deleuze's campaign against interiority is already underway in his 1946 article "From Christ to the Bourgeoisie," published when he was only twenty-one. Intriguingly, the article argues that the Synoptic Christ embodies an external spirituality: "[Christ's] presence . . . imposes itself on the open road, . . . in the fields, by the sudden revelation of a possible world. . . . The paradox of the Gospel is the exteriority of an interiority," a paradox "essentially expressed in the notion of parable" (Deleuze, *Letters and Other Texts*, 268–69).

INTRODELEUZE (WHO AND WHY?)   21

concept of meaning. To interpret, for Deleuze—to excavate, dredge up, or otherwise recover putatively lost or hidden meanings—is to make a fetish of the unseen, the opaque, the esoteric, the phantasm: in a word, the *secret* (Deleuze and Parnet, *Dialogues II*, 46–47). Books become boxes, as we saw earlier, reliquaries for secret meanings, even, or especially, the books within the Book of books, the Box of boxes; and the long-stored semantic contents of those stacked biblical boxes must, in consequence, now be delicately extracted, whole and entire, without damaging them. Interpretation-fixation was a disease, for Deleuze, one he named interpretosis, as we already noted.[40]

But Deleuze himself was an interpretosis survivor. His 1964 book *Proust and Signs* was dedicated to the meticulous interpretation of those titular signs. "To learn is first of all to consider a substance, an object, a being as if it emitted signs to be deciphered, interpreted," the book's introduction announced (4). "Everything that teaches us something emits signs; every act of learning is an interpretation of signs or hieroglyphs" (4).

But that was before Gilles met Félix. Among the many things Deleuze borrowed from Guattari (never to return) was the *machine*,

> "The emergence of the machine marks a date, a change, different from a structural representation" (Guattari, *Molecular Revolution*, 112).[41]

a concept Deleuze used to hone the edges of his emerging antihermeneutic. *Proust and Signs* went through two expanded editions in consequence. The 1976 edition contained an entire new Part II comprising five chapters and titled "The Literary Machine." Introducing that machine, Deleuze stated, "To the *logos* . . . whose meaning must be discovered in the whole and to which it belongs, is opposed the antilogos, machine and machinery whose meaning (anything you like) depends solely on its functioning." As such, the literary machine poses "no problem of meaning" but "only a problem of use" (*Proust and Signs*, 146). Pragmatics displaces semantics, and function displaces interpretation.

What the literary machine functions to produce—and it is a machine precisely because it produces (*Proust and Signs*, 146)[42]—are *effects*. More

---

[40] See p. 3 earlier.

[41] The borrowing was, however, reciprocal. Guattari's "Machine and Structure," quoted here, was a 1969 paper (published in 1971) in which Guattari, prior to meeting Deleuze, drew on Deleuze's *Difference and Repetition* and *The Logic of Sense* to fuel his machine concept.

[42] The neo-Marxist factory-floor origins of the machine megatrope are very much in evidence in Guattari's "Machine and Structure" (*Molecular Revolution*, 111–19).

22   THE BIBLE AFTER DELEUZE

precisely, it produces "literary effects" that are analogous to "electric effect[s]" or "electromagnetic effect[s]" (153). Deleuze might equally have said that literature is a machine for producing *affects*. Indeed, Deleuze and Guattari do say as much many years later. Artists, not least literary artists, "are presenters of affects, the inventors and creators of affects" (*What Is Philosophy?*, 175). And such affects are indeed electrifying. They generate, and manifest themselves within, "compounds of sensations that transform themselves, vibrate, couple, or split apart" (175).

Deleuze and Claire Parnet had earlier described in the following terms the being—or, better, the becoming—of characters in the literature that most interested them: "They are collections of intensive sensations, each is such a collection, a packet, a bloc of variable sensations" (*Dialogues II*, 39–40). To assume, however, that these sensations are purely subjective, that they flash and sputter only within the individual interiority of the reader, would be to miss the distinctive Deleuzian point. Sensations are creatures of the interstice,

> **"Sensation has one face turned toward the subject (the nervous system, . . . 'instinct,' 'temperament' . . .), and one face turned toward the object (the 'fact,' the place, the event). Or rather, it has no faces at all, it is both things indissolubly, it is Being-in the World, as the phenomenologists say" (Deleuze, *Francis Bacon*, 31).**

the in-between. But they are also creatures of the outside. Sensations emerge between the literary work and its audience, so that work and audience—and, tenuously tethered to both of them, the work's producer, its author—constitute a single body of sensation, a seething, continuously changing symbiosis that exceeds all three agents and assumes a life of its own independent from any of them. Think, for example, of the theopolitical reception histories of the book of Exodus or the book of Revelation—less linear histories, however, than zigzagging series of discontinuous becomings and consequential collective sensations. The final chapter of the present book attempts to follow Revelation's darting, flowing, sensation-suffused passage through the swampland of recent US politics.

Deleuze and Guattari's term for this process of fusion, separation, and unbounded becoming, not least as it pertains to literature, is *affect* (*What Is Philosophy?*, 173). Literature invents previously "unknown or unrecognized affects and brings them to light as the becoming of . . . characters"

INTRODELEUZE (WHO AND WHY?) 23

(174)—Eve, Moses, David, Mary, Jesus, Paul . . .—such becomings symbiotically enfolding with the becomings of audiences

> "I *become* in the sensation and something *happens* through the sen-
> sation, one through the other, one in the other" (Deleuze, *Francis*
> *Bacon*, 31).

and, retrojectively, of authors, in an "enterprise of co-creation" that is a singular instance of the capacity of life to continually generate "zones" in which
"living beings whirl around" each other endlessly (Deleuze and Guattari,
What Is Philosophy?, 173). Within the "zone of indetermination, of indiscernibility" that literature creates,

> "This is a 'logic of the senses' . . . which is neither rational nor cerebral"
> (Deleuze, *Francis Bacon*, 37).

authors, works, and audiences "endlessly reach that point that immediately precedes their natural differentiation" (Deleuze and Guattari, *What Is*
Philosophy?, 173), so that Paul, for instance, writing before the emergence of
the narrative gospels, might well be speaking for innumerable readers-and-
hearers-to-come of the crucifixion sequence in those gospels, that singularly
intense bloc of all but unbearable sensations, when he says, "I have been crucified with Christ, and it is no longer I who live but Christ who lives in me"
(Gal 3:19–20). And this, too, "is what is called an affect" (173).

The literary machine is a producer of affects, then. As a machine, moreover, literature raises "no problem of meaning" but "only a problem of use."
So Deleuze argued in the machine-enabled expansion of *Proust and Signs*
(146), as we already saw. Guattari, meanwhile, also writing on Proust, was
saying such things as that "readers of the *Recherche* . . . do not read a book,
they use a tool" (*The Machinic Unconscious*, 303). "One does not interpret a
content" in this machine-book; rather, "one makes it work" by activating it as
"a pragmatic field, a knot of machinic propositions" (304).[43]

From such individual pronouncements it was but a short step to the
dual-authored antihermeneutic manifesto with which *A Thousand Plateaus*

---

[43] My simplifying summary of Guattari's immensely dense and extraordinarily rich engagement
with Proust's novel (*The Machinic Unconscious*, 229–331), which, unlike Deleuze's engagement with
it, reads like a spillover from *A Thousand Plateaus*.

24 THE BIBLE AFTER DELEUZE

begins. "We will never ask what a book means, as signified or signifier," Deleuze and Guattari announced;

> we will not look for anything to understand in it. We will ask what it functions with, in connection with what other things it does or does not transmit intensities,[44] in which other multiplicities its own are inserted and metamorphosed, and with what Bodies without Organs[45] it makes its own converge. A book exists only through the outside and on the outside. So a book itself is a little machine [*Ainsi, un livre étant lui-même une petite machine*]. . . . The only question is which other machine the literary machine can be plugged into, must be plugged into in order to work. (4)[46]

This is not simply a lyrical restatement of the theory of intertextuality, it should be noted; for the other machines into which the literary machine can be plugged are both textual and nontextual, discursive and nondiscursive, organic and nonorganic, human and nonhuman. All of which is to say that "literature is an assemblage [*agencement*]" (4).

Disassembling the Assemblage

What is an assemblage—aside from being the unifying concept of *A Thousand Plateaus* (so Deleuze, *Two Regimes of Madness*, 174–75) and, arguably, the concept from that concept-profuse experiment whose impact on contemporary thought has been most extensive?[47] The most complete

[44] Here a synonym for "affects."

[45] A proper introduction to these singular bodies will have to await pp. 99–101 below. Suffice it for now to mention that whereas *le(s) corps sans organes* is ordinarily in lowercase in the Deleuzian corpus, it appears sometimes in lowercase and sometimes in uppercase in English translations. For consistency (and because it pleases me), I have opted for "Body/Bodies without Organs" throughout this book.

[46] Translation lightly modified.

[47] Already in 2015 Ian Buchanan could write, "My university library catalogue lists over 8,000 journal articles across all disciplines with the word 'assemblage' in the title" ("Assemblage Theory and Its Discontents," *Deleuze Studies* 9, no. 3 [2015]: 382). What of biblical studies? Assemblage theory animates the following, at least: Rhiannon Graybill, *Are We Not Men? Unstable Masculinity in the Hebrew Prophets* (Oxford: Oxford University Press, 2016), esp. 37-39, 121-42; Stephen D. Moore, *Gospel Jesuses and Other Nonhumans: Biblical Criticism Post-Poststructuralism*, Semeia Studies 89 (Atlanta: SBL Press, 2017), 41-59; Dong Hyeon Jeong, "Simon the Tanner, Empires, and Assemblages: A New Materialist Asian American Reading of Acts 9:43," *The Bible and Critical Theory* 16, no. 1 (2020): 41-63; and A. Paige Rawson, "Reading (with) Rhythm for the Sake of the (I-n-)Islands: A Rastafarian Interpretation of Samson as Ambi(val)ent Affective Assemblage," in *Religion, Emotion, Sensation: Affect Theories and Theologies*, ed. Karen Bray and Stephen D. Moore, Transdisciplinary Theological Colloquia (New York: Fordham University Press, 2020), 126-44.

model of the Deleuzoguattarian assemblage is that found in the "Postulates of Linguistics" plateau of *A Thousand Plateaus* (88–91; see also 323–37 passim; 503–5). Later, in chapter 4, we will circle the device fully and peer into it closely (it has axes, sides, segments, and cutting edges), and we also ponder it in other chapters. For now, some preliminary observations. The assemblage preexisted *A Thousand Plateaus*. Deleuze and Guattari's previous collaboration, *Kafka: Toward a Minor Literature*, ended with a chapter titled "What Is an Assemblage?"[48] The assemblage concept emerged both from their entranced exploration of Kafka's narrative worlds and their earlier concept of "desiring-machines" (*machines désirantes*).[49]

"Kafka doesn't think only about the conditions of alienated, mechanized labor," Deleuze and Guattari muse, "but . . . he [also] considers men and women to be part of the machine not only in their work but even more so in their adjacent activities, in their leisure, in their loves, in their protestations, in their indignations" (*Kafka*, 81). The mechanic remains part of the machine even during her off-hours, since the machine is "a social machine" whose gears are human agents no less than nonhuman agents (81).[50] And the machine's engine? "The machine is desire . . . because desire never stops making a machine in the machine and creates a new gear alongside the preceding gear, indefinitely" (82). To say the same thing differently, what desire does is *connect*, and so "that which makes a machine . . . are connections," and that intricately interconnected machine in turn is "a social assemblage of desire" (82).[51]

[48] Not that this chapter contained the first mention in *Kafka* of the assemblage. True to form, Deleuze and Guattari scattered the term liberally around the book long before telling us what they meant by it.

[49] The desiring-machines thrum through the pages of *Anti-Oedipus*, Deleuze and Guattari's first joint venture. The assemblage idea "replaced" the desiring-machines idea (Deleuze, *Two Regimes of Madness*, 177), both as a result of Deleuze and Guattari's ongoing quest to find ever more potent concepts "to upset the order" (Deleuze, *Desert Islands*, 278) and because the desire in desiring-machines had come to be too closely identified with, misunderstood as, sexual desire (Deleuze and Parnet, *Dialogues II*, 101).

[50] The social machine concept also has its rhizomatic roots in Deleuze and Guattari's *Anti-Oedipus*. It runs through the book. Particularly pertinent for the *Kafka* material we are considering is the following statement: "The social machine . . . has [human beings] for its parts even if we view them *with their machines*" (*Anti-Oedipus*, 141).

[51] The idea that desire is what drives the assemblage is considerably less prominent in *A Thousand Plateaus*, although periodically reiterated in passing (see 229 and 399 for the most explicit statements).

26   THE BIBLE AFTER DELEUZE

All elementary thus far, as Deleuzoguattarese goes. And things get even simpler in the *Abécédaire* experiment that Deleuze later conducts with Claire Parnet:[52]

> So, what was an assemblage? . . . I would maintain that there were four components of an assemblage. . . . This said very roughly, . . . maybe there are six. . . .

> 1) An assemblage referred to "states of things." . . . For example, . . . I like this café, I don't like that café, the people that are in a particular café, etc., that's a "state of things."
> 2) Another dimension of assemblages: *les énoncés*, little statements, each person has a kind of style, his/her way of talking. . . . In the café, for example, . . . one has a certain way of talking with one's friends, so each café has its style. I say the café, but it applies to all kinds of other things. . . . History in the space of five years can produce a new kind of statement. . . . For example, in the Russian revolution, when did statements of a Leninist kind appear, how, in what form?... It's very complex. In any case, every assemblage implies styles of enunciation.
> 3) An assemblage implies territories, each of us chooses or creates a territory, even just walking into a room, one chooses a territory. I walk into a room that I don't know, I look for a territory. . . .
> 4) And then there are processes of what one has to call deterritorialization. . . .

> I would say that an assemblage encompasses these four dimensions: states of things, enunciations, territories, movements of deterritorialization. It's within these [dimensions] that desire flows (*L'Abécédaire*, n.p.).

But concepts that start simply in the Deleuzian thought-world rarely remain so. If a zoom-lens focus on the assemblage sends us to the corner café, a wide-angle focus quickly induces vertigo: "Assemblages . . . are populated

---

[52] *L'Abécédaire de Gilles Deleuze, avec Claire Parnet* (Gilles Deleuze's Alphabet Book, with Claire Parnet), an eight-hour filmed "interview" with (a terminally ill) Deleuze conducted by Parnet in which they work through each letter of the alphabet in succession, Parnet proposing a word beginning with a particular letter ("'A' is 'Animal' . . . ") and Deleuze extemporizing on it. (Details of the film and its transcription and translation may be found in the Abbreviations.)

by . . . various multiplicities (packs, masses, species, races, populations, tribes . . .)" (Deleuze and Parnet, *Dialogues II*, 79). Moreover, an assemblage can be a police van one moment and a getaway vehicle the next. Assemblages lock us up and let us escape. On the one hand, the "segments" that constitute assemblages "capture desire by territorializing it, fixing it in place" (Deleuze and Guattari, *Kafka*, 86). On the other hand, assemblages also possess deterritorializing "lines of flight" that arise from the plane of immanence: "The assemblage extends over or penetrates *an unlimited field of immanence* that . . . liberates desire from all its concretizations and abstractions, or, at the very least, fights actively against them in order to dissolve them" (86). We should not be surprised at the vertiginous vista now visible through the window of the corner café (causing several of the patrons to splutter on their espresso). All roads lead to the plane of immanence sooner or later in Deleuze's ontologically flat thought-world.

And this particular road also leads us back to the opening salvo of *A Thousand Plateaus*. Having declared a book, any book, to be an assemblage, Deleuze and Guattari continue, "One side of a machinic assemblage faces the strata,[53] which doubtless make it a kind of organism, or signifying totality, or determination attributable to a subject; it also has a side facing a *Body without Organs*,[54] which is continually dismantling the organism, causing asignifying particles or pure intensities to pass or circulate" (4). There is much to be unpacked here, an entire suitcase of arguments and assumptions that have profound ramifications for the Bible and its interpretation (beginning with the fact that the suitcase equips us to engage with the Bible in a mode other than interpretation), but that unpacking will have to await chapter 1.

What at its most mundane, however, at the humdrum level of yet another cog in the multigeared social machine, is the book assemblage? As an assemblage, a book "is made of variously formed matters" (or "materials": *matières*), Deleuze and Guattari explain (*A Thousand Plateaus*, 3). What matters, what materials, might these be? They do not say precisely, but let us take our clue from one of their aphorisms: "There is no difference between what a book talks about and how it is made" (4). Let the variously formed matters/materials, then, of which the book assemblage talks, whether explicitly or implicitly, while being made be: *innumerable antecedent books* (a bottomless

---

[53] We revisit the strata in a subsequent chapter. Suffice it for now to say that they correspond, more or less, to the "concretizations" of the previous quotation: all that immobilizes desire and locks it in place.

[54] Here a nonsynonymous synonym for the plane of immanence.

28   THE BIBLE AFTER DELEUZE

ocean of books in the case of biblical scholarship); *the writer's consequently throbbing brain;*

> "The writer invents assemblages, starting from assemblages that have invented the writer" (Deleuze and Parnet, *Dialogues II*, 52).[55]

assorted mobile and mutating affects;

> "Affects circulate and are transformed within the assemblage" (Deleuze and Guattari, *A Thousand Plateaus*, 257).

processed wood pulp (trees falling, all but unheard, in the forest so that technical works of biblical scholarship can plummet, all but unread, into the void); *electronic circuits;*

> "The life of modern machines, a genuine non-organic life, totally distinct from the organic life of carbon, is channeled through silicon[,] . . . a silicon-assemblage" (Deleuze, *Two Regimes of Madness*, 178).

the laws of genre; other discursive conventions;

> "Knowledge is a practical assemblage, a 'mechanism' of statements and visibilities" (Deleuze, *Foucault*, 51).

state censors; tenure and promotion committees; publishing houses and editorial boards;

> "Writing is . . . either . . . a way of reterritorializing oneself, conforming to a code of dominant utterances, to a territory of established state of things . . . or else . . . it is becoming, becoming something other" (Deleuze and Parnet, *Dialogues II*, 74).

the reader's increasingly drowsy brain; communities of reception (as we say in biblical studies; *collectivities of circulation* would better accord with Deleuzespeak); *societies of control;*

---

[55] Translation lightly modified.

> "*Control societies* are taking over from disciplinary societies [. . .]
> forming a system of varying geometry whose language is *digital* (though
> not necessarily binary)" (Deleuze, *Negotiations*, 178).

and so on. But all connected—assembled, arranged[56]—by desire. "To desire is to construct an assemblage," Deleuze again asserts. Indeed, "There is no desire that does not flow . . . within an assemblage" (Deleuze and Parnet, *L'Abécédaire*, n.p.). All of which is to say, "Desire only exists when assembled or machined" (Deleuze and Parnet, *Dialogues II*, 96). And the *object* of desire? "Desire is a machine, and the object of desire is another machine connected to it" (Deleuze and Guattari, *Anti-Oedipus*, 26).

To inquire, however, about the *source* of desire is to be pointed once again toward the plane of immanence; which is to say that, for Deleuze, there is no source as such for desire. The post-psychoanalytic concept of desire that he and Guattari developed in their first collaboration, *Anti-Oedipus*, flows on into their *Kafka* book and beyond into *A Thousand Plateaus*. "It appeared to us that desire was a process," Deleuze explains, "and that it unrolled a *plane of consistency*, a field of immanence, a 'Body without Organs' . . . crisscrossed by particles and flows that escape objects and subjects. . . . Desire is therefore not interior [*intérieur*] to a subject . . . : it is strictly immanent to a plane it does not preexist" (Deleuze and Parnet, *Dialogues II*, 89).[57] More emphatically stated: "The plane of immanence has nothing to do with an interiority; it is like the Outside [*le Dehor*] where all desires come from" (96–97). Desire is external because it is social; indeed, human desire, for Deleuze as for Guattari, is coextensive with the social, as we see in chapter 3. But desire also exceeds the human, is outside the human, because it is not a preserve of the human. Desire flows through assemblages, magnetically (if transitorily) conjoining components that might or might not be human, that might equally be nonhuman animals, plants, or

> "The assemblage's only unity is that of co-functioning: it is a symbiosis. . . . It is never filiations which are important, but alliances, alloys;

---

[56] As the anglophone translators of Deleuze and Parnet's *Dialogues* note, the French word *agencement*, usually rendered as "assemblage," "has both an active and a passive sense, 'a way of assembling or arranging' as well as the resulting 'ordering or arrangement'" (xiii). Ian Buchanan ponders at much greater length the nuances of *agencement* and the challenges of rendering it in English; see his *Assemblage Theory and Method* (New York: Bloomsbury Academic, 2021), 18–21.

[57] My translation.

30   THE BIBLE AFTER DELEUZE

> these are not successions, lines of descent, but contagions, epidemics, the
> wind" (Deleuze and Parnet, *Dialogues II*, 69).

anything whatsoever. Desire, thus transhumanly conceived, exists processually in ontologically heterogenous assemblages; has its "source" in other assemblages from which, and through which, it has flowed; and has as its "destination" still other assemblages—infinite other assemblages—to which, and toward which, it is bound.

Unpoststructuralist Deleuze

Returning to our parable of the Box and the Machine, we can now better understand, following our detour through the desire-transmitting circuits of the assemblage concept, why Deleuze and Guattari insist that to explain what a book is, and how it operates, by appealing to a transcendently anterior author-creator resplendent with unfathomable interiority "is to overlook [the] working of matters [in assemblages], and the exteriority of their relations. It is to fabricate a beneficent God to explain geological movements" (*A Thousand Plateaus*, 3). How, then, are the complex movements of the textual machine—glacially slow movements alternating with faster-than-light movements, and every speed in between—

> "A book . . . is made of variously formed matters, and very different dates
> and speeds" (3).

to be explained?

The textual machine is always rotating, ever spinning, within larger extratextual machines. Asked once about the relationship of his textual practice to deconstruction, Deleuze replied, "As for the method of textual deconstruction, I know what it is, and I admire it" (Derrida was in the room at the time),[58] "but it has nothing to do with my own method. . . . For me, a text is nothing but a cog in a larger extratextual practice. It's not about using deconstruction, or any other textual practice, to do textual commentary; it's about seeing what one can do with an extratextual practice that extends the text"

---

[58] The occasion was *Nietzsche aujourd'hui?* (Nietzsche Today?), a 1972 colloquium held at Cerisy-la-Salle in Normandy. Deleuze and Derrida were two of its headliners.

(*Desert Islands*, 260). How might the text be activated so as to be extended, so as to extend itself? By plugging into (other) social machines, as Deleuze and Guattari will later explain—a "war machine," say,

> "The assemblage that draws lines of flight is of the war machine type.... This machine ... *in no way has war as its object*, but rather the emission of quanta of deterritorialization.... War ... is only the abominable residue of the war machine, either after it has allowed itself to be appropriated by the State apparatus, or even worse has constructed itself as a State apparatus capable only of destruction" (Deleuze and Guattari, *A Thousand Plateaus*, 229–30, their emphasis).

or a "love machine," or a "revolutionary machine" (*A Thousand Plateaus*, 4).

Few texts have, of course, been so extended, so overextended, as the biblical texts, becoming huge, constantly whirring cogs in extratextual practices that themselves constitute continent-spanning social machines (even if the population-controlling capacities of those machines have grown ever more depleted on certain continents since the dawn of post-Christian time). To ask whether these vast social machines have been war machines, love machines, or revolutionary machines

> "Until now, there has not existed in the revolutionary field a machine that didn't reproduce something else: a State apparatus, the very institution of repression.... Today we're looking for the new mode of unification in which ... all the marginal discourses can subsist, so that all these escapes ... can graft themselves onto a war machine that won't reproduce a State or Party apparatus" (Deleuze, *Desert Islands*, 279–80).

would be facile. They have, of course, been all three at once, a machinic Trinity whose interpenetrating operations have rivaled in complexity the inner life of Christianity's Triune God.

Deleuze was holding his philosophical cards close to his chest when he politely put down deconstruction, in Derrida's presence, at the Cerisy-la-Salle colloquium. There was a great deal more Deleuze might have said, for by then he had rejected not only the hypertextualism, but also the panlinguism, of both structuralism and (what would soon be named) poststructuralism as encapsulated and perpetuated in such slogans as, "It is language which speaks" (Barthes); "The unconscious is structured like a language" (Lacan);

32   THE BIBLE AFTER DELEUZE

"The ... text is produced through the ... simultaneous affirmation and negation of another text" (Kristeva); and "There is nothing outside the text" (Derrida).[59]

It was not that Deleuze was uninterested in language. Language fascinated him sufficiently that he devoted one of his two most ambitious early books, *The Logic of Sense*, to the evanescent phenomenon of

> "Sense, ... an incorporeal, complex, and irreducible entity, at the surface of things, a pure event which inheres or subsists in the proposition" (*The Logic of Sense*, 19).

linguistic meaning. Moreover, "The Postulates of Linguistics" chapter of *A Thousand Plateaus* is, arguably, one of its most consequential; the "On Several Regimes of Signs" chapter pairs with it; and still other chapters of the book also have trenchant things to say about language. And Deleuze's last solo book, *Essays Critical and Clinical*, is unified by an intense preoccupation with literary language. Yet Deleuze was not a philosopher of language at base, which is to say that the internal operations of language or the relations of the linguistic and the extralinguistic were not of first importance for him. As such, although his work was technically poststructuralist (certainly from *Anti-Oedipus* onward),

> "The [structuralist] imperialism of the signifier does not take us beyond the question, 'What does it mean?'" (Deleuze and Guattari, *Anti-Oedipus*, 208).

it was also out of step with the movement that would be assembled retroactively under the poststructuralist banner. Deleuze thought to a different drumbeat,[60] but that is precisely why his work is attracting unprecedented

[59] Roland Barthes, "The Death of the Author" (1967), in his *Image, Music, Text*, trans. Stephen Heath (New York: Hill and Wang, 1977), 143; Jacques Lacan, *The Seminar of Jacques Lacan. Book XI: The Four Fundamental Concepts of Psychoanalysis*, ed. Jacques-Alain Miller, trans. Alan Sheridan (New York: Norton, [1964] 1998), 20; Julia Kristeva, *Sèméiotikè. Recherches pour une sémanalyse* (Paris: Seuil, 1969), 257, my translation; Jacques Derrida, *Of Grammatology*, trans. Gayatri Chakravorty Spivak, 40th ann. ed. (Baltimore: Johns Hopkins University Press, [1967] 2016), 158.

[60] As did Guattari. Their mutual distance from both structuralist and poststructuralist orthodoxies is encapsulated in an exchange between Guattari and an interviewer in which the latter interjects, "The dominant theoretical approaches in France, which have developed out of structuralism, close ranks around the linguistic signifier, disregarding non-discursive resonances and emotional pathways connected to them. They disregard what you call *non-verbal intensities* that blaze existential territories and 'pathic' routes." Guattari replies, "Right. The linguistic signifier in no way encloses all of the components combining to produce subjectivity" (Guattari, "From Transference,"

INTRODELEUZE (WHO AND WHY?) 33

attention in the prolonged post-poststructuralist, or para-poststructuralist, moment in which theory currently finds itself.

Not a philosopher of language, Deleuze was instead a philosopher of— what? Of becoming, certainly, as of affect and sensation, also of difference,

> "We tend to subordinate difference to identity in order to think it.... In other words, we do not think difference in itself.... The powers of difference [may] be reached only by putting into question the traditional image of thought" (Deleuze, *Difference and Repetition*, xv–xvi).

of virtuality, and, relatedly, of the event in its special Deleuzian sense,

> "Any event is a fog of a million droplets" (Deleuze and Parnet, *Dialogues II*, 65).

all of which is to say that Deleuze was a philosopher of flux

> "Flux is reality itself" (Deleuze and Guattari, *A Thousand Plateaus*, 361).

for whom every discrete being or concrete existent, every system or structure, was a chaotic quantity of ever-mobile particles and ever-fleeing flows

> "Chaos is defined not so much by its disorder as by the infinite speed with which every form taking shape in it vanishes" (Deleuze and Guattari, *What Is Philosophy?*, 118).

conceptually captured or slowed so as to be rendered perceptible; and as a philosopher of flux,

> "Desire is present wherever something flows and runs" (Deleuze and Guattari, *Anti-Oedipus*, 105).

---

243). Guattari was particularly critical of postmodernism, which he saw as a reduction of the materiality of the social to "erratic clouds of floating discourse in a signifying ether" (*Schizoanalytic Cartographies*, 39). Against postmodern panlinguism, Guattari pitted "concrete social Assemblages, which . . . call into question many other things than linguistic performances: ethological and

34 THE BIBLE AFTER DELEUZE

Deleuze was also a philosopher of desire. Most of all (as is implicit in all the terms of this chain), Deleuze was a philosopher of immanence.

Of these various "ofs," however, it is Deleuzian affect that has most excited the academic imagination in recent years, being swept up into a multidisciplinary turn in the humanities to emotions and other associated states, a turn precipitated in part by Deleuzian affect itself, and one that has even entailed a modest affective swerve in biblical studies.[61] But what, again, *is* affect, specifically in the Deleuzian sense?

The Deleuze Affect

Unemotional Affect

First, a paradox. Affect theory has arguably been the most impactful theoretical product of the current century thus far, and Deleuze has been the most influential resource for affect theory.[62] Yet affect is a rather reclusive presence, all told, in the Deleuzian corpus. Several of Deleuze's most prominent solo works (*Difference and Repetition, The Logic of Sense, Proust and Signs, The Fold...*), and two of his joint works with Guattari (*Anti-Oedipus, Kafka*), refer either infrequently or not at all to affect. Where is affect mainly to be found, then, in Deleuze's oeuvre?

Deleuze derived his concept of affect from Baruch Spinoza,[63] the philosopher he most revered,

---

ecological dimensions, economic, aesthetic, corporeal... components that are irreducible to the semiology of language" (39).

[61] Maia Kotrosits's *How Things Feel: Biblical Studies, Affect Theory, and the (Im)personal*, Brill Research Perspectives in Biblical Interpretation 1 (Leiden, The Netherlands: Brill, 2016) exhaustively takes stock of the first shoots of affect theory in biblical studies. Work that has appeared since her survey includes Moore, *Gospel Jesuses and Other Nonhumans*, 15–59; Fiona C. Black and Jennifer L. Koosed, eds., *Reading with Feeling: Affect Theory and the Bible*, Semeia Studies 95 (Atlanta: SBL Press, 2019); Michal Beth Dinkler, *Literary Theory and the New Testament*, Anchor Yale Bible Reference Library (New Haven, CT: Yale University Press, 2019), 163–78; the biblical essays in Bray and Moore, eds., *Religion, Emotion, Sensation*; and Jimmy Hoke, *Feminism, Queerness, Affect, and Romans: Under God?*, Early Christianity and Its Literature 30 (Atlanta: SBL Press, 2021).

[62] See pp. 7–8 earlier, which, however, only scratches the surface of Deleuze's impact, both direct and diffuse, on affect theory. Even a scholar as critical as Ruth Leys of the Deleuzian construal of affect concedes, "Probably the most influential figure in the rise of the new affect theory is Deleuze" (*The Ascent of Affect: Genealogy and Critique* [Chicago: University of Chicago Press, 2017], 312 n. 13).

[63] A name also emblazoned in the origin story of biblical studies as an academic discipline, as it happens. We turn to that other Spinoza in due course.

INTRODELEUZE (WHO AND WHY?) 35

> "Spinoza is the Christ of philosophers" (Deleuze and Guattari, *What Is Philosophy?*, 60).

and with few exceptions the preponderance of affect as a topic in Deleuze's solo books is proportionate to the prominence of Spinoza in those books. Affect thus looms large in Deleuze's introductory book on Spinoza—*Spinoza: Practical Philosophy*; and in Deleuze's more technical book on Spinoza—*Expressionism in Philosophy: Spinoza*—affect shows up on almost every page. The exceptions to the Spinoza rule of thumb are Deleuze's two film books, *Cinema 1* and *Cinema 2*; in both of them, but especially the first, affect is also an important theme, even though Spinoza is not mentioned in the first book and is barely mentioned in the second. And in Deleuze and Guattari's *What Is Philosophy?*, their final collaboration,[64] affect receives more sustained attention (163–99) than in any of their previous joint efforts. But none of that seems sufficient to explain why Deleuze is commonly seen as the proto-affect theorist par excellence, and, as such, the source for what is arguably the predominant form of contemporary affect theory.

This is where Brian Massumi reenters the plot,[65] affect theory in the Deleuzian mode being in no small part a Massumian creation, beginning with Massumi's 1987 translation of Deleuze and Guattari's *Mille plateaux*. Massumi's "Notes on the Translation" opens with a much-quoted definition of "affect/affection" (*A Thousand Plateaus*, xvi), thereby conjuring the impression that affect looms larger in the book than it actually does. But it was Massumi's *Parables for the Virtual* (2002), which we encountered earlier, that proved to be the primary progenitor for affect theory in the Deleuzian mode. Massumi acknowledges that "it is Gilles Deleuze who reopened the path" to the (previously neglected) thinkers who subtend Massumi's book, Spinoza and Henri Bergson above all,[66] and the book is suffused with concepts that Deleuze had taken from those thinkers and made his own—preeminently, affect, intensity, movement, sensation, and virtuality.

In the minds of most who know anything about affect theory, an emphatic distinction between affect and emotion is the distinguishing trait of

---

[64] In name, anyway. *What Is Philosophy?* was written by Deleuze alone. That Guattari's name appears as coauthor is Deleuze's acknowledgment of the extent to which the book's ideas, arguments, and terminology were products of his long-standing collaboration with Guattari. See, further, François Dosse, *Gilles Deleuze and Félix Guattari: Intersecting Lives*, trans. Deborah Glassman (New York: Columbia University Press, 2010), 456.

[65] We met Massumi earlier in p. 8.

[66] Massumi, *Parables for the Virtual*, 32.

36 THE BIBLE AFTER DELEUZE

the Deleuze-Massumi current of affect theory, setting it apart from both the psychobiological current associated with Silvan Tomkins and Eve Sedgwick and the cultural current[67] associated with Sara Ahmed, Lauren Berlant, Ann Cvetkovich, and many others. The classic statement of the affect/emotion distinction, however, one commonly cited, is found, not in any work by Deleuze, but in Massumi's "The Autonomy of Affect" (which we also encountered earlier), an essay subsequently reprinted in his *Parables for the Virtual*:

> An emotion is a subjective content, the sociolinguistic fixing of the quality of an experience which is from that point onward defined as personal. Emotion is qualified intensity,[68] the conventional, consensual point of insertion of intensity into semantically and semiotically formed progressions, into narrativizable action-reaction circuits, into function and meaning. It is intensity owned and recognized. It is crucial to theorize the difference between affect and emotion.[69]

Massumi, it is important to note, is not claiming in *Parables for the Virtual* that his sharp-edged affect/emotion distinction derives from Deleuze. As affect theory has circulated through the humanities and social sciences, however, the assumption that the distinction was Deleuze's before it was Massumi's has become commonplace.[70]

Before we can properly ponder whether or to what extent Massumi's surgical separation of emotion from affect is also a Deleuzian operation, we need to descend deeper into Deleuze's concept of affect—a descent too rarely undertaken in any case,[71] and not undertaken at all in previous biblical-critical engagements with affect, which is the primary reason for

---

[67] Or cultural lens, as Karen Bray and I have dubbed it: "The cultural lens, most readily found in queer and feminist cultural studies and critical race theory, . . . resists categorizing affects as presocial and focuses instead on how they are produced through cultural and historical structures of power" (Bray and Moore, "Introduction: Mappings and Crossings," in *Religion, Emotion, Sensation*, 5).

[68] "For present purposes, intensity will be equated with affect" (Massumi, *Parables for the Virtual*, 27).

[69] Massumi, *Parables for the Virtual*, 28.

[70] Due in no small part to Massumi's translator's note on affect in *A Thousand Plateaus*. His eight-line definition of "affect/affection" begins, "Neither word denotes a personal feeling (*sentiment* in Deleuze and Guattari)" (xvi). That may be true of *A Thousand Plateaus*. As we shall see, however, *sentiment* regularly denotes affect in Deleuze's two books on Spinoza.

[71] Relatively speaking, of course; the "Deleuze and . . ." industry is vast, as we saw. Nevertheless, there have been far fewer dedicated studies of Deleuze's concept of affect than one might expect. Particularly fine is Gregory J. Seigworth's "From Affection to Soul," in *Gilles Deleuze: Key Concepts*, 2nd ed., ed. Charles J. Stivale (New York: Routledge, 2014), 181–91. As I write, a book-length study of the topic is on the near horizon, D. J. S. Cross's *Deleuze and the Problem of Affect*, forthcoming from Edinburgh University Press.

INTRODELEUZE (WHO AND WHY?)   37

the extended exploration that follows. What was Deleuzian affect before the emergence and coalescence of affect theory? It begins as yet another simple-seeming path that, once again, opens up on vertiginous vistas.

What Spinoza's Body Can Do

To engage with Deleuze on affect is to engage with Deleuze on Spinoza on affect, as intimated above; for Deleuze draws his theory of affect from Spinoza's *Ethics* as though from a bottomless well—

> "This book, one of the greatest in the world" (Deleuze, *Essays Critical and Clinical*, 138).

the *Ethics* being the Dutch philosopher's magnum opus published posthumously in 1677,

> "He does not publish his book because he knows that if he publishes it, he'll find himself in prison" (Deleuze, "The Velocities of Thought," Lecture 1, n.p.).

the year of his death from a lung disease, sibling to the illness that propelled Deleuze through a third-floor window more than three centuries later.

Let us peer over Deleuze's shoulder, then, as he gazes rapt into the *Ethics*, mesmerized by the darting movements within its tranquil depths. But why not drink directly from the source and simply read Spinoza ourselves? Because the Spinoza-Deleuze symbiote exceeds the pre-Deleuzian Spinoza. As Deleuze once remarked while lecturing on Spinoza, "He is speaking through my mouth; he didn't say it this way because he died too young" ("Spinoza's Concept of *Affect*," n.p.).

Spinoza's Latin features two affect-words, *affectus* and *affectio*. Deleuze influentially renders *affectus* as *l'affect*, "affect" in English. "Some [French] translators translate . . . *affectus* as 'feeling' [*sentiment*]," he notes, "but I don't see the necessity . . . since French offers the word 'affect'" ("Spinoza's Concept of *Affect*," n.p.).[72] *Affectus*, affect, is a body-word; it plays a prominent role in

---

[72] Deleuze was, however, inconsistent on this issue of translation. In his *Expressionism in Philosophy*, for example, we read, "From a given idea of an affection there necessarily flow 'affects' or feelings (*affectus*)" (220). Indeed, *sentiment* ("feeling") is a synonym for "affect" (*affectus*) throughout

38   THE BIBLE AFTER DELEUZE

Spinoza's attempt to answer a driving question of his *Ethics*: "What can a body do?"[73] Affect is also an action-word; it names the perpetual becoming, the incessant movement—at times glacially slow, at other times lightning fast—

> "Spinozists . . . think in terms of speeds and slownesses, of frozen catatonias and accelerated movements" (Deleuze, *Practical Philosophy*, 128).

that is the essential condition of the human body, or any body,

> "A body can be anything; it can be an animal, a body of sounds, a mind or an idea; it can be a linguistic corpus, a social body, a collectivity" (127).

in the Spinozan-Deleuzian conception. "How does Spinoza define a body?" Deleuze asks. "In the first place, a body . . . is composed of an infinite number of particles; it is the relations of motion and rest, of speeds and slownesses between particles, that define a body, the individuality of a body" (123). Affect, *affectus*, as both corporeal and actional, is the continual passage or transition from state to state within the perpetual motion machine that is the body. As Deleuze phrases it, "From one state to another . . . there are transitions, passages that are experienced, durations through which we pass. . . . The continual durations or variations . . . are called 'affects,' or feelings (*affectus*)" (48–49).

When Deleuze teams up with Guattari, the vocabulary of passage and transition becomes more exuberant, most especially when it is the Body without Organs that is its object,[74]

> "After all, is not Spinoza's *Ethics* the great book of the BwO?" (Deleuze and Guattari, *A Thousand Plateaus*, 153).

---

this book, Deleuze's most ambitious exposition of Spinoza, and also throughout *Practical Philosophy*, his later Spinoza book. That does not mean, of course, that the term "feeling" in these books can simply be conflated with the term "feeling" as contemporary affect theorists such as Ann Cvetkovich use it.

[73] "What Can a Body Do?" is the title of a chapter of Deleuze's *Expressionism in Philosophy* (217–34). Spinoza's own formulation of the problem reads, "Nobody as yet has determined the limits of the body's capabilities" (*Ethics*, in *Spinoza: The Complete Works*, ed. Michael L. Morgan, trans. Samuel Shirley [Indianapolis: Hackett, 2002], 280)—a statement Seigworth and Gregg style as "one of the most oft-cited quotations concerning affect" ("An Inventory of Shimmers," 3).

[74] A body in whose company we shall spend much time in subsequent chapters, even venturing more thorough definitions of it.

INTRODELEUZE (WHO AND WHY?)   39

the body, which, among other things, is the affective body (cf. Deleuze, *Essays Critical and Clinical*, 131) amped up to its full capacity: "Nothing but bands of intensity, potentials, thresholds, and gradients" (Deleuze and Guattari, *Anti-Oedipus*, 19). And later: "The body is now nothing more than a set of valves, locks, floodgates. . . . Only intensities pass and circulate. . . . [It is] defined by axes and vectors, gradients and thresholds, . . . dynamic tendencies involving energy transformations and kinematic movements" (Deleuze and Guattari, *A Thousand Plateaus*, 153). And, soon after, in Deleuze's solo book on the painter Francis Bacon: "It is an intense and intensive body. It is traversed by a wave that traces levels or thresholds. . . . [It is] flesh and nerve; a wave flows through it and traces levels upon it; a sensation is produced when the wave encounters the Forces acting on the body"—and much more in this language-imploding vein (*Francis Bacon*, 39–40).

This, then, is the kind of machine that a body is.[75] But the body, thus conceived, is bound up with a certain concept of power, since Spinoza's "entire *Ethics* presents itself," on Deleuze's reading, "as a theory of power [*puissance*]" (*Practical Philosophy*, 104).[76] Power as it relates to a body is precisely the power to act, and the name for such a power is nothing other than *affect*: "There is a continuous variation in the form of an increase-diminution . . . of someone's power [*puissance*] of acting or force of existing. . . . It really is existence in the street. It's necessary to imagine Spinoza strolling about—and he truly lives existence as this kind of continuous variation. . . . This . . . melodic line of continuous variation will define affect (*affectus*)" (Deleuze, "Spinoza's Concept of Affect," n.p.).[77] Or somewhat more soberly: "These are passages, becomings, rises and falls, continuous variations of power that pass from one state to another. We will call them *affects*" (Deleuze, *Essays Critical and Clinical*, 139).[78]

---

[75] At least when described by the Spinoza-Deleuze symbiote. The Nietzsche-Deleuze symbiote proposes a different, but related, description: "What is the body? . . . What defines a body is [the] relation between dominant and dominated forces. Every relationship of forces constitutes a body—whether it is chemical, biological, social or political. Any two forces, being unequal, constitute a body as soon as they enter into a relationship. This is why the body is always the fruit of chance, in the Nietzschean sense, and appears as the most 'astonishing' thing, much more astonishing, in fact, than consciousness and spirit" (Deleuze, *Nietzsche and Philosophy*, 39–40).

[76] *Puissance*, "power to," as distinct from *pouvoir*, "power over," correspond to Spinoza's *potentia* and *potestas*, respectively. *Potentia/puissance* is potential or capacity. One of the basic arguments of the *Ethics*, for Deleuze, is its denial that God possesses "any power [*potestas*] analogous to that of a tyrant, or even an enlightened prince." Instead, God's essence is pure *potentia*, infinite capacity, specifically, "a capacity for being affected" (*Practical Philosophy*, 97; see also Deleuze, *Expressionism in Philosophy*, 102).

[77] Translation lightly modified.

[78] I am quoting here, as so often in this section, from "Spinoza and the Three 'Ethics'" (*Essays Critical and Clinical*, 138–51), which amounts to Deleuze's final statement on Spinoza.

40   THE BIBLE AFTER DELEUZE

All this may sound a tad solipsistic, Spinoza strolling about, absorbed only in Spinoza, acutely attuned to his internal power gauge, his capacity meter, its numbers flickering upward or downward as his power of acting, his force of existing, increases or diminishes, the *causes* of these continuous oscillations being only of secondary importance to him relative to the fluctuations themselves. But we have merely been peering curiously into the affect machine; now we need to circumambulate it, so far as that is possible (we shall soon discover that its outer perimeter extends to infinity).

Affectus is only one of the two Spinozan affect-words, as noted earlier, the other being *affectio* (a maddeningly hard-to-translate term, as we see shortly). To risk oversimplifying the convolutedly complex, if *affectus* concerns what is continually going on *in* a body, *affectio* concerns what is continually going on *between* bodies. *Affectio* is deceptively easy to define. It is "the state of a body insofar as it suffers the action of another body," or, which is to say the same thing, "the trace of one body upon another" (Deleuze, *Essays Critical and Clinical*, 138), an "imprint" or "effect" of, say, some other body "on the soft and fluid parts of our own body" (Deleuze, *Expressionism in Philosophy*, 147).

Bodies undergoing *affectio*, however, need not be human. As we noted earlier, a body, for Deleuze (as for Spinoza, although less insistently), can be human or nonhuman, corporeal or incorporeal, individual or collective, molecular or massive. That is why Deleuze does not hesitate to ascribe affect to inanimate objects on occasion:

> **"And why is expression not available to things? There are affects of things"** (*Cinema 1*, 97).

a knife, rain, a metal bridge, an entire city considered independently of its human inhabitants (97, 111). The two bodies may be as dissimilar and distant from each other as the sun and a human being (to take an example Spinoza ponders and to which Deleuze repeatedly returns). Notwithstanding the immense expanse separating these two bodies, however, *affectio* here, as always, names an immediacy of impact. *Affectio* is the "instantaneous effect" of another body upon my own body (Deleuze, *Essays Critical and Clinical*, 139), of any body upon any other body. Spinoza "does not believe in action at a distance," observes Deleuze ("Spinoza's Concept of *Affect*," n.p.).

How best to translate *affectio*, then? "Affection" is the English word long conscripted to render this Spinozan term. Deleuze himself routinely translates *affectio* as *l'affection*, which his English translators duly render

INTRODELEUZE (WHO AND WHY?)   41

in turn as "affection." Whatever might be said about *l'affection* in contemporary French usage, however, "affection" in contemporary English usage is too tightly tied to "fondness" and other warm, fuzzy feelings to mean much of what Spinoza's *affectio* means—at least without drawing on affection's archaic semantic reserves.[79] Admittedly, I do not have a more adequate English equivalent for *affectio* to propose. But this Latin term, lovingly massaged and elaborately dressed up by Deleuze, admits of succinct definition, at least. *Affectio* may be said to be *freeze-frame affect*, affect arrested in the instant (although really the micro-instant), and, also, *intercorporeal affect* (affect in/ as the in-between). And *affectus*, by contrast, may be said to be *instant-by-instant affect*, unfolding affect, affect in passage, in transition, in duration, and, also, *intracorporeal affect*.

Any disentangling of *affectio* and *affectus* is, however, purely notional, a sound of one hand clapping. And once *affectio* is conceptually conjoined, rejoined, with *affectus*, Spinoza is effectively de-solipsistized. Now Spinoza strolls through the streets of The Hague as a fully functional affect-machine. A balmy April sun beams down on him out of a pellucid sky. He feels his power of acting,

> **"The most beautiful thing is to live on the edges, at the limit of [one's] own power of being affected"** (Deleuze, "Spinoza's Concept of *Affect*," n.p.).

his force of existing, increase. Entire sentences of the *Ethics*, his constant companion, begin to write themselves automatically

---

[79] Of the twenty-one senses that the *Oxford English Dictionary* lists for "affection" (eleven of them labeled "obsolete" and three "rare"), the following (quoted in full) is the one closest in meaning to Spinoza's *affectio* and Deleuze's *l'affection*:

Any state or condition of the body, whether due to external or internal influence. *Obsolete.*
?1541 R. COPLAND *Galen's Fourth Bk. Terapeutyke* sig. Aiij, in *Guy de Chauliac's Questyonary Cyrurgyens* Euery vlcere is eyther symple and alone without other dysposytyon or affectyon begynnynge with it.
1665 R. SOUTH *Serm. preached before Court* 3 To place men with the furious affections of hunger, and thirst in the very bosome of Plenty.
1701 W. COCKBURN *Profluvia Ventris* 86 They stimulating the musculous Fibres of the Stomach, must create an affection in proportion to the Stimulating.
1757 E. BURKE *Philos. Enq. Sublime & Beautiful* IV. §1. 117 Why certain affections of the body produce such a distinct emotion of mind.
1798 A. CRICHTON *Inq. Mental Derangem.* II. 157 Laughter is, for the most part, an affection of the body, arising from certain thoughts which occur without the intervention of the will.

42   THE BIBLE AFTER DELEUZE

> "What Spinoza is going to name God, in the first book of the *Ethics*, . . . is
> going to be the strangest thing in the world" (Deleuze, "The Velocities of
> Thought," Lecture 1, n.p.).

in his head. A flower-seller whose beguiling aspect causes unexpected excitations within the philosopher extends a luscious red tulip to him, inviting him to savor its subtle fragrance. Encountering not just one but two bodies with which his own body *can enter into composition* (as the Spinozan-Deleuzian idiolect would have it),

> "Spinoza never ceases to be amazed by the body. He is not amazed
> at having a body, but by what the body can do" (Deleuze and Parnet,
> *Dialogues II*, 60).

temporarily combining with them to constitute a more powerful whole, each body (philosopher, flower-seller, flower) becoming subindividualities[80] of a newly composed and composite individual—why, then Spinoza experiences an exponential augmentation of his power of acting,

> "This frugal, propertyless life, undermined by illness, this thin, frail
> body, this brown, oval face with its sparkling black eyes—how does one
> explain the impression they give of being suffused with Life itself, of
> having a power identical to Life?" (Deleuze, *Practical Philosophy*, 12).

an exhilarating increase of his force of existing. Spinoza continues on his way with a new spring in his step. Taking his usual shortcut through an alley, however, the philosopher experiences an abrupt, altogether shocking encounter with the contents of a chamber pot casually cast through an attic window. His power of acting and force of existing plummet precipitously.

Of course, these are but the more dramatic moments in Spinoza's affect-imbued meander through the market. "You understand that a body is necessarily composite to infinity," Deleuze is telling his lecture audience as we once again slip into the back row ("Spinoza's Concept of *Affect*," n.p.). And later: "Hence I am affected in an infinity of ways." But the "infinite set of

---

[80] A term that occurs several times in Deleuze's lectures on Spinoza's concept of affect but not in either of his books on Spinoza.

extensive parts" that is my body, that "belongs to me" as such, "is not separable from other sets, equally infinite, that act on it . . . and do not belong to me." My skin particles, for instance, or Spinoza's skin particles, are not separable, ultimately, from the air particles

> "The dying rat enters into composition with the air" (Deleuze and Guattari, *A Thousand Plateaus*, 262).

"that come to strike them" ("Spinoza's Concept of *Affect*," n.p.). Of course, most of what Spinoza's body does, in its capacity to affect and be affected, is more microparticular even than that, meaning that most of it occurs below the threshold of consciousness. Where precisely a body begins or ends, philosophically or even scientifically, no one as yet can say. In this zone of indistinction

> "A zone of indistinction, of indiscernibility, . . . an extreme proximity, an absolute contiguity" (Deleuze, *Essays Critical and Clinical*, 78).

affect has its home.

At the Beach with Spinoza and Deleuze

Spinoza takes the concept of affect to infinity, then. Deleuze follows him there. Once again, he and Spinoza are gazing into the sun. "There are people on the beach," Deleuze remarks to Spinoza, "but they don't understand, they don't know what the sun is, they live badly." Spinoza nods glumly. Affected by the sun, enveloped in *affectio*, these scantily clad beachgoers, oblivious to the odd philosophical couple pensively regarding them from afar, feel the sun's "particles act on [their] particles," an effect that is "a pleasure or a joy." But they experience the sun only as an external or extrinsic body, distinct and distant from their own. This is "the sun of the first kind of knowledge"—of first-level affect, if you will (Deleuze, "Spinoza's Concept of *Affect*," n.p.).

There is also, however, a "second kind of knowledge" whereby one begins to "leave behind" the zone of distinction. One now knows "how to compose the relations of [one's] body" with the relations of the sun,

44 THE BIBLE AFTER DELEUZE

> "The street enters into composition with the horse, just as . . . the beast
> and the full moon enter into composition with each other" (Deleuze and
> Guattari, *A Thousand Plateaus*, 262).

so much so that "[one is] not far from being able to say, 'the sun, I am something of it,'" to experience "a kind of communion with the sun." Deleuze's
foremost example of second-level affective knowledge is the kinetic painting
technique of Vincent van Gogh, who (Deleuze claims) composed the relations of his body with the majestic movements of the sun. He did not "have
the same relation to his canvas depending on whether the sun [was] high
or . . . about to set. Van Gogh painted on his knees." Indeed, the sublime spectacle of the setting sun compelled van Gogh to prostrate himself before it, "to
paint almost lying down so that [his] eye had the lowest horizon line possible." Van Gogh "[began] to enter into a kind of communication with the
sun," a zone of intimate accord with the sun (Deleuze, "Spinoza's Concept of
Affect," n.p.).

But even that is only the second kind of knowledge of the sun. "What
would the third kind be?" Deleuze inquires of Spinoza, who has removed his
buckled shoes and white stockings to wade in the surf. It is a rhetorical question, Spinoza having already provided the all but undiscoverable answer in
the fifth book of his *Ethics* through "a method of invention that . . . proceed[s]
by intervals and leaps, hiatuses and contractions, somewhat like a dog
searching rather than a reasonable man explaining" (Deleuze, *Essays Critical
and Clinical*, 149). Like a dog or like a mystic. "This is where there is something irreducibly mystical [*C'est là qu'il y a quelque chose d'irréductiblement
mystique*] in Spinoza's third kind of knowledge," muses Deleuze ("Spinoza's
Concept of *Affect*," n.p.).[81] At this level of knowledge, which is also the ultimate level of affect, one can affirm absolute union with the sun, "so much so
that the rays by which the sun affects me are the rays by which I affect myself,
and the rays by which I affect myself are the rays of the sun that affects me."
But how? "Not at all because there is an identification" between the sun's fiery
body and my watery body, insists Deleuze, much less a relationship of resemblance. My essence remains distinct from that of the sun, but it is no longer
the distinction of two entities that are extrinsic to each other. Rather, I have

---

[81] Translation modified. Deleuze has already asked himself, "What would the third kind [of know-
ledge] be?" and answered, "In abstract terms it would be a mystical union [*une union mystique*]"
("Spinoza's Concept of *Affect*," n.p.).

arrived at a "mode of intrinsic distinction." The sun and I are distinguished from each other "on the inside" (Deleuze, "Spinoza's Concept of *Affect*," n.p.).

On the inside of what? In Spinozan terms, on the inside of the one substance (*substantia*) that, for him, is the only substance that exists, and each and every body (micro- or macro-, human or nonhuman, animate or inanimate), even each and every human thought, is but a "mode" (*modus*) or particular modification (*modification*) of that single infinite substance

> "The world of Spinoza is . . . truly the most anti-hierarchical world that philosophy has ever produced! . . . All beings are equal . . . ? . . . A stone and a sage, a pig and a philosopher, all are of equal value? . . . Of course they're of equal value! . . . Spinoza will never give up on that" (Deleuze,
> "The Velocities of Thought," Lecture 2, n.p.).

—a substance that, moreover, is beholden to no preexisting or external Creator, because Spinoza's concept of substance is sufficiently capacious that even God can be folded into it without remainder. More precisely, this infinite substance *is* God, for Spinoza.

Once again: The sun and I are distinguished from each other "on the inside," insists Deleuze, but which inside would that be? In Deleuzian terms, it is the inside of the plane of immanence, Deleuze's reconceptualization of Spinoza's single substance. Of course, the single substance and the plane of immanence are not identical; too much water has flowed under the philosophical bridge for that. Far from declaring his own distance from Spinoza, however, upstream in that roiling current, Deleuze is instead content to assert that Spinoza is already in the *Ethics* transforming the single-substance concept in its relative simplicity into a more evolved, a more involved, plane-of-immanence concept: "What is involved is no longer the affirmation of a single substance, but rather the laying out of a *common plane of immanence* on which all bodies, all minds, and all individuals are situated" (Deleuze, *Practical Philosophy*, 122, his emphasis). They are situated and constantly resituated, always in motion, always "being woven" by the "gigantic shuttle" that is the plane of immanence (Deleuze and Guattari, *What Is Philosophy?*, 38). Within that woven fabric there are no absolute outsides, no actual insides, but only *folds* in the fabric,

> "A fold is always folded within a fold, like a cavern in a cavern" (Deleuze,
> *The Fold*, 6).

46   THE BIBLE AFTER DELEUZE

seeming insides that are folds of an ostensible outside, "as if the ship were a folding of the sea" (Deleuze, *Foucault*, 97). Or as if the sun were a folding of the sky and the painter prostrate before the sun were a folding of the earth, which in turn were a fabric continuous with the sky into which it fades at the horizon.

All of which is to say that affect, for Deleuze as for Spinoza, exceeds the human. At the third level of affect, indeed, that is putting it all too mildly; at this level, affect infinitely exceeds the human. But even at the first level of affect, the level of bodies affecting other bodies and being affected by them in turn—the hedonistic bodies on Deleuze's beach, say, splashing contentedly on the edges of the larger aqueous body that borders it, conceiving of the ocean and one another only as bodies entirely external to their own— most of what transpires eludes easy capture by concepts such as "the human" or "the individual," "person" or "identity." Affect is too fine-grained, too microparticular, for such macroconceptual containers. At its most granular, affect entails relations, not between fully formed, cleanly delineated bodies, so much as "between differential velocities, between deceleration and acceleration of particles. A composition of speeds and slownesses on a plane of immanence" (Deleuze, *Practical Philosophy*, 123).

And even when we descend much closer to the level of lived actuality, much in the domain of affect hovers elusively on the imperceptible side of the threshold of conscious awareness. Now Guattari joins Spinoza and Deleuze on the beach. Affect is "hazy, atmospheric," he interjects—yet "nevertheless perfectly apprehensible" in that it engenders "threshold effects," those momentary bodily transitions from state to state that Spinoza termed *affectus*.[82] Why affect remains hazy, however, is that it is nondiscursive, which Guattari parses as, "Not founded upon systems of distinctive oppositions inflected according to sequences of linear intelligibility" ("Existential Affects," 158). Indeed, the moment one attempts "to quantify an affect," one loses what is proper to it, Guattari muses (159), watching affect dissipate even as he speaks. This prompts Deleuze to declare, "Every mode of thought insofar as it is non-representational will be termed affect" ("Spinoza's Concept of *Affect*," n.p.). Nondiscursive, then, and nonrepresentational, and as such maddeningly elusive. Yet, paradoxically, also insistently proximate.

---

[82] Which is also the plural form of this Latin noun.

INTRODELEUZE (WHO AND WHY?)   47

"Affect sticks to subjectivity," Guattari continues. "It is a glischroid matter," viscous in the extreme ("Existential Affects," 158).[83] It clings, it catches, it gloms onto. Affect sticks to enunciation in particular, Guattari thinks, hearing the breathless exclamations and inarticulate shrieks of the bathers romping in the shallows and throwing themselves into the waves. Aloud he adds, "Only, an affect sticks just as well to the subjectivity of the one who is its utterer as it does to the one who is its addressee; and, in so doing, it disqualifies the enunciative dichotomy between speaker and listener" (158). Affect exceeds the seemly separation of persons, then, even of complete strangers in bathing suits intent on appearing oblivious to one another, precisely because affect is "essentially a pre-personal category" that comes from a nonplace that is not simply within the person but is "unlocatable" with regard both to its ultimate origin and final destination. An affect "speaks through me" more than it "speaks to me" (160). On the beach, affect is babbling continually in and through bodies exquisitely equipped to transmit it. Spinoza, savoring the clamorous silence, smiles.

Spinoza's Bliss

And the relationship of affect to emotion? That's more complex. Massumi's pronouncement on that relationship—a pronouncement of divorce—is commonly seen as definitive of the Deleuze-Massumi brand of affect theory, as noted earlier, notwithstanding the fact that Massumi does not claim to be channeling Deleuze in severing affect from emotion. But Massumi does claim that this affect-emotion separation, together with other related distinctions and formulations, finds "a formidable philosophical precursor" in Spinoza.[84] Is this claim compelling?

States that sound suspiciously like emotions bubble up constantly in both Spinoza's *Ethics* and Deleuze's explications and elaborations of it.[85] Most

[83] Readers of Sara Ahmed may be struck by Guattari's assertion that affect "sticks" (*l'affect colle*). Independently of Guattari's 1989 article, apparently, the insistence that affect (or emotion; Ahmed refuses the affect/emotion dichotomy) "sticks" and is "sticky" runs like a refrain through her *The Cultural Politics of Emotion* (New York: Routledge, 2004; expanded 2nd ed. 2014) in particular.

[84] Massumi, *Parables for the Virtual*, 28.

[85] Even if one breaks with the tradition of rendering Spinoza's *affectus* as "emotion," a tradition enshrined in Morgan and Shirley, *Spinoza: Complete Works* (see n. 73 in this chapter), although not in *The Collected Works of Spinoza*, ed. and trans. Edwin Curley, 2 vols. (Princeton, NJ: Princeton University Press, 1985–2016). Deleuze also sets that tradition aside; the French term *l'émotion* does not appear in either of his Spinoza books.

48   THE BIBLE AFTER DELEUZE

significantly, joy (*laetitia*) and its antonym sadness (*tristitia*) feature prominently in the *Ethics*,

> "There is a Spinoza-assemblage: soul and body, relationships and encounters, power to be affected, affects which realize this power, sadness and joy which qualify these affects" (Deleuze and Parnet, *Dialogues II*, 62).

impelling Deleuze to describe the *Ethics* not only as "a philosophy of pure affirmation," but as "a philosophy of the joy corresponding to such affirmation" (*Expressionism in Philosophy*, 272).

The joy and, indeed, the sadness are both products of the affect-machine that is the Spinozan-Deleuzian body. Deleuze describes the machine's oscillating motion: "When we encounter an external body that does not agree with our own . . . , it may be said that our power of acting is diminished or blocked, and the corresponding passions are those of *sadness*." But "when we encounter a body that agrees with our nature, . . . we may say that its power is added to ours; the passions that affect us are those of *joy*, and our power of acting is increased or enhanced" (*Practical Philosophy*, 28). Spinoza inhales the fragrance of the bloom offered to him by the flower-seller and feels a sought-after sentence of his *Ethics* stir at the threshold of the articulable. *Spinoza is filled with joy.* Spinoza later scurries back to his garret following the mortifying incident in the alley,

> "Everything is simply an encounter in the universe, a good or a bad encounter. Adam eats the apple. . . . Adam has a bad encounter" (Deleuze and Parnet, *Dialogues II*, 60).

his philosophical musings abruptly snuffed out like a candle. *Spinoza is filled with sadness.*

Not joy in the sense of happiness, Massumi would object (he doesn't pronounce on Spinozan sadness, so far as I know). For Massumi, Spinoza's joy, as expressed in his *Ethics*, is "on a different axis" from happiness. It is "joy as affirmation, an assuming by the body of its potentials, its assuming of a posture that intensifies its powers of existence. The moment of joy is the co-presence of those potentials, in the context of a bodily becoming."[86] To most ears, I suspect, that moment, so described, sounds like a supremely happy one.

---

[86] Brian Massumi, *Politics of Affect* (Malden, MA: Polity Press, 2015), 44. Massumi is pondering Spinoza's "joy" in tandem with Nietzsche's "gaiety." He later revisits the theme in a yet more austere

INTRODELEUZE (WHO AND WHY?)   49

More compelling is Massumi's assertion that joy in the Spinozan mode has the potential to "be very disruptive," to "even be very painful," to be "an experience that overcomes you," and "can actually destroy [you]," [87] a caveat that would seem to apply at least to the elevated version of Spinozan joy associated with what Deleuze terms the third kind of knowledge, which is also third-level affect. This is also what Deleuze labels the "mystical" variant of affect ("Spinoza's Concept of *Affect*," n.p.), as we saw earlier, and the joy corresponding to it is "no longer defined by an increase of our perfection or power of acting but by the full, formal possession of that power or perfection" (Deleuze, *Practical Philosophy*, 51), its "full actualization" (*Expressionism in Philosophy*, 130).

Just how elevated is this third-level joy? For such joy, "we must reserve the name *beatitude* [*béatitude*]," Deleuze insists (*Practical Philosophy*, 51) [88]

> "We will say of pure immanence that it is A LIFE [*UNE VIE*] and nothing else. . . . A life is the immanence of immanence, absolute immanence: it is complete power [*puissance*], complete bliss [*béatitude*]" (Deleuze, *Pure Immanence*, 27).

—a name he also reserves for the title of the climactic chapter of his other Spinoza book, the chapter on the third kind of knowledge (*Expressionism in Philosophy*, 303–20). [89] But third-level joy is a thoroughly exceptional state, for Spinoza as for Deleuze. For the most part, all we may attain are joys of a lesser kind (Deleuze, *Practical Philosophy*, 27–28, 50; *Expressionism in Philosophy*, 310–11), the kind that do not flirt with the madness Massumi evokes, lesser joys that bubble up frequently and unapologetically in Spinoza's *Ethics* and Deleuze's books and lectures on Spinoza. There is, as

register: "[Spinozan] joy is not 'happy,' and it does not connote the attainment of satisfaction. These 'hedonistic' distinctions simply do not apply to affect. They apply to emotions: the psychological capture of affect for the interiority of a supposedly individual subject. Subjects feel good about themselves emotionally (or not), in the personal refuge of their putative interiority. Affect feels out the world" (208–9).

[87] Massumi, *Politics of Affect*, 44–45. Massumi's examples of persons thus destroyed, plunged into madness, are Nietzsche himself, but especially Antonin Artaud (the French literary artist and actor who, as we see later, was a crucially important figure for Deleuze).

[88] My translation.

[89] Ironically in light of Massumi's squeamishness about a joy-happiness equation, Martin Joughin, translator of Deleuze's *Spinoza et le problème de l'expression*, is squeamish about rendering Spinoza's *beatitudo* as "beatitude," arguing that it is better translated as "happiness": "I would happily render *beatitudo* simply by 'happiness,' had not Spinoza's French translators and Deleuze used *béatitude* rather than *bonheur*" ("Translator's Notes" in Deleuze, *Expressionism in Philosophy*, 412).

50   THE BIBLE AFTER DELEUZE

Martin Joughin notes, a "distinction between Spinozist 'joy' in general and a beatific joy or *jouissance*—the full possession of joy in a sort of dispossession of oneself" ("Translator's Notes" in *Expressionism in Philosophy*, 412). In claiming in blanket fashion that Spinozist joy "is not 'happy,' and . . . does not connote the attainment of satisfaction," Massumi erases that distinction.[90]

What of emotion more broadly in Deleuzian thought? How does it relate to affect? The partition between affect and emotion for Deleuze (as for Guattari) is considerably more porous than Massumi's partition. The following statement from *A Thousand Plateaus*, for instance, would be all but unimaginable from the lips of Massumi: "Affect is the active discharge of emotion [*l'émotion*]" (400). Earlier, in Deleuze and Guattari's *Anti-Oedipus*, affect collapses entirely into emotion on occasion: "The basic phenomenon of hallucination (*I see, I hear*) and the basic phenomenon of delirium (*I think . . .*) presuppose an *I feel* [*Je sens*] at an even deeper level. . . . [They] are secondary in relation to the really primary emotion [*l'émotion vraiment primaire*], which in the beginning only experiences intensities, becomings, transitions" (18). Later in *Anti-Oedipus*, this "really primary emotion" is described as "the intensive emotion, the affect [*l'émotion intensive, l'affect*]" (84). Ultimately, it is the envelopment or enfolding of emotion in the Spinozan concept of affect that comes to expression in these statements.

Yet, Deleuze's distance from Massumi should not be exaggerated either. That distance closes to a hairline crack at times, at least when it comes to the affect-feeling distinction, as in the following assertions by Deleuze: "Affects aren't feelings [*Les affects ne sont pas des sentiments*], they're becomings that spill over beyond whoever lives through them (thereby becoming someone else)" (*Negotiations*, 137). And again: "[Desire] is an affect, as opposed to a feeling" (*Two Regimes of Madness*, 130). And more elaborately: "The body has autonomous external reactions. The body is an animal. What the body does it does alone"—which, as Deleuze notes, puts yet another spin on Spinoza's famous formula, "We do not know what a body can do" (*Essays Critical and Clinical*, 123). Specifically, "the body never ceases to act and react *before the mind moves it*" (123, emphasis original).[91] This is where emotion comes in, but always a few steps behind. Consider the following: (1) The animal that

---

[90] Massumi, *Politics of Affect*, 208.

[91] The body is not a mere instrument of the mind, not "a means or vehicle for the mind, but rather a 'molecular sludge' that adheres to all the mind's actions," molecular sludge being "the body's final state" (Deleuze, *Essays Critical and Clinical*, 123). The body, then, is both a live animal and a dead animal at one and the same time.

INTRODELEUZE (WHO AND WHY?)   51

is my body suddenly encounters another animal that is an (uncaged) lion. (2) My body reacts by trembling. (3) I feel the emotion of fear. Deleuze draws this example from William James, pronouncing accurate James's logical separation of micromoments 2 and 3 (*Essays Critical and Clinical*, 123–24).

In fact, Deleuze would extend in crawling slow motion the microduration separating these micromoments (and in a way that causes the crack between him and Massumi to widen once again): "The mind begins by coldly and curiously regarding what the body does, it is first of all a witness; then it is affected, it becomes an impassioned witness, that is, it experiences for itself affects that are not simply effects of the body, but veritable *critical entities* that hover over the body and judge it. Spiritual entities or abstract ideas are not what we think they are: they are emotions or affects [*ce sont des émotions, des affects*]" (*Essays Critical and Clinical*, 124). But if affects are, or can be, emotions, for Deleuze ("emotion" being a term he uses infrequently), then, conversely, emotions are, or can be, affects; and we have glimpsed the immensity of affect in Deleuzian thought, a vastness rhizomatically rooted in Spinozan soil (specifically, in Spinoza's infinite single substance out of which Deleuze's plane of immanence grows), which makes Deleuze's emotions altogether different from emotions as ordinarily conceived.

... and the Bible?

Spinoza's Bible

As it happens, Spinoza is hailed as the foreparent, not only of affect theory in certain of its most influential contemporary manifestations, but also of critical biblical scholarship. While humanist philology and heterodox Protestantism undoubtedly paved the path for the Jewish excommunicant's radical reappraisal of the Bible,[92] Spinoza's *Theological-Political Treatise* (1670) is commonly seen as the first defiant throwing down of the rationalist gauntlet in the frequently bloody arena of post-Reformation biblical hermeneutics, which necessitated not only that the *Treatise* be published

---

[92] In 1656, the Talmud Torah congregation of Amsterdam issued a writ of *ḥerem* (effectively, the Jewish equivalent of Roman Catholic *vitandus*, excommunication) against the twenty-three year old Spinoza. Subsequently, Spinoza was adopted by assorted Protestant freethinkers, most notably, the dissenting Protestant sect known as the Collegiants, among which he became an influential, and controversial, figure.

52 THE BIBLE AFTER DELEUZE

anonymously and in Latin rather than Dutch, but that its publisher and place of publication be misidentified on its title page. It was condemned at the Reformed Synod of Dort in 1673 and formally banned the following year, which did not, however, prevent it from being expeditiously translated into Dutch, French, and English and being hotly debated in elevated circles all across Europe.

The *Theological-Political Treatise* argued that the Bible cannot reasonably be said to derive its authority from any transcendent deity (there being no such entity in the Spinozan cosmos). To properly apprehend the Bible, one must approach it like any other object in Nature (Nature being all there is, for Spinoza): "For the method of interpreting Nature consists essentially in composing a detailed study of Nature from which . . . we can deduce the definitions of the things of Nature. Now in exactly the same way the task of Scriptural interpretation requires us to make a straightforward study of Scripture, and from this . . . to deduce by logical inference the meaning of the authors of Scripture."[93] Thus understood, the Bible should be seen, not as a book designed to impart scientific or philosophical truth, but only to compel obedience. To quote the summative title of one of the *Treatise*'s chapters, "It is shown that Scripture teaches only very simple doctrines and inculcates nothing but obedience, and that concerning the nature of God it teaches only what men can imitate by a definite code of conduct."[94]

But what of affect? Inextricably embedded as the Bible is in Spinoza's single substance (Nature or God),

> "The eternal and infinite being, whom we call God, or Nature [*Deus, sive Natura*]" (Spinoza, *Ethics*, 321).

how might the Bible be said to participate in third-level affect in particular, affect of the "mystical" kind, as we saw, the kind most attuned to the more sublime attributes of the single substance? Even if one side of the biblical text—the recto side, if you will—necessarily faces what Deleuze and Guattari term "the strata" (*A Thousand Plateaus*, 4),

> "Strata are acts of capture" (40).

---

[93] Baruch Spinoza, *Theological-Political Treatise*, trans. Samuel Shirley, 2nd ed. (Indianapolis: Hackett, 2001), 87.

[94] Spinoza, *Theological-Political Treatise*, 153.

INTRODELEUZE (WHO AND WHY?)   53

which, among other things, is also the domain of "order-words" (76), words that, as Spinoza would phrase it, are designed to "inculcate nothing but obedience,"[95] might the other side of the biblical text, the verso side, not face—not open like a floodgate, indeed—on the infinite potentiality, the incalculable virtuality, of the single substance or plane of immanence, what Deleuze and Guattari also term the Body without Organs: "A book is an assemblage.... One side ... faces the strata ...; it also has a side facing a Body without Organs" (*A Thousand Plateaus*, 4)?[96] Might all of the foregoing not be visible in the somber sentences of the *Theological-Political Treatise*, glowing through them and pulsing within them? Apparently not. If third-level affect coursed visibly through the pages of the *Treatise*, then that text would be the charter document, not of biblical criticism in the ancient-contextual and authorial-intentionalist mode, but of biblical criticism in modes yet to be implemented or even imagined.

That is not to say that affect is not an explicit theme in the *Theological-Political Treatise*. On the contrary, affect is a prominent theme in it, at least in its preface. But it is affect of a more stunted sort than we find in the *Ethics*, completed four years after the *Treatise*. Briefly put, affect (*affectus*) is framed negatively in the *Treatise*. Fear is the foremost affect in it, the one that enslaves entire populations to superstition; and hatred, rage, and other destructive affects follow in its wake.[97] Affect is a synonym for passion (*passio*) in the *Treatise*, and as such the antonym of reason (*ratio*).[98]

By the time we arrive at the *Ethics*, however, affect and reason have been reconciled. Reason has developed the capacity to generate positive affects that constrain the negative affects. And in place of the *Treatise*'s cynical concept of affect derived from sordid human dysfunction—a concept that dictates why Spinoza's Bible needs to be a book of commands, an instrument of control—the *Ethics* presents us with an elegant geometry of affect that proceeds in serene deductive fashion from the primary affects to their complex combinations.[99] The distance affect has traveled in the relatively short

---

[95] Spinoza, *Theological-Political Treatise*, 153.

[96] Much more on the strata and the BwO in chapter 1.

[97] Spinoza, *Theological-Political Treatise*, 1–3, 7–8.

[98] Representative in this regard is the following statement: "Superstition, like all other instances of hallucination and frenzy, ... is sustained only by hope, hatred, anger and deceit. For it arises not from reason but from affect [*affectus*], and affect of the most powerful kind" (Spinoza, *Theological-Political Treatise*, 2, translation modified).

[99] The phrase "geometry of affect" is no metaphor here. The work's full Latin title is *Ethica, ordine geometrico demonstrata* [Ethics, Demonstrated in Geometrical Order], and it is Euclidean is format, each of its books constituting a series of definitions, axioms, propositions, proofs, corollaries, and the like.

54   THE BIBLE AFTER DELEUZE

interval between the preface to the *Treatise* and the final book of the *Ethics* is astounding. Affect has ascended out of the mud and attained beatitude.[100]

Deleuze's Bible?

The path of the present book, in contrast, leads into the mud; by the time we arrive at its final two chapters, those on race and racism, pandemic plague and Trumpism, we are thigh-deep in the stuff. But there are glimpses of beatitude along the way. Here is how the book unfolds.

Chapter 1, "TEXT (the Bible without organs)," is propelled by several questions that are really one question: What is a biblical text, and how does it do what it does? What am I reading when I read my Bible with Deleuze or Deleuze and Guattari? The answer, once we arrive at it (following some stage-setting preliminaries involving Foucault), turns out to be fivefold. First, I am reading (in) flux and as such affectively. Second, I am reading (in) an assemblage and as such in prepersonal and transpersonal interrelationality. Third, I am reading a book—*the* Book, indeed—of order-words and as such resistantly. Fourth, I am reading a book that expresses everything while communicating nothing. Fifth, I am reading a book of two warring deities. One of these deities is an ultraterritorializing God, an altogether despotic deity, Deleuze and Guattari's "lobster God." The other deity is an all but inarticulable God but one worthier of the name, a God who may not be a God at all, as God is customarily conceived, a God better conceived as a Body without Organs, Deleuze and Guattari's most intractable and most intriguing paratheological term.

Chapter 2 unfolds under the title "BODY (why there are no bodies in the Bible, and how to read them anyway)." In the field of early Christian studies, as in the field of classics, the ancient body has gradually dissolved, its surfaces and contours becoming ever more indistinct. It has been reconceived and remolded by third-wave gender theory but also by queer theory: discursivity and performativity, whether explicitly named or not, have become key for work on it. But is the constructed body, discursive or performative, the only body that theory and criticism, including biblical criticism, are equipped to access? Might Deleuzian theory enable us to exit the Foucauldian-Butlerian

---

[100] Further on the evolution of Spinozan affect from the *Theological-Political Treatise* to the *Ethics*, see Chantal Jaquet, *Affects, Actions and Passions in Spinoza: The Unity of Body and Mind*, trans. Tatiana Reznichenko (Edinburgh: Edinburgh University Press, 2018), 47–74.

INTRODELEUZE (WHO AND WHY?)   55

paradox of a body that has no articulable existence anterior to the discourses and performances that enflesh it by bestowing legible form on it? What narratological form might such exiting take as we engage with, say, the Jesuses of the Synoptic Gospels and their abiding affects? How might we imagine ancient literary bodies differently? Such rethinking might begin with the observation that early Christian narratives, like all narratives, contain no corporeal entities whatsoever, no bodies as such to know, whether human or nonhuman, but only incorporeal bodies (in the Deleuzian sense), which demand a different kind of knowing, a different mode of engagement, and hence a return to theoretical first principles.

Chapter 3, "SEX (a thousand tiny sexes, a trillion tiny Jesuses)," intensifies the post–Foucault/Butler thrust of the previous chapter. Queer theory's standard origin story centers on Foucault and Butler, together with Eve Sedgwick and Teresa de Lauretis. This chapter proceeds down a less-traveled road, one well signposted in recent decades but yet to be explored in biblical studies. Its point of departure is the iconoclastic theory of desire set forth in Deleuze and Guattari's *Anti-Oedipus*. The difference this rerouting makes is considerable, yielding a concept of the gendered body that is neither discursive (à la Foucault) nor performative (à la Butler) but virtual; a concept of sexuality that overflows the human/nonhuman binary containers no less than the heterosexual/homosexual containers; and an alternative version of queer theory's "antisocial thesis" that precedes Lee Edelman's Lacanian version by more than thirty years—namely, Guy Hocquenghem's Deleuzoguattarian version. Deleuze's own engagement with Hocquenghem also fuels this chapter. How might Deleuze and Guattari's hyperqueer theory (for that is what their concept of sexuality amounts to) translate into biblical reading? Addressing this question through an extended analysis of the Gospel of Mark is actually the main business of chapter 3.

Chapter 4 is titled "RACE (Jesus and the white faciality machine)." One of the preeminent products of the European colonization of the Majority World was a racially white Jesus, a transfiguration of the Eastern Mediterranean Jewish Jesus refracted in the pages of the New Testament. Deleuzoguattarian theory provides a particularly potent resource for peeling back and scrutinizing the layers of whiteness Jesus has accrued, and for opening up the "abstract machine of faciality" (as Deleuze and Guattari style it) that produced, and still produces, whiteness as such. The most radical analysis of whiteness, indeed, to have emerged out of, or to the side of, French poststructuralism is the "Year Zero: Faciality" chapter of Deleuze and Guattari's *A*

56 THE BIBLE AFTER DELEUZE

Thousand Plateaus, a chapter that, as it happens, assigns pivotal significance to Jesus as the retroactive linchpin of the faciality machine that produces, and reproduces, white masculinity as Christian universalism. Bringing Deleuze and Guattari into dialogue with seminal Black thinkers on race—notably W. E. B. Du Bois, Frantz Fanon, and Stuart Hall—my own chapter attempts to ponder anew the intersections of Christianity, empire, and whiteness, together with certain of the New Testament texts that white Christendom claims as its own.

Chapter 5, finally, "POLITICS (beastly boasts, apocalyptic affects)," is a tale about a democracy, a despot, a pandemic, and an ancient prophet. Deleuze cowrote a memorable essay on the book of Revelation. This chapter appropriates his reading tactics, together with those of contemporary affect theory, to connect Revelation with the Trump presidency, post-Trump Trumpism, and the COVID-19 pandemic. Specifically, the chapter relates Revelation's Beast to Trump and Trumpism noneschatologically in a nonrepresentational reading strategy. The chapter's operative assumption, adapted from Deleuze, is not that Trump or the pandemic were prophesied in Revelation, but rather that Revelation possesses multiple sockets into which the pandemic, the Trump presidency, and now the Trump legacy may be plugged and thereby illuminated. The chapter connects Revelation's visions with consequential recent events, then, not by reading for relations of resemblance or analogy between these visions and events but rather by reading the events as though they were intricately folded into the visions, coextensive with and co-implicated in them in a continuous plane of interimbrication. The chapter takes the form of a simultaneous plague journal and reign-of-the-Beast journal, and ends with a post-Beast postscript.

At least two things will be immediately apparent from these chapter previews. First, the book's main title plays fast and loose with the book's contents. That title is a sobriquet for the book's less sexy real title: *The Bible, with Special Reference to the Synoptic Gospels and the Book of Revelation, after Deleuze and Guattari*. Second, the book contains no overarching, unifying argument, incrementally crafted, each chapter ending by deftly handing off the rhetorical baton to its successor chapter. Each chapter is rather a freestanding essay, essentially, although the chapters may reference each other at times or gesture back to the introduction.

The chapter sequence, however, is not random. The text chapter (chapter 1), which, among other things, is a Bible-as-Body-without-Organs chapter, sets up the (official) body chapter (chapter 2); which flows into the sex chapter (chapter 3), which, of course, is yet another body chapter; which runs into the race chapter (chapter 4), sex and race being a long-established couple; which topples over into the politics chapter (chapter 5), which at base is another race and racism chapter.

Of my hope for the book as a whole, I would simply say what Deleuze once (with immeasurably less reason for modesty) said of his own books: "The question facing every writer is whether or not people have some use, however small, to make of the book, in their own work, in their life, and their projects" (*Two Regimes of Madness*, 180).

1

TEXT (the Bible without organs)

What am I reading when I read my Bible with Deleuze? With Deleuze and Guattari? "What am I reading?" questions are the driving ones propelling this chapter forward. What it means to read the Bible, or any other text, with Deleuze and Guattari emerges in sharper relief, however, when set against the backdrop of what it means to read a text, not least a biblical text, with or through Michel Foucault,

> "I read what [Foucault] wrote with a passion.... I had the feeling, with no sadness, that in the end I needed him and he did not need me" (Deleuze, *Two Regimes of Madness*, 281).

another of Deleuze's most important intellectual influences. We begin with Foucault, then, move to Deleuze on Foucault, and then to Deleuze and Guattari, all the while asking, what Bible, what Bibles, do these theoretical shifts, these differently calibrated machines,

> "They are machines that make one see" (339).

make visible?

Part I: At the Bible Study with Foucault and Deleuze

What Is a Biblical Author?

Foucault's Discourse

For Foucault, it wasn't so much that there was nothing *outside* the text, as Derrida had infamously asserted, as that there was nothing *inside* the text: no intrinsic formal properties, no inherent semantic content, no anterior authorial intentions awaiting rediscovery, no slumbering princess in a concealed

---

The Bible after Deleuze. Stephen D. Moore, Oxford University Press. © Oxford University Press 2023.
DOI: 10.1093/oso/9780197581254.003.0002

TEXT (THE BIBLE WITHOUT ORGANS)   59

inner chamber awaiting an interpretive kiss. Mind you, all of that is merely implicit in Foucault. It was not in the interiority of *texts* that Foucault disbelieved so much as in the interiority of *discourse*, an altogether more expansive category. For Foucault, discourse has no concealed core, no hidden nucleus of meaning;

> "That everything is always said in every age is perhaps Foucault's greatest historical principle: behind the curtain there is nothing to see, but it was all the more important each time to describe the curtain, or the base, since there was nothing either behind or beneath it" (Deleuze, *Foucault*, 54).

instead, it only has "external conditions of existence" determined by "chance series of . . . events."[1]

(Ah, *The Archaeology of Knowledge and the Discourse on Language*. . . . How many hapless students have I inflicted this dry-as-dust text on over the decades? And why do I find myself trudging yet again through its arid wastes, mesmerized by the dazzling glint of sunlight on this turn of phrase, that sentence or passage?)

What discourse, in the Foucauldian sense, was not: "Groups of signs," such signs in turn being "signifying elements referring to contents or representations."[2] (Never confuse me for Saussure, Foucault was silently insisting.) What discourse, in the Foucauldian sense, was: "Practices that systematically form the objects of which they speak,"[3] practices that, in consequence, are also "place[s] in which a tangled plurality . . . of objects is formed and deformed, appears and disappears."[4] Objects such as texts, even?

That texts are discursive constructions through and through is fully implicit in Foucault's "archaeological" theory of knowledge, although he does not announce it explicitly. Foucault was surprisingly uninterested in the discursive constructedness of textual bodies, given that the discursive constructedness of human bodies was one of his enduring obsessions,[5] and what are texts but bodily prostheses? Logically, texts, too, would be

---

[1] Michel Foucault, *The Archaeology of Knowledge and the Discourse on Language*, trans. A. M. Sheridan Smith (New York: Pantheon Books, [1969] 1972), 229.

[2] Foucault, *The Archaeology of Knowledge*, 49.

[3] Foucault, *The Archaeology of Knowledge*, 49.

[4] Foucault, *The Archaeology of Knowledge*, 48.

[5] An obsession I turn to in the opening section of the next chapter.

60   THE BIBLE AFTER DELEUZE

factory products of those multiple Foucauldian institutional sites in which discourses of knowledge, and hence of truth and power, are continually manufactured and manipulated—"the prodigious machinery of the will to truth," as Foucault somberly puts it, "with its vocation of exclusion."[6]

Foucault's Bible

What, then, am I reading when I read my Bible with Michel Foucault (peering suspiciously over my shoulder)? Easier to answer is the question, what am I reading when I read *biblical scholarship* with Michel Foucault? I'm not sure it's ever been remarked just how much of Foucault's "What Is an Author?" and "The Discourse on Language" read as though he were pronouncing specifically on the discipline of biblical studies.[7]

For instance, biblical authors, as commonly (re)constructed by biblical scholars, might be said to epitomize what Foucault termed *the author function* [*la fonction auteur*]: "In a civilization like our own there are a certain number of discourses that are endowed with the 'author function,' while others are deprived of it."[8] This author function, moreover, fully matured, is of relatively recent vintage. It coalesced only when texts became "goods caught up in a circuit of ownership," as began to happen in eighteenth-century Europe with the formal codification of copyright law.[9]

More below on the mercantile origins of the author function. Not coincidentally, as we shall see, we biblical scholars began to take our first toddling steps in this period. So vital, indeed, was the invention of the author function to our emerging disciplinary identity that, to this very day, we still cling collectively to the interpretive strategies it thrust into our hands:

---

[6] Foucault, *The Archaeology of Knowledge*, 220.

[7] He wasn't, of course, but it's illuminating, even at this far distant remove from these remarkable lectures, to read him as though he were. Foucault delivered "What Is an Author?" to the Société Française de Philosophie in 1969 and "The Discourse on Language" (literally, "The Order of Discourse": *L'Ordre du discours*) at the Collège de France in 1970. See Michel Foucault, "What Is an Author?," in *Aesthetics, Method, and Epistemology*, ed. James D. Faubion, trans. Robert Hurley et al., Essential Works of Foucault, 1954–1984 (New York: New Press, 1998), vol. 2, 205–22; "Appendix: The Discourse on Language," in Foucault, *The Archaeology of Knowledge*, 215–37. The latter essay overlaps with the former and reads like an outgrowth of it.

[8] Foucault, "What Is an Author?," 211.

[9] Foucault, "What Is an Author?," 212.

TEXT (THE BIBLE WITHOUT ORGANS)   61

We [still] ask of each poetic or fictional [or rhetorical, or historical, biblical] text: From where does it come, who wrote it, when, under what circumstances, or beginning with what design? The meaning ascribed to it and the status or value accorded it depend on the manner in which we answer these questions. And if a text should be discovered in a status of anonymity [or pseudonymity] ... the game becomes one of rediscovering the author. Since literary anonymity is not tolerable, we can accept it only in the guise of an enigma.[10]

But the cerebral multiplayer game that is biblical historical criticism is devoted not only to the rediscovery of the author as a historical individual, the rightful owner of the text's long-lost meanings, the semantic treasures buried within it; the modern author-concept has other functions in addition. The apostle Paul, collectively refashioned as an author in the modern mold,

> "What is Paul?" (1 Cor 3:5).

would, perhaps, be the consummate biblical-scholarly example of these additional functions. The author, thus reconceived, is also "the principle of ... unity" in any body of writing that perches on the precipice of incoherence (which is to say, any body of writing whatsoever),

> "At first, the threat is imperceptible, but a few steps suffice to make us
> aware of an enlarged crevice; the whole organization of the surface
> has already disappeared. ... Nonsense ... has consumed everything"
> (Deleuze, *The Logic of Sense*, 82).

enabling critics to have recourse to such concepts as authorial "evolution, maturation, or influence" as they attempt to impose order on its vertigo-inducing movements.[11] The author, thus deployed, "serves to neutralize the contradictions that may emerge." More precisely, the author, thus reinvented, is the meticulously constructed place "where incompatible elements are at last tied together."[12] Notably few Pauline scholars have managed to embrace a differently constructed Paul, a disunified, self-contradictory, incoherent Paul,

---

[10] Foucault, "What Is an Author?," 213.
[11] Foucault, "What Is an Author?," 215.
[12] Foucault, "What Is an Author?," 215.

62 THE BIBLE AFTER DELEUZE

an apostle-in-fragments Paul. Such a Paul—a Paul ignominiously stripped of his author function—would leave the Pauline specialist fully as naked as the shivering apostle, deprived of the need for their expert discourse on him.

For Foucault, moreover, the birth of the modern concept of authorship coincided with the birth of capitalism. More precisely, the concept of the author as legitimate owner of the text's semantic contents was an oblique expression of the mercantile ethos of European capitalism in its emergent phase. Even to this day, and as is exceptionally evident in the high-walled disciplinary enclave known as critical biblical scholarship, the author function

> allows a limitation of the cancerous and dangerous proliferation of significations within a world where one is thrifty not only with one's resources and riches, but also with one's discourses and their significations. The author is the principle of thrift [*économie*] in the proliferation of meaning. As a result, we must entirely reverse the traditional idea of the author. We are accustomed . . . to saying that the author is the profuse creator [*l'instance créatrice jaillissante*] of a work in which he deposits, with infinite wealth and generosity, an inexhaustible world of significations. . . . The truth is quite the contrary: the author . . . is a certain functional principle by which, in our culture, one limits, excludes, and chooses. . . . One can say that the author is an ideological product, since we represent him as the opposite of his historically real function.[13]

As a Pauline scholar, one might live that contradiction robustly and unreflectingly. One might devote an entire prolific publishing career to the two-hundred-odd pages that comprise the undisputed Pauline letters in one's *Novum Testamentum Graece* (cherished, ceaselessly pored-over pages, become papery extensions of one's own bodily tissue), all the while teaching one's elective courses exclusively on Paul (if one were so fortunate as to enjoy an academic position that afforded such specialization—or any full-time academic position at all). The *founding assumption* of this all-consuming professional endeavor would be that Paul richly repays the labor, Paul being conceived as "the profuse creator" of a wholly unique and inestimably valuable body of work "in which he has deposited . . . an inexhaustible world of significations."[14] Yet the *operative assumption* of one's scholarly practice

---

[13] Foucault, "What Is an Author?," 221–22, translation lightly modified.
[14] Foucault, "What Is an Author?," 221.

TEXT (THE BIBLE WITHOUT ORGANS)   63

(seeping over into one's pedagogical practice) would be that explicating precisely what Paul's letters mean, from the micro- to the macro-level,

"There are some things in them hard to understand" (2 Pet 3:16).

entails walking the finest of fine exegetical lines, so much so, indeed, that none of one's fellow laborers in the Pauline vineyard, much as one admires and appreciates their expertise and insights, have managed to get all the details exactly right—and fortunately so, for that is precisely what enables one to make one's own exquisitely nuanced, yet sufficiently substantial, contribution to Pauline knowledge. In the process, the ancient author whose often obscure pronouncements one has devoted so much of one's professional life to deciphering has become "the principle of thrift in the proliferation of meaning."[15]

Of course, Paul is more than just another author for Pauline specialists, more than just another author function. Paul would be a signal instance of what Foucault names *founders of discursivity* (*fondateurs de discursivité*).[16] Like Marx or Freud (Foucault's own examples), Paul is not merely the author of his own works. Paul has produced something else in addition, something that far exceeds those works. Paul has established an infinitely proliferating possibility for critical discourse—on Paul, first and foremost, but not only on Paul. As a founder of discursivity, Paul has generated a colossal scholarly appendage to supplement his own slim epistolary corpus. As he marches through Philippi, Thessalonica, or Corinth, Paul is blithely unaware of what is germinating within him, which, when it finally bursts forth from his martyred body and begins to enlarge exponentially, will cause him to become, not the founder of Christianity, as has often been said of him, but the founder of Christian discursivity.

One could go on this vein. Foucault's "The Discourse on Language," sister text to "What Is an Author?," maps onto the discipline of biblical studies as effortlessly as the latter. Look no further than the principal themes of "The Discourse on Language": *disciplinarity* ("Disciplines constitute a system of control in the production of discourse");[17] *authorship* (once again); *commentary* ("Commentary's only role is to say *finally*, what has silently been

---

[15] Foucault, "What Is an Author?," 221.
[16] Foucault, "What Is an Author?," 217.
[17] Foucault, "The Discourse on Language," 224.

64   THE BIBLE AFTER DELEUZE

articulated *deep down*. It must . . . say, for the first time, what has already been said,

> "Heavenly or subterranean, sense is presented as Principle, Reservoir, Reserve, Origin. As heavenly Principle, it is said to be fundamentally forgotten and veiled or, as subterranean principle, it is said to be deeply erased, diverted, and alienated. But beneath the erasure and the veil, we are summoned to rediscover and to restore" (Deleuze, *The Logic of Sense*, 72).

and repeat tirelessly what was, nevertheless, never said");[18] *doctrine* (which is institutional no less than religious, binding its adherents "to certain types of utterance while consequently barring them" from other types of utterance);[19] and *fellowships of discourse*, the latter dedicated to the preservation and proliferation of arcane or expert discourse, its circulation "within a closed community, according to strict regulations" and entailing an "ambiguous interplay of secrecy and disclosure."[20] Much of "The Discourse on Language" reads like a description of the discipline of biblical studies meticulously compiled by an alien visitor to the annual meeting of the Society of Biblical Literature, that twelve-hundred-session grand spectacle of biblical-scholarly hyperactivity, the overloaded but enthralled alien clutching its program book in one hand, its Tanakh in another, and its Greek New Testament in a third as it scurries from session to session.

Knowledge, Power, Desire

Solid or Liquid?

The immense utility of "early" Foucault for defamiliarizing the profession of biblical scholarship should by now be apparent. But what precisely is the Foucauldian text and, by extension, the Foucauldian Bible? Is it solid

> "Your writing has to be liquid or gaseous simply because normal perception and opinion are solid, geometric" (Deleuze, *Negotiations*, 133).

---

[18] Foucault, "The Discourse on Language," 221, emphasis in original.
[19] Foucault, "The Discourse on Language," 226.
[20] Foucault, "The Discourse on Language," 225–26.

TEXT (THE BIBLE WITHOUT ORGANS)   65

or is it liquid? Earlier I attempted to ferret out Foucault's theory of the text only to be promptly detoured, firmly ushered, into his theory of discourse. The reason is not hard to discern. From its very first mention in "What Is an Author?" the text concept is subordinated to the author concept. Indeed, the text is of interest only insofar as it is an indexical sign of the author, Foucault proposing "to deal solely with the relationship between text and author and with the manner in which the text points to this 'figure' that, at least in appearance, is outside and antecedes it."[21] For Foucault's theory of the text proper—a theory in miniature, however, always a side dish and never the main course—we need to turn back to his *Archaeology of Knowledge*.

Early in his reflections on what he calls the "facts of discourse"[22]—its normative rules, classificatory principles, and institutionalized categories—Foucault acknowledges the ostensible solidity of the book and the oeuvre, but only in order to liquefy it. "There is the material individualization of the book," muses Foucault, "which occupies a determined space, which has an economic value, and which itself indicates, by a number of signs, the limits of its beginning and its end"[23]—none more insistently than the book that takes its name from the Greek and Latin words for book(s), one might add, which begins with the words "In the beginning . . ." (Gen 1:1) and ends with the end of everything (but in the form of a new beginning that loops back to the old beginning, the book thereby locking shut with an audible click: "Then I saw a new heaven and a new earth" [Rev 21:1]). "And then there is the establishment of an oeuvre," continues Foucault, "which we recognize and delimit by attributing a certain number of texts to an author"[24]—the seven "undisputed" texts apportioned to Paul, say, to return to our earlier example.

Foucault's rhetorical materialism, however, immediately dissolves in his discursivism. "Is not the material unity of the volume a weak, accessory unity in relation to the discursive unity of which it is the support?" he asks.[25] Which discursive unity in the case of the Bible? we might ask in turn. Scholarly discourse on the Bible is conducted in a different (even if overlapping) domain from confessional discourse on it. Foucault, however, has anticipated our objection. "But is this discursive unity itself homogeneous . . . ?" he interjects. The ostensible solidity, the boundedness, of the material text is the product

---

[21] Foucault, "What Is an Author?," 205.
[22] Foucault, *The Archaeology of Knowledge*, 22.
[23] Foucault, *The Archaeology of Knowledge*, 23.
[24] Foucault, *The Archaeology of Knowledge*, 23.
[25] Foucault, *The Archaeology of Knowledge*, 23.

66 THE BIBLE AFTER DELEUZE

of a heterogenous field of discourse that is itself unbounded: "The book is not simply the object that one holds in one's hands; and it cannot remain within the little parallelepiped that contains it."[26] For instance, as soon as I apply to my own NRSV Bible, whose solid heft I register on my outstretched hand, the probe of a certain line of questioning, its reassuring "self-evidence" flows away from it like sand; "it indicates itself, constructs itself, only on the basis of a complex field of discourse."[27] What more may be said about this discursive, text-productive field? Foucault elaborates: "The frontiers of a book are never clear-cut: beyond the title, the first lines, and the last full stop, beyond its internal configuration and its autonomous form, it is caught up in a system of references to other books, other texts, other sentences: it is a node within a network."[28]

Earlier, when reflecting on the opening pages of Deleuze and Guattari's *A Thousand Plateaus*, I remarked that their pronouncements on what a book is, and what it does, do not amount to a simple recycling of the theory of intertextuality, there being too much of the nontextual and the nondiscursive, and even the nonorganic and the nonhuman, in the Deleuzoguattarian conception of the book-machine. Foucault, in contrast, in telling us what a book is and is not, does seem to have implicit recourse to the (then still novel) concept of intertextuality. (It is not a term Foucault ever uses explicitly in his writings, so far as I am aware.) As has often been remarked, Foucault's concept of intertextuality has more "political edge" than that of, say, Julia Kristeva or Roland Barthes, Foucault characteristically attending to the constraints exercised by institutions, disciplines, and professions on the circulation of, and attribution of meaning to, textual "nodes" in the intertexual "network."[29] When all is said and done, however (or so it seems to me, anyway), the Foucauldian text inhabits a universe that is decidedly bookish, a universe whose most evolved, most adapted life form is none other than *homo academicus*.

---

[26] Foucault, *The Archaeology of Knowledge*, 23.
[27] Foucault, *The Archaeology of Knowledge*, 23.
[28] Foucault, *The Archaeology of Knowledge*, 23.
[29] Foucault, *The Archaeology of Knowledge*, 23.

TEXT (THE BIBLE WITHOUT ORGANS) 67

Foucault's Power

How else might Foucault's concept of the book be distinguished from Deleuze's? This is where Deleuze's own book on Foucault is instructive. Deleuze reminds us that Foucault's oeuvre is animated by two successive, preeminent obsessions: an obsession with knowledge (*savoir*) that culminated with *The Archaeology of Knowledge*, and an obsession with power (*pouvoir*) that began in earnest with *Discipline and Punish* and emerged fully with *The History of Sexuality*. Foucault's author concept and text concept were both products of Foucault's knowledge period.

In Deleuze's comparative analysis of Foucault's *savoir* and *pouvoir* phases, he is, in familiar Deleuzian fashion, assimilating Foucault's thought to his own and creating a Foucault-Deleuze symbiote in the process. First of all, Deleuze assimilates the Foucauldian construal of knowledge to the Deleuzoguattarian concept of "strata" (*les strates*). Foucauldian knowledge is "stratified" (Deleuze, *Foucault*, 73–74) because it imposes form on "unformed, unstable *matières*" (matters, materials), "imprisons intensities," and generally perpetrates "acts of capture" (Deleuze and Guattari, *A Thousand Plateaus*, 40). Foucauldian knowledge, thus recast, behaves like a "black hole" that "strives to seize whatever comes within its reach" (40). In a word, it "territorializes" (40).[30] Less paranoiacally put, "Knowledge concerns formed matters . . . and formalized functions" (Deleuze, *Foucault*, 73). The Bible would be one such formed matter with a formalized function, or several, beginning with its traditional function as the material medium of "God's Word." Much that the Bible has effected does reduce to acts of capture, although, of course, that is not all the Bible has done.

Foucault's concept of power, somewhat paradoxically, signifies, for Deleuze, the opposite of knowledge's territorializing impulse.[31] That is not to

---

[30] Extrapolating freely from Deleuze, *Foucault*, 73–74, which does not refer explicitly to *A Thousand Plateaus*.

[31] The paradox is already fully present in *La volunté de savoir* (The Will to Knowledge), the inaugural volume of Foucault's *The History of Sexuality*, which famously (if implicitly) refuses the Marxist proclivity to locate power in state apparatuses: "By power, I do not mean 'Power' as a group of institutions and mechanisms that ensure the subservience of the citizens of a given state" (*The History of Sexuality*, vol. 1, 92). The paradox is compounded by the fact that Foucault's resoundingly positive reading of power is accomplished in French not through the use of *puissance* but rather through the use of *pouvoir* (see p. 39 n. 76 earlier on the *pouvoir/puissance* distinction). In the book's celebrated and controversial power chapter (officially its method chapter: *Méthode*, 121–35 of *La volunté de savoir*), the term *puissance* is used only once (123), and even then as a synonym for *pouvoir*. Deleuze follows Foucault in using *pouvoir* when analyzing and recasting Foucault's theory of power, even though *puissance* is Deleuze's preferred power-word elsewhere. Michel Foucault, *Histoire de la*

68 THE BIBLE AFTER DELEUZE

say, however, that in the passage from *savoir* to *pouvoir* we leave behind once and for all the bumper-car ride that is stratified knowledge, with its constant interruptions, collisions, and containments (a bumper car in which Michel was always more comfortable than Gilles), in order to ride the roller coaster that is its converse. The knowledge/power relationship, as Deleuze states it, is rather one of "mutual presupposition" and "mutual immanence" (*Foucault*, 74). What, then, is Foucauldian power when pressed through a Deleuzian wringer?

In good Foucauldian fashion, power, for Deleuze, is defined as much by what it is not as by what it is,[32] and what it is not, preeminently, is knowledge: "The practice of power remains irreducible to any practice of knowledge" (Deleuze, *Foucault*, 74). Deleuze concurs with Foucault's claim that power's theater of operations is microphysical. "But we must not take 'micro' to mean a simple miniaturization of visible and articulable forms," Deleuze insists; "instead it signifies another domain, . . . a dimension of thought that is irreducible to knowledge" (74).

To articulate the inarticulable dimensions of power, Deleuze has recourse to his own concepts of affect and virtuality. Power, for Foucault, "is a relation between forces" (Deleuze, *Foucault*, 70);

"Force is what enables" (Deleuze, *Nietzsche and Philosophy*, 50).[33]

in consequence, an exercise of power is affective, since force is nothing other than the "power to affect [*pouvoir d'affecter*] other forces" and "be affected" by them in turn (Deleuze, *Foucault*, 71). Consideration of the virtual dimension of power, meanwhile, brings us back to the domain of knowledge; for "relations between forces will remain transitive, unstable, faint, almost virtual, at all events unknown, unless they are carried out by the formed or stratified relations which make up forms of knowledge" (74). Power, as "almost virtual," then is "actualized" by the forms of knowledge, those stratifications that generate institutions, "not just the State, but also the Family, Religion, Production, the Marketplace, . . . Morality, and so on" (75).

---

sexualité, tome 1: *La volunté de savoir* (Paris: Gallimard, 1976); ET: *The History of Sexuality*, vol. 1: *An Introduction*, trans. Robert Hurley (New York: Random House, 1978).

[32] "By power I do not mean . . ."; "Power's conditions of possibility must not be sought in . . ."; "Power is not something that . . ."; and so on (Foucault, *The History of Sexuality*, vol. 1, 92ff.).

[33] *La force est ce qui peut* (my translation).

TEXT (THE BIBLE WITHOUT ORGANS)   69

Tucked tidily among these institutions, no doubt—indeed, prominently displayed in certain of them—would be the Bible. And what precisely would its relationship to power be, in the counterintuitive Foucauldian sense of the term? An utterly oblique relationship, according to the Foucault-Deleuze symbiote. Power in the microphysical Foucauldian mode, even the kind of microphysical power specific to the institution of "the Christian Religion," would not originate in the Bible or radiate outward from it, for power relations in this mode "do not emanate from a central point or unique locus of sovereignty, but at each moment move 'from one point to another' in a field of forces, marking inflections, resistances, twists and turns," constituting "an exercise of the non-stratified," and evading "all stable forms of the visible and the articulable" (Deleuze, *Foucault*, 73).[34] All of which would mean what, precisely, for our understanding of the Bible and what it "at each moment" does?

Deleuze's Desire

Deleuze's *Foucault* enables us to formulate a Foucauldian-Deleuzian answer to that question; but it is a stunted answer ultimately, not nearly as rich and multifaceted as the Deleuzian-Guattarian answer toward which the present chapter is progressing. The real differences between Deleuze and Foucault are not to be found in Deleuze's 1986 book on Foucault but rather in the lengthy note Deleuze had sent his longtime friend in 1977, published many years later as "Desire and Pleasure,"[35] in which he set forth a detailed critique of Foucault's concept of power, which critique further exacerbated an already opening rift between Deleuze and Foucault,[36] and which rift Deleuze is apparently attempting to repair in his book on Foucault (even though Foucault is already dead by then), as well as defend Foucault from his (other) critics. It reads as a book written as an act of love.

---

[34] The unattributed internal quotation, "from one point to another," appears to be from Foucault, *The History of Sexuality*, vol. 1, 93.

[35] Gilles Deleuze, "Désir et plaisir," *Magazine littéraire* 325 (October 1994): 59–65; ET: "Desire and Pleasure," in Deleuze, *Two Regimes of Madness*, 122–33.

[36] Details culled from François Dosse, *Gilles Deleuze and Félix Guattari: Intersecting Lives*, trans. Deborah Glassman (New York: Columbia University Press, 2010), 316–17, in combination with James Miller, *The Passion of Michel Foucault* (New York: Simon & Schuster, 1993), 297–98.

70   THE BIBLE AFTER DELEUZE

The critique elaborated in "Desire and Pleasure," gentle in tone[37] but scathing in substance, does not carry over into *Foucault*, then. But what was that substance? For Deleuze, desire, not power, is the primordial soup of the social. To speak about the social, for Deleuze, is to speak about assemblages, but assemblages are, at base, assemblages of desire,[38]

> **"How can the assemblage be refused the name it deserves, 'desire'?"**
> **(Deleuze and Parnet, *Dialogues II*, 70).**

not assemblages of power (Deleuze, *Two Regimes of Madness*, 124). "Of course, an assemblage of desire will include power arrangements," Deleuze concedes, but such arrangements are merely components of the larger assemblage (125). Power arrangements would take the form of territorialization or reterritorialization, but the assemblage "would also include points of deterritorialization" (125). Deleuze and Guattari had already argued in their *Kafka* book that deterritorialization and desire, not territorialization and power, are what ultimately drive the assemblage. On the one hand, the assemblage "is segmental," and its segments "are powers [*pouvoirs*]" that "capture desire by territorializing it, fixing it in place, . . . extracting from it an image of transcendence" (*Kafka*, 85–86). On the other hand, the assemblage not only has "*points of deterritorialization*," and "always *a line of flight* [*une ligne de fuite*] by which it escapes itself,"

> **"Lines of flight . . . never consist in running away from the world but rather in causing runoffs, as when you drill a hole in a pipe" (Deleuze and Guattari, *A Thousand Plateaus*, 204).**

but it "extends over or penetrates *an unlimited field of immanence* [aka the plane of immanence] that makes the segments melt and that liberates desire from all its concretizations . . . or, at the very least, fights actively against them in order to dissolve them" (Deleuze and Guattari, *Kafka*, 86, emphasis in original).[39]

---

[37] The gentleness will not come through in my summary of its arguments. François Ewald, however, who had originally delivered this peculiar third-person letter ("With regard to Michel . . ."; "The danger is: does Michel . . . ," etc.) from Deleuze to Foucault, aptly noted in his editorial foreword to the letter's publication seventeen years after Deleuze had composed it, "The following text is not just unpublished. There is something intimate, secret, confidential about it" (http://www.artdes.monash.edu.au/globe/delfou.html).

[38] See p. 25 earlier.

[39] Translation lightly modified.

TEXT (THE BIBLE WITHOUT ORGANS)   71

Consequently, Deleuze is not convinced by Foucault's nonrepressive, ultraproductive conception of power.[40] Within assemblages of desire, power arrangements do have a "repressive effect" for Deleuze (*Two Regimes of Madness*, 126). This leads to Deleuze's statement of what he takes a society to be:

> For me, a society, a social field . . . , first and foremost, . . . leaks out on all sides. . . . It . . . escapes in all directions. These lines of flight are what come first (even if first is not chronological). Far from being outside the social field, . . . lines of flight constitute its rhizome

> **"There are multiplicities which constantly go beyond binary machines. . . . There are centres everywhere, like . . . black holes which do not let themselves be agglomerated. . . . Non-parallel evolutions . . . which leap . . . between completely heterogeneous beings. . . . The rhizome is all this"** (Deleuze and Parnet, *Dialogues II*, 26).[41]

> or cartography. Lines of flight are almost the same thing as movements of deterritorialization. . . . They are points of deterritorialization in assemblages of desire. . . . Lines of flight are not necessarily revolutionary, . . . but they are what power arrangements are going to seal off and tie up. (Deleuze, *Two Regimes of Madness*, 127)[42]

And later: "Lines of flight, movements of deterritorialization . . . have no equivalent in Michel's work" (129).

Crudely put, if, for Foucault, the social is a closed system, a pressure cooker, so to speak, even the resistance

> **"Lines of resistance, or what I call lines of flight"** (Deleuze, *Two Regimes of Madness*, 132).

---

[40] Foucault's overarching question in his book is: "Do the workings of power . . . really belong primarily to the category of repression?" (*The History of Sexuality*, vol. 1, 10). And his answers are typified by the following statement: "Relations of power are not in superstructural positions, with merely a role of prohibition . . . ; they have a directly productive role, wherever they come into play" (94).

[41] The rhizome is all this and much more, being the overarching concept of the opening sequence of *A Thousand Plateaus* ("Introduction: Rhizome," 3–25).

[42] Translation lightly modified.

72   THE BIBLE AFTER DELEUZE

that power invariably elicits itself being internal to power ("Where there is power, there is resistance, and yet . . . this resistance is never in a position of exteriority in relation to power"),[43] the social, for Deleuze, is an open system, a sieve, if you will. So leaky is the social, for Deleuze, so constituted at base by innumerable flows, by escapes in all directions at once, that the fundamental "problem for a society is how to stop" those flows (*Two Regimes of Madness*, 280).[44] That is where power, where power arrangements, come in, but in a secondary (logical if not chronological) role. Deleuze continues: "What surprised Foucault was that faced with all these powers, all of their deviousness . . . , we can still resist.[45] My surprise is the opposite." Resistance "is flowing everywhere," yet those in power "are able to block it." For Foucault, the social is "an architecture," but for Deleuze it "is a fluid, or . . . a gas" (280).

And the Bible, as a specific assemblage of desire within a social field, within multiple social fields, thus reconceived? What should we expect it to be or do? To this (presumably) perforated book, perpetually stoppered and sealed, yet ever flowing and fleeing, we turn once again.

Part II: At the Bible Study with Deleuze and Guattari

For Deleuze and Guattari, as we have already seen, to read is to plug a text into something else,

> "The only question is which other machine the literary machine can be plugged into, must be plugged into in order to work" (*A Thousand Plateaus*, 4).

and this plugging, this interconnecting, it might be argued, is intrinsic even to the most orthodox modes of scholarly investigation. As an emblematic instance of this procedure in biblical scholarship, consider the following research report from the *Journal of Biblical Literature*: "I have checked all 4,030 instances of χρῆσις in the TLG into the fifth century CE. Of the verb, χράομαι, I have checked all 21,845 instances in the same time period in first-person

---

[43] Foucault, *The History of Sexuality*, vol. 1, 95.

[44] We are no longer in "Desire and Pleasure" now but rather in a 1986 interview with Deleuze that appears in *Two Regimes of Madness* under the title "Foucault and Prison" (272–81).

[45] Hence the ultimately awkward position that resistance holds in Foucault's theory of power: "[Resistances] are the odd term [lit., 'the other term,' *l'autre terme*] in relations of power" (*The History of Sexuality*, vol. 1, 96).

TEXT (THE BIBLE WITHOUT ORGANS) 73

singular, third-person singular, third-person plural indicative, subjunctive, and optative, and infinitive and feminine participle."[46] 25,875 times this inhumanly assiduous scholar plugged one or the other of his two Greek terms, *chrēsis* and *chraomai*, into the vast electrotextual circuit that is the Thesaurus Linguae Graecae, and not once did either of them light up. (To compound the surreality of the exercise, his argument depended on them *not* lighting up.) But his matter-of-fact description of his vision-imperiling research procedure electrified me. It constituted an iconic verbal cartoon of the inherited disciplinary mindset of biblical studies that I have always loved and loathed (but loved more than loathed, all told).

So let's plug in, then, although not into TLG but ATP, *A Thousand Plateaus* and its companion texts. What am I reading when—driven and desperate; desperate but still driven—I read my Bible with Deleuze, with Deleuze and Guattari, with Deleuze and Parnet?

In Flux, in Assemblage

Hydraulic Hermeneutics

First and foremost, I am reading (in) flux. I am reading a text that is a Heraclitean stream. I never step, or sink, into the same Bible twice, nor is the "I" doing the stepping or sinking the same I from reading to reading or even from syllable to syllable. This Bible-in-flux, this ever-streaming semiosis, demands a hydraulic hermeneutic (which, admittedly, might be no hermeneutic at all, hermeneutics likely being unable to subsist on a liquid diet) rather than a text-theory of solids in which seeping fluids, semiotic leakages, and other uncontrollable spillages would be a deviation,

"A hydraulic model, rather than . . . a theory of solids treating fluids as a special case" (Deleuze and Guattari, *A Thousand Plateaus*, 361).

a danger in need of damming, of containment. The Bible and I move together, align and realign together, become together;

---

[46] David J. Murphy, "More Evidence Pertaining to 'Their Females' in Romans 1:26," *Journal of Biblical Literature* 138, no. 1 (2019): 223 n. 5.

74   THE BIBLE AFTER DELEUZE

> "While you turn in circles ..., there are becomings which are silently at
> work, which are almost imperceptible. We think too much in terms of
> history.... Becomings belong to geography, they are orientations, direc-
> tions, entries and exits" (Deleuze and Parnet, *Dialogues II*, 2).

in that moment-by-moment encounter we each become something other
than we were a split second earlier.

A perpetually becoming Bible read by a continuously changing reader
cannot be an "object" distinguishable from a "subject." Neither of us are solid
enough for that ontological standoff. Neither of us are set-in-stone objects;
neither of us are substantial subjects. We meet midstream

> "The narrow stream which belongs neither to the one nor the other, but
> draws both into a ... heterochronous becoming" (Deleuze and Parnet,
> *Dialogues II*, 35).

in a transpersonal medium of floating affects. I dissolve in, become with, become one with an ostensible object that is utterly unlike me:

> "Becomings are not phenomena of imitation or assimilation, but of
> ... non-parallel evolution" (2).

an intricate artifact of processed wood pulp and printer ink, as nonsentient
and insensate as a stone. Yet it and I enter and inhabit a zone of indiscernibility in relation to each other. We do not face each other, we do not face off,
even when we disagree (as we often do); instead, we trade properties, we exchange affects,

> "Flows of intensity, their fluids, ... their continuums and conjunctions of
> affects" (Deleuze and Guattari, *A Thousand Plateaus*, 162).

we flow together even while seeming to be solid.

A hydraulic hermeneutic requires a piscatorial trope—a piscatorial parable, even. The one that follows swims lazy circles in one of the many rock
pools of *A Thousand Plateaus*: "Animal elegance, the camouflage fish,
the clandestine: this fish is crisscrossed by abstract lines that resemble
nothing, that do not even follow its organic divisions; but thus disorganized,

TEXT (THE BIBLE WITHOUT ORGANS)   75

disarticulated, it worlds with the lines of a rock, sand, and plants, becoming imperceptible" (280). Becoming imperceptible in the zone of indiscernibility

> "Zone of indiscernibility, . . . diffusion throughout a microphysical fabric" (226).

renders impossible the traditional critical task—not least the traditional biblical-critical task—of confidently distinguishing the fish from the flow, the reader from the text. We co-create each other continually in our encounter. But we do not do so in isolation.

The Assembled Bible

For what I am also reading when I read my Bible with Deleuze and his collaborators is, of course, an assemblage. More precisely, I am reading *in* an assemblage, one of which the text and I are equally components, and that assemblage in turn is intricately interconnected with, nested within, a multiplicity of other assemblages, the resulting composite being so convoluted, so colossal

> "An assemblage . . . brings into play within us and outside us populations, multiplicities, territories, becomings, affects, events" (Deleuze and Parnet, *Dialogues II*, 51).

as to beggar description. We gazed out on this disorienting vista earlier,[47]

> "The problem of *consistency* concerns the manner in which the components of a territorial assemblage hold together. But it also concerns the manner in which different assemblages hold together. . . . It may even be the case that consistency finds the totality of its conditions only on a properly cosmic plane, where all the disparate and heterogeneous elements are convoked" (Deleuze and Guattari, *A Thousand Plateaus*, 327).

but it merits further reflection.

[47] See p. 26.

76 THE BIBLE AFTER DELEUZE

Even at its most rudimentary, the assemblage is not one. Oversimplifying somewhat for now, reserving the complexities for later,[48] we may say that it is both *an assemblage of expression* (the discursive register) and *an assemblage of bodies* (the extradiscursive register). The assemblage of expression is composed of verbal productions, both spoken and written, of speech acts of all kinds—many of them momentously consequential in the case of biblical speech acts (more on which later). Intricately imbricated with the assemblage of expression—indissociable from it, indeed, caught up with it in a continuous feedback loop—is the assemblage of bodies, including textual bodies, such as the biblical text. There is, however, no biblical *text*, but only biblical *texts*—an incalculable multiplicity of them. And each biblical text, as singular material body,[49] enters into assemblage with a heterogeneity of other bodies,

> "We are now in the intra-assemblage. Its organization is very rich and complex" (Deleuze and Guattari, *A Thousand Plateaus*, 323).

both nonhuman and human. Indeed, it is always interlinked with such bodies, shifting in and out of them, shuttling between them: bodies of paper; bodies of plastic, fiberglass, steel, aluminum, copper, gold (and the other material components of your computer and mine); human bodies, individually and in community, not least "communities of reception" (a simplifying term that itself conceals complex congeries of nested assemblages); and other-than-human organic bodies, which, although blithely incognizant of biblical pronouncements on their subordinate relations to human bodies,

> "Little Hans's horse [an omnibus-pulling draft horse, collapsed in the street, flogged by its enraged owner, witnessed by Freud's Little Hans] is . . . an element or individual in a machinic assemblage: draft horse-omnibus-street. It is defined by . . . active and passive affects . . . : having

[48] See especially pp. 201–202.
[49] Elsewhere I have written personally of two such biblical text-bodies, also in relation to Deleuzian theory: my dog-eared first-edition NRSV, which I compulsively clutch and wave about in class, and my still more ancient several-editions-out-of-date UBS Greek New Testament, another classroom fetish object for me (my twenty-eighth edition of Nestle-Aland, the current scholarly standard, sits in pristine neglect in my office), each unsubstitutably singular text indelibly marked not only by my copious, all-but-illegible scribbles but by the secretions and excretions of my sebaceous and sudoriferous glands, so that I am bonded chemically and intercellularly as well as psychically and affectively with these now moldering books. Stephen D. Moore, *Untold Tales from the Book of Revelation: Sex and Gender, Empire and Ecology* (Atlanta: Society of Biblical Literature, 2014), 160–62.

> eyes blocked by blinders, having a bit and a bridle, . . . pulling heavy
> loads, being whipped, . . . making a din with its legs. . . . These affects cir-
> culate and are transformed within the assemblage: what a horse 'can do'"
> (Deleuze and Guattari, *A Thousand* Plateaus, 257).[50]

are nonetheless momentously affected by them.

The Book of Order-Words

Capture and Escape

Much more needs to be said about biblical pronouncements as they per-
tain to, as they press upon, bodies of all kinds. For what am I also reading
when I read my Bible if not a book of colossally consequential speech acts?
At times they flow torrentially through its pages and burst explosively out of
them, staging spectacular lines of flight, escapes in all directions, multiple
deterritorializations in the social field. More often, however, they engender
controlling, constrictive power arrangements designed to plug or seal potential flows before they occur, to anticipate and forestall lines of flight, to
thoroughly territorialize

> "The *territorial machine* is . . . the first form of socius, the machine of
> primitive inscription, the 'megamachine' that covers a social field"
> (Deleuze and Guattari, *Anti-Oedipus*, 141).

in advance:

> "Be fruitful and multiply, and fill the earth and subdue it; and have do-
> minion over the fish of the sea and over the birds of the air and over every
> living thing that moves upon the earth" (Gen 1:28);

> "Your desire shall be for your husband, and he shall rule over you" (Gen 3:16);

> "To your descendants I give this land" (Gen 15:18);

---

[50] "What a horse 'can do'" (poignantly) echoes and redirects Spinoza's affect-related question,
"What can a body do?" (see p. 37 earlier).

78 THE BIBLE AFTER DELEUZE

> "Flows of women and children, flows of herds and of seed, sperm flows, . . . menstrual flows: nothing must escape coding.[51] The primitive territorial machine, with its immobile motor, the earth, is already a social machine, a megamachine, that codes the flows of production"
> (Deleuze and Guattari, *Anti-Oedipus*, 142).

"Let my people go" (Exod 5:1);

"You shall not allow a witch to live" (Exod 22:18);

"You shall love your neighbor as yourself" (Lev 19:18);

"If a man lies with a male as with a woman, both of them have committed an abomination; they shall be put to death" (Lev 20:13);

"You shall not murder" (Deut 5:17);

"You shall annihilate them—the Hittites and the Amorites, the Canaanites and the Perizzites" (Deut 20:17);

"Do justice, . . . love kindness, . . . and walk humbly with your God" (Mic 6:8);

"Just as you did it to one of the least of these . . . , you did it to me" (Matt 25:40);

"His blood be on us and on our children!" (Matt 27:25);

"Go therefore and make disciples of all nations" (Matt 28:19);

"Love your enemies, do good to those who hate you, bless those who curse you, pray for those who abuse you" (Luke 6:27);

"Love one another as I have loved you" (John 15:12);

---

[51] "Coding" (*codage*) connotes control in Deleuzoguattarese. "Precapitalist social machines . . . code the flows of desire" (*Anti-Oedipus*, 139).

TEXT (THE BIBLE WITHOUT ORGANS)   79

"It is good for a man not to have sexual relations with a woman" (1 Cor 7:1);

"Women should be silent in the churches" (1 Cor 14:34);

"Slaves, obey your earthly masters in everything" (Col 3:22);

"I permit no woman to teach or to have authority over a man" (1 Tim 2:12);

> "Man is the molar entity par excellence, whereas becomings are molecular.... [Man] is this central Point that moves across all of space or the entire screen, and at every turn nourishes a certain distinctive opposition . . . : male-(female), adult-(child), white-(black . . .), rational-(animal). The central point . . . thus has the property of organizing binary distributions within the dualism machines, and of reproducing itself in the principal term of the opposition" (Deleuze and Guattari, *A Thousand Plateaus*, 292).

"Let us love one another, because love is from God. . . . Whoever does not love does not know God, for God is love" (1 John 4:7–8);

and far too many other life-or-death, death-in-life, or life-not-death injunctions of this sort to list.

The Bible is a book of "order-words," then,[52]

> "Language is made not to be believed but to be obeyed" (Deleuze and Guattari, *A Thousand Plateaus*, 76).

of orders both explicit and implicit. The question of what the Bible *does* (the pragmatic question) better reveals what it is than the question of what it *means* (the hermeneutical question). And what the Bible does, the Christian Bible in particular, what it has done overwhelmingly, though by no means

---

[52] Deleuze and Guattari introduce and elaborate on the concept of order-words (*mots d'ordre*) in *A Thousand Plateaus*, 75–85.

80 THE BIBLE AFTER DELEUZE

invariably, since the emergence of imperial Christendom, is throw cordons of regulation around entire human populations—and even around nonhuman populations—by means of order-words, declaimed directly or obliquely, that reach manifestly or invisibly into bodies to align or realign them in relation to other bodies. (I am waxing more Foucauldian than Deleuzian for now, focusing on the immensity of the container rather than the perforations in its fabric.) *The Bible pronounces on how bodies may interact and intermingle* ("'The people of Israel . . . have not separated themselves from the peoples of the land. . . . The holy seed has mixed itself with the peoples of the land. . . .' When I heard this, I tore my garments and my mantle, and pulled hair from my head and beard, and sat appalled"—Ezra 9:1–3; "Come out of her, my people, so that you do not take part in her sins!"—Rev 18:4); *it proclaims certain bodies to be subordinate or inferior to other bodies* ("The fear and dread of you shall rest on every animal of the earth"—Gen 9:2; "Cursed be Canaan; lowest of slaves shall he be to his brothers"—Gen 9:25; "Honor your wife as the weaker vessel"—1 Pet 3:7; "irrational animals, mere creatures of instinct, born to be caught and killed"—2 Pet 2:12);

> "Every animal has a world, and it's curious because there are a lot of humans . . . who do not have a world. They live the life of everybody else" (Deleuze and Parnet, *L'Abécédaire*, n.p.).[53]

it declares still other bodies to be deficient on other grounds, when not altogether abominable ("No one who has a blemish shall draw near [to God in the sanctuary], one who is blind or lame, or one who has a mutilated face or a limb too long, . . . or a hunchback, or a dwarf, or a man with . . . crushed testicles"—Lev 21:18–20; "Effeminate males [*malakoi*] . . . will [not] inherit the kingdom of God"—1 Cor 6:9); *it assigns some bodies to eternal life and consigns others to eternal damnation* ("Come, you that are blessed by my Father, inherit the kingdom prepared for you from the foundation of the world. . . . You that are accursed, depart from me into the eternal fire prepared for the devil and his angels"—Matt 25:34, 41);

> "The dark and wondrous theory of damnation" (Deleuze, *The Fold*, 71).

---

[53] Translation lightly modified.

TEXT (THE BIBLE WITHOUT ORGANS)   81

and, more generally, it catches countless bodies up in the multiple assemblages in which the Bible is itself caught, which is to say, socioreligious and sociopolitical assemblages of all kinds.

Incorporeal Transformations

The Bible's full biopolitical reach is intensified immeasurably by the fact that corporeal transformations are not all it brings about. It also effects what Deleuze and Guattari call *incorporeal transformations* (*A Thousand Plateaus*, 80–91, 107–9).[54] The words "I now pronounce you wife and wife," for example, uttered in a context and by an authority that would make them legally binding, would effect an incorporeal transformation in the bodies over which the words were spoken. "The incorporeal transformation is recognizable by its instantaneousness, its immediacy, by the simultaneity of the statement expressing the transformation and the effect the transformation produces," which is why many order-words that engender such changes "are precisely dated . . . and take effect the moment they are dated" (81).

The concept of incorporeal transformations is immensely relevant to the question of what the Bible does and how it does it, since so many of the Bible's pronouncements purport to effect alterations that do not entail bodily transmutation

> "Contrast . . . bodies with these incorporeal events which would play
> only on the surface, like a mist over the prairie (even less than a mist,
> since a mist is after all a body)" (Deleuze, *The Logic of Sense*, 5).

but are profoundly consequential nonetheless. They mobilize, reorient, or re-purpose bodies without reshaping or remodeling them in a manner accessible to empirical verification.

Many of these incorporeal transformations might be said to occur primarily within the narrative worlds of the biblical texts:

---

[54] Deleuze originally derived the concept of incorporeals from ancient Stoic philosophy, for which he possessed an immense and enduring admiration, seeing Stoicism as the first philosophical school "to reverse Platonism" (*The Logic of Sense*, 7). For Deleuze's most sustained discussions of incorporeals (*asōmata*, in Stoic parlance, as opposed to *sōmata*, "bodies"), see *The Logic of Sense*, 4–11, 142–47, together with Deleuze and Parnet, *Dialogues II*, 60–66.

82   THE BIBLE AFTER DELEUZE

"Samuel took a phial of oil and poured it on [Saul's] head, and kissed him; he said, 'The Lord has anointed you ruler over his people Israel'" (1 Sam 10:1);

"I am a herdsman, and a dresser of sycamore trees, and the Lord took me from following the flock, and the Lord said to me, 'Go, prophesy to my people Israel'" (Amos 7:14–15);

"And when day came, [Jesus] called his disciples and chose twelve of them, whom he also named apostles" (Luke 6:13);

"[Jesus] breathed on [his disciples] and said to them, 'Receive the Holy Spirit. If you forgive the sins of any, they are forgiven them; if you retain the sins of any, they are retained'" (John 20:22–23).

Even such incorporeal transformations, however, can impinge forcefully on extratextual flesh-and-blood bodies. For example, the restriction of apostolic incorporeal transformation to male bodies in the canonical gospels and the Acts of the Apostles (Matt 10:1–2; Mark 3:14; Luke 6:13; Acts 1:21–26; cf. John 6:70; contrast Rom 16:7) has been employed throughout Christian history to exclude women from ordination, that particular incorporeal transformation being controlled by male ecclesial authorities. As with a high-pressure liquid or gas, however, incorporeal transformation is not easily contained, as the battle tales and victory songs of women's ordination

> "From all these bodily struggles, there arises an ... incorporeal vapor"
> (Deleuze and Parnet, *Dialogues II*, 63).

amply testify.

Many other incorporeal transformations promptly overspill the porous boundaries of the biblical texts to sweep up individual readers, liturgical audiences, and entire faith communities in their metamorphic flows:

"I will take you as my people, and I will be your God" (Exod 6:7);

"I [Moses] am making this covenant ... not only with you who stand here with us today before the Lord our God, but also with those who are not here with us today" (Deut 29:14–15);

TEXT (THE BIBLE WITHOUT ORGANS)   83

"He took a loaf of bread . . . and said, 'Take; this is my body.' Then he took a cup, and . . . said to them, 'This is my blood of the covenant' " (Mark 14:22–24);

> **"The wound is something I receive in my body, in a particular place, at a particular moment, but there is also an eternal truth of the wound as . . . incorporeal event" (Deleuze and Parnet, *Dialogues II*, 65).**

"If you confess with your lips that Jesus is Lord and believe in your heart that God raised him from the dead, you will be saved" (Rom 10:9);

"There is no longer Jew or Greek, . . . slave or free, . . . male and female; for all of you are one in Christ Jesus" (Gal 3:28).

Still further incorporeal transformations enacted within the biblical texts spill out of them like toxic waste to envelop certain other bodies and transmute them into objects of hate—abominable bodies, devilish bodies, bodies deserving only of annihilation:

"For a man to lie with a male as with a woman is abomination [*tôʿēḇâ*]; they shall assuredly be put to death [*môt yûmātû*]" (Lev 20:13);

"Jesus said to [the Jews (*hoi Ioudaioi*)], . . . 'You are from your father the devil. . . . The reason you do not hear [the words of God] is that you are not from God' " (John 8:42–47);

"The woman was clothed with purple and scarlet, . . . and on her forehead was written a name, a mystery, 'Babylon the great, mother of whores and of earth's abominations [*bdelygmatōn*]' [. . .] They . . . will hate the whore; they will make her desolate and naked; they will devour her flesh and burn her up with fire" (Rev 17:4–5, 16).

Ordinary Pragmatics

Further incorporeal transformations await us in subsequent chapters, as do further musings on what incorporeal transformations do and how they do it.

84   THE BIBLE AFTER DELEUZE

I conclude for now with a brief reflection on their potential significance for biblical studies. The normally sedate subfield of linguistics known as pragmatics, a little bruised and bewildered following its encounter with Deleuze and Guattari, is defined by them as "a politics of language" (*A Thousand Plateaus*, 82).[55] If pragmatics is a politics of language,

> "Language . . . gives life orders. Life . . . listens and waits" (*A Thousand Plateaus*, 76).

and, as such, an investigation of how order-words work, then biblical pragmatics in the Deleuzoguattarian mode, whether conceived as a supplement to, or a supplanter of, standard biblical hermeneutics, would be a politics of biblical language, an analysis of biblical order-words, both explicit and implicit; the corporeal and incorporeal transformations they effect; and the nested assemblages of desire and power

> "For everything which changes passes along that line: assemblage" (Deleuze and Parnet, *Dialogues II*, 75).

in which they are enmeshed.

From the abstruse to the ordinary. Last night, leafing through a past issue of the journal *Biblical Interpretation*, I came across an article in which the author, Helen John, a white, British, professionally credentialed biblical scholar, reports on her experience of reading the Gospel of Mark with groups of what, in such studies, are usually termed "ordinary readers" (a term John also uses, although she seems to prefer "grassroots interpreters"), in this case, nonacademic African Christians, Aawambo

---

[55] Deleuze and Guattari's theory of language (whose spiky surface we have barely scratched; we explore it further in the section that follows) is a highly eclectic arrangement of assorted elements (an assemblage, if you will), principal among them being: ancient Stoic reflection on incorporeality, linguistic sense being conceived by Deleuze, as a result of his engagement with Stoicism, as "a nonexisting entity," "an incorporeal . . . entity, at the surface of things, a pure event which inheres or subsists in the proposition" (Deleuze, *The Logic of Sense*, xiii, 19); J. L. Austin's and John Searle's speech-act theory; C. S. Peirce's semiotics; and, most especially, Louis Hjelmslev's glossematics (already in *Anti-Oedipus*, 241–43; Deleuze and Guattari elevate Hjelmslev over Saussure [more on Hjelmslev later]), all pressed through a Spinozan sieve.

villagers from Owamboland in northern Namibia.[56] What most arrested me in John's article was a quotation from Gerald West, a white South African pioneer of the "reading with" strategy that John was employing with the Aawambo Bible study groups. Writes West, "Contextual Bible reading is not about understanding the Bible better. The Bible is read for change. The Bible as a site of struggle itself . . . is wrestled with (or re-read) until it contributes to real, substantive, systemic change."[57] Like Deleuze and Guattari, then, contextual Bible readers of the kind with which West has worked so extensively would not look for anything to understand in the Bible, but would ask only what it can be used for, what it can do, what transformations it can effect. No doubt, contextual Bible study can work perfectly well without recourse to Deleuze and Guattari's para-poststructuralist pragmatics. Still, the parallel is thought-provoking, suggesting unpredictable convergences and unanticipable alliances in the "immense outside" (*A Thousand Plateaus*, 23) in which reading of any kind, including Bible reading, is conducted.

A Bible That Expresses Everything While Communicating Nothing

What else does the Bible express when translated into Deleuzoguattarese? *Expression* is, indeed, another key concept for Deleuze and Guattari. Brian Massumi has produced an incisive exposition of Deleuze and Guattari's theory of expression. In what follows I gloss Massumi glossing Deleuze and Guattari and relate what they have to say about expression in general to biblical expression in particular.

---

[56] Helen C. John, "Conversations in Context: Cross-Cultural (Grassroots) Biblical Interpretation Groups Challenging Western-Centric (Professional) Biblical Interpretation," *Biblical Interpretation* 27, vol. 1 (2019): 36–68. John's article has since been incorporated into her *Biblical Interpretation and African Traditional Religion: Cross-Cultural and Community Readings in Owamboland, Namibia,* Biblical Interpretation Series 176 (Leiden, The Netherlands: Brill, 2019).

[57] Gerald O. West, "Reading the Bible with the Marginalised: The Value/s of Contextual Bible Reading," *Stellenbosch Theological Journal* 1, vol. 2 (2015): 240, quoted in John, "Conversations in Context," 44. West's observations are by no means unusual, it would appear. Already in 1983 Carlos Mesters could write of Christian base communities in Brazil, "The emphasis is not placed on the [biblical] text's meaning in itself but rather on the meaning the text has for the people reading it . . . . The common people are putting the Bible in its proper place, the place where God intended it to be. They are putting it in second place. Life takes first place!" ("The Use of the Bible in Christian Communities of the Common People," in *The Bible and Liberation: Political and Social Hermeneutics,* ed. Norman K. Gottwald [Maryknoll, NY: Orbis Books, 1983], 122).

86   THE BIBLE AFTER DELEUZE

Schleiermacher's Shadow

What is expression? Introducing the collection *A Shock to Thought: Expression after Deleuze and Guattari*, Massumi reflects:

> Expression conjures up the image of a self-governing, reflective individual whose inner life can be conveyed at will to a public composed of similarly sovereign individuals—rational atoms of human experience in voluntary congregation, usefully sharing thoughts and experiences. In a word: "communication." Communicational models of expression share many assumptions. These include the interiority of individual life, its rationality, an effective separation into private and public spheres, . . . the possibility of transparent transmission between privacies or between the private and the public, and the notion that what is transmitted is fundamentally information.[58]

None of this would raise any biblical-scholarly eyebrows. When it comes to communing with biblical authors, most of us still labor in the shadow of Schleiermacher, for whom every act of understanding was but the obverse of an act of expression. Within the terms of this hermeneutic, the act of interpretation reverses the act of expression, faithfully follows it back to its presumed origin, an interior space within an individual psyche. The responsible interpreter attempts to re-create the context in which the author wrote ("One has only understood what one has reconstructed . . . in its context"), in order to re-create in turn the intentions presumed to explain why the author wrote what they did ("Every utterance corresponds to a sequence of thoughts of the utterer").[59] The putative intention-filled interiority of biblical authors and redactors has been the Holy Grail of a great many biblical scholars over

---

[58] Brian Massumi, "Introduction: Like a Thought," in *A Shock to Thought: Expression after Deleuze and Guattari*, ed. Massumi (New York: Routledge, 2002), xiii.

[59] The parenthetical quotations are from Friedrich Schleiermacher, *Hermeneutics and Criticism: And Other Writings*, trans. and ed. Andrew Bowie, Cambridge Texts in the History of Philosophy (Cambridge: Cambridge University Press, 1998), 228–29. Without referencing Schleiermacher explicitly or the philosophical, theological, or biblical-scholarly traditions appended to his name, Foucault articulates their enabling assumptions: "Usually, the historical description of things said is shot through with the opposition of interior and exterior; and wholly directed by a desire to move from the exterior . . . towards the essential nucleus of interiority. To undertake the history of what has been said is to re-do, in the opposite direction, the work of expression: to go back from statements preserved through time and dispersed in space, toward that interior secret that preceded them" (*The Archaeology of Knowledge*, 120–21).

TEXT (THE BIBLE WITHOUT ORGANS)   87

a great many decades.[60] These collective quests rely on communicational models of expression that share many overarching assumptions.

Massumi, however, continues, "All of these assumptions have been severely tested by structuralist, poststructuralist, postmodern, and postpostmodern thought."[61] Deleuze and Guattari are among those who hold that communication "is a questionable concept."[62] No surprise there. The surprise is rather that they hold fast to the concept of expression while jettisoning the concept of communication. But how can expression express without communicating? Because, as we shall see, expression does not simply reproduce the content of a communication.

First consider how the traditional model works:

> Traditionally, for communicational purposes, expression is anchored to a "content." The content is viewed as having an objective existence prior and exterior to the form of its expression. . . . Expression faithfully conveys content: re-presents it at a subjective distance. . . . In this model, content is the beginning and end of communicative expression: at once its external cause and its guarantee of validity.[63]

This is the container model of communication, a commonplace one in biblical studies. The biblical scholar reaches out blindly but confidently over the historical void separating her from the biblical author and feels for the precious parcel of semantic content she is certain is being passed to her. Gripping it tightly she hauls it out of the gloom and triumphantly holds it aloft.

The container model, therefore, is also a *retrieval* model. Its opposite would be the *constructive* model whereby the assorted discourses of knowledge covertly conspire to produce that which they purport to describe. Through a sleight of hand so subtle that even she herself is unaware of it, the biblical scholar would have fabricated in the concealing gloom of the historical void the very parcel of semantic content she appears to extract from it. Foucault has provided a particularly elegant articulation of the constructive model, as we have seen. Foucault's constructivism, however, appears to have

---

[60] Not equally across all biblical genres, however. Intentionalism tends to flare far more brightly in an exegesis of the Letter to the Galatians, say, than in an exegesis of the Song of Songs.

[61] Massumi, "Like a Thought," xiii.

[62] Massumi, "Like a Thought," xiii. "Language Is Informational and Communicational" is both the title and the target of the first section (75–85) of the "Postulates of Linguistics" chapter of Deleuze and Guattari's *A Thousand Plateaus*.

[63] Massumi, "Like a Thought," xiv–xv.

88　THE BIBLE AFTER DELEUZE

no place for expression. His archaeology of knowledge "suspends the theme of expression [*l'expression*]," which he sees as properly belonging to "the task of hermeneutics."[64]

Deleuze's Event

Neither Deleuze nor Guattari are content with the constructive model. Massumi articulates the problem: "A subject is made to be in conformity with the system that produced it, such that the subject reproduces the system. . . . Where, in the conformity and correspondence between the life-form of the subject and the system of power that produced it, has the potential for change gone?"[65] We recall how Deleuze distinguished his own view of the social from that of Foucault—Deleuze's surprise that power somehow manages to contain so much of the resistance that everywhere flows through the social versus Foucault's surprise that faced with the omnipresence of power, resistance is possible at all (*Two Regimes of Madness*, 280).

The constructive model of communication is too constrictive for Deleuze, as for Guattari. It accords too much authority to language, discourse, and culture; to codes, conventions, and regulations; to the always already said and the always about to be said; to the predictable and the preordained. Rather than allowing expression to be subsumed in, swallowed up by, discursive construction, Deleuze and Guattari retrieve expression and recode it. The system—any system—does not simply reproduce itself, replicate itself recursively through the human subjects through which it expresses itself. Expression also expresses the never previously expressed, the until now unthought, for expression is an *event*. But what is an event?

The event (a crucial concept for Deleuze even before his collaborations with Guattari)[66] is a flash of lightning, whether literal or metaphorical: "Before the flash there is only potential, in a continuum of intensity: a

---

[64] Foucault, *The Archaeology of Knowledge*, 164, 162; cf. 55, 117, 139, 210. Foucault subsumes expression in what we have been calling communication: "If one speaks . . . unreflectingly of an author's *oeuvre*, it is because one imagines it to be defined by a certain expressive function. One is admitting that there must be a level (as deep as is necessary to imagine it) at which the *oeuvre* emerges, in all its fragments, even the smallest, most essential ones, as the expression of the thought, the experience, the imagination, or the unconscious of the author, or, indeed, of the historical determinations that operated upon him" (24).

[65] Massumi, "Like a Thought," xvi-xvii.

[66] The event (*l'événement*) looms especially large in Deleuze's *The Logic of Sense*, and, later, in *The Fold*.

field of charged particles. The triggering of the charge is a movement immanent to the field of potential, by which it plays out the consequences of its own intensity."[67] The literary act would, or at least could,

> "Making an event . . . is the most delicate thing in the world: the opposite of making a drama or making a story. Loving those who are like this: when they enter a room they are not persons, characters or subjects, but an atmospheric variation, a change of hue, an imperceptible molecule, . . . a fog or a cloud of droplets. . . . Great events, too, are made in this way. . . . It is not easy to think in terms of the event" (Deleuze and Parnet, *Dialogues II*, 66).[68]

be such an event.

To recode literature, however—biblical literature included—as an event of expression is not to resurrect a Romantic conception of literary genius. Massumi again:

> It is important not to think of the creativity of expression as if it brought something into being from nothing. There is no tabula rasa of expression. It always takes place in a cluttered world. Its field of emergence is strewn with the after-effects of events past, already-formed subjects and objects and . . . systems of capture . . . : nets aplenty. In order to potentialize a new type, the atypical expression must evade these already established articulations. It must extract itself from captures ready and waiting, falling for an instant through the propositional mesh.[69]

The source of the atypical expression (needless to say by now) would not be the interiority of a classically humanist authorial subject: a Shakespeare, a Fourth Evangelist, a Yahwist. Deleuze and Guattari's author would be fully as dead

---

[67] Massumi, "Like a Thought," xxiv.

[68] As this quotation obliquely signals, the event is yet another facet of a particular cluster of Deleuzian concepts, each designed to articulate differently, to make thinkable from different angles, the conditions in which newness (that which is always other than it might have been) continually bursts forth in the world, concepts that (among others) also include affect, becoming, and virtuality. The event is aligned especially closely with the virtual: "The event is not the state of affairs. It is actualized in a state of affairs, in a body, in a lived, but it has a shadowy and secret part that is continually subtracted from or added to its actualization" (Deleuze and Guattari, *What Is Philosophy?*, 156).

[69] Massumi, "Like a Thought," xxix.

90   THE BIBLE AFTER DELEUZE

> "The death of writing is like the death of God or the death of the father: the thing was settled a long time ago, although the news of the event is slow to reach us" (Deleuze and Guattari, *Anti-Oedipus*, 240).

as that of Roland Barthes. Expression, for Deleuze and Guattari, is impersonal. It is agency without an agent, subjectivity without a subject. Where, then, is expression located? Expression is not rooted in an individual body,[70] being too immense for a single body to contain, even a biblical-authorial body.

And yet expression needs human bodies in order to flow: "If expression's charge of potential were not incarnated in an individual body," it "would dissipate, unperceived, like the lightning flash you just missed seeing."[71] Again, where is expression located? "Expression is abroad in the world—where the potential is for what may become. It is non-local, scattered across a myriad struggles over what manner of life-defining nets will capture and contain that potential in reproducible articulations.... Determinate minds, subjects, bodies, objects, and institutions are the result."[72]

Back in the Box

Implicit in the foregoing is another tenet: Expression is also and always susceptible to dilution or domestication, to capture or control. The event of the lightning flash, whether literal or literary, may become a conduit "for a mythic form of expression. Zeus, for example, emerges to take the credit."[73] Or Matthew or John does, taking credit for forms of expression that previously did not need their names. "A creator now owns the deed. A subject has been added to the expression, a doer to the deed. The energies creative of the flash have extended into myth creation: from physical ontogenesis to mythopoiesis.... The heroic subject has emerged to claim his object.... The flash has gone from the expressive to the possessive."[74]

---

[70] Massumi, "Like a Thought," xxi.
[71] Massumi, "Like a Thought," xxix.
[72] Massumi, "Like a Thought," xxi.
[73] Massumi, "Like a Thought," xxv.
[74] Massumi, "Like a Thought," xxv.

The heroic authors of the biblical tradition, most of all the pseudonymous authors—Moses, David, Solomon, Pseudo-Paul, Pseudo-Peter, and the rest—are mythopoetic constructs. They march in to claim the texts

> "It is the mark that makes the territory" (Deleuze and Guattari, *A Thousand Plateaus*, 315).

they did not write. But even the nonpseudonymous biblical authors participate in a territorial process. The texts become their mirrors before which they preen. The properties the texts are thought to reflect become the authors' properties, their features. And it is not only the precritical biblical tradition that has engaged in this exercise, awarding vast tracts of text to Moses, sizeable swaths to Solomon and to the apostle John, extending Paul's already substantial territory, and so on. Critical scholarship on Mark, say, of the past century or so has successively transformed him from modest compiler of traditions, to seminal theologian, to ingenious literary author, to proto-postmodernist. With every reconfiguration of the textual mirror there is a corresponding reconfiguration of the evangelist. And those surface images are invariably imagined to contain concealed depths. The evangelist is equipped with an imagined interiority replete with imagined intentions of which both the content and the form of his gospel are imagined to be the product, the expression. Again, this is the container model of communication, which is also the book-as-box model that we encountered earlier.[75] How might the container, the box, be broken open so as to release

> "Whenever a territorial assemblage is taken up by a movement that deterritorializes it . . . , we say that a machine is released" (Deleuze and Guattari, *A Thousand Plateaus*, 333).

what it locked within it?

A Machine Is Released

For Deleuze and Guattari, as we have seen, every utterance is an order-word, whether explicit or implicit, overt or covert. And the order-word is more than

---

[75] See pp. 12–13.

92   THE BIBLE AFTER DELEUZE

a word; more often it is a string of words. The string may be of any length, presumably, up to and including the book-utterance:

> "If you do not diligently observe all the words . . . written in this book, . . . then the Lord will overwhelm both you and your offspring with severe and lasting afflictions. [. . .] The Lord will . . . take delight in prospering you, . . . when you obey . . . his commandments . . . that are written in this book" (Deut 28:58–59; 30:9–10);

> "O that my words were written down! O that they were inscribed in a book!" (Job 19:23);

> "Thus says the Lord, the God of Israel: Write in a book all the words that I have spoken to you" (Jer 30:2);

> "These things have been written so that you may believe that Jesus is the Messiah, the Son of God" (John 20:31);

> "Blessed is the one who keeps the words of the prophecy of this book" (Rev 22:7).

The obverse side of the order-word thesis, however, one implicit in Deleuze's view of the social as constituted more by flows than by stoppages, now needs to be stated. It's rather obvious, really. Order-words cannot compel obedience, cannot predetermine their reception. That language can be disobeyed is more important ultimately for Deleuze, as for Guattari, than that language issues orders. That the never-before-seen-or-said is not only a permanent possibility but a constant reality conditions Deleuze and Guattari's theory of literature, for example,

> "The ultimate aim of literature is to set free" (Deleuze, *Essays Critical and Clinical*, 4).

far more than the other permanent possibility: "the reduction of literature to an object of consumption conforming to the established order" (Deleuze and Guattari, *Anti-Oedipus*, 133).

Placing unanticipatable emergence at the center of a model of expression again differentiates it from the communicational model in which an intended

TEXT (THE BIBLE WITHOUT ORGANS)   93

content is transmitted from the interiority of a speaker or writer to the interiority of a hearer or reader. In a successful act of communication thus conceived, the form of the content received corresponds with the form of the content expressed. What precisely Paul intended to say in Romans about the law-grace relationship as it intersects with the Jew-Gentile relationship—the presumed content of his expression (let us say for the sake of argument), with all its exquisite theological nuance and circumstantially determined contours—is finally apprehended adequately by a present or future Pauline scholar and entrusted to an article, monograph, or commentary that then becomes the repository of that necessarily rephrased but accurately captured content. Even if many Pauline scholars are too sophisticated hermeneutically to put stock in such teleology, most operate nonetheless as though it were their professional raison d'être.

How else might expression and its decoding and recoding be understood? This brings us to what Massumi calls "the cornerstone" of Deleuze and Guattari's theory of expression "in their solo as well as collaborative writings."[76] Its inspiration is the writings of linguist Louis Hjelmslev, whose theories, articulated long before the ascent of French structuralism, Deleuze and Guattari assimilate to their own,

> "His *form* is our *code*. His *substance* is our *flow*. They belong to the same semiotic machine" (Guattari, *The Anti-Oedipus Papers*, 202).[77]

hailing him as the anti-Saussure, effectively, in *Anti-Oedipus* (242–43), and, tongue-in-cheek, in *A Thousand Plateaus* as "the Danish Spinozist geologist, . . . that dark prince descended from Hamlet" (43).[78]

The Deleuzoguattarian Hjelmslev proposes "a purely immanent theory of language" that dismantles the "transcendent" scaffolding of Saussurian linguistics (*Anti-Oedipus*, 242).[79] Hjelmslev renames Saussure's signifier *the expression plane* and his signified *the content plane*. Expression, for Hjelmslev,

---

[76] Massumi, "Like a Thought," xviii.

[77] This claim occurs in "Hjelmslev and Immanence," Guattari's impassioned, occasionally critical, but ultimately enthusiastic appraisal of Hjelmslev's potential contributions to his and Deleuze's theoretical enterprise (*The Anti-Oedipus Papers*, 201–23).

[78] "Geologist" because the compliment occurs in the plateau titled "10,000 B.C.: The Geology of Morals (Who Does the Earth Think It Is?)" (*A Thousand Plateaus*, 39–74). It is not known whether or not Hjelmslev ever actually read Spinoza. Hjelmslev's magnum opus, which Deleuze and Guattari cite, is *Prolegomena to a Theory of Language*, trans. Francis J. Whitfield (rev. ed.; Madison: University of Wisconsin Press, [1943] 1961).

[79] We have occasion later to unpack Saussure's theory of language (see especially pp. 195–197).

94 THE BIBLE AFTER DELEUZE

is the material substance of the linguistic sign (the spoken or written word, say), but Hjelmslev refuses any conception of content as immaterial meaning. Content is content only because it is the content of an expression, while expression is expression only because it is the expression of a content. The co-constitutive reciprocity of content and expression is what attracts Deleuze and Guattari to Hjelmslev's linguistic theory: expression is no longer subordinate to content, because content no longer preexists expression; and since content no longer precedes expression, content no longer predetermines expression.

Yet content and expression are not merely alternative names for a single linguistic form. On the contrary,

> "Form is not a passive receptacle, an eternal feminine" (Guattari, *The Anti-Oedipus Papers*, 203).

content and expression each possess their own form. This element of Hjelmslev's linguistic theory, as Deleuze and Guattari construe it, enables it to exit the representationalist hall of mirrors in which thinking on language has traditionally been conducted.[80] As they phrase it, "Precisely because content, like expression, has a form of its own, one can never assign the form of expression the function of simply representing, describing, or averring a corresponding content: there is neither correspondence nor conformity. The two formalizations are not of the same nature; they are independent, heterogeneous" (*A Thousand Plateaus*, 86).

Paul's Innumerable Letters to the Romans

Let an example illustrate what is in play and at stake here. If Paul's Letter to the Romans is a form of expression[81] in the sense proposed by Deleuze and Guattari, following Hjelmslev, its form—or, more precisely, its forms—of

---

[80] And not only thinking on language. Deleuze and Guattari's sole criticism of Hjelmslev (at least in *Anti-Oedipus* and *A Thousand Plateaus*) is that he fails to see that his theory far exceeds the linguistic (*A Thousand Plateaus*, 43), and even the human: "Not only do plants and animals, orchids and wasps, sing or express themselves, but so do rocks and even rivers, every stratified thing on earth" (44).

[81] I say "a form of expression" simply for convenience. "The" Letter to the Romans, as material artifact, is multiple, existing as translations, in more than fifteen hundred languages, of a Greek "original" that itself is a scholarly construction made from thousands of (mostly fragmentary) ancient manuscripts.

content are incommensurably different from that form of expression. What is more, its forms of content are virtually infinite.[82] They include any and every way Romans, or any portion of Romans, has ever been actualized by any and every reader or hearer of Romans. These innumerable forms of content include an epochal actualization by a certain sixteenth-century German monk whose anguished and obsessive meditations on Romans 1:17[83] impelled him to actions that transformed Europe and the world irreversibly; they include a less momentous, but nonetheless impactful, actualization by the faithful of Westboro Baptist Church in Topeka, Kansas, for whom the most important verses in the New Testament are Romans 1:26–27 ("Their women exchanged natural intercourse for unnatural. . . . Men committed shameless acts with men. . . .") and which they paraphrase as "God hates fags," infamously emblazoning those words on placards and brandishing them at LGBTQ pride parades, funerals of murder victims of antiqueer violence, and other such events;[84] they even include an actualization by a singularly unscholarly New Testament scholar who, in an essay on the same verses of Romans, contended that the letter as a whole is best regarded as a saga of soteriological transformation, since the Jesus of Romans appears to be a woman forever in the process of becoming a man.[85]

But back to Massumi on Deleuze and Guattari's theory of expression:

> The reciprocal actions of content and expression have to pass a gap of nonresemblance which breaks . . . the symmetry between content and expression assumed by the communicational model. . . . What happens in the break is the crux of the matter for Deleuze and Guattari. . . . There is no logical or teleological reason why that particular articulation had to be. Its

---

[82] Using "virtual" here in its special Deleuzian sense (which we explore in detail in chapter 3).

[83] "At last, by the mercy of God, meditating day and night, I gave heed to the context of the words, namely, 'In [the gospel] the righteousness of God is revealed, as it is written, "He who through faith is righteous shall live"' [Rom 1:17, quoting Hab 2:4]. There I began to understand that the righteousness of God is that by which the righteous lives by a gift of God, namely by faith . . . . I felt that I was altogether born again and had entered paradise itself through open gates." Martin Luther, *Luther's Works*, vol. 34, *Career of the Reformer IV*, ed. Helmut T. Lehmann and Lewis W. Spitz (St. Louis, MO: Concordia, 1960), 336–37.

[84] At the time of writing, the church's website is, in fact, (still) titled "God Hates Fags" (www.godhatesfags.com), and the death of its notorious spiritual leader, Fred Phelps, in 2014 does not appear to have significantly diminished its sense of its mission.

[85] Stephen D. Moore, "Sex and the Single Apostle," in his *God's Beauty Parlor: And Other Queer Spaces in and around the Bible*, Contraversions: Jews and Other Differences (Stanford, CA: Stanford University Press, 2001), 133–72.

96   THE BIBLE AFTER DELEUZE

power was the cumulative result of a thousand tiny performative struggles peppered throughout the social field.[86]

In my own case, my actualization of Romans by means of queer theory depended upon an incalculable number of performative struggles both tiny and tremendous, few of them involving me personally, but ranging from the LGBTQ activism of the late 1980s and early 1990s associated especially with the group Queer Nation, in symbiotic relationship with which the term "queer theory" was coined and the academic phenomenon bearing that name was launched; more proximate struggles within the United Methodist Church around LGBTQ issues and the courageous stand the UMC seminary in which I teach has long taken in that particular struggle (the courage being displayed by certain UMC faculty in the seminary, I hasten to add, of which I am not one), making this seminary a safe space in which to pursue queer-affirming projects such as that Romans experiment; and so on down to an extremely fine-grained micropolitical level that would be impossible to detail adequately, "the fog of a million droplets" of which Deleuze and Parnet write (*Dialogues II*, 65).

Summoning Forth a People to Come

Another way of articulating this complexity is to affirm that expression always occurs in an assemblage. Indeed, Deleuze and Guattari's detailed assemblage model has, as its "first, horizontal axis, . . . two segments, one of content, the other of expression" (*A Thousand Plateaus*, 88). And the expression segment of the general assemblage is parsed out as, in effect, a sub-assemblage, "a collective assemblage of enunciation" (88). The singular is always already collective for Deleuze and Guattari. As Massumi explains,

> Deleuze and Guattari . . . argue that even the most ostensibly personal expression may be directly political, in that it envelops a potential collective. For example, the subject of literary expression, to the extent that it is effectively creative, is not the individual author but a "people to come". . . . The atypical expression emits the potential for an unlimited series of further (collective) expressions by individuals who will retrospectively be assigned

[86] Massumi, "Like a Thought," xix.

by a propositional system of capture to membership in a group (psychoso-cial type, class, ethnicity, nation).[87]

This people to come, birthed by atypical expression

> "The poet . . . is one who lets loose molecular populations in hopes that
> this will sow the seeds of, or even engender, the people to come [*le peuple
> á venir*], that these populations will pass into a people to come, open a
> cosmos" (Deleuze and Guattari, *A Thousand Plateaus*, 345).

—atypical expression later dubbed "biblical," for instance—perennially vul-nerable to propositional capture, might also be a religion, even a "world religion," to come. How complete will its capture be? If we're talking about Christianity, its capture will be conspicuously evident from the fourth cen-tury onward and the unexpected interpenetration (painful and ecstatic by turns) of the (orthodox) Christian faith and the imperial Roman state. "A complementary order of conventional performative expressions will help manage this new form of content. The force of collective, expressive emer-gence will be streamed into stratified functions of power."[88]

But the capture need not, indeed cannot, be absolute. What Deleuze and Guattari call "lines of flight" emerge in the form of an "unless" clause: "Unless: the collectivity in the making resists pick-up by an estab-lished stratum," retaining "a shade of the unclassifiable and a margin of un-predictability in the eyes (or net) of existing systems of reference, no matter how hard those systems try fully to contain them."[89] The Christian collec-tivity in the making, for example—even once the collectivity being assem-bled is overwhelmingly an imperial enterprise—will still have those strange, stammering,

> "[Make] the standard language stammer, tremble, cry, or even sing: this
> is the style, the 'tone,' the language of sensations, or the foreign language
> within language that summons forth a people to come" (Deleuze and
> Guattari, *What Is Philosophy?*, 176).

---

[87] Massumi, "Like a Thought," xxviii.
[88] Massumi, "Like a Thought," xxviii.
[89] Massumi, "Like a Thought," xxviii.

98 THE BIBLE AFTER DELEUZE

people-to-come-summoning biblical books. And if several centuries of incessant biblical-scholarly labor (a colossal labor of confinement?) has taught us anything at all, it is that these books

> "... Visions and Auditions that no longer belong to any language....
> They are ... the outside of language" (Deleuze, *Essays Critical and
> Clinical*, 5).

cannot be completely confined. They continue unceasingly not just to engender stultifying effusions of sameness, oppressive confirmations of existing arrangements,

> "On a vertical axis, the assemblage has ... *territorial sides*, or
> reterritorialized sides, which stabilize it ... " (Deleuze and Guattari, *A
> Thousand Plateaus*, 88).

but also to engender the previously unthought and untried, the socially innovative and experimental,

> "... and *cutting edges of deterritorialization*, which carry it away" (*A
> Thousand Plateaus*, 88).

to foster a de-stagnating ethics of emergence

> "... the projection of a human group still to be discovered" (Guattari,
> *Chaosophy*, 102).

that would also be a deterritorializing ethics of collective expression.

How Do You Make Yourself a Bible without Organs?

There is yet more, very much more, that a Deleuzoguattarian engagement with the Bible might entail. Let us return to one of the more intriguing statements from the opening pages of *A Thousand Plateaus* and ponder it further. "A book is an assemblage," Deleuze and Guattari declare, one side of which "faces the strata, which doubtless makes it a kind of organism, or signifying totality, or determination attributable to a subject" (4). The other

TEXT (THE BIBLE WITHOUT ORGANS) 99

side of the book-assemblage, meanwhile, "fac[es] a *Body without Organs* [*un corps sans organes*], which is continually dismantling the organism, causing asignifying particles or pure intensities to pass or circulate" (4).

The Body without Organs: A Brief Biography

The Body without Organs (to begin with the most intractable but also the most interesting term) is so colossally overdetermined in the Deleuzian and Deleuzoguattarian oeuvre as to render it incapable of univocal definition. The Body without Organs (often abbreviated as the BwO) makes its first appearance in Deleuze's 1969 book *The Logic of Sense*,[90]

> "... a glorious body ..., the superior body or Body without Organs" (*The Logic of Sense*, 88).

after which it winds its way circuitously through Deleuze's solo works, Guattari's solo works, and Deleuze and Guattari's collaborative works,

> "From time to time we have written about the same idea, and have noticed later that we have not grasped it at all in the same way: witness 'Bodies without Organs'" (Deleuze and Parnet, *Dialogues II*, 17).

amassing ever new conceptual valences along the way. Deleuze derived the Body without Organs concept from avant-garde literary artist and actor Antonin Artaud (a crucial figure for Foucault as for Deleuze), specifically, from Artaud's 1947 radio play, *To Have Done with the Judgment of God*.[91] Near the end of the solo performance play (which, however, never aired) the protagonist declaims,

> When you will have made him a body without organs,
> then you will have delivered him from all his automatic reactions

---

[90] See Deleuze, *The Logic of Sense*, 88, 92–93, for the explicit mentions of the Body without Organs. In effect, however, the entire chapter in which these mentions occur, "Thirteenth Series of the Schizophrenic and the Little Girl" (82–93), is an exploration of the Body-without-Organs concept. The schizophrenic of the title is Antonin Artaud and the little girl is Lewis Carroll's Alice, a recurrent presence in this book on sense and nonsense.

[91] See "*To Have Done with the Judgment of God*, a radio play (1947)," in *Antonin Artaud: Selected Writings*, ed. Susan Sontag (Berkeley: University of California Press, 1976), 555–72.

100 THE BIBLE AFTER DELEUZE

and restored him to his true freedom.[92]

Among the many resources Deleuze discovered in the unexpected recesses of the seemingly slim Body-without-Organs concept was a counterweapon against biopolitical appropriations of the human body to regulate identities and control behavior. Let a quick example illustrate such resistance—an example that invokes neither Artaud nor Deleuze, however, or explicitly adduces the BwO concept (which, for me, only adds to its interest). An arresting BwO moment occurs in Judith Butler's *Gender Trouble*, specifically in an anecdote Butler tells about feminist-queer theorist and novelist Monique Wittig. Wittig had famously argued that "lesbians are not women,"[93] because the term and concept "woman" assumes meaning only within the heterosexual sex/gender system and "a reproductive discourse that marks and carves up the female body into artificial 'parts' like 'vagina,' 'clitoris,' and 'vulva.' At a lecture at Vassar College, Wittig was asked whether she had a vagina, and she replied that she did not."[94]

Among the many things the Body without Organs appears to be, for Deleuze and Guattari, is the incarnation of Spinoza's dictum that "nobody as yet has determined the limits of the body's capabilities."[95] So redolent with sheer potentiality and raw virtuality is the Body without Organs

> "The Body without Organs is an affective, intensive, anarchist body that consists solely of poles, zones, thresholds, and gradients. It is traversed by a powerful, nonorganic vitality" (Deleuze, *Essays Critical and Clinical*, 131).

that it utterly resists being organized as a set of predetermined organs with predictable functions.[96] As such, it is also "the body without an image" (Deleuze and Guattari, *Anti-Oedipus*, 8),

---

[92] Artaud, "*To Have Done with the Judgment of God,*" 571.

[93] Monique Wittig, *The Straight Mind and Other Essays* (Boston: Beacon Press, 1992), 20.

[94] Judith Butler, *Gender Trouble: Feminism and the Subversion of Identity* (New York: Routledge, 1990), 157 n. 54.

[95] Baruch Spinoza, *Ethics*, in *Spinoza: The Complete Works*, ed. Michael L. Morgan, trans. Samuel Shirley (Indianapolis, IN: Hackett, 2002), 280.

[96] Just as the book can be boxed in, for Deleuze—conceived *as* a box, indeed (see pp. 12–13 earlier)—so too can the body: "The body itself [as] a box containing organs as so many parts" (*Essays Critical and Clinical*, 15).

TEXT (THE BIBLE WITHOUT ORGANS)   101

> "Antonin Artaud discovered this one day, finding himself with no shape
> or form whatsoever, right there where he was at that moment" (8).

which is to say, among other things,

> "The BwO is what remains when you take everything away" (Deleuze
> and Guattari, *A Thousand Plateaus*, 151).

that it is also nonrepresentational. It is an exquisitely sensitive,

> "But what is a Body without Organs? The spider . . . receives only the
> slightest vibration at the edge of her web, which propagates itself in her
> body as an intensive wave and sends her leaping. . . . She answers only to
> signs . . . surging through her body" (Deleuze, *Proust and Signs*, 182).

altogether receptive surface of preprocessed sensations and zones of affective
intensity.

But the Body without Organs is not simply the zero-degree human body,
the body in which affect theorists of the Deleuzian lineage delight (although
it is that as well). The Body without Organs is much vaster than the human
body, as vast even as the earth

> "The earth . . . is a Body without Organs" (Deleuze and Guattari, *A
> Thousand Plateaus*, 40).

—specifically, an earth scoured clean of human reformation and deformation,

> "And the earth was without form, and void" (Gen 1:2, KJV).

an earth without (human) form and void (of human exploitation).[97]

We are now in a position to make (further) sense of the "strata." The book-
assemblage, as we saw, "faces the strata" on one side, "which doubtless make
it a kind of organism, or signifying totality, or determination attributable to a

---

[97] My eco-paraphrase of Deleuze and Guattari, *A Thousand Plateaus*, 40. For the sake of (relative)
simplicity, I am glossing over, here and in what follows, the amoebalike splittings that fissured the
Body without Organs during its sinuous passage from *The Logic of Sense* through *Anti-Oedipus* to
A Thousand Plateaus and beyond, resulting in at least three different Bodies without Organs: a full
BwO, an empty BwO, and a cancerous BwO (see further *A Thousand Plateaus*, 162–66).

102 THE BIBLE AFTER DELEUZE

subject," while it faces a Body without Organs on the other side (Deleuze and Guattari, *A Thousand Plateaus*, 4). The strata, evoking stubborn sedimentation and obdurate coagulation (502), are structures that impose form on "unformed" matter (40, 503),

> **"The Body without Organs and its intensities are not metaphors, but matter itself" (Deleuze and Guattari, *Anti-Oedipus*, 283).**

so much so, indeed, that "stratification is like the creation of the world from chaos, a continual, renewed creation" (Deleuze and Guattari, *A Thousand Plateaus*, 502). And God saw that the strata were good? The God of the strata did, presumably. We'll meet this God in a moment. First, we should note that Deleuze and Guattari's own view of the strata is considerably less positive. They do concede that a degree of stratification is necessary and that "every undertaking of destratification . . . must . . . observe concrete rules of extreme caution" (503). At base, however, they construe the strata as "acts of capture" that "operate by . . . territorialization" (40).

As Deleuze and Guattari's word of caution implies, the saga of the strata does not unfold exclusively on the cosmic level. In Deleuze's *Foucault*, the strata are "historical formations, positivities or empiricities. As 'sedimentary beds' they are made from things and words, from seeing and speaking, from the visible and the sayable, from bands of visibility and fields of sayability, from contents and expressions" (47). Already in *Anti-Oedipus*, indeed, the strata are, among other things, the social itself,

> **"Doubtless the Body without Organs haunts all forms of socius" (Deleuze and Guattari, *Anti-Oedipus*, 281).**

conceived as territory and territorialization, making the Body without Organs "the limit of the socius" (281), "the ultimate residuum of a deterritorialized socius" (33).

But the strata are also "judgments of God" (Deleuze and Guattari, *A Thousand Plateaus*, 40)—and the Deleuzoguattarian God, it must be said, is a highly judgmental and thoroughly reactionary entity, a grand amalgam of every negative Christian-God stereotype that ever was, stereotypes for which the Bible is the privileged source and sacred storeroom. "Stratification in general is the entire system of the judgment of God," is Deleuze and Guattari's religiopolitical summation of the situation (40;

cf. 502). Judgment is stratification, coagulation, sedimentation because it reifies existing social structures. "Judgment prevents the emergence of any new mode of existence" (Deleuze, *Essays Critical and Clinical*, 135).[98] As always in the Deleuzoguattarian universe, however, deterritorializing flows, lines of flight,

> "There is always something that flows or flees, that escapes the ... overcoding machine" (Deleuze and Guattari, *A Thousand Plateaus*, 216).

manage to proliferate nonetheless. "The earth, or the Body without Organs, constantly eludes . . . judgment, flees and becomes destratified, decoded, deterritorialized" (40).

"Since strata are judgements of God," Deleuze and Guattari remark tongue-in-cheek, "one should not hesitate to apply all the subtleties of medieval scholasticism and theology [to them]" (*A Thousand Plateaus*, 58). But there are more promising, less impoverished places in their oeuvre on which theology (although not of the scholastic sort) might alight. The real Deleuzian and Deleuzoguattarian "God-words" (the scare quotes are essential here since none of these words denote transcendent entities but are instead names of immanence) are found elsewhere in their corpus—elsewhere than in the term "God," that is.

Preeminent among such "God-words" would be the plane of immanence,

> "The plane of immanence is . . . that which must be thought and that which cannot be thought" (Deleuze and Guattari, *What Is Philosophy?*, 59).

Deleuze's para-poststructuralist recasting of Spinoza's single substance,[99] itself an immanentist, pantheistic recasting of the transcendent deities of orthodox Judaism and Christianity

---

[98] From Deleuze's "To Have Done with Judgment" in his *Essays Critical and Clinical*, 126–35. Deleuze's main interlocutor in the essay, after Artaud, is Nietzsche, whom he sees as having uncovered the life-suppressing mechanism of the philosophical-theological category of judgment while demonstrating that "there exists a justice that is opposed to all judgment" (127).

[99] On which see Deleuze's *Practical Philosophy*, 122–30, together with his *Expressionism in Philosophy*, 11, and my own earlier reflections on pp. 45–46 on the single substance/plane of immanence relationship.

> "Spinoza has had such a strong reputation for materialism even
> though he never ceases to speak of the mind and the soul, a reputation
> for atheism even though he never ceases to speak of God" (Deleuze,
> "Spinoza's Concept of *Affect*," n.p.).

and the production of a liminal theism that is all but indistinguishable from atheism.

But "Body without Organs" is a synonym for "plane of immanence" often enough in the Deleuzian corpus as to cause it to exhibit symptoms of divinity through contagion. "In effect, the Body without Organs is itself the plane of consistency [= plane of immanence]," we read in Deleuze and Guattari's *A Thousand Plateaus* (40; see also 43, 56, 72, etc.), while in Deleuze and Parnet's *Dialogues II* we read of desire unrolling upon "a plane of consistency, a field of immanence, a 'Body without Organs'" (89).[100] It is in Deleuze and Guattari's *Anti-Oedipus*, however, that we find the most explicit statement on the relationship of the Body without Organs to Spinoza's single substance: "The Body without Organs is the immanent substance, in the most Spinozist sense of the word" (327). Not surprisingly, Deleuze and Guattari show little interest in explicitly slapping the worn and tattered "God" label on the Body without Organs; their instinct, indeed, is the opposite: "The Body without Organs is not God, quite the contrary" (13). They immediately add, however, "But the energy that sweeps through it is divine" (13).[101]

The Lobster God Battles the BwO God

Where does all of this leave us in relation to the Bible? The Bible-as-assemblage, we might say, faces in two directions at once, and what it turns its two faces toward might be construed as two Gods (a term around which the reader is invited to continue placing scare quotes, even though only one of these Gods is terrifying). On one side is the ultraterritorializing

---

[100] Translation lightly modified.

[101] Deleuze's musings on the Body without Organs in his Bacon book also take us to the brink of theology: "The phenomenological hypothesis is perhaps insufficient because it merely invokes the lived body. But the lived body is still a paltry thing in comparison with a more profound and almost unlivable Power [*Puissance*] .... Beyond the organism, but also at the limit of the lived body, there lies what Artaud discovered and named: the Body without Organs" (*Francis Bacon*, 39). Bradley H. McLean has attempted to relate the BwO to Christian theology, and Christianity more broadly, as noted earlier (p. 9 n. 23), and so has Matthew G. Whitlock in "The Wrong Side Out With(out) God: An Autopsy of the Body Without Organs," *Deleuze and Guattari Studies* 14, no. 3 (2020): 507-32.

TEXT (THE BIBLE WITHOUT ORGANS) 105

God, the God who operates through constant "acts of capture," through "imprisoning intensities and locking singularities into systems" (Deleuze and Guattari, *A Thousand Plateaus*, 40). Confronted by "flows in all directions," "free intensities," "nomadic singularities," and "mad or transitory particles" (40), this despotic deity has only one instinctive reaction: Snip, snip go its giant double pincers. Hence the infamous Deleuzoguattarian declaration that "God is a Lobster" (40). This arthropod God crawls around in the Bible, and crawls out of it. It is the God of peremptory commands.

But the Bible-as-assemblage also faces the Body without Organs, as we earlier saw (in wonder and in awe), which would be the other God, the God by any other name, the God more worthy of the name. This BwO God and the Lobster God also face each other, but only in battle. The BwO God experiences the constricting actions of the Lobster God as monstrous oppression: "So many nails piercing the flesh,

> **"He cannot bear the BwO. . . . He pursues it and rips it apart" (Deleuze and Guattari, *A Thousand Plateaus*, 159).**

so many forms of torture. In order to resist . . . , the Body without Organs presents its smooth, slippery, opaque, taut surface as a barrier. . . . It sets up a counterflow of amorphous, undifferentiated fluid. . . . It utters only gasps and cries

> **"The BwO howls" (Deleuze and Guattari, *A Thousand Plateaus*, 159).**

that are sheer unarticulated blocks of sound" (Deleuze and Guattari, *Anti-Oedipus*, 9).

The judgment of the Lobster God "weighs upon . . . the BwO; it is the BwO that undergoes it" (Deleuze and Guattari, *A Thousand Plateaus*, 159). The self-loathing Lobster God

> **"Anything in the seas or the streams that does not have fins and scales . . . , they are detestable to you and detestable they shall remain" (Lev 11:10–11).**

seeks to crush the Body-without-Organs God under immovable order-words, the same stratifying, segmenting order-words

106 THE BIBLE AFTER DELEUZE

> "The human being is a segmentary animal. Segmentarity is inherent to
> all the strata composing us. . . . Life is spatially and socially segmented"
> (Deleuze and Guattari, *A Thousand Plateaus*, 208).

we heard intoned over it earlier ("If a man lies with a male . . . they shall be
put to death"; "You shall annihilate them—the Hittites and the Amorites, the
Canaanites and the Perizzites"; "Women should be silent in the churches";
"Slaves, obey your earthly masters" . . .), causing the Body-without-Organs
God to writhe in indescribable anguish.

Beneath the strata accumulating above it, however, the BwO God (which,
as pure virtuality, is the true creator God) is creating. Most of its creations are
seized and stratified by the Lobster God (the creator pretender) even as they
are actualized; notably, "the first things to be distributed on the Body without
Organs are races, cultures,

> "These are the families of Noah's sons, according to their genealogies,
> in their nations; and from these the nations spread abroad on the earth
> after the flood" (Gen 10:32).

and their gods" (Deleuze and Guattari, *Anti-Oedipus*, 85).

Yet the BwO God is forever escaping in every direction from the Lobster
God. For ultimately the Body-without-Organs is a "cosmic egg" always about
to burst open and out of which might emerge anything and everything imaginable—"worms, bacilli, Lilliputian figures, animalcules, and homunculi,
with their organization and their machines, minute strings, ropes, teeth,
fingernails, levers and pulleys, catapults. . . " (Deleuze and Guattari, *Anti-
Oedipus*, 281)—along with much that is not yet imaginable. It creates continually, and not all its creations are chaotic. Constantly emerging from the
chaos, projected from its virtual depths,

> "The earth was a formless void and darkness covered the face of the
> deep" (Gen 1:2).

is "the shadow of 'people to come'" (Deleuze and Guattari, *What Is
Philosophy?*, 218), that same people whom we encountered earlier,
summoned forth by specific order-words that we also listed (the all-but-
unactualizable absolute love commands in particular), a people perpetually
in partial emergence, the perennial prey of the Lobster God.

TEXT (THE BIBLE WITHOUT ORGANS)   107

Two Gods, then, but also two books, a Lobster God book and a BwO book. That's what the Bible is. But is it the Lobster God book before it is the BwO book (logically, not chronologically, speaking), or vice versa? On this Deleuze and Guattari are, in effect, emphatic: "Under no circumstances must it be thought that absolute deterritorialization comes... afterwards" (*A Thousand Plateaus*, 56)—after absolute stratification, that is. "In fact, what is primary is an absolute deterritorialization, an absolute line of flight . . . —that of the plane of consistency or Body without Organs. . . . It is the strata that are always residue, not the opposite. The question is not how something manages to leave the strata but how things get into them in the first place" (56). The Lobster God, then, is a predator but also an interloper. The Bible is the BwO book before it is the Lobster book.

Where is the BwO, book or God, located in relation to each of us? It is always behind us, but it is also always ahead of us, pulling us forward into the blind gloom: "You never reach the Body without Organs, you can't reach it, you are forever attaining it, it is a limit" (Deleuze and Guattari, *A Thousand Plateaus*, 150). Yet it subsists, it insists, in the most intimate proximity to us: "You're already on it, scurrying like a vermin. . . . On it we sleep, live our waking lives, fight . . . and are fought . . . , experience untold happiness and fabulous defeats; . . . on it we love" (150). All of which is to say that although the Body without Organs exceeds us infinitesimally yet infinitely, it not only creates us but we also create it. We become with it, we emerge with it, we emerge within it.

How, then, do you make yourself a Body without Organs?[102] Deleuze and Guattari believe they have the answer:

> This is how it should be done. Lodge yourself on a stratum, experiment with the opportunities it offers, find an advantageous place on it, find potential movements of deterritorialization, possible lines of flight, experience them, produce flow conjunctions here and there, try out continua of intensities segment by segment, have a small plot of new land at all times. It is through a meticulous relation with the strata that one succeeds in freeing lines of

[102] The sixth plateau of *A Thousand Plateaus* is titled "November 28, 1947: How Do You Make Yourself a Body without Organs?" (149–66). The titular date is when Antonin Artaud recorded *Pour en finir avec le jugement de Dieu* (To Have Done with the Judgment of God) for French radio, a performance subsequently denounced as offensive by the radio station director and never aired, as mentioned earlier.

108   THE BIBLE AFTER DELEUZE

flight, causing conjugated flows to pass and escape and bringing forth continuous intensities for a BwO. (*A Thousand Plateaus*, 161)

The Body without Organs, thus fashioned, might, as it flows and meanders, meet the BwO God (rivers do flow into each other) as the latter wends its way, craftily and cautiously, through the Bible,

> "... a stream without beginning or end that undermines its banks and picks up speed in the middle" (*A Thousand Plateaus*, 25).

managing to survive, even thrive, in the inhospitable biblical lands, the militarized biblical territories, ever imperiled by the Lobster God, the patrolling and controlling God.

The BwO God grows, as bodies tend to do, but of necessity it grows as a weed

> "Explain to us the parable of the weeds of the field" (Matt 13:36).

in between the tightly cultivated, sternly regimented spaces maintained and policed by the despotic other God, the spaces and places ordinarily associated with religion. The weed encroaches cunningly on these spaces and places and flourishes abundantly between,

> "That's it, a rhizome, or weed.... The weed overflows.... It grows between" (Deleuze and Parnet, *Dialogues II*, 30).

around, and beyond them. The weed lives wildly, exuberantly, excessively in the supposedly waste spaces left uncolonized by the forces of rigid, replicating, straight-row cultivation. Eventually, left to its own resourceful devices, the weed might even prevail, by means mysterious yet mundane,

> "Master, did you not sow good seed in your field? Where, then, did these weeds come from?" (Matt 13:27).

over the divine despot, however unfruitful and unlovely the weed might seem to that other God and its docile adorers, since, after all, "the weed produces

TEXT (THE BIBLE WITHOUT ORGANS)   109

no lilies, no battleships, no Sermons on the Mount" (Deleuze and Guattari, *A Thousand Plateaus*, 18-19).[103]

Well, maybe a Sermon on the Mount.

What, then, am I reading when I read my Bible, with, or even without, Deleuze and Guattari? Abysmally awful things. *God*awful things, to be technical. Again, what am I reading when I read my Bible, with, or even without, etc.? Gloriously sublime things; ethically energizing things; life-affirming things,

> **"A life is everywhere, in all the moments that a given living subject goes through.... Small children, through all their sufferings and weaknesses, are infused with an immanent life that is pure power and even bliss"**
> **(Deleuze, *Pure Immanence*, 29–30).**

> **"He called a child, whom he put among them, and said, 'Truly I tell you, unless you change and become like children, you will never enter the kingdom of heaven'" (Matt 18:3).**

even.

And the execrable and the excellent are intricately intertwined, intimately conjoined, invariably and irreparably in this Assemblage of assemblages. And within it and beyond it, the colossally clawed Lobster and the sinuously serpentine Body without Organs (its infinite tail forever disappearing down its bottomless gullet in its looping movement from the virtual to the actual and back again) are

> **"On that day the Lord with his cruel and great and strong sword will punish Leviathan the fleeing serpent, Leviathan the twisting serpent"**
> **(Isa 27:1).**

---

[103] "Introduction: Rhizome" is the sequence with which *A Thousand Plateaus* begins (3–25), as we noted earlier, and "Follow the plants" (11) is the directive that resounds from it. In time, that exhortation became a rallying cry (one of several) for the emergent field of critical plant studies (on which see Hannah Stark, "Deleuze and Critical Plant Studies," in *Deleuze and the Non/Human*, ed. Jon Roffe and Hannah Stark [New York: Palgrave Macmillan, 2015], 180–96, together with Jeffrey T. Nealon, *Plant Theory: Biopower and Vegetable Life* (Stanford, CA: Stanford University Press, 2016], 83–107). Deleuze himself described his "research undertaken with Guattari" as "invok[ing] a vegetal mode of thought" (*Difference and Repetition*, xvii).

110   THE BIBLE AFTER DELEUZE

> "Let an incorporeal rise to the surface like a mist over the
> earth . . . : not the sword, but the flash of the sword" (Deleuze, *Essays
> Critical and Clinical*, 22).

locked in eternal combat.

2

BODY (why there are no bodies in the Bible, and how to read them anyway)

What is a body when it is literary? When it is biblical-literary? What, for instance, is a body in the Synoptic Gospels?[1] What, for that matter, is *the* body in the Synoptics—"the Synoptic body," if you will? *A curiously elusive entity* would appear to be the answer. The Synoptic body, it seems, is susceptible to a highly contagious condition that currently threatens all ancient bodies. The ancient body has been gradually dissolving in recent decades, its surfaces and contours becoming ever blurrier rather than ever more distinct as scholars have crowded around it, optical instruments in hand. Dimly legible, inscribed on a tag tied around a toe of this deliquescent body, is the legend "Property of Michel Foucault"; and so the present chapter, like the previous one, is another tale that begins with Foucault and proceeds to Deleuze. Ultimately, the questions the chapter asks and eventually attempts to answer are: What is a body when it is literary *and* Deleuzian? What would the Synoptic body look like made over as a Deleuzian body?

---

[1] The "Synoptic Gospels" concept itself is a curious corporeal phenomenon, being what Deleuze and Guattari might term an *incorporeal transformation* (see pp. 81–83 in this volume) of the three textual bodies that early Christian tradition had named the Gospels According to Matthew, Mark, and Luke. In 1774, J. J. Griesbach pronounced these three gospels *Synoptic* (a Greek-derived neologism to express his conviction that they needed to be *viewed together*, as an intertwined threesome), thereby establishing (or, at any rate, formalizing) an apparently unbreakable bond between the three that endures to this day. See Johann Jakob Griesbach, *Libri historici Novi Testamenti Graece. Pars prior, sistens synopsin Evangeliorum Matthaei, Marci et Lucae* (Halle: Curtius, 1774).

The Bible after Deleuze. Stephen D. Moore, Oxford University Press. © Oxford University Press 2023.
DOI: 10.1093/oso/9780197581254.003.0003

112 THE BIBLE AFTER DELEUZE

Part I: The Eclipse of the Ancient Body

Bodies Discoursed and Performed

Foucault's Body

Paradoxically, the eclipse of the ancient body coincides with the emergence of the ancient body. Introducing an ancient-body book in the field of classics, Gloria Ferrari ponders how and why it was that the human body as such became "an important topic" in the humanities and social sciences in the latter decades of the twentieth century.[2] Among the catalysts she identifies are feminist studies, queer theory, and postcolonial theory, all multifaceted lenses that disclose how "dominant ideologies identify, shape and control particular bodies."[3] But if one were to single out the primary catalyst, she contends, "most would agree that it was the work of Michel Foucault."[4] Foucault's distinctive brand of body constructivism—his radical reconception of the body as a discursive object, culturally constituted from head to toe—untethered debate on the ontological and epistemological status of the body from the discipline of philosophy, enabling the body to become "a central concern in studies of culture and society and the proper subject of historical inquiry."[5] Because the second and third volumes of Foucault's *History of Sexuality* dealt with Greek and Roman antiquity respectively,[6] Foucault's impact on the field of classics in particular "has been considerable," Ferrari argues.[7]

Many classicists would concur with this judgment. Never mind that Foucault was seen by many traditionally minded classicists as a bull in the

---

[2] Gloria Ferrari, "Introduction," in *Bodies and Boundaries in Graeco-Roman Antiquity*, ed. Thorsten Fögen and Mireille M. Lee (Berlin: Walter de Gruyter, 2009), 1.

[3] Ferrari, "Introduction," 1.

[4] Ferrari, "Introduction," 1.

[5] Ferrari, "Introduction," 1.

[6] Michel Foucault, *The History of Sexuality*, vol. 2: *The Use of Pleasure*, trans. Robert Hurley (New York: Pantheon Books, [1984] 1985); vol. 3: *The Care of the Self*, trans. Robert Hurley (New York: Pantheon Books, [1984] 1986). The fourth volume of *Histoire de la sexualité* finally appeared thirty-four years after its author's death, and is now also available in English; see *The History of Sexuality*, vol. 4: *Confessions of the Flesh*, trans. Robert Hurley (New York: Pantheon Books, [2018] 2021). In it, Foucault ponders pronouncements on sexual desire by a host of ancient Christian authors, ranging from Justin Martyr and Clement of Alexandria to Augustine and Jerome.

[7] Ferrari, "Introduction," 1.

BODY (WHY THERE ARE NO BODIES IN THE BIBLE)   113

disciplinary china shop, or that feminist classicists quickly (and rightly) took Foucault to task for his egregious androcentrism. Foucault intensified an already incipient interest in the body in the field of classics; provoked a sweeping reappraisal of what a body, not least an ancient body, is or was; and modeled a sophisticated methodology for analyzing that newly complexified object. The Foucauldian body was an elaborately fabricated discursive product,

"I am fearfully and wonderfully made" (Ps 139:14).

whether it was the medical body, the penal body, the ancient sexual body, the Victorian sexual body, or any other body that caught his interest; and Foucault devoted volume after volume to tracing the meticulous cultural fashioning of these various corporeal entities.[8]

Early Christian Body-Talk

And just as Foucault's example impacted the field of classics, so too has it impacted the fields of New Testament and early Christian studies (albeit more obliquely), classics having always been the foremost interdiscipline for the latter fields.[9] The ancient Christian body that more and more gender analysts in New Testament and early Christian studies have wanted to talk about is, at base, a Foucauldian-Butlerian body (Foucault's corporeal constructivism having been extended to its limits in Judith Butler's theory of gender performativity)[10]—whether or not the names of Foucault and Butler are

---

[8] Nevertheless, Foucault resisted being labeled a social constructivist (just as he also resisted being labeled either a structuralist or a poststructuralist). When asked, for example, whether homosexuality was an innate predisposition or the result of social conditioning, he responded, "On this question I have absolutely nothing to say. 'No comment.'" Michel Foucault, "Sexual Choice, Sexual Act" (1982), in his *Ethics: Subjectivity and Truth*, ed. Paul Rabinow, trans. Robert Hurley et al. (New York: New Press, 1997), 142.

[9] Peter Brown's *The Body and Society* was a more proximate conduit for Foucault's influence on early Christian studies. In his introduction to the twentieth-anniversary edition of the book (a pivotal study of early Christian marriage and sexual practices), Brown fulsomely acknowledges its debt to Foucault. Peter Brown, *The Body and Society: Men, Women, and Sexual Renunciation in Early Christianity*, 20th ann. ed., with a new introduction (New York: Columbia University Press, 2008), xxxv–xxxvii.

[10] Famously for Butler, gender is the cumulative product of a socially scripted set of stylized actions, which combine and conspire to generate retroactively the illusion that gender is natural and innate, "expressed" by the speech, gestures, and other behaviors that in fact engender it (*Gender Trouble: Feminism and the Subversion of Identity* [New York: Routledge, 1990], 128–41). In short, gender is performative, "a practice of improvisation within a scene of constraint," as Butler would later say (*Undoing Gender* [New York: Routledge, 2004], 1).

114 THE BIBLE AFTER DELEUZE

explicitly invoked in such ancient Christian body-talk.[11] In other words, what so many of us in New Testament and early Christian studies have wanted to teach, present on, and write about is how Jesus, Paul, or other leading men in ancient Christian literature *perform* masculinity, not least how they so often seem to fail as men when measured against the inflexible gender yardsticks of ancient Mediterranean culture that determined which forms of speech and behavior counted as masculine and which as feminine;

> "Does not nature itself teach you that if a man wears long hair, it is de-grading to him, but if a woman has long hair, it is her glory?" (1 Cor
> 11:14–15).

or how female characters in ancient Christian literature perform gender in ways that subtly, or not so subtly, subvert the hegemonic gender scripts; or how eunuchs tear up and rewrite those scripts altogether. In general, we have delighted in exploring how gender, and even sex, appear to float free of anatomy in such literature.

Consequently, in much early Christian body-talk, the ancient body has receded behind ancient discourses on the body. It has slipped below or slid behind such discourses, has eluded them or been elided by them,

> "He was lifted up, and a cloud took him out of their sight" (Acts 1:9).

becoming all but inaccessibly ineffable. The ancient Christian body that more and more analysts have held up for observation has been a socially inscribed body, a culturally encrypted body, a discoursed body "all the way down." As such, it has been tightly, even if often invisibly, tethered to the Foucauldian body.

This tethering is tangible in the most ambitious example of mascu-linity studies within New Testament studies, Colleen Conway's *Behold the Man: Jesus and Greco-Roman Masculinity*. A section of the book aptly ti-tled "The Paradoxical Body" begins with an ostensible truism: "The body

---

[11] In the earliest New Testament body book worthy of the name, Dale B. Martin's *The Corinthian Body* (New Haven, CT: Yale University Press, 1995), Foucault is barely mentioned and Butler not at all. Nevertheless, Martin's Corinthian body is a Foucauldian body through and through, Martin's conception of the ancient body having been shaped by sectors of the field of classics that in turn had been informed by Foucault's body-discursivism. An exhaustive list of New Testament and early Christianity body books (never mind articles and essays) that work out of a constructivist and per-formative paradigm would by now be extremely long.

BODY (WHY THERE ARE NO BODIES IN THE BIBLE) 115

is perhaps the most obvious entrée into issues of sexuality and gender."[12] Nevertheless, continues Conway, "what has become increasingly clear" (clear in the field of classics first and foremost, one might add, and primarily as a result of the Foucault effect) "is that ancient masculinity was constituted more by the shape of one's life than the shape of one's body."[13] Indeed, "the body was ultimately not of primary importance in the achievement of ideal masculinity."[14] Why not? Because "the core of masculine identity resided not in the body per se but rather in what one did with, and allowed to be done to, one's body."[15] To rephrase this statement in Butlerian terms (and Butler does make cameo appearances in Conway's monograph), the core of masculine identity resided not in the body per se but in bodily performativity.

What the Jesus, or Jesuses, of the New Testament "allowed to be done to" their bodies has been of particular interest for analysts of New Testament masculinities. For example, when Brittany Wilson in her monograph on masculinity in Luke-Acts[16] comes to take the measure of the Lukan Jesus's manliness against Greco-Roman gender protocols, she is immediately drawn to the Lukan passion narrative. Indeed, Wilson's chapter on the Lukan Jesus's masculinity is primarily a reflection on the fate of the Lukan Jesus's body during his final hours. Wilson's verdict on that publicly displayed body is that its owner fails so abysmally to protect its boundaries that his status as a man is fatally undermined.[17] Yet, even though Wilson homes in with laser-sharp focus on the Lukan Jesus's body, both earthly and risen, in her critical appraisal of his masculinity,

"Look at my hands and my feet; see that it is I myself" (Luke 24:39).

the body that invariably appears in her lens is an overwritten body, an inscribed body, an encoded body. Wilson is able to read it, to decipher it, only by overlaying it with the ancient Mediterranean gender scripts that classicists have meticulously reconstructed.

---

[12] Colleen M. Conway, *Behold the Man: Jesus and Greco-Roman Masculinity* (New York: Oxford University Press, 2008), 16.

[13] Conway, *Behold the Man*, 16.

[14] Conway, *Behold the Man*, 17.

[15] Conway, *Behold the Man*, 21.

[16] Brittany E. Wilson, *Unmanly Men: Refigurations of Masculinity in Luke-Acts* (New York: Oxford University Press, 2015).

[17] Wilson, *Unmanly Men*, 234–35.

116   THE BIBLE AFTER DELEUZE

Undeniably, much of importance may be decrypted in the overwritten literary bodies of antiquity. The arrival of disability studies in New Testament studies further underscores this importance. Louise Lawrence's *Sense and Stigma in the Gospels*, a seminal instance of New Testament disability studies, illustrates the social constructivist assumptions about the body that undergird this still emerging field. Lawrence identifies "embodiment" and "performance" as two crucial concepts she will "think with" throughout her book. For her, as for the disability theorists who have informed her, the body is not a "static fact"; rather, when it comes to bodies, there is only "purposefully enacted role-play."[18] Moreover, for Lawrence, bodily performers, not least the blind, deaf, leprous, "demon-possessed," and other disabled characters in the New Testament narratives, can subtly subvert and tactically convert the stereotypes and stigmas that prop up the biopolitical binaries of physiological normality and abnormality, ability and disability that construct and contain them.[19]

Bodies in a Noumenal Night

Phenomenal Bodies, Noumenal Bodies

The question such analysts of New Testament bodies as we have been considering tacitly ask is not so much "Is there a text in this class?" (à la Stanley Fish) as "Is there a body in this text?" And the answer they implicitly supply is that there is no body as such in the text, only *representations* of bodies (but there *is* class in those representations to the extent that they are classed representations, sexed and gendered representations, and racial/ethnic representations through and through).

This has been an extremely productive vein of research. I myself have devoted endless hours to mining it. But theory has now entered another era (as theory is wont to do), and I have been following its transformation with fascination (as I am wont to do), and thinkers who once seemed strikingly different from each other now seem surprisingly similar. To be more precise, they now seem surprisingly *Kantian*.

---

[18] Louise J. Lawrence, *Sense and Stigma in the Gospels: Depictions of Sensory-Disabled Characters*, Biblical Refigurations (New York: Oxford University Press, 2013), 3.
[19] Lawrence, *Sense and Stigma in the Gospels*, 2–3, 20–21.

BODY (WHY THERE ARE NO BODIES IN THE BIBLE) 117

First of all (since we have just been talking about it), the bracketing of the material body in favor of the discursive body that has become a stock feature of gender analysis in New Testament and early Christian studies may be said to be broadly Kantian in its lineaments. In Kantian terms, the body in such scholarship—and most particularly in body theory of the Foucauldian or Butlerian stripe—would be the *noumenon*, the *Ding an sich*, the body as such or in itself, as distinct from the *phenomenon*, the body as empirically apprehended by the senses. The noumenal body would be unknowable in principle—"this unknown something" (*dieses unbekannte Etwas*)—unavailable to sensory perception.[20]

In the brief but heady heyday of postmodernism in biblical studies (essentially, the 1990s), Kant was the preeminent embodiment of the "Enlightened modernity" whose antithesis we imagined postmodern theory, emblematized by poststructuralist theory, to be. And in many ways Kantian philosophy was precisely that. But it is now possible to see just how many structuralists, and even poststructuralists, were the unacknowledged progeny of old man Kant, beginning with Ferdinand de Saussure himself. For Saussure's linguistic theory, which fueled French structuralism, setting it on fire, and much of French poststructuralism besides (for what was early Derridean philosophy, to cite the most conspicuous example, but super-Saussureanism without metaphysical guardrails?),[21] was a Kantian byproduct—Kantianism without any explicit evocation of Kant. The enabling gesture of Saussurean linguistics was a rigorous bracketing of what Saussure termed "the thing" (*la chose*)[22]— the actual concussion-dealing tree, say,[23] which you had better not walk into but could consign to the outer darkness of your linguistic theory, effectively rendering it the Kantian *noumenon* in your linguistic-philosophical system

---

[20] Immanuel Kant, *Prolegomena to Any Future Metaphysics That Will Be Able to Come Forward as Science with Selections from the Critique of Pure Reason*, ed. and trans. Gary Hatfield; rev. ed. (Cambridge: Cambridge University Press, [1783, 1781] 2004), 66. Kant insists, "This rule . . . brooks no exception whatsoever: that we do not know and cannot know anything determinate about [the *noumena*], because our pure concepts of the understanding as well as our pure intuitions refer to nothing but objects of possible experience, hence to mere beings of sense, and that as soon as one departs from the latter, not the least significance remains for those concepts" (67).

[21] To the extent that Derrida radicalized Saussure's conception of language as a system of differences without positive terms and set it loose on metaphysics.

[22] See Ferdinand de Saussure, *Course in General Linguistics*, ed. Charles Bally and Albert Sechehaye with Albert Riedlinger, trans. Wade Baskin (New York: McGraw-Hill, [1915] 1966), 66: "The linguistic sign unites, not a thing and a name, but a concept and a sound-image."

[23] "Tree" (*arbre*) being the word Saussure famously chose to illustrate his sign theory (*Course in General Linguistics*, 66–67).

118   THE BIBLE AFTER DELEUZE

> "... a sword ... to guard the way to the tree of life" (Gen 3:24).

—coupled with an exclusive focus on what Saussure termed the signifier (the sound-image "tree," whether spoken or written) and the signified (the mental concept of a tree derived from sensory experience), both of which functionally become the Kantian *phenomena* in the system.[24]

Foucault had far less to say about Saussure than did other French intellectuals of his era. Interestingly, however, Foucault in his passing references to him in *The Order of Things* styles Saussure's theory of language a theory of representation.[25] What of Foucault's own theory of language, or, better, his theory of discourse? Is it, too, representationalist at base, notwithstanding Foucault's own critique of representationalism?[26] Might Saussure's Kantian bracketing of the referent, the *Ding an sich*, a seminal representationalist move, not also be said to be the indispensable Foucauldian move? Might Foucault's overarching project not be said to amount to an elaborate exorcism of the Transcendent Thing,

> "Is not this thing ... a fraud?" (Isa 44:20).

the Object-in-Itself? What Foucault did not wish to do: "To neutralize discourse, to make it the sign of something else, and to pierce through its density in order to reach what remains silently anterior to it."[27] What Foucault did wish to do: "To dispense with 'things' [*choses*]. . . . To substitute for the enigmatic treasure of 'things' anterior to discourse, the regular formation of objects that emerge only in discourse"—things or objects appearing to possess a "rich, heavy, immediate plenitude": such is the hyperproductive power of discourse.[28] And preeminent, for Foucault, among the *thingly* objects, the *objective*-seeming things conjured up by discourse was the human body channeling the discourse.

---

[24] Further on Saussure's account of the linguistic sign (including its implicit Kantianism), see pp. 195–198 in the present volume.

[25] Michel Foucault, *The Order of Things: An Archaeology of the Human Sciences*, trans. anon. (New York: Routledge, [1966] 1989), 74, 320; cf. 312.

[26] See "The Limits of Representation" in *The Order of Things*, 235–71. The French title of the book, *Les mots et les choses* (Words and Things), indicates how central the issue of representation is to it as a whole.

[27] Michel Foucault, *The Archaeology of Knowledge and the Discourse on Language*, trans. A. M. Sheridan Smith (New York: Pantheon Books, [1969] 1972), 47.

[28] Foucault, *The Archaeology of Knowledge*, 47. Indeed, for Foucault, it is discourse, not things or objects, that possesses a "ponderous, awesome materiality" (216)—a telling inversion of the relationship of reality and language as ordinarily conceived.

BODY (WHY THERE ARE NO BODIES IN THE BIBLE)   119

Foucauldian discursive body-constructivism, which, I am arguing, is representationalist in its essence,[29] did not, however, achieve its neo-Kantian apogee with Foucault himself. It was further intensified by Judith Butler. In a much-admired early article titled "Foucault and the Paradox of Bodily Inscriptions," Butler undertook to out-Foucault Foucault, arguing, in effect, that Foucault's claim in *The History of Sexuality* that cultural construction *of* the body may be understood as cultural inscription *on* the body regresses from the proper rigor of Foucauldian body theory by positing a body that possesses ontological status prior to and apart from such inscription, a notion Butler herself rejects.[30] Butler does not merely out-Foucault Foucault, however, she also out-Kants him, arguing, in effect, that Foucault's discursive body is still excessively phenomenal and insufficiently noumenal.

Even as the body is thrust on stage, therefore, in Butler's gender theory, to perform in the spotlight, so indelibly and deeply inscribed, so completely constructed is this performing body as to fade to invisibility and recede to infinity even in the act of presenting itself, in effect slipping out through the back door of the theater and vanishing into a noumenal night. Butler chronicled early reactions of disquiet to her insufficiently solid body—"What about the materiality of the body, Judy?"—and did so in a book whose very title, *Bodies That Matter*, bespoke her determination to restore due gravity to the weighty corporeal entity her theory appeared to have rendered weightless.[31]

---

[29] It is with fear and trembling that I charge Foucault with representationalism. If representationalism is what Foucault's concept of discourse ultimately amounts to, it is an exquisitely nuanced representationalism (so much so as to pass muster even with Deleuze, apparently, although Deleuze does label Foucault's archaeological project "a sort of neo-Kantianism" [*Foucault*, 60]). A more adequate appraisal of Foucault's relationship to representation would need to incorporate his own reflections on Kantianism in *The Order of Things*, his philosophical engagements with postrepresentational art, and much else besides—all of which Petra Carlsson Redell does expertly and impressively in her *Foucault, Art, and Radical Theology: The Mystery of Things* (New York: Routledge, 2019), 9–12, 20–35. Ultimately, however, I am not altogether convinced that Foucault escaped the representational enclosure. And even if he did, certain of his most influential appropriators in Anglo-American theory have worked with theories of representation that lack Foucauldian nuance—Judith Butler, for instance, as I argue later, but also Edward Said, whose *Orientalism* (New York: Pantheon Books, 1978) was a descent, inspired by Foucault's concept of discourse (3), into the dense, multifaceted matrix of Western representations of "the Orient," coupled with a strategic (neo-Kantian) bracketing of the experiential, embodied lives of actual "Oriental" persons, Middle Eastern persons, mainly—"a brute reality obviously greater than anything that could be said about them in the West," as Said put it, immediately adding, "About that fact this study of Orientalism has very little to contribute, except to acknowledge it tacitly" (5).

[30] Judith Butler, "Foucault and the Paradox of Bodily Inscriptions," *Journal of Philosophy* 86, no. 11 (1989): 601–7; see esp. 601–3. The statement by Foucault to which Butler is responding occurs in his *History of Sexuality*, vol. 1: *An Introduction*, trans. Robert Hurley (New York: Random House, [1976] 1978), 148. Butler reprises her argument in abbreviated form in her *Gender Trouble*, 130–31.

[31] Judith Butler, *Bodies That Matter: On the Discursive Limits of "Sex"* (New York: Routledge, 1993), ix. She remarks, "I took it that the addition of 'Judy' was an effort to dislodge me from the more formal 'Judith' and to recall me to a bodily life that could not be theorized away" (ix).

120   THE BIBLE AFTER DELEUZE

But she can hardly be said to have succeeded. Prominent among the many "turns" that queer theory has taken since its Foucauldian-Butlerian-Sedgwickian heyday is a "post-Butlerian" turn, and our next chapter follows the Deleuzian lane in that particular highway turnoff. In the meanwhile, certain pronouncements from Chrysanthi Nigianni and Merl Storr's introduction to *Deleuze and Queer Theory* are highly pertinent to our current topic:

> What strikes and troubles one in the field known as "Queer Theory" is primarily an insistence on performativity as the only adequate way to perceive the social world and the real and the consequent refusal to "see" a positive (rather than constitutive) outside, a "beyond" of the signifier, discourse, language: a short-sightedness in relation to body and materiality.... Is after all the heterosexual matrix of imposed naturalized performances the only reality we can imagine? Is language the only air we can breathe? Is text the only land we can inhabit? Is parody the only resistance we can imagine?[32]

And a little later: "I am here to welcome the return of 'real' bodies and 'real' matter. A body whose forces and potentialities cannot be reduced to its cultural representations and the norms of gender; a matter that is no longer seen as static and passive, a blank slate written on by language and culture."[33]

What It Means to Be a Body

Analogous concerns have been voiced by at least one prominent analyst of ancient social body scripts, gender scripts in particular. Jennifer Glancy has been one of the most incisive decrypters of ancient Christian corporeality, most of all in her book *Corporal Knowledge: Early Christian Bodies.*

---

[32] Chrysanthi Nigianni and Merl Storr, "Introduction: . . . so as to know 'us' better. Deleuze and Queer Theory: two theories, one concept—one book, many authors . . . ," in *Deleuze and Queer Theory*, ed. Chrysanthi Nigianni and Merl Storr, Deleuze Connections (Edinburgh: Edinburgh University Press, 2009), 3.

[33] Nigianni and Storr, "Introduction," 5 (the editors shuttle between "I" and "we" throughout their introduction). (Early) Butler is likewise the foil of several other essays in *Deleuze and Queer Theory* and of much other work of a similar (often Deleuzian) ilk. As it happens, Butler's *Undoing Gender* includes a brief section titled "Deleuze," which includes the following statement: "I confess . . . that I am not a very good materialist. Every time I try to write about the body, the writing ends up being about language. This is not because I think that the body is reducible to language; it is not. Language emerges from the body, constituting an emission of sorts. The body is that upon which language falters, and the body carries its own signs, its own signifiers, in ways that remain largely unconscious" (198).

BODY (WHY THERE ARE NO BODIES IN THE BIBLE)   121

Interestingly, Glancy too reveals that "Foucault's influence" on her project has been "pervasive but diffuse."[34] Yet hers "is not a book about Foucault. After we have said everything about early Christian bodies that Foucault helps us say, those bodies will still have more stories to tell."[35] The latter statement gestures to a challenge that Glancy has set herself in this book, and even her failures to meet it are instructive. Already in her first chapter, Glancy is worried that "at this point in [her] discussion, early Christian bodies may seem remote, more ghost than matter."[36] Attempting to put flesh on these spectral bodies, she turns to "the corporal vernacular at work in the Gospel of Mark."[37]

Detailed analysis of Mark's representations of bodily gestures, bodily deportment, and other bodily movements and dispositions then follows. In particular, Glancy ponders the action of various Markan characters, most notably the Syrophoenician woman (Mark 7:24–30), of throwing themselves at Jesus's feet or otherwise abasing themselves before him. "Although the varying postural descriptions may evoke somewhat different images, each is an act of self-lowering that participates in a corporal vernacular expressing emotion, social location, and perception of power."[38] Through these stylized actions, the characters enact a nonverbal sociocultural script that would have been readily legible to ancient Mediterranean audiences.

But in focusing on these formulaic movements, does Glancy really succeed in fleshing out the bodies that enact or perform them? Or is the body still a secondary effect of a primary regimen of socially scripted gestures and postures, the paradoxical product of the actions it ostensibly enables? In other words, have we really exited the Foucauldian-Butlerian paradox of a body that has no articulable existence anterior to the discourses that bestow legible form on it or "enflesh" it,

> "They . . . thought that they were seeing a ghost" (Luke 24:37).

no expressible essence apart from the performativity that conjures it into being?

---

[34] Jennifer A. Glancy, *Corporal Knowledge: Early Christian Bodies* (New York: Oxford University Press, 2010), 4.

[35] Glancy, *Corporal Knowledge*, 4.

[36] Glancy, *Corporal Knowledge*, 15.

[37] Glancy, *Corporal Knowledge*, 15.

[38] Glancy, *Corporal Knowledge*, 15–16.

122 THE BIBLE AFTER DELEUZE

Even Glancy herself seems less than satisfied with her corporal analysis of Markan characters. Following the exercise summarized earlier, and another on the Johannine episode of the man born blind (John 9:1–12), she confesses,

> I have a long-standing frustration with analyses of bodies that tell us nothing about what it means to be a body. . . . In focusing on the . . . body of John's vision-impaired beggar, for example, we overlook the question of whether the world was blear or crisp when the beggar first glimpsed it; what visual sense he made of a world he had previously known through hearing and touch; whether the mud Jesus rubbed into the blind man's eyes was gritty and slimy on the thin flesh of his eyelids.[39]

The same line of questioning could, of course, be put to the entire throng of newly sighted bodies in the Synoptic Gospels (Matt 9:27–31; 12:22; 15:30–31; 20:29–34; 21:14; Mark 8:22–26; 10:46–52; Luke 4:18; 7:21–22; 18:35–43). "If we think about such questions at all," Glancy muses, "we bracket them as homiletic."[40] She promises that the final chapter of her book, "an extended treatment of Mary's body in childbirth," will finally press beyond "a semiotic or representational approach to bodies" to what she terms "a phenomenological approach."[41] The experiment turns out to be an intriguing one, despite the laboring body of the Matthean and even the Lukan Mary being absent from it, Glancy opting to focus instead on the *Infancy Gospel of James* and other extracanonical sources.

What resources might Deleuzian thought offer for "press[ing] beyond a semiotic or representational approach to bodies"? Glancy's monograph is titled *Corporal Knowledge*, but the early Christian narratives with which it wrestles contain no corporeal entities, no bodies as such to know, only incorporeal bodies, which demand a different kind of knowing, an incorporeal knowledge, and a return to theoretical first principles.

[39] Glancy, *Corporal Knowledge*, 21.
[40] Glancy, *Corporal Knowledge*, 21.
[41] Glancy, *Corporal Knowledge*, 22.

Part II: The Ponderous Weight of the Incorporeal Synoptic Body

The term "incorporeal" promptly puts the diligent reader of Deleuze in mind of the concept of incorporeals he adopted, and adapted, from ancient Stoic philosophy,[42] and that concept is fundamental to all that follows here. To rethink *literary* bodies as incorporeals, however, is to improvise, since it is not something Deleuze himself did directly. What follows, then, attempts to expand "what the Deleuzian body can do."[43] It harnesses that capacious conceptual body to rethink Synoptic character bodies as *incorporeal* (which, as we shall see, is quite different from thinking of them as representational), while rethinking Synoptic readerly bodies as fully *corporeal*, which is to say as affective and immanent.

Nonrepresenting the Synoptic Body

Does Writing Represent?

What is a body when it is incorporeal? How might one write about such a paradoxical non-object? Specifically, how might one write about the incorporeal bodies of the Synoptic Gospels? For there are, of course, no bodies in the Synoptics, strictly speaking: no human bodies, no animal bodies, no bodies of any kind. There are only *representations* of bodies in the Synoptics, one might say, most *would* say. But are they really representations? If that is what they are, then they are representations more abstract, more oblique than any modern or postmodern work of visual art.

Specifically, the words in the Synoptics that denote or connote bodies are inherently devoid of any relation of *resemblance* to physical bodies. As ordinarily conceived, visual representation (sculpture, painting, drawing, photography, film) entails a relation of resemblance to the object represented. Even the Alexamenos graffito, a crude drawing of two figures, one of them a crucified donkey-headed man—possibly the earliest extant visual depiction of Jesus—would be classified by most as representational, notwithstanding

---

[42] See p. 81 n. 54 above.

[43] Joe Hughes's phrase; see his "Introduction: Pity the Meat? Deleuze and the Body," in *Deleuze and the Body*, ed. Laura Guillaume and Joe Hughes, Deleuze Connections (Edinburgh: Edinburgh University Press, 2011), 5.

124   THE BIBLE AFTER DELEUZE

the fact that the caricatured anthropoid at its center has an animal head: nonexistent entities lend themselves as readily as existent entities to visual representation as commonly conceived. Linguistic representation, in contrast, including literary representation (at least when conducted in nonpictographic alphabets), entails no relation of resemblance between the word and its referent: the word "Jesus," in any language, is precisely as like or unlike the particular historical person who became the preeminent bearer of that name as the words "James," "Jacqueline," or "jack-in-the-box."

Is the concept of representation rendered void in the absence of any relation of resemblance? For Deleuze, resemblance is one of "the four iron collars of representation" (*Difference and Repetition*, 262).[44] How might the absolute dissimilarity of the word "Jesus" and the specific, ancient, bipedal, large-brained primate most often designated by that name be conceived within a Deleuzian theory of representation? As involving a "relaxed" relation of resemblance (127)? The Christian soteriological tradition, after all, turns on the idea that resemblance without likeness is possible, as Deleuze himself reminds us. Human beings were created "in the image and likeness of God, but through sin we have lost the likeness while remaining in the image" (127; cf. Deleuze, *The Logic of Sense*, 257).[45]

When likeness is entirely absent, however, Deleuze beholds, not resemblance (however attenuated), but rather the *phantasma* or simulacrum

> "Simulacra are . . . demonic images, stripped of resemblance" (Deleuze,
> *Difference and Repetition*, 127).

that so alarmed Plato. The effects of resemblance produced by simulacra

> "If we say of the simulacrum that it is . . . an infinitely loose resemblance,
> we then miss the essential. . . . The simulacrum is an image without re-
> semblance" (Deleuze, *The Logic of Sense*, 257).

are illusory. The simulacra appear "like a flash of lightning" even in the inhospitable sky above Plato's *Republic*—Plato who wished only to banish them, to exorcise them, thereby denying them "the possibility of a world of their own" (Deleuze, *Difference and Repetition*, 128). Although Deleuze does not say so

---

[44] The other three are identity, opposition, and analogy.

[45] The image-without-likeness idea may be traced at least as far back as Irenaeus (*Against Heresies* 1.6.1).

BODY (WHY THERE ARE NO BODIES IN THE BIBLE)   125

explicitly, such a world would contain (it might even center on) the realm of written signs.[46]

The Ruse of Resemblance

But back to the name. The example of the name is not incidental to our elusive topic, the body in the Synoptic Gospels. In common with much ancient literature (not least the literature of the Hebrew Bible, as Erich Auerbach long ago observed),[47] and in contrast with most modern literature, the Synoptics are almost entirely devoid of descriptions of human bodies. Proper names and personal pronouns are employed to fill that void. Undescribed bodies dangle pendulously from appellative hooks: "Jesus," "Peter," "Mary," "the Pharisee," "the leper," "the women". . . . Physical portraiture in antiquity, whether verbal and visual, tended to be bound up with physiognomy: interpreting physical characteristics as expressive of moral character. It has been argued that the Synoptic Evangelists were not enamored of physiognomy (none of their gospels contains a physical description of their protagonist), and that at least one of them, Luke, sought to subvert physiognomic conventions.[48] Physiognomics, in any case, does not enable us to defamiliarize the phenomenon of literary representation; for physiognomy was representational through and through. In physiognomy, outward aspect (straight eyebrows, outward-curving eyebrows, downward-curving eyebrows . . .) was relentlessly made to represent inner disposition (gentleness, cynicism, irascibility . . .). Framing the dearth of physical descriptions in our target texts with more recent conceptual resources, however, yields the following heuristic proposition: The Synoptic Gospels are largely innocent of *the ruse of resemblance*.

The ruse of resemblance:

---

[46] For Plato, poetic discourse, in particular, is the domain of *phantasmata*, simulacra (*Republic* 10.598e–599e).

[47] Erich Auerbach, *Mimesis: The Representation of Reality in Western Literature*, trans. Willard R. Trask (Princeton, NJ: Princeton University Press, [1946] 1953), 7–11.

[48] See Mikeal C. Parsons, *Body and Character in Luke and Acts: The Subversion of Physiognomy in Early Christianity* (Grand Rapids: Baker Academic, 2006). Callie Callon, *Reading Bodies: Physiognomy as a Strategy of Persuasion in Early Christian Discourse*, Library of New Testament Studies 597 (New York: Bloomsbury, 2019), investigates physiognomy in extracanonical early Christian discourse, finding Jesus to be a physiognomic anomaly therein ("a physically unappealing Jesus" [131]), even in a milieu in which Christian authors regularly sought to capitalize rhetorically on physiognomic principles.

126   THE BIBLE AFTER DELEUZE

> "The smile on the canvas is made solely with colors, lines, shadow, and light. . . . It is the . . . affect of the material itself, the smile of oil" (Deleuze and Guattari, *What Is Philosophy?*, 166).

What you see on the surface of this ceiling mural from the Catacomb of Callixtus is not a maze of lines, a chaos of colors. Rather, it is a young man bearing a sheep on his shoulders, his left hand firmly gripping its legs. It is, indeed, Jesus as Good Shepherd. He stands foregrounded in an illusory space whose imagined depths seem (to our modern, perspective-accustomed eyes, at least) to contain foreshortened trees toward which we might casually stroll in our imaginations, picking our way around the immobile youth and the other sheep at his feet.[49] Revelation 1:12–16, the book's head-to-toe description of the glorified Son of Man (physiognomy in a Jewish apocalyptic register?), spectacularly enacts the ruse of resemblance:

> ". . . the effect of the functioning of the simulacrum as machinery" (Deleuze, *The Logic of Sense*, 263).

What is present to your mind as you pore over this text or hear it declaimed aloud is not a muddle of random squiggles on papyrus or paper, or a cacophony of random sounds emitted by a human vocal apparatus, but an anthropomorphic entity whose divine nimbus and consequent anomalous corporeal composition presses your imagination to its limits (and beyond).

In the Synoptic Gospels, in contrast, nobody—and, more to the point, no body—is accorded a remotely comparable description. And it is not only detailed descriptions of glorious bodies—angelic, transfigured, risen, returning on the clouds—that are lacking in these singularly skeletal narratives. (Matthew 17:2, hardly ample, comes closest to being the rule-proving exception: "And his face shone like the sun, and his clothes became dazzling white"; cf. Mark 9:3; Luke 9:29; Exod 34:29; Dan 10:5–6.) Descriptions of inglorious bodies are equally lacking, which is to say that there is also nothing comparable in the Synoptics to the arrestingly ordinary (and consummately physiognomic) verbal portrait of Paul found in the *Acts of Paul and Thecla*: "A man small of stature, with a bald head and crooked legs, in a good state of body,

---

[49] I am riffing here on Michel Foucault's ruminations on representation in his *This Is Not a Pipe*, ed. and trans. James Harkness (Berkeley: University of California Press, [1968] 1983), 43–44. Foucault's own example is a different mural, but he does apply to it the phrase, "the ruse of a convincing resemblance [*la ruse d'une ressemblance qui convainc*]" (43).

BODY (WHY THERE ARE NO BODIES IN THE BIBLE)   127

with eyebrows meeting and nose somewhat hooked, full of friendliness; for now he appeared like a man, and now he had the face of an angel" (3.3).[50]

In the Synoptic Gospels, in contrast, there are only proper names and personal pronouns; condensed descriptive tags; and sporadic mentions of specific body parts. Regarding Mark's "John the Baptizer," for instance, there is mention only of a "waist," which is wrapped with "a leather belt," which in turn serves to accessorize "clothing made of camel's hair" (Mark 1:6; cf. Matt 3:4). This, however, is considerably more than we are told about Jesus's appearance when he arrives on the scene soon thereafter (Mark 1:9), or about Simon, Andrew, James, or John, his first followers (1:16–20), or about most of the characters in this narrative. To these minimalistic verbal indexes, implied bodies are imaginatively appended by audiences. How else might the matter be phrased?

What Is a Body When It Is Incorporeal?

Making Sense of Sense

Synoptic bodies are Janus-faced entities that, like all literary bodies, turn in two directions simultaneously. One face is turned to the verbal fragments that tether the bodies to their respective narratives. We may express this in shorthand as: One face is turned to the word. Another face, meanwhile, is turned to the world, meaning the world "outside" the text—the world in which the text is, however, itself a moving part, a cog in a complex sociopolitical machine, and in relation to which it assumes agency (more on which later). Incorporeal literary bodies, including Synoptic bodies, shimmer, specterlike, along the surface that simultaneously separates and conjoins word and world.

How does this work? Synoptic bodies, being incorporeal, are *not* sense objects since they are not apprehended through the senses. Yet Synoptic bodies *are* sense objects in the other sense of "sense": they manifest themselves

---

[50] Translation from *New Testament Apocrypha*; vol. 2: *Writings Relating to the Apostles; Apocalypses and Related Subjects*, ed. Wilhelm Schneemelcher and R. McL. Wilson (Louisville, KY: Westminster/ John Knox Press, 1992).

128 THE BIBLE AFTER DELEUZE

> "The metaphysical property that sounds acquire in order to have a sense"
> (Deleuze, *The Logic of Sense*, 166).

the moment we begin to "make sense of" the text. Sense (*sens*) is incorporeal, for Deleuze (*The Logic of Sense*, 19)—which is not to say, however, that it exists only in the mind. Its mode of operation is such that it skirts altogether the mental/material opposition (20, 28).

Sense is also an effect, "a language effect" that is akin to an "optical effect" or a "sound effect" (Deleuze, *The Logic of Sense*, 70). This is not to imply, however, that sense is merely "an appearance or an illusion." Rather, "it is a product" that "extends itself" over a surface (70). The surface of a text, let us say.[51] Sense is "an incorporeal effect" that is also "a surface effect" (70),

> "The incorporeal is not high above" (*The Logic of Sense*, 130).

one "inseparable from the surface that is its proper dimension" (72).

But this surface is also a border. Sense is the "boundary," the "frontier," between language and things (*The Logic of Sense*, 22, 28). In the case of the text, sense is like a ground mist that hugs its surface (cf. 5) and spreads out over its entire extent (cf. 70). And it is in the "flat world of the sense-event" (22) that the incorporeal bodies of the Synoptic Gospels produce and reproduce themselves incessantly. But this flat world is by no means a world without gravity, without weight, as we are about to see.

What Can an Incorporeal Body Do?

How do audiences of the Synoptics *make sense* of the incorporeal bodies of these minimal-body

> "... only the skeleton of sense, or a paper cutout" (Deleuze and Guattari,
> *Kafka*, 21).

narratives? These mainly undescribed, minimally invoked bodies might be said to possess a "minimum of being"; they are not beings as such but

---

[51] Thereby narrowing Deleuze's own focus, which is on the operations of sense in language in general.

BODY (WHY THERE ARE NO BODIES IN THE BIBLE)   129

"quasi-beings" or "extra-beings" (Deleuze, *Difference and Repetition*, 156).[52] Synoptic audiences, however, possess knowledge of innumerable corporeal bodies, beginning with their own, and it is that encyclopedic body-knowledge, at once intimate and abstract, that enables these audiences to ascribe phantom substance to the implied, incorporeal bodies

> "...incorporeal...entities we detect at the same time that we produce them, and which appear to have been always there" (Guattari, *Chaosmosis*, 17).

of the Synoptic narratives. These incorporeal bodies do not *exist* so much as they *insist* (Deleuze, *Difference and Repetition*, 156): they press insistently, and affectively, upon the imagination, the emotions, the intellect. Although incorporeal, they exercise agency in the corporeal realm. They cause events to occur not just in the world of words but also in the world of things. Most obviously, the incorporeal bodies of the Synoptic Jesuses have, through the ages and in alliance with the incorporeal bodies of other New Testament Jesuses, created entire worlds of things, while obliterating other worlds of things. In the process, they have moved countless corporeal bodies in ways that have been sublimely life-transforming, horrifyingly destructive, or stultifyingly mundane.

Because these incorporeal, undescribed Synoptic bodies can always be—indeed, must always be—actualized differently by different readers or hearers, they may also be categorized as *virtual* bodies. Indeed, Synoptic bodies are real although incorporeal,

> "The virtual must be defined as strictly a part of the real object—as though the object had one part of itself in the virtual into which it plunged as though into an objective dimension" (Deleuze, *Difference and Repetition*, 209).[53]

and the real is indissociable from the virtual. But because these virtual Synoptic bodies are minimally defined—line drawings of the most

---

[52] Deleuze is not speaking specifically of incorporeals here but rather of sense and its products more generally.

[53] Consequently, "virtual" in the Deleuzian sense must be distinguished from the "virtual reality" sense, the latter connoting an irreal dimension rather than a dimension of reality. More on the virtual later in this chapter and in the next.

130   THE BIBLE AFTER DELEUZE

rudimentary kind, figuratively speaking—their capacity for variant actualizations is multiplied exponentially. They can be fleshed out in endless variations and through infinite permutations,

> **"Actualization is creation" (Deleuze, *Bergsonism*, 98).**

as the history of Christian art alone superabundantly testifies. As such, whereas the bodies in the Synoptic Gospels—whether cursorily described, conspicuously underdescribed, or altogether undescribed—constitute a finite series, limited in number, the incorporeal bodies assembled on the innumerable borders between the words of those gospels and the worlds in and through which those incorporeal bodies assume imagined flesh, and thereby live and act, constitute an infinite series. These virtual bodies have inestimable effects and generate incalculable affects in the faith communities and wider worlds that ceaselessly and compulsively actualize them.

Assembl(ag)ed Bodies

The incorporeal human bodies of the Synoptic Gospels travel, then. They travel in the narrative wor(l)ds of those gospels, and, far more extensively, in their extratextual worlds. But they do not travel alone. Most often they are coupled with, or conjoined to, incorporeal nonhuman bodies: animal bodies and further other-than-human bodies, including "inanimate" bodies—although the latter often exercise as much agency as "animate" bodies. The Markan account of Jesus's postbaptismal "testing" (*ēn . . . peirazomenos*), for instance (1:12–13), is a scene with six actors (or, better, actants), only one of which is human. "The Spirit" thrusts Jesus into "the wilderness" (the latter an important actant in Mark, one with the uncanny capacity to cause the remote past to reactualize transformatively in the present: see 1:2–4; 6:31–44; 8:1–9; together with Isa 40:3; Exod 16; Num 11; 2 Kgs 4:42–44),

> **"It is not enough to say that it is a landscape. . . . What it lays out are paths. . . . These . . . trajectories are inseparable from becomings"** (Deleuze, *Essays Critical and Clinical*, 66-67).

where he is "tempted by Satan" and is "with the wild beasts" (*meta tōn thēriōn*),

BODY (WHY THERE ARE NO BODIES IN THE BIBLE) 131

"What does it mean to have an animal relationship with an animal?"
(Deleuze and Parnet, *L'Abécédaire*, n.p.).

and where "the angels minister to him." The human being is a notably passive player, a relatively inert body, in this transspecies, interbeing drama.

Human bodies in the Synoptics, as this scene illustrates, frequently exist in symbiotic, temporary relationships with nonhuman bodies. Such examples abound; what follows is but a sample of them. A "paralytic" (*paralytikos*) is accompanied, not by any physical description, but by a "pallet" (*krabbatos*), which, when the man is lying prone on it, announces that he is a disabled body, but when he is carrying it, that he is able-bodied (Mark 2:3–12; see also Matt 9:2–8; Luke 5:18–26). The ancient grammar of disability here employs things in apposition to words (or, more precisely, "thing-words" in apposition to "person-words"). The Matthean Peter is presented with keys—"the keys [*tas kleidas*] of the kingdom of heaven" (Matt 16:19)—that will shadow him through the history of Christian art, distinguishing him from every other generic, male, bushy-bearded Christ follower in that tradition (such as Paul with his sword). The anointing woman is nameless, faceless, and wordless in each of her Synoptic appearances. She would be nothing whatsoever, however, a perfect blank, were it not for her alabaster jar of ointment, an agential object that imparts agency to her in turn (Mark 14:3–9; Matt 26:6–13; Luke 7:36–50; cf. John 12:1–8).

Jesus is also coupled with agential objects. In all three Synoptics, he is clothed with a cloak of healing, which exercises agency independently of him, curing those who touch it (Mark 5:27–30; see also Mark 6:56; Matt 9:20–22; 14:35–36; Luke 8:43–44; Acts 19:11–12). Most obviously, of course, Jesus is also coupled in all three Synoptics with a terrifying instrument of torturous execution—a cross—long before he is physically pinioned to it. The Synoptic Jesuses are never unaccompanied by their crosses, indeed, even when those crosses are not invoked by name. The incorporeal crosses, retrojective constructs, cause each Synoptic Jesus to cast a perpetual cruciform shadow (a shadow longest and deepest in Mark, as is customarily observed). So symbiotically bonded with their crosses are the Synoptic Jesuses that to be a true Christ-follower in these gospels is to become a cross-bearer in turn (Mark 8:34; Matt 16:24; Luke 14:27)—to carry one's cross around "daily" (*kath' hēmeran*), adds Luke's Jesus (9:23), plunging from the grotesque into the surreal.

132 THE BIBLE AFTER DELEUZE

Jesus Triumphant, meanwhile, in all three Synoptics is as blank affectively as a freshly scrubbed slate, but is symbiotically, and semiotically, supplemented by a colt (Mark 11:1–10; Luke 19:28–38), or a colt together with an ass (Matt 21:1–9; cf. Zech. 9:9),

> "The horse, and the child, . . . become events, in assemblages that are inseparable from an hour, a season, an atmosphere, . . . a life" (Deleuze and Guattari, *A Thousand Plateaus*, 262).

which, singly or in tandem, declaim to the multitude the message Jesus himself need not speak. Postresurrection, finally, Jesus Triumphant is conjoined with the throne that his cross has refolded to become—"the throne of his glory [*ho thronos doxēs autou*]" (Matt 19:28; 25:31; see also Mark 14:62; Luke 1:32; 22:69). The throne loudly proclaims his glory

> ". . . a faceified object" (Deleuze, *Cinema 1*, 97).

even when he sits mute upon it, its agency rendering his unnecessary.

In short, corporeal human bodies in the Synoptics live, move, and have their "quasi-being" or "extra-being" (Deleuze, *Difference and Repetition*, 156) in assemblages. Deleuze and Guattari's assemblage theory enables us to ponder where and how the corporeal interacts with the incorporeal when the virtuality of a Synoptic Gospel is actualized through an act of reading or hearing. Deleuze and Guattari distinguish "collective assemblages of enunciation" from "machinic assemblages of bodies," as we noted previously, the former pertaining to words and their effects, and the latter pertaining to material bodies and their affects (*A Thousand Plateaus*, 88). Enunciative assemblages interlock intricately, and productively, with machinic assemblages. In the case in question (if the setting were liturgical), a human reader (a corporeal body) reads a Synoptic Gospel (another corporeal body) aloud to a human audience (an assembly of further corporeal bodies), and in the machinic conjoining of these different corporeal entities, incorporeal bodies, both human and nonhuman, are produced, and interact in turn: John the Baptizer, the Jordan River, Jesus, the Spirit, the heavenly voice, the wilderness, Satan, the wild beasts, the angels, the first disciples. . . .

Incorporeal bodies, Synoptic or otherwise, are not as different from corporeal bodies as we might imagine. The corporeal/incorporeal distinction does not imply a solidity, a fixity on the part of corporeal bodies (those of

BODY (WHY THERE ARE NO BODIES IN THE BIBLE)   133

readers or hearers, for example) in contrast to the fluidity, the mutability of incorporeal bodies (those of the Synoptic Jesuses, for example, or the other human characters who constellate around them). The corporeal body, too, is a creature of flux,

> "It is rather a gaseous state. Me, my body, are . . . a set of molecules and atoms which are constantly renewed" (Deleuze, *Cinema 1*, 58).

caught up in perpetual becoming, incessantly changing. In the event of reading, corporeal bodies-in-process intermingle with incorporeal bodies-in-process, and do so in assemblages

> "[An assemblage] is an assemblage of possible fields, of virtual as much as constituted elements" (Guattari, *Chaosmosis*, 35).

that shuttle constantly between virtuality and actuality.

The incorporeal body acts upon the corporeal body even as the corporeal body acts upon the incorporeal body. Something passes from one to the other, and is immediately passed back in a different form, in a recursive loop. That which passes also transforms. For the collective assemblages of enunciation in which the Synoptics are ceaselessly caught up include multiple instances of language use that effect "incorporeal transformations attributed to bodies" (Deleuze and Guattari, *A Thousand Plateaus*, 88)—in other words, that trigger incorporeal changes in corporeal bodies.[54]

What Else Can an Incorporeal Body Do?

Incorporeal transformations must be distinguished from corporeal transformations. The latter abound in the Synoptics; they are the indispensable stuff of its multitudinous miracle tales: "'Be made clean!' Immediately his leprosy was cleansed"; "'Go; let it be done for you according to your faith.' And the servant was healed in that hour"; "He touched her hand, and the fever left her" (Matt 8:3, 13, 15). *Incorporeal* transformations operate differently, as we saw earlier. The alterations they bring about do not entail bodily metamorphosis but are equally real nonetheless: "The judge's

---

[54] A phenomenon we first considered in chapter 1.

134 THE BIBLE AFTER DELEUZE

sentence . . . transforms the accused into a convict," just as the words "I love you" transform the utterer into a lover, and the words "Nobody move!" transform airline passengers into hostages (Deleuze and Guattari, *A Thousand Plateaus*, 80–81).[55] Incorporeal transformations also occur within the narrative worlds of the Synoptics. For example, the Synoptic Jesuses announce to two different Synoptic characters (or four depending on how we count: three of them are the "same" paralyzed person in parallel pericopae), "Your sins are forgiven" (Matt 9:2; Mark 2:5; Luke 5:20; 7:48 [the addressee here is the anointing woman]), while the Lucan Jesus declares to Zacchaeus, "Today salvation has come to this house" (19:9).

But these Synoptic narratives, both in their constituent components and in their entirety, are themselves immensely powerful machines for producing incorporeal transformations in the extranarrative worlds

> "The incorporeal universes of classical antiquity . . . underwent a radical reshaping with the trinitary revolution of Christianity" (Guattari, *Chaosmosis*, 62).

in which their ever-changing audiences live processually, move incessantly, and have their being-as-becoming. Only consider the following three statements that flow out of the Gospel of Luke.

First, Luke 1:35: "The angel said to [Mary], 'The Holy Spirit will come upon you, and the power of the Most High will overshadow [*episkiasei*] you;

> "The question is fundamentally that of the body. . . . This body is stolen first from the girl . . . in order to impose a history, or prehistory, upon her" (Deleuze and Guattari, *A Thousand Plateaus*, 276).

therefore the child to be born will be holy; he will be called Son of God.'" Not only do the words pronounced over the previously obscure peasant woman or girl by a named angel, Gabriel (cf. Luke 1:19; Dan 8:15–16; 9:21; *1 Enoch* 20:7; 40:9; 54:6), "sent by God" (Luke 1:26) to her village, effect a preconception incorporeal transformation of the embryo soon to form in her womb, the words also effect an incorporeal transformation of the woman

---

[55] In effect, this is the speech act theory of J. L. Austin and John Searle joined to Deleuze's theory of incorporeals (those two intertwined theoretical strands being woven into Deleuze and Guattari's assemblage theory, which in turn is woven into Deleuze's neo-Spinozan philosophy of immanence with its signature concept of the plane of immanence).

BODY (WHY THERE ARE NO BODIES IN THE BIBLE) 135

herself—multiple future incorporeal transformations, in fact, each more wondrous than the next,

> "She never ceases to roam upon a Body without Organs" (Deleuze and Guattari, *A Thousand Plateaus*, 277).

as the immense virtual power of this sparse narrative is progressively actualized through the ages. As Gabriel utters the formula of transformation over her, future-Mary becomes Theotokos, "God-bearer"; she also becomes the Immaculate Conception (another prime Marian title), conceived and born, like her Son, without the stain of original sin; she is made immortal, too, not dying when her earthly life has run its course, but "assumed" instead into heaven—and not to live out her (now endless) days in a pearly gated retirement community but rather to preside as Queen of Heaven (yet another signal Marian title) side by side with her regal Son and his almighty Father— these successive incorporeal transformations, along with other lesser transformations too numerous to name, wrought by dogmatic ecclesiastical pronouncements that all flow from the originary angelic pronouncement.[56]

The extent to which that originary, fictive, angelic pronouncement has affected individual Roman Catholic and Eastern Orthodox lives through the ages—the depth with which the once-calloused hands of Mary of Nazareth have reached into faith communities as a result of that formula of transformation—is, of course, inestimable. A minor personal example: Although I am a cisgender man (most of the time), one of my two middle names is Mary. The year of my birth was declared the Marian Year by the Roman Catholic Church, and in (then) hyper-Catholic Ireland where I was born, numerous parents bestowed Mary's name not only on female infants as a first name but also on male infants as a middle name,

> "... proper names which are not people but events" (Deleuze and Parnet, *Dialogues II*, 79).

hidden folds in the flimsy fabric of their identities.

---

[56] For a different attempt to focus the Lukan annunciation scene through a Deleuzian lens, see Em McAvan, "The Becoming-Girl of the Virgin Mary," *Rhizomes* 22 (2011): http://www.rhizomes.net/issue22/mcavan/index.html.

136   THE BIBLE AFTER DELEUZE

Other enormously consequential incorporeal transformations wrought by the Gospel of Luke (and the other canonical gospels) concern Jesus, needless to say. Particularly notable among them is his own incorporeal self-transformation

> "Communing with Christ is . . . an intermingling of bodies . . . no less 'real' for being spiritual" (Deleuze and Guattari, *A Thousand Plateaus*, 81).

at his final meal with his disciples: "Then he took a loaf of bread . . . and gave it to them, saying, 'This is my body [*touto estin to sōma mou*] . . .'" (Luke 22:19; cf. Matt 26:26; Mark 14:22; 1 Cor 11:24). But this incorporeal transformation is also a corporeal substitution in that the primary physical encounter with Jesus henceforth, for innumerable Christ-followers throughout Christian history, will be with a body of bread with wine for blood. We return in the next chapter to this singularly surreal body, at once comforting and terrifying.

Jesus' final incorporeal transformation in Luke (as in Matthew and Mark) is the most momentous of all. "Why do you look for the living among the dead?" the "two men" (*andres duo*, later identified as angels—Luke 24:23) inquire of the women who have arrived at Jesus' tomb to anoint his corpse. "He is not here, but was raised [*ouk estin ōde, alla ēgerthē*],"[57]

> "Let an incorporeal rise . . ." (Deleuze, *Essays Critical and Clinical*, 22).

the men continue (24:6). As with any incorporeal transformation, the person uttering the formula of transformation must be properly accredited (Deleuze and Guattari, *A Thousand Plateaus*, 82). For a transformation as epochal as this one, a transcendent agent, such as an angel, is needed to speak the words (the same authority to whom Luke earlier had recourse in the announcement to Mary)—or, better still, two angels. It is no longer sufficient, apparently, that this pivotal incorporeal transformation formula be uttered by an agent as ambiguous as Mark's "young man" (*neaniskos*—16:5–6; cf. 14:51–52),

---

[57] Words present in the majority of ancient manuscripts, Codex Bezae being the most important exception. Their absence would impact significantly the corporeal/incorporeal dynamics of Luke 24. As it happens (and unrelated to manuscript variants), the Johannine resurrection narrative lacks the "He is risen" incorporeal transformation formula (see John 20:11–14), Jesus having already uttered the formula over himself in 11:25: "I am the resurrection and the life." (The Johannine Jesus loves to upstage the Synoptic Jesuses.)

BODY (WHY THERE ARE NO BODIES IN THE BIBLE)   137

who, if he possesses angelic credentials, never presents them (or has them presented on his behalf, as in Luke 24:23).

Even as the transformation formula is solemnly uttered in the Lukan tomb, Jesus is instantaneously transferred, teleported, from the numberless company of "the dead" (*hoi nekroi*) to become "the living one" (*ho zōn*—24:5). Now he is in a position to appear to his disciples, first on the road to Emmaus (24:13–32) and then in the upper room in Jerusalem (24:33–53; cf. Acts 1:13a)—exceedingly strange and interesting appearances that we ponder later.[58] Suffice it for now to note that in the final appearance, Jesus seems to exist in a liminal state between incorporeality ("They . . . thought that they were seeing a ghost [*pneuma*]"—24:37) and corporeality ("A ghost does not have flesh and bones [*sarka kai ostea*] as you see that I have"—24:39), to flicker unstably between the two.

The Lukan disciples seem terrified by what they see, and the Lukan Jesus seems confused by what he has become, but Paul had earlier announced his full confidence in the reality of risen incorporeality. Paul sounds the formula of transformation: "But now [*nuni de*] Christ has been raised from the dead [*egēgertai ek nekrōn*]" (1 Cor 15:20). Raised in what form? What is "sown" (*speiretai*) is a "physical body" (*sōma phychikon*), Paul asserts, but what is raised is a "spiritual body" (*sōma pneumatikon*—15:44), whether in the case of Jesus as "the first fruits" of a general resurrection (15:20) or in the case of anyone who dies believing in him.

A *sōma pneumatikon* is what the risen Lukan Jesus does not want to be ("Touch me and see; for a *pneuma* does not have flesh and bones . . . "— Luke 24:39), but Paul is adamant that that is precisely what the risen Jesus is. Deleuze and Guattari want to know, What can this incorporeal body, this *sōma pneumatikon*, do?;

> "We know nothing about a body until we know what it can do" (*A Thousand Plateaus*, 257).

they circle and touch it curiously in response to Jesus' invitation. It can do much more than the corporeal body, the *sōma phychikon*, is Paul's emphatic answer. "What is sown is perishable [*speiretai en phthora*]," Paul declares, but "what is raised is imperishable [*egeiretai en aphtharsia*]" (1 Cor 15:42).

---

[58] See pp. 176–177 and 223–225.

138 THE BIBLE AFTER DELEUZE

And history has proven Paul right. It was the incorporeal body of the dead but imperishable Nazarene that gradually acquired world-spanning bulk and ponderous weight as Paul and an ever-swelling army of missionaries proclaimed the resurrection formula of incorporeal transformation over Jesus' butchered remains across the Roman Empire and many other empires to come. From the corporeal-seeming risen incorporeality of this long-dead figure has flowed, not only the Christian religion, as we say (in actuality, all the Christian religions that have ever been), but also the glorious and gory, abundant and atrocious histories of so much of humanity.

Why the Synoptic Gospels Represent Nothing

All this is to say that the Synoptic narratives do intervene—have always intervened—intensively in the worlds of their audiences. But how precisely? Not as agents external to those worlds, certainly. The Synoptic narratives are themselves material artifacts and hence worldly as well as word-ly, fully implicated in sociopolitical realities, folded into them. Furthermore and relatedly, the Synoptic narratives do not exercise agency through strategies of representation—specifically, through representing bodies, whether human or nonhuman, in a nonbodily medium; for what we call "literary representations" are themselves bodies (Deleuze and Guattari, *A Thousand Plateaus*, 86),

> "Writers generate real bodies" (Deleuze, *Negotiations*, 134).

and, as such, possess bodily agency.

"Every word is physical," indeed, "and immediately affects the body" (Deleuze, *The Logic of Sense*, 87). Written words, like spoken words, are material objects in the material world: inked letters on papyrus, printed letters on paper, electronic letters on a visual display terminal. Entirely unhindered by their absolute nonresemblance to our own organic bodies, these bodies of inscription act on us, move us, attract us, repel us—viscerally and affectively,

> "We ceaselessly jump from one register to another, in which signs are at work in things . . . just as things extend into . . . signs . . . . We constantly pass from order-words to the 'silent order' of things . . . and vice versa" (Deleuze and Guattari, *A Thousand Plateaus*, 87).

BODY (WHY THERE ARE NO BODIES IN THE BIBLE) 139

which is to say instantaneously. There is no palpable delay, no perceptible interval between our automatic visual or aural decoding of a written
or spoken word in the semantically seething sentence of a Synoptic narrative, or any narrative, and our being affected by that word. We do
not need to put the sentence on hold or hit a mental pause button while
we rummage through our immense inner encyclopedia for the appropriate referent of the word. Rather, the word, whatever it may be—
sat . . . grass . . . loaves . . . fish . . . broke . . . ate . . .—immediately, and
autonomously, generates an incorporeal body that affects our own body as
reader or hearer, that corporeal body acting, reacting,

"The skin is what is deepest" (Deleuze, *The Logic of Sense*, 10).[59]

"before the mind moves it" (Deleuze, *Essays Critical and Clinical*, 123).

In other words, "one does not proceed from sounds to images and from
images to sense"; rather, sense is the sphere in which one always already finds
oneself, that which makes speech possible in the first place (Deleuze, *The
Logic of Sense*, 28). And also writing and reading, for that matter. Sense is
metaphysical, for Deleuze—as we saw earlier, he remarks on "the metaphysical property that sounds acquire in order to have a sense" (166)—but it is a
"metaphysics in motion, in action" (Deleuze, *Difference and Repetition*, 8),
an immanent metaphysics as opposed to the kind that hovers high overhead.
This immanent metaphysics "carr[ies] out immediate acts"; it "produc[es]
within the work a movement capable of affecting the mind outside of all
representation"; it "invent[s] vibrations, rotations, whirlings, gravitations,
dances or leaps which directly touch the mind" (8).

If sense is immanent, immediate, and if Synoptic narratives are producers
of sense, what kind of body are they in consequence? Guattari's ruminations
on what literary and other "virtual machines" are, and how they operate, may
be plugged into the Synoptic text-machines, causing their sense-producing
display panels to activate:

Strange contraptions, you will tell me, these machines of virtuality, these
blocks of mutant percepts and affects,[60] half-object and half-subject. . . .

---

[59] Translation lightly modified.

[60] For Deleuze and Guattari, sensation is "a compound of percepts and affects" (*What Is Philosophy?*,
164). Percepts are not perceptions; prepersonal, impersonal, they do not entail a distinction between

140   THE BIBLE AFTER DELEUZE

> They have neither inside nor outside. They are limitless interfaces which
> secrete interiority and exteriority. . . . They are becomings. . . . One gets to
> know them not through representation but through affective contamina-
> tion. They start to exist in you, in spite of you. And not only as crude, un-
> differentiated affects, but as hyper-complex compositions. . . . But whatever
> their sophistication, a block of percept and affect . . . agglomerates in the
> same transversal flash the subject and object, the self and other, the material
> and incorporeal. . . . In short, affect is not a question of representation . . . but
> of existence. I find myself transported into a . . . blazing becoming. . . . I have
> crossed a threshold. . . . Before the hold of this block of sensation, . . . every-
> thing was dull, beyond it, I am no longer as I was before, I am swept away by
> a becoming other. (*Chaosmosis*, 92–93)

Alternatively, of course, everything may simply remain monochromatic.
Dullness is the default atmosphere that envelops too many Sunday-morning
performances of Synoptic Gospel fragments. But blazing becomings,
sweepings away, are ever pulsing virtually below the dusty ecclesiastical
threshold, and occasionally that virtuality blazes into actuality.

The Mundane Miracle of Reading (Everywhere Enacted Daily)

Textbodies, Readerbodies, Jesusbodies

How do the incorporeal bodies of a Synoptic narrative connect with the corporeal body of a reader or hearer? The incorporeal body is not a bodiless
ghost or spirit that wafts out of the text, hovers over it, and only then enters
the body of the reader or hearer, possessing it. Like the Synoptic superdemon,
Legion (Mark 5:1–20; Matt 8:28–34; Luke 8:26–39), which can exit the
demoniac's body only by entering the bodies of the herd of swine feeding
nearby, incorporeal bodies require corporeal bodies in order to exist. Like
Legion, too, now careening suicidally toward the Sea of Galilee in multiple
porcine bodies, incorporeal bodies also have the capacity to inhabit more
than one body simultaneously:

---

perceiver and perceived, subject and world. "We are not in the world, we become with the world"
(169), and the percept is "a perception in becoming" (Deleuze, *Essays Critical and Clinical*, 88). As
such, it (logically) precedes perception, just as the affect precedes emotion.

BODY (WHY THERE ARE NO BODIES IN THE BIBLE) 141

"It is a peculiarity of demons to . . . leap over the barriers . . . , thereby confounding the boundaries between properties" (Deleuze, *Difference and Repetition*, 37).

the textbody, the readerbody, the multibody of a liturgical audience.

While the corporeal bodies remain separate entities (relatively speaking) in the text-audience commingling, the incorporeal bodies that emerge from this coupling manifest themselves in a nonspace that is neither one nor the other: neither the space of the text nor yet the space of the reader/ hearer. Channeling Deleuze, we might say that the textbody and the reader/ hearerbody form "a zone of indistinction, of indiscernibility," as though, un-accountably, they had somehow "reached the point immediately preceding their respective differentiation" (Deleuze, *Essays Critical and Clinical*, 78). This is the mundane miracle of reading, everywhere enacted daily. And whereas corporeal bodies are mortal and finite, incorporeal bodies are, in principle, potentially eternal, available for infinite actualizations, each one different, as they manifest themselves in and through countless corporeal entities.

The Synoptic Jesus' dogged refusal to die, the mega-trope with which each of the three Synoptics ends, makes him a particularly apt emblem of the in-corporeal body, all the more so since his risen body also resists knowability (Matt 25:37–39, 44; Luke 24:15–16; cf. John 20:14–15), a peculiarity we ponder later.[61] The potential unknowability of all bodies (not just textual or risen ones) is a source of fascination for Deleuze and Guattari. "We know nothing about a body until we know . . . what its affects are," they write (*A Thousand Plateaus*, 257), by which they do not mean a body's capacity to feel or emote so much as its capacity to act upon other bodies, thereby augmenting or diminishing their power to act in turn. "We know nothing about a body until we know . . . how [its affects] can or cannot enter into com-position with . . . the affects of another body, either to . . . exchange actions and passions with it or to join with it in composing a more powerful body" (257).

The Synoptic Gospels have been particularly potent bodies of this kind, corporeal bodies with immeasurable incorporeal dimensions, embedded in infinitely open-ended, intricately nested assemblages. Each Synoptic Gospel interacts continually with its two Synoptic companions, thereby augmenting its individual power. The immense potency of the Synoptic Gospels in human

---

[61] See pp. 176–176 and 223–231.

142 THE BIBLE AFTER DELEUZE

history, however, has derived primarily from another relationship—a relationship of intimate proximity, of immediate contiguity—to another body, a temporally distant human body. Each Synoptic Gospel is, first and foremost, the surface, the skin, connecting the corporeal body of "the Jesus behind the Gospels" (as we like to say) with the boundless multiplicity of the incorporeal Jesuses incessantly actualized by the inexhaustible heterogeneity of hearers and readers in their dizzyingly different sociocultural locations.[62]

But things are considerably more complex even than that, and not only because the once corporeal Jesus now possesses the power to manifest himself incorporeally and hence multiplicitously. New Testament scholars are fastidious curators of the differences (even, or especially, the minute differences) between each Synoptic Jesus. We are less attentive to the differences *within* each Synoptic Jesus—not to mention the differences within the Composite Christ, the Synoptic (and Johannine) amalgam with whom the rest of the gospel-reading world is content to commune.

Channeling Deleuze once more, we might affirm that "two bodies coexist" within the Pan-Synoptic Composite Christ, "each of which reacts upon and enters into the other: a *body of judgment*, with its . . . differentiations . . . , its hierarchies;

> "Those who are ashamed of me and of my words in this adulterous and sinful generation, of them the Son of Man will also be ashamed when he comes in the glory of his Father with the holy angels" (Mark 8:38).

> "All the nations will be gathered before him, and he will separate people one from another as a shepherd separates the sheep from the goats" (Matt 25:32).

> "I confer on you, just as my Father has conferred on me, a kingdom, . . . and you will sit on thrones judging [*krinontes*] the twelve tribes of Israel" (Luke 22:29–30).

but also a *body of justice* in which the . . . differentiations [are] lost, and the hierarchies thrown into confusion,

---

[62] The arguments made in these pages by means of Deleuze and Guattari's concepts of incorporeality, virtuality, and actualization could also be made in a different register by means of their concepts of content and expression (see pp. 85–98 earlier).

BODY (WHY THERE ARE NO BODIES IN THE BIBLE)   143

"Among the Gentiles ... their rulers lord it over them, and their great ones are tyrants over them. But it is not so among you. ... For the Son of Man came not to be served but to serve" (Mark 10:41–45).

"Blessed are you who are poor. ... But woe to you who are rich" (Luke 6:20, 24).

a body that retains nothing but intensities that make up uncertain zones,

"He broke it ... and said, 'Take; this is my body.' Then he took a cup, and ... all of them drank from it. He said ..., 'This is my blood ...' " (Mark 14:22–24).

"Jesus himself came near and went with them, but their eyes were kept from recognizing him" (Luke 24:15–16).

[a body] that traverse[s] these zones ... and confront[s] the powers in them,

"He set his face to go to Jerusalem" (Luke 9:51).

"When he entered Jerusalem, the whole city was in turmoil, asking, 'Who is this?' " (Matt 21:10).

[an] anarchic body" (Deleuze, *Essays Critical and Clinical*, 131, emphasis added). These two incorporeal Jesusbodies—the body of judgment and the body of justice—perpetually confront and constrain each other within and across the Synoptic Gospels. And each invested reader or hearer, each community of faith—or, more accurately, each heterogeneous collectivity of faith, unfaith, and indeterminate in-betweenness—actualizes both Jesusbodies simultaneously and incompletely, and lives both of them in contradiction.

The Parable of the Tick

Let us turn back, finally, to the intricate, occluded operations of the textbody-readerbody assemblage. What kind of conjoined body or symbiotic entity does a Synoptic Gospel and its reader form? "With what can we compare [it], or what parable will we use for it?" (Mark 4:30; cf. Luke 13:18). A Synoptic

144   THE BIBLE AFTER DELEUZE

Gospel—like any canonical gospel, like any scriptural text, bloated with readings, insatiable for interpretations—may be likened to a tick. "Attracted by the light, it hoists itself up to the tip of a branch; it is sensitive to the smell of mammals, and lets itself fall when one passes beneath . . . ; it digs into its skin, at the least hairy place it can find. Just three affects; the rest of the time the tick sleeps, . . . indifferent to all that goes on in the immense forest" (Deleuze and Guattari, *A Thousand Plateaus*, 257). Ever indifferent yet always ravenous, the tick-text slumbers on the bookshelf, on the lectern, sightlessly alert to every warm-blooded readerbody within its range,

> "Look at the tick, admire that creature . . . defined by three affects, . . . all it is capable of. . . . What power, nevertheless!" (Deleuze and Parnet, *Dialogues II*, 60).

a micromachine of pure impersonal desire.

The Parable of the Orchid and the Wasp

But perhaps Deleuze and Guattari's parable of the orchid and the wasp (*A Thousand Plateaus*, 10)

> "A wasp-becoming of the orchid, an orchid-becoming of the wasp . . ." (Deleuze and Parnet, *Dialogues II*, 2).

better captures the intricate interactivity of the gospelbody-readerbody assemblage. Let the orchid be the gospel and let the wasp be the reader. Certain orchids cunningly simulate the reproductive organs and pheromones of female wasps, impelling maddened male wasps to attempt copulation with them, the males thereby becoming unwitting vehicles for the orchid's pollen as they visit, and fertilize, other orchids. Effectively, the wasp becomes a cog in an alien organic machine:

> "A machine captures within its own code a code fragment of another machine, and thus owes its reproduction to [that] machine: the red clover and the bumble bee; or the orchid and the male wasp" (Deleuze and Guattari, *Anti-Oedipus*, 285).

BODY (WHY THERE ARE NO BODIES IN THE BIBLE)   145

the orchid's reproductive apparatus. Analogously, the unwitting reader mistakes a Synoptic Gospel for something human (it is not; it is nonsentient matter through and through) and attempts to unite with it, to enter its mysterious inner spaces, or allow it to enter her, his, their intimate inner reaches. Beyond interspecies copulation, this is animate-inanimate copulation (to have recourse to that admittedly crude binary distinction). In the process, the gospel propagates and ensures its perpetuation. Manifested in this unnatural mating dance and its consummation, especially when viewed in the longue durée of Christian history, is the "aparallel evolution" of two bodies "that have absolutely nothing to do with each other" (Deleuze and Guattari, *A Thousand Plateaus*, 10).

And that, ultimately, is why there are no human bodies in the Synoptic Gospels, or even any representations of human bodies: the very concept of representation blindly glosses over the irreducible difference between text and reader. The abstract surface squiggles that constitute the Synoptic Gospels, their flat, depthless bodies, have even less to do with human bodies, ontologically speaking, than orchids have to do with wasps. Orchids and wasps, texts and readers, gospels and communities of reception are all "interkingdoms, unnatural participations" (Deleuze and Guattari, *A Thousand Plateaus*, 242). Their encounters can be understood only in terms of

"The assemblage is . . . symbiosis" (Deleuze and Parnet, *Dialogues II*, 52).

symbiosis. And in this ceaseless symbiotic process, each unalike body—the textual body, the readerly body (never as self-contained as it feels itself to be), the corporate body of readers-in-community (often packlike and prone to contagion)—constantly becomes more and other than it was, and always in communion with what it is not.

3

SEX (a thousand tiny sexes, a trillion tiny Jesuses)

This chapter explores one of the less-traveled roads of queer critical thought in general, which is a path yet to be pursued in biblical studies in particular. Like "classic" queer theory, epitomized by Butler's *Gender Trouble*,[1] this trajectory's roots also lie in French thought, not that of Foucault or Lacan, however, but—no surprise—that of Deleuze, alone and with Guattari.[2] To preview the path to be traversed, the difference this relocated point of origin makes for the capacities of queer thought is considerable, yielding, among other innovations, a concept of the gendered body that is neither discursive (à la Foucault) nor performative (à la Butler) but virtual; a concept of sexuality that overflows the human/nonhuman binary containers no less than the hetero/homo containers; and an alternative version of queer theory's "antisocial thesis" that precedes Lee Edelman's influential Lacanian version[3] by more than thirty years, namely, Guy Hocquenghem's *Homosexual Desire*, a manifesto sprung from a manifesto to the extent that it extends the

---

[1] Judith Butler, *Gender Trouble: Feminism and the Subversion of Identity* (New York: Routledge, 1990).

[2] Dedicated attempts to articulate a Deleuzian or Deleuzoguattarian queer theory have included Michael O'Rourke, ed., *The Becoming-Deleuzoguattarian of Queer Theory*, Rhizomes 11/12 (Fall 2005/Spring 2006); Chrysanthi Nigianni and Merl Storr, eds., *Deleuze and Queer Theory*, Deleuze Connections (Edinburgh: Edinburgh University Press, 2009); David V. Ruffolo, *Post-Queer Politics*, Queer Interventions (Farnham, UK: Ashgate, 2009); Nick Davis, *The Desiring-Image: Gilles Deleuze and Contemporary Queer Cinema* (Oxford: Oxford University Press, 2013); and Rachel Loewen Walker, *Queer and Deleuzian Temporalities: Toward a Living Present* (New York: Bloomsbury Academic, 2021). Also pertinent are Frida Beckman, *Between Desire and Pleasure: A Deleuzian Theory of Sexuality*, Plateaus—New Directions in Deleuze Studies (Edinburgh: Edinburgh University Press, 2013); Frida Beckman, ed., *Deleuze and Sex*, Deleuze Connections (Edinburgh: Edinburgh University Press, 2011), and Anna Hickey-Moody, *Deleuze and Masculinity* (New York: Palgrave Macmillan, 2019), together with Jasbir K. Puar, *Terrorist Assemblages: Homonationalism in Queer Times*, Next Wave: New Directions in Women's Studies (Durham, NC: Duke University Press, 2007), which draws strategically (even if not extensively) on Deleuze and Guattari.

[3] Lee Edelman, *No Future: Queer Theory and the Death Drive* (Durham, NC: Duke University Press, 2004). (All too) briefly, the antisocial thesis in queer theory is radically anti-assimilationist. What the homophobic forces of right-wing reaction have gotten right, for Edelman—more right, indeed, than the left—is that queerness, fully embraced, threatens "the wholesale rupturing of the social fabric" (*No Future*, 14).

The Bible after Deleuze. Stephen D. Moore, Oxford University Press. © Oxford University Press 2023.
DOI: 10.1093/oso/9780197581254.003.0004

SEX (A THOUSAND TINY SEXES, A TRILLION TINY JESUSES)   147

sexual politics of Deleuze and Guattari's *Anti-Oedipus*.[4] The loop formed by Deleuze's own subsequent engagement with Hocquenghem is also part of the tale to be spun, as are Deleuze's, and Deleuze and Guattari's, further pronouncements on sex. How might Deleuze and Guattari's hyperqueer theory (which is what their concept of sex amounts to) translate into biblical hermeneutics—or, since Deleuze and Guattari rejected the enabling assumptions of hermeneutics, as we saw earlier,[5] into biblical *his*meneutics, *their*meneutics, or *queer*meneutics? That is the driving question of the train of thought now beginning to chug down our less-traveled road, one without a pre-laid track.

Part I: The Deleuzian Queer

Desiring and Naming

Desire on the Factory Floor

Anti-Oedipus unveils with brio a materialist theory of desire. It refuses the capitalist separation of labor and libido, production and reproduction. For the neo-Marxist authors of *Anti-Oedipus*,

> **"I think Félix Guattari and I have remained Marxists, in our two different ways" (Deleuze, *Negotiations*, 171).**

the unconscious is a factory (Deleuze and Guattari, *Anti-Oedipus*, 24, 49, 55). The unconscious "engineers, it is machinic" (53). A factory is nothing, indeed, without machines, and what "pound away and throb" in the unconscious are "desiring-machines [*machines désirantes*]" (54), defined by their capacity for

---

[4] Guy Hocquenghem, *Homosexual Desire*, trans. Daniella Dangoor, Series Q (Durham, NC: Duke University Press, [1972] 1993). The Edelman "precursor" more commonly identified is Leo Bersani; see his "Is the Rectum a Grave?," *October* 43 (Winter 1987): 197–222, and especially his *Homos* (Cambridge, MA: Harvard University Press, 1995). For an "early" assertion that the antisocial thesis may be traced back to Hocquenghem, see Tim Dean, "The Antisocial Homosexual," *PMLA* 121, no. 3 (2006): 827.

[5] See pp. 20–21.

148   THE BIBLE AFTER DELEUZE

> "What defines desiring-machines is precisely their capacity for an un-
> limited number of connections, in every sense and in all directions"
> (Guattari, *Chaosophy*, 96).

unlimited connectivity. Desiring-machines were actually what early Freud unearthed in the unconscious as "the domain of free syntheses where everything is possible: endless connections, nonexclusive disjunctions, nonspecific conjunctions, partial objects and flows" (Deleuze and Guattari, *Anti-Oedipus*, 54). But later Freud lost his nerve,

> "The Freudian Unconscious has . . . lost the seething richness and disqui-
> eting atheism of its origins" (Guattari, *Chaosmosis*, 10).

burying the desiring-machines in the back lawn of the Holy Family's home and taking up residence himself in that bourgeois domicile (Deleuze and Guattari, *Anti-Oedipus*, 51–56).

The Neopronominal Revolution

What are the ramifications of Deleuze and Guattari's hyperconnective theory of desire[6] for sex and sexuality in general and sexual identity in particular? Sexual identity dissolves instantly in the theory, for reasons outlined shortly, which places Deleuze and Guattari at one end of the queer identity spectrum. But it is not a lonely place to be. Queer theory, even or especially in its "classic" manifestations, has tended overwhelmingly to lean anti-identitarian: look no further than the subtitle of Butler's *Gender Trouble*, which, of course, is *Feminism and the Subversion of Identity*, or Edelman's oft-repeated dictum: "For queerness can never define an identity; it can only ever disturb one."[7]

Who or what clusters at the identitarian end of the spectrum? Millions more people than at the other end, needless to say, an exponentially expanding multitude. And an ever-greater number of them employ an elaborate taxonomic idiom to label themselves and others, an in-group language that has become ever more exquisitely precise. (Learning while) teaching gender

---

[6] Further on which see pp. 25, 29–30, and 69–72 earlier.
[7] Edelman, *No Future*, 17.

SEX (A THOUSAND TINY SEXES, A TRILLION TINY JESUSES)   149

and sexuality seminars over several decades has positioned me to observe, to experience, firsthand the incremental increase of exactitude displayed in, say, the circle of self-introductions, that affect-suffused first-day-of-class ritual: "I'm a cisgender male feminist LGBTQIA ally"; "I'm a genderqueer nonbinary AFAB". . . . I was reminded of that self-naming ritual recently as I perused the elegant, often moving, online article collection *Audre Lorde Now*,[8] sex/gender self-identifications interlacing intersectionally with racial/ethnic self-identifications as the contributors introduce themselves as, for example, "an Afro-Cuban feminist activistx, non-binary, fantastically fat, trans masculine historian," or "a Puerto Rican/Irish multi-gendered street scholar and freedom maker."[9]

It all amounts to a glorious full turning of the circle whose constricting origins

> "[Masoch] was . . . disturbed when Krafft-Ebing used his name to designate a perversion" (Deleuze, *Coldness and Cruelty*, 10).

Foucault chronicled in his history of sexuality. Once again, in other words, "perverse" sex is proving an "incitement to discourse" of Foucauldian proportions. The eruptive discoursing of sex in the eighteenth and especially nineteenth centuries was a time for a parade of "figures, scarcely noticed in the past, to step forward and speak, to make the difficult confession of what they were."[10] More particularly, however, it was the age of nascent psychiatry and psychology and rampant sexology, and consequently for the taxonomic "entomologizing" of a multitude of "perverts," ranging from "Krafft-Ebing's zoophiles and zooerasts" to "Rohleder's auto-monosexualists," and on to "mixoscopophiles, gynecomasts, presbyophiles, sexoesthetic inverts, and dyspareunist women."[11]

The significance of the contemporary counterpart, the proliferation of queer (counter)names, the ever more precise terminological encapsulation

---

[8] Lorde being widely seen as, among other things, the preeminent "precursor" for the queer-of-color trajectory in queer studies, principally because of her *Sister Outsider: Essays and Speeches* (Berkeley, CA: Crossing Press, 1984).

[9] Conor Tomás Reed, ed., *Audre Lorde Now*, CUNY Center for the Humanities, July 16, 2020: https://www.centerforthehumanities.org/news/audre-lorde-now. The two contributors whose self-descriptions I quote are, respectively, Tito Mitjans Alayón and Reed.

[10] Michel Foucault, *The History of Sexuality*, vol. 1: *An Introduction*, trans. Robert Hurley (New York: Pantheon Books, 1978), 39. "The Incitement to Discourse" is the title of the book's first chapter.

[11] Foucault, *The History of Sexuality*, 43.

150 THE BIBLE AFTER DELEUZE

of sexual identities, sub-identities, and sub-sub-identities should not be underestimated. It represents a quiet—when not clamorous—sexual and hence social revolution, creating potent pockets of countercommunity within the larger society. But is the distance between nineteenth-century sexological taxonomy, epitomized by Richard von Krafft-Ebing's *Psychopathia Sexualis* (1886),

> "The sadomasochistic entity was not invented by Freud; we find it in the work of Krafft-Ebing, Havelock Ellis and Féré" (Deleuze, *Coldness and Cruelty*, 38).

and, say, the "Terms, Definitions & Labels" webpage of Amherst College's Queer Resource Center ("Accomplice," "AFAB," "AMAB," "Ally," "Allyship," "Androgyny," "Aromantic," "Asexual" . . .)[12] really the yawning gulf it might seem to be, containment of sexual otherness on one side of the divide, sexual self-realization on the opposite side? Deleuze would likely not think so, were he still among the living, and for reasons worth pondering.

The Proletariat of Eros (Producing the Product Society Cannot Want)

Clubbing with Deleuze and Hocquenghem

Deleuze would sit out the contemporary identitarian dance, in other words, morosely nursing his drink in a corner of the club.[13] But why precisely? Not because of his sexual orientation but rather because of his philosophical orientation, which precludes him from believing in identity. More

---

[12] See https://www.amherst.edu/campuslife/our-community/queer-resource-center/terms-definitions. This useful and informative glossary of almost a hundred terms ends, tellingly, with this caution: "Again, this is not an exhaustive list of terms and definitions! New language emerges as our understandings of these topics change and evolve." Such resources now abound and continue to multiply.

[13] Deleuze's presence in the club, however, and even less that of Guattari, would not raise any eyebrows. In contemporary idiom, Guattari was an LGBTQIA+ ally of the first order. In particular, he was an active force in the *Front homosexuel d'action révolutionnaire*, launched in 1970 (Deleuze was also a member), and organizer of the 1973 incendiary queer publication-event, *Trois milliards de pervers* (Three Billion Perverts; Deleuze and Foucault were among its three dozen or so contributors), for which he was legally prosecuted, tried, and fined for "affronting public decency." See Guattari, *Chaosophy*, 215–24, which includes Guattari's notes for his (militant) self-defense in his trial. Foucault also testified in the trial.

SEX (A THOUSAND TINY SEXES, A TRILLION TINY JESUSES)   151

precisely, Deleuze's philosophical convictions compel his *refusal* of the concept of identity. Again, why? To fully fathom his philosophical resistance to the concept, we would need to wade through all 350 pages of his *Difference and Repetition*—pages that call us cumulatively, however, to "a world of differences implicated one in the other, to a complicated, properly chaotic world *without identity*" (57, emphasis in original). Deleuze's *political* aversion to the concept of identity (to the extent that the Deleuzian political may be disentangled from the Deleuzian philosophical) is easier to encapsulate. Brian Massumi's foreword to *A Thousand Plateaus* captures it well: "The annals of official philosophy are populated by 'bureaucrats of pure reason' who speak in 'the shadow of the despot' and are in historical complicity with the State. . . . Theirs is the discourse of sovereign judgment, of stable subjectivity legislated by 'good' sense, *of rocklike identity*, 'universal' truth, and (white male) justice."[14] Identity, for Deleuze, possesses a sinister aspect even when presenting a benign face. It yanks on the reterritorializing tether even while masquerading as an exhilarating line of flight.

As much as anything, that tether might be said to be "a line of rigid segmentarity on which everything seems calculable and foreseen, the beginning and end of a segment, the passage from one segment to another" (Deleuze and Guattari, *A Thousand Plateaus*, 195). Rigid segmentarity is the substratum of normativity—heteronormativity, homonormativity, chrononormativity, and all the other meganormativities

> "We don't use the words 'normal' and 'abnormal'" (Deleuze, *Desert Islands*, 262).

routinely invoked by queer theorists. "Not only are the great molar aggregates segmented (States, institutions, classes), but so are people as elements of an aggregate, as are feelings as relations between people; they are segmented, not in such a way as to disturb or disperse, but on the contrary to ensure and control the identity of each agency, including personal identity" (Deleuze and Guattari, *A Thousand Plateaus*, 195). And not least sexual identity. "The fiancé can say to the young woman, Even though there are differences between our segments, we have the same tastes and we are alike. I am a man,

---

[14] Brian Massumi, "Translator's Foreword: Pleasures of Philosophy," in Deleuze and Guattari, *A Thousand Plateaus*, ix, emphasis added. The internal quotations are from Deleuze's "Nomadic Thought" (*Desert Islands*, 259).

152 THE BIBLE AFTER DELEUZE

you are a woman; you are a telegraphist, I am a grocer; you count words, I weigh things: our segments fit together, conjugate. Conjugality. A whole interplay of well-determined, well-planned territories. They have a future but no becoming" (195). Becoming marks the place of the queer—or, more precisely, names the process of queering—in Deleuzian thought. And identity is the antonym of becoming, in Deleuzese as in Deleuzoguattarese.

Enter Guy Hocquenghem clutching his *Homosexual Desire*. It's still fifteen years before the first attested use of the term "identity politics," but that's all he wants to talk about as he joins Deleuze in his lonely corner of the club. Specifically, Hocquenghem wants to say exquisitely nuanced and thoroughly iconoclastic things about queer sexual identity, but such discourse is still in the Stone Age. He and Deleuze have only one word between them to articulate all that needs to be said on this intractably slippery topic, that word being *homosexualité*. They grunt their word, they snarl it, they screech it; they leap up and down excitedly, bare their teeth, and thump their chests.

Channeling *Anti-Oedipus* Hocquenghem announces, " 'Homosexual desire'—the expression is meaningless."[15] Ah, the book's title is a spoof, then. Deleuze chuckles appreciatively. "There is no subdivision of desire into homosexuality and heterosexuality," Hocquenghem continues. "Properly speaking, desire is no more homosexual than heterosexual. Desire emerges in a multiple form, whose components are only divisible *a posteriori*, according to how we manipulate it. Just like heterosexual desire, homosexual desire is an arbitrarily frozen frame in an unbroken and polyvocal flux."[16] What, then, is desire chipped free from its frozen frame, reanimated, and released into the wild? There is a certain ineffability to desire in the Deleuzoguattarian sense, as Hocquenghem recognizes. For him, as for Deleuze and Guattari, homosexuality is no longer the love that dare not speak its name. Rather, "both heterosexuality and homosexuality are the precarious outcome of a desire which knows no name."[17]

Desire, so unnamed, touches everything intimately and queers everything utterly. Straight sex and sexuality are customarily distinguished from queer sex and sexuality. But there are no straight lines in desire any more than in nature. Desire queers heterosex completely while revealing homosex to be insufficiently queer. Bisexuality also dissolves in desire's incessant flux. Deleuze and Guattari declare, "Sexuality . . . is badly explained by the binary

---

[15] Hocquenghem, *Homosexual Desire*, 49.
[16] Hocquenghem, *Homosexual Desire*, 49–50.
[17] Hocquenghem, *Homosexual Desire*, 75.

SEX (A THOUSAND TINY SEXES, A TRILLION TINY JESUSES)   153

organization of the sexes, and just as badly by a bisexual organization within each sex. Sexuality brings into play . . . *n* sexes. . . . Sexuality is the production of a thousand sexes, which are so many uncontrollable becomings" (*A Thousand Plateaus*, 278).

Sexuality thus reconceived, as Deleuze reflects in dialogue with Hocquenghem,

> "Every day a thousand kinds of homosexual behavior challenge the classifications imposed on them" (Hocquenghem, *Homosexual Desire*, 148).

> "Far from closing itself in on the identity of a sex, this homosexuality opens itself up to a loss of identity" (Deleuze, *Desert Islands*, 287).

"open[s] itself up to all sorts of possible new relations, micrological or micropsychic, essentially reversible, transversal relations, with as many sexes as there are assemblages, not even excluding [most shockingly of all?] new relations between men and women. . . . It is no longer about being a man or woman, but inventing sexes" (Deleuze, *Desert Islands*, 287).[18]

Neither Hocquenghem nor Deleuze, however, want to see the queer slink quietly away, stripped of all sexual specificity. For both of them, the queer, potentially at least, is still a scare figure of the first order. Hocquenghem contends that if "the homosexual phantasy . . . contains a complex knot of dread and desire, . . . is more obscene than any other and at the same time more exciting, . . . arousing mixed feelings of horror and desire," then it must be that "homosexuality expresses some aspect of desire" that "appears nowhere else" and "haunts the 'normal world.'"[19] Homosexuality "produces itself without reproducing," so that every homosexual is "the end of the species." They "can only be a degenerate, for [they do] not generate."[20] The

[18] From Deleuze's "Preface to Hocquenghem's *L'Après-Mai des faunes*" (*Desert Islands*, 284–88). Hocquenghem's second queer manifesto, *L'Après-Mai des faunes: Volutions* (The After-May of the Fauns: Volutions; Paris: Bernard Grasset, 1974), for which Deleuze wrote the preface, has yet to be translated (in its entirety, anyway) into English. So too Hocquenghem's *La Colère de l'agneau* (The Wrath of the Lamb; Paris: Albin Michel, 1985), a queer-themed historical novel about the apostle John.
[19] Hocquenghem, *Homosexual Desire*, 50.
[20] Hocquenghem, *Homosexual Desire*, 107–8. These are representative excerpts from Hocquenghem's extended articulation of what would in due course—stamped not with his name, as noted earlier, but with those of Bersani and Edelman—be termed the antisocial thesis in queer theory. Edelman himself, however, acknowledges that he sees Hocquenghem's position on queers—which Edelman summarizes as, "we do not intend a new politics, a better society, a brighter tomorrow, since all of these fantasies reproduce the past, through displacement, in the form of the future"—as anticipating his own (*No Future*, 30–31).

154 THE BIBLE AFTER DELEUZE

homosexual, or, as we would now say, the queer, thereby eludes both the capitalist calculus of *production*, being a worker like no other who produces the product society cannot want,

> "... the queer as a proletariat of Eros" (Deleuze, *Desert Islands*, 287).

and the heterogenital calculus of *reproduction*, falling outside the "social" altogether, entering into a perverse "relationship with the Outside" (Deleuze, *Desert Islands*, 285)—indeed, becoming the Outside inside the social.

Millisexuality

All of this, however, amounts to only one end of the sexual continuum in this particular body of (proto-)queer theory, the militant end. Its other end is extraordinarily ordinary. Since desire is coextensive with the social in the theory,

> "It is not possible to attribute a special form of existence to desire, a mental or psychic reality that is . . . different from the material reality of social production" (Deleuze and Guattari, *Anti-Oedipus*, 30).

"sexuality is everywhere" (293). Aislinn O'Donnell notes how "intimacy is 'desexualized'" and "the erotic is demystified" in Deleuzian thought, becoming less an "ecstatic" experience

> than a dimension of everyday encounters, habits, practices and even infrastructures. . . . One imagines here moments like sitting in a ward, drawing or gently massaging the bodies of women who are HIV+ with stage 3 or 4 AIDS, or the tender camaraderie of a group of ex-political prisoners which forecloses ready stereotypes about men and soldiers, or an ant struggling to climb up a leaf, writing, or the look in a student's eyes at the encounter with a new thought.[21]

---

[21] Aislinn O'Donnell, "Beyond Sexuality: Of Love, Failure and Revolutions," in Beckman, *Deleuze and Sex*, 217. Tellingly, most of the essays in *Deleuze and Sex* are interchangeable with most of the essays in *Deleuze and Queer Theory* (see n. 2 in this chapter).

SEX (A THOUSAND TINY SEXES, A TRILLION TINY JESUSES) 155

The example of the ant and the leaf is especially significant. The "everywhere" where desire, sex, and sexuality are active is one that precedes, exceeds, eludes, and elides the human. "Everywhere there is libido as machine energy," and to cordon off conceptually what humans do with humans sexually from what occurs between "the red clover and the bumble bee, the wasp and the orchid" (Deleuze and Guattari, *Anti-Oedipus*, 323) is to misapprehend how that libidinal megamachine operates. Anthropocentric queer theory, we should conclude, is insufficiently queer, is too conserving of the human with its self-constituting, speciesist, subjugation of the nonhuman. Queer theory in the Deleuzoguattarian mode, meanwhile,

> "Assembling an infernal desiring-machine, putting desire in contact with a libidinal world of . . . flows and schizes that constitute the nonhuman element of sex, . . . crossing, mixing, overturning structures and orders— mineral, vegetable, animal . . .—always pushing forward a process of deterritorialization" (Guattari, *Chaosophy*, 100).

spills over into ecotheory:

> If we consider the great binary aggregates, such as the sexes or classes, it is evident that they also cross over into molecular assemblages of a different nature, and that there is a double reciprocal dependency between them. For the two sexes imply a multiplicity of molecular combinations bringing into play not only the man in the woman and the woman in the man, but the relation of each to the animal, the plant, etc.: a thousand tiny sexes. (Deleuze and Guattari, *A Thousand Plateaus*, 213)

Millisexuality? Well, why not?[22]

---

[22] Especially as "polysexuality" is already taken. The term was still available in 2011 when Ronald Bogue featured it in the title of his contribution to *Deleuze and Sex* ("Alien Sex: Octavia Butler and Deleuze and Guattari's Polysexuality," in Beckman, *Deleuze and Sex*, 30–49). By now in LGBTQIA+ culture, however, "polysexuality" has displaced "bisexuality" as the preferred term for "attraction to all genders." Perhaps even to all one thousand of them? Again, why not?

156 THE BIBLE AFTER DELEUZE

Part II: Queer Mark

The Coming, and Becoming, of Christ

Millisexuality and Mark

Tweaking Deleuze and Guattari's claim that "a schizophrenic out for a walk is a better model [of active desire] than a neurotic lying on the analyst's couch" (*Anti-Oedipus*, 2), we might say that a millisexual out for a walk is a better model of active desire than two or even many subjects, queer or otherwise, having sex on the analyst's couch. Such a stroll in the wild, however, would be no walk in the park. For to immerse oneself utterly in millisexuality— whatever that might mean, the "whatever" necessarily being unknowable in advance—would to risk being seen as mentally disabled at best and a danger to society at worst.

In response to the ever implicit (when not confrontationally explicit) question of sexual identity, the millisexual would answer, like the much-maligned "demoniac" of Mark 5:1–20, "My name is Legion; for we are many" (5:9). Impelled by inhuman desire, the millisexual would transition between the human-animal body and the nonhuman-animal body: "And [they] came out of [of the human being]

> "What demons do is jump across intervals. [...] Becoming ... is the demonic element par excellence" (Deleuze and Parnet, *Dialogues II*,
> 40, 42).

and entered the pigs" (5:13). The millisexual might even be driven by desire to seek intimate union with, utter immersion in, an aqueous body: "And the herd, numbering about two thousand [each with a thousand tiny sexes, moreover], rushed down the steep bank into the sea" (5:13). Such desire, altogether untrammeled, would propel the millisexual *outside*,

> "What we're trying to do is put libido in relation with an 'outside'"
> (Deleuze, *Desert Islands*, 229).

cause them to be expelled from the social body: "He lived among the tombs; and no one could restrain him any longer . . . ; for he had often been restrained with shackles and chains, but the chains he wrenched apart, and the shackles he broke

SEX (A THOUSAND TINY SEXES, A TRILLION TINY JESUSES)   157

in pieces" (5:3–4). And abandoning himself, themselves, outright to transspecies and transelemental desire might not end well for the millisexual: "[They] rushed down the steep bank into the sea, and were drowned" (5:13). With millisexuality, then, we find ourselves returned effectively to the Deleuzoguattarian proto-version of the antisocial thesis in queer theory and to a sexual subject whose mode of existence is one of extreme marginality and absolute precarity.

Mark's Jesus, however, notwithstanding his own perpetually precarious positionality and self-elected marginality, shows surprisingly little empathy for millisexuality in the episode we have been considering, seeing it only as a malignant condition requiring eradication. That is not to say, however, that the Gospel of Mark is, overall, inimical to queerness, or even to hyperqueerness on the outsized Deleuzoguattarian scale. For queerness has long stirred within this singular narrative, causing it to pace restlessly within the apostolic family circle that early became its cage.[23] Let's retitle it *The Queer Gospel of Mark* in honor of *The Secret Gospel of Mark*, that sublimely queer,

> "But the youth, looking upon (Jesus), loved him and began to beseech him that he might be with him. . . . And after six days Jesus told him what to do and in the evening the youth comes to him, wearing a linen cloth over his naked body. And he remained with him that night, for Jesus taught him the mystery of the kingdom of God."[24]

even if possibly forged, fragmentary text, which scholars call *Secret Mark* for short to show they are intimate with it, whether or not they believe in it.[25] Let's refer to our text as *Queer Mark*, then.

---

[23] Construction of the cage began with Papias's early-second-century claim that although the author of this gospel "had not heard the Lord nor had he accompanied him," he did accompany Peter and dutifully transcribed the authoritative words that issued from the chief apostle's mouth (*Exposition of the Sayings of the Lord*, quoted in Eusebius, *Church History* 3.39.15, NPNF trans.).

[24] Morton Smith's translation of what he argued were fragments of an alternative version of canonical Mark preserved in a previously unknown letter of Clement of Alexandria (*Clement of Alexandria and a Secret Gospel of Mark* [Cambridge, MA: Harvard University Press, 1973], 446–47). Smith, a distinguished historian of antiquity, claimed to have found the letter in the Mar Saba monastery outside Jerusalem in 1958. Three other scholars went in search of the letter in 1976 and found it. Sometime after 1990, however, the pages with the fragments mysteriously vanished, having been photographed, however, in the interim.

[25] In an intriguing essay, Alexis G. Waller has passed the highly fraught scholarly debate on the authenticity of Secret Mark, which has now raged for nearly half a century, through the prisms of queer

158   THE BIBLE AFTER DELEUZE

Virtually Queer

How does Queer Mark begin? Improbably, as we shall see, but that too is significant. Queerness, fully torqued theoretically, is regularly conceived as an active process of emergence whereby what is and what was is remade as what has never yet been. José Esteban Muñoz's oft-cited pronouncement is paradigmatic here: "I contend that if queerness is to have any value whatsoever, it must be viewed as being visible only in the horizon."[26] Queerness, thereby unhooked once again from the identitarian peg,

> "[What] happens to the libido . . . happens from far off on the horizon,
> not from within" (Deleuze, *Desert Islands*, 229).

finds its corollary in the Deleuzian concept of the virtual.[27] Necessarily oversimplifying, we might say that queerness and virtuality are but two names for a single project: counteractualization of the present.[28]

Deleuze occasionally assigns a creative agency to virtuality that borders on the theological (even while sensibly remaining on the atheological side of the line), remarking, for example, that "it is on the basis of [the] reality [of the virtual] that existence is produced" (*Difference and Repetition*, 211)—which returns us to Queer Mark. Within its tortuously torqued narrative world, virtuality would be the impersonal omnicreative agency that the protagonist personifies as parental. "Abba, Father, for you all virtualities are actualizable" (*panta dynata soi*—Mark 14:36), he pleads, knowing that he has reached a

---

theory and affect theory; see her "The 'Unspeakable Teachings' of *The Secret Gospel of Mark*: Feelings and Fantasies in the Making of Christian Histories," in *Religion, Emotion, Sensation: Affect Theories and Theologies*, ed. Karen Bray and Stephen D. Moore, Transdisciplinary Theological Colloquia (New York: Fordham University Press, 2020), 145–73.

[26] José Esteban Muñoz, *Cruising Utopia: The Then and There of Queer Futurity* (New York: New York University Press, 2009), 11. And again: "Queerness is not yet here. . . . [W]e are not yet queer. . . . The future is queerness's domain" (1). The present, in contrast, "is a prison house," a "totalizing rendering of reality" (1).

[27] Arguing from different premises (different from mine and different from each other's), Claire Colebrook and Mikko Tuhkanen also identify the Deleuzian virtual with the queer. See Claire Colebrook, "On the Very Possibility of Queer Theory," and Mikko Tuhkanen, "Queer Hybridity," in Nigianni and Storr, *Deleuze and Queer Theory*, 16–23 passim and 104–5, respectively. For a rare biblical-critical engagement with the Deleuzian virtual, see George Aichele, *Simulating Jesus: Reality Effects in the Gospels*, Bible World (London: Equinox, 2011), esp. 2–47.

[28] Cf. Colebrook, "On the Very Possibility," 20.

SEX (A THOUSAND TINY SEXES, A TRILLION TINY JESUSES) 159

life-or-death fork in his tale. Functionally speaking, virtuality absorbs the actuality of the character whom we call "God" in this narrative,[29]

> "Then a cloud overshadowed them, and from the cloud there came a voice" (Mark 9:7).

> "Every actual surrounds itself with a cloud of virtual images" (Deleuze and Parnet, *Dialogues II*, 148).

or, to say the same thing another way, "[this] actual character is no more than a virtuality" (*Dialogues II*, 150). As such, the God of this gospel bristles with queer potential. How much of it is actualized in the narrative?

Queer Mark begins improbably, as we had begun to say, with its protagonist embarking on an ostensibly impossible mission. A minor member of a conquered people,

> "A minor people, eternally minor, taken up in a becoming-revolutionary . . . Always in becoming, always incomplete" (Deleuze, *Essays Critical and Clinical*, 4).

an unknown peasant from an undistinguished hamlet, his first words in the narrative ("The time is fulfilled, and God's Empire [*hē basileia tou theou*] is at hand"—1:15) are an announcement of a virtual empire, an empire in emergence, that of this subject people's deity, an empire to rival, even to supplant, the already actual, all-encompassing present empire, that of Rome. But he will not throw himself alone into the iron-fanged maw of the imperial megamachine. In the scene that tradition has dubbed "the call of the first disciples" (1:16–20), he summons four fellow-nonentities to follow what they cannot know in a mission they cannot comprehend.

An immensely alluring man appears out of nowhere in this scene. He beckons imperiously and four other men follow him silently. Queer virtuality here engineers an emergence at once momentous and mundane. Peasant A puts one foot in front of the other on the path that was not there a moment ago but has now opened up in front of him,

---

[29] Here I am crudely reanimating the theological skin that Deleuze's concept of the virtual has sloughed off—the roots of the concept in Duns Scotus, Spinoza, and Leibniz, which concept reaches Deleuze having already been "secularized" by its passage through Bergson. See Deleuze, *Expressionism in Philosophy*, 49, 63–65, 227–28; *Bergsonism*, 96–98.

160 THE BIBLE AFTER DELEUZE

> "... paths leading to radically mutant forms of subjectivity" (Guattari,
> *Chaosmosis*, 89).

and peasants B, C, and D plod after him. Significantly, the path promptly leads
away from the heteropatriarchal family: "Immediately . . . they left their father
Zebedee in the boat with the hired help and followed him" (1:20). And it is not
only the father who is abandoned; the mention of Peter's mother-in-law (1:30–
31) evokes the unmentioned wives (contrast Luke 18:29) whom Peter and his
fellow revolutionaries-in-becoming have left behind in order to be with Jesus.
By 3:31–35, the queer counterfamily has been formed and Peter has himself become Jesus' mother: "They said to him, 'Your mother and your brothers and
sisters are outside, asking for you.' And he replied, 'Who are my mother and
my brothers?' And looking at [his disciples] seated in a circle around him [*kai
periblepsamenos tous peri auton kyklō kathēmenous*], he said, 'Here are my
mother and my brothers!'" (3:34; see also 10:28–30).

Our Walk with Jesus

Just as significantly, and implicit in some of what has already been said, our
protagonist is mentally disabled, psychically queer. He hears voices ("You
are my Son, the Beloved; with you I am well pleased!"—1:11). He has consequential encounters with long-dead people ("Elijah and Moses, who were
talking with Jesus"—9:4) and other nonexistent entities ("He was . . . tempted
by Satan . . . and the angels waited on him"—1:12–13). Indeed, he is assailed
by specters ("Whenever the unclean spirits saw him, they . . . shrieked, 'You
are the Son of God!'"—3:11). His sizable family, which includes his mother
and at least six siblings (6:3), is deeply disturbed by his bizarre behavior: "His
family [*hoi par' autou*] . . . went out to restrain him [*kratēsai auton*], for they
were saying, 'He has gone out of his mind [*exestē*]!'" (3:21).[30] In short, he is
schizophrenic. But Deleuze and Guattari would not hold that against him.

---

[30] The scholarly consensus takes the ambiguous phrase *hoi par' autou* (literally, "those with him")
to refer to Jesus' family here (as in Prov 31:21 LXX; Susanna 33; Josephus, *Ant.* 1.193), and *exestē* (in
this context at least) to denote mental derangement. Both interpretations may be traced at least as
far back as Jerome, who writes in his letter to Eustochium, "In the gospel [of Mark] we read that even
his kinsfolk desired to bind him as one of weak mind" (*Letter 108*, NPNF trans.), and in his Vulgate
renders *exestē* as *in furorem versus est* (loosely, "he is become mad").

SEX (A THOUSAND TINY SEXES, A TRILLION TINY JESUSES)   161

For them, schizophrenia is a revelatory state suffused with revolutionary potential.[31]

Our boy likes to walk, so let's walk with him (which is precisely the idea that his "first followers" had). When it comes to the desiring-machines everywhere operational in both the psychic and social spheres, "[a] schizophrenic out for a walk is a better model than a neurotic . . . on the analyst's couch," as we noted earlier (Deleuze and Guattari, *Anti-Oedipus*, 2). Everywhere the "whirr of machines"—plant machines, animal machines, celestial machines—"all of them connected to those of his body" (2). Indeed, our hero will hold the earth itself up as the quintessential embodiment of the pure virtuality that is the inflowing Queerdom of God. "Listen!" he exclaims. "A sower went out to sow. And as he sowed, some seed fell along the path. . . . Other seed fell into the good earth [*tēn gēn tēn kalēn*] and brought forth grain, growing up and increasing and yielding thirty and sixty and a hundredfold" (4:3–8). A little later he muses, "God's Empire [*hē basileia tou theou*] is as if someone would scatter seed on the earth [*epi tēs gēs*], . . . and the seed would sprout and grow, he does not know how. The earth [*hē gē*] produces of itself, first the stalk, then the head, then the full grain in the head" (4:26–27). Once again, he gropes for an analogy;

> **"What is the nature of this one and simple Virtual?"** (Deleuze,
> *Bergsonism*, 96).

once again, the earth-machine generates one: "With what can we compare God's Empire, or what parable shall we use for it? It is like a mustard seed, which, when sown on the earth [*epi tēs gēs*], is the smallest of all seeds . . . yet . . . becomes the greatest of all shrubs, and puts forth large branches, so that the birds of the air can dwell in its shade" (4:30–32). What of eschatology, that pulsing virtuality so weighty for the Markan Messiah?

---

[31] Deleuze and Guattari have been accused of romanticizing schizophrenia. Their (anti-)method of schizoanalysis, however—which, among other things, apprehends schizophrenia positively as an expansive model for thought—far from being dreamed up in an academic office or seminar room, emerged primarily out of Guattari's clinical work with schizophrenics at La Borde, the innovative psychiatric facility in the Loire Valley where he spent his entire professional career. In "La Borde: A Clinic Unlike Any Other," Guattari writes, "Psychosis can show its true face only in a collective life developed around it . . . , a face that is . . . one of a different relation to the world" (*Chaosophy*, 176). For Deleuze's preliminary, pre-Guattarian appropriation of schizophrenia for philosophical thought, see his *The Logic of Sense*, 82–93. Deleuze and Guattari's *Anti-Oedipus*, whose concluding chapter is an exhaustive exposition of schizoanalysis (273–382), may be seen in hindsight as a particularly early example of critical disability studies.

162   THE BIBLE AFTER DELEUZE

Eschatology, counterintuitively, is eschat*ecology* in Mark, for the earth is also model and mentor here, as we later learn: "From the fig tree learn its lesson:

> "Follow the plants" (Deleuze and Guattari, *A Thousand Plateaus*, 11).

as soon as its branch becomes tender and puts forth its leaves, you know that summer is near" (13:28).

All of this is sexual, as we saw earlier, the incessant interactions and intra-actions of the thousand tiny sexes:

> "Fluids and flows, matter and particles . . . appear to us more adequate than the reduction of sexuality to the pitiful [family] secret" (Deleuze and Guattari, *Anti-Oedipus*, 292).

the sower emitting his seed; the earth receiving the seed; the seed gestating unseen within the earth; the earth bearing the plant, slowly thrusting it forth; Jesus ingesting the plant in reverent wonder, taking it into the secret recesses of his body

> "The wisdom of the plants: even when they have roots, there is always an outside where they form a rhizome with something else—with the wind, an animal, human beings . . ." (Deleuze and Guattari, *A Thousand Plateaus*, 11).

while he ponders "the mystery [*to mystērion*] of God's Empire" (4:11) to which the plant bears silent testimony.[32] Yes, from the fig tree and its fellow plants he is "learning his lesson" (13:28), and the lesson is an eschatological one; but it is less a case of a Second Coming than a Thousandth, even a Trillionth Coming. Who or what is coming, emerging, becoming in Queer Mark in and through this protracted labor? Who or what but

> "The . . . stroll of the schizo, [an] outing in the mountains and under the stars, the immobile voyage in intensities on the Body without Organs" (Deleuze and Guattari, *Anti-Oedipus*, 292).

---

[32] For a different set of Deleuzian reflections on vegetal thought in Mark, see Dong Hyeon Jeong, *With the Wild Beasts, Learning from the Trees: Animality, Vegetality, and (Colonized) Ethnicity in the Gospel of Mark*, Semeia Studies (Atlanta: SBL Press, forthcoming).

SEX (A THOUSAND TINY SEXES, A TRILLION TINY JESUSES)   163

a Body without Organs?

The Crucified Body without Organs

How to Make Yourself a Bloody Body without Organs

The Body without Organs is an exquisitely slippery Deleuzian concept,

> **"The Body without Organs presents its smooth, slippery . . . surface"**
> **(Deleuze and Guattari, *Anti-Oedipus*, 9).**

as we discovered earlier. What this body is without is less organs than organization—specifically, organization of a hierarchical or static sort, regulated by unquestioned conventions, inflexible habits, or predictable behaviors. And in a society that is rigidly hierarchical or assiduously self-perpetuating, one that misconstrues what contingently is for what necessarily must be, to expose the Body without Organs

> **"The Body without Organs is the deterritorialized socius, the wilderness**
> **. . . , the end of the world, the apocalypse" (176).**

is to assail naturality, to assault normativity. That is why the jaws of the disciples drop in unison when their mentor announces, "You know that those purporting to rule the Gentiles [read: Romans] lord it over [*katakyrieuousin*] them, and their exalted ones wield authority over [*katexousiazousin*] them. It is not so among you, however; but whoever among you would be exalted must be your servant [*diakonos*], and whoever would be first must be slave [*doulos*] of all" (Mark 10:42–44).

They should not, however, be shocked. The Body without Organs has been manifesting itself for months in their midst, exposing itself through the hierarchy-stripping utterances of the outrageous unman they have been following. The BwO has taken the form of "a little child" (*paidion*) as their unleaderly leader has dissolved the seeming boundaries between himself and it, "enfolding" the child in his arms (*enagkalisamenos auto*) and thereby becoming a man-child assemblage so that he is able to say, "Whoever receives one such child in my name receives me" (9:36–37). Indeed, the disciples will themselves need to undergo the becoming-child process

164 THE BIBLE AFTER DELEUZE

> "People always think of a majoritarian future (... when I have power). Whereas the problem is that of a minoritarian-becoming, not pretending, not playing or imitating the child, the madman, ... the foreigner, but becoming all these, in order to invent new forces" (Deleuze and Parnet, *Dialogues II*, 5).

in order to actualize the virtual, nonimperial, divine empire: "Whoever does not receive God's Empire as a little child will never enter it" (10:15).

What is more, the Body without Organs—the dehierarchized, demasculinized body, access to which equips one to actualize that virtual empire—need not be "whole." It can be a nonstandard body, a reconfigured body, for physical disability will pose no obstacle to entry: "If your hand causes you to stumble, cut it off. ... And if your foot causes you to stumble, cut it off. ... And if your eye causes you to stumble, tear it out. ..." For it is preferable "to enter God's Empire" as a Body without (certain) Organs (literally), "to enter life disabled" (*kyllon eiselthein eis tēn gēn*) with the queer disabled Messiah, than to be cast into Gehenna having never accessed one's BwO (9:43–48).[33]

Being a solid, upstanding citizen, however, a pillar of normativity in the temple of mammon, replete with social status epitomized by wealth, will pose a near-insurmountable obstacle to actualization of the virtual divine empire: "How hard it will be for those who have wealth [*ta chrēmata echontes*] to enter the Empire of God! ... It is easier for a camel to pass through the eye of a needle" (10:23, 25). It will be altogether easier for children, servants, and slaves, for "many who are first will be last, and the last will be first" (10:31; see also 9:35). And foremost among those privileged to be last, the very last of the last, are those who not only possess slave status but, even or especially if they are not actual slaves but are emulating the example of their servile master, abandon themselves voluntarily, even eagerly, to "the slave's punishment":[34]

---

[33] As Margrit Shildrick observes, the Body without Organs is a term "that ha[s] the potential to radically disrupt the devaluation of the disabled body" ("Prosthetic Performativity: Deleuzian Connections and Queer Corporealities," in Nigianni and Storr, *Deleuze and Queer Theory*, 115). See further Shildrick's *Dangerous Discourses of Disability, Subjectivity and Sexuality* (New York: Palgrave Macmillan, 2009), 157–59, together with Jasbir K. Puar, "Bodies with New Organs: Becoming Trans, Becoming Disabled," in her *The Right to Maim: Debility, Capacity, Disability* (Durham, NC: Duke University Press, 2017), 33–62.

[34] As Valerius Maximus styled crucifixion (*Memorable Deeds and Sayings* 2.7.12), writing under Tiberius, the same emperor whose crucified subjects included Jesus of Nazareth. Much earlier,

SEX (A THOUSAND TINY SEXES, A TRILLION TINY JESUSES)   165

"If anyone desires to come after me, let them . . . take up their cross and follow me. For whoever would save their life will lose it, and whoever loses their life . . . will save it" (8:34–35). Sheer, utter insanity? Why, yes, absolutely. But to construct a Body without Organs is to flirt with madness,

> **"The BwO is always swinging between the surfaces that stratify it and the plane [of immanence] that sets it free. If you free it with too violent an action, . . . you will be killed, plunged into a black hole" (Deleuze and Guattari, *A Thousand Plateaus*, 161).**

as our hero early discovered (we are returned to 3:21–22 and the straitjacket incident: "They went out to restrain him").

As we are seeing once again, then, the Body without Organs is neither an achieved state nor a static entity but an "exercise [in] experimentation," "a set of practices," a process of becoming, a perpetually receding horizon (Deleuze and Guattari, *A Thousand Plateaus*, 149–50). But is the BwO an individual body or a social body? It is both and neither, because it exceeds the social, as ordinarily understood, through a process that evacuates the "I":

> We are in a social formation; first see how it is stratified . . . ; then descend from the strata to the deeper assemblage within which we are held; gently tip the assemblage, making it pass over to the side of the plane of consistency.[35] It is only there that the BwO reveals itself for what it is: connection of desires, conjunction of flows, continuum of intensities. You have constructed your own little machine, ready when needed to be plugged into other collective machines. . . . For the BwO is . . . necessarily a Collectivity (assembling elements, things, plants, animals, tools, people, powers, and fragments of all of these; for it is not "my" Body without Organs, instead the "me" [*moi*] is on it, or what remains of me, . . . changing in form, crossing thresholds). (161)

Cicero had described crucifixion as "the worst extreme of the tortures inflicted upon slaves" (*Verrene Orations* 2.5.169, LCL trans.).

[35] Aka the plane of immanence, as we saw earlier (p. 13 n. 25).

166   THE BIBLE AFTER DELEUZE

All of which is to say: "And while they were eating, he took a loaf of bread, blessed it, broke it, gave it to them and said, 'Take; this is my body'" (Mark 14:22).

Jesus's Haemosexuality

One man surrenders his body to a group of other men ("the twelve"—see Mark 14:17), invites them to devour it, but only as a proleptic preenactment of his subsequent self-submission to still other groups of men (14:43, 46; 15:1, 16) who will humiliate him abjectly (14:65; 15:16–20; see also 15:29–32, 35–36), flog him mercilessly (15:15), and penetrate him viciously with sharp objects (15:24),

> "So many nails piercing the flesh, so many forms of torture.... [The BwO] utters only gasps and cries that are sheer unarticulated blocks of sound" (Deleuze and Guattari, *Anti-Oedipus*, 9).

this self-annihilating self-surrender (14:48-49; see also 8:31; 9:12b, 31; 10:33-34, 38, 45; 14:8, 21a) being performed in obedience to the imagined desires of yet another male

> "[He] appears to be held by real chains, but in fact he is bound by his word alone" (Deleuze, *Coldness and Cruelty*, 75).

> "The flux of pain and humiliation is expressed as a contractual assemblage" (Deleuze and Parnet, *Dialogues II*, 121).

—the paternal personification of the virtual that is to be actualized through the abysmal suffering of our hero: "Abba, Father, for you all virtualities are actualizable [*panta dynata soi*]; remove this cup from me, yet not what I desire but what you desire [*all' ou ti egō thelō alla ti su*]" (14:36).

That *desire* is the fulcrum of the entire ordeal-to-come is no accident, for "the BwO *is* desire; it is that which one desires and by which one desires" (Deleuze and Guattari, *A Thousand Plateaus*, 165, emphasis added). As such the BwO is ineluctably sexual, but it is also infinitely more than sexual. The desire that is the BwO both incorporates and transcends sexual desire as ordinarily conceived: "The organs distribute themselves on the BwO," but the organs, far from being sexual organs in any simple sense, "are no longer anything more than intensities that are produced, flows, thresholds, and

SEX (A THOUSAND TINY SEXES, A TRILLION TINY JESUSES)   167

gradients" (164). A thousand sexes yet again, in other words, even a hundred thousand,

> "Making love is not just becoming as one, or even two, but becoming as a hundred thousand . . . . Not . . . two sexes, but *n* sexes" (Deleuze and Guattari, *Anti-Oedipus*, 296).

all of them differently actualized—but actualized in the instance we are considering by means of a systematically flayed back and an extended bodily suspension on nails driven through flesh.

And subsequently actualized to infinity by the almost absurdly anodyne reenactment of that atrocious ordeal

> "[This] cannot be regarded as pornography; it merits the more exalted title of 'pornology' [. . .] Pornological literature . . . confront[s] language with its own limits, with what is in a sense a 'nonlanguage' (violence that does not speak, eroticism that remains unspoken)" (Deleuze, *Coldness and Cruelty*, 18, 22).

through the liturgical consumption of bread. Once again: "He took a loaf of bread, blessed it, broke it, gave it to them and said, 'Take; this is my body'" (Mark 14:22; see also Matt 26:26; Luke 22:19; 1 Cor 11:23–24).[36] A trillion tiny Jesuses and a trillion tiny sexes, then, differently actualized for each Eucharistic participant, down through the ages and around the planet, reverently or indifferently ingesting the broken body-bread and thereby initiating its intimate passage through the hidden depths of their own body from mouth to anus.

But that is merely the first course; the second is still to come: "And taking a cup and giving thanks he gave it to them and all of them drank from it. And he said to them, 'This is my blood of the covenant, which is spilled [*ekchynnomenon*] for many" (Mark 14:23–24; see also Matt 26:27–28; Luke 22:17, 20; 1 Cor 11:25). Implicit, then, in the elaborately choreographed all-male exchange that begins at the Last Supper and climaxes with Jesus' death-torture is not *homo*sexuality so much as *haemo*sexuality.

---

[36] In pronouncing on the Eucharist here and in what follows, I am glossing over all the fine doctrinal distinctions that were matters of life or (grisly) death in early-modern Europe and that continue to define and divide Christian denominations today.

168   THE BIBLE AFTER DELEUZE

As Gretchen Riordan notes in her essay "Haemosexuality," even in contemporary cultural circles in which sexual fetishism in general raises few eyebrows, "blood is considered an inappropriate fetish object," and in psychiatric literature blood fetishism is commonly categorized as a mental disorder[37]—except, of course, when it is embedded in an organized religion. Then one can report not only on having intimate interactions with a man who, according to the historical record, has been dead for almost two thousand years, one can even declare that eating his body and drinking his blood is an essential element of that relationship; and to confess such beliefs and practices, far from causing you to be forcibly "restrained" or to have people say that you have "gone out of [your] mind" (Mark 2:21), is instead widely seen as the very badge of decent respectability and moral rectitude.

Let's peer more closely into the cup, brimming over with his blood, that our hero is handing us across the table. "This is my blood" is the only invocation of the Greek word *haima* in this gospel, but it is a momentous one. The non-biological counterfamily that the protagonist earlier proclaimed himself and his disciples to be (3:31–35; see also 10:29–30) now becomes a family bound by blood—consanguineal, yet neither patrilineal nor matrilineal because not the product of reproductive sexual activity. Within this queer family circle, which, by the time we arrive at the Last Supper, has narrowed to a fortified all-male enclave ("When it was evening, he came with the twelve"—14:17),[38] the excluded female abruptly erupts in the form of what Riordan might call "labial machines." They "populate many territories; they are located on the face, they are female genitals, or they can be created almost anywhere on a body by cutting."[39] In the course of his flogging, labial machines emerge everywhere on the protagonist's back; further labial machines open as he is nailed to his cross. They bleed profusely, and this is the very blood that fills the cup he extends proleptically to his genderqueer family prior to his ordeal, the blood, fervently imbibed, overflowing their own facial labial machines to soak their beards.

The Last Supper, then, is the initiatory rite and covenantal ritual of a haemosexual community. Riordan writes:

---

[37] Gretchen Riordan, "Haemosexuality," in Beckman, *Deleuze and Sex*, 75. Riordan's essay does not engage with the Christian Eucharist and barely mentions Christianity. Having read no more than its title, however, I knew the essay had long been waiting, with ever-mounting impatience, to be plugged into the Markan passion narrative.

[38] A statement that must be set beside 15:41: "And there were many . . . women who had come up with him to Jerusalem."

[39] Riordan, "Haemosexuality," 86.

SEX (A THOUSAND TINY SEXES, A TRILLION TINY JESUSES)   169

"Haemosexual" describes a wide variety of ways of encountering blood. Rather than transcribe them into conventional sexual acts, haemosexual encounters may be described as a multiplicity of connections that compose an experiment to create a bloody BwO. For example: Eyes closed, passive, nostrils flaring as they follow the ferrous scent. Lips slightly parted, swollen like two grapes about to burst. Tongue escaping its clammy cavern, anxious for the taste of copper and salt, iron and sugar . . . . A ferrous taste, a meaty scent, a sweet aftertaste.[40]

Or, at least, a communion wafer melting on the tongue,[41] or a torn fragment of loaf dipped in wine, fleetingly tantalizing the taste buds—the most anodyne engagements of all with the horrifically tortured man who is the pivot of the Christian religion, the blood-bespattered man who has been an object of haemosexual desire for countless devotees throughout Christian history. "Loving haemosexually . . . means opening one's lips to the intensities that flow across a bloody BwO."[42] And these intensities, these affects, continue to flow freely

> "These incorporeal events . . . A body penetrates another and coexists with it in all of its parts, like a drop of wine in the ocean" (Deleuze, *The Logic of Sense*, 5–6).

even when the blood is incorporeal.

The Risen Body without Organs

How to Make Yourself a Glorious Body without Organs

The bloody BwO that the Markan Messiah constructs opens up an immensely productive process of virtuality, and opens it up, specifically, within the (ostensibly) empty tomb. This tomb, "hewn out the rock," is where the bloody BwO is laid following its removal from the cross (15:46). Deleuze has, in effect, written about the final transformation of the queer, disabled Markan Jesus: "For the schizophrenic . . . it is . . . a question of . . . transforming the painful passion of

---

[40] Riordan, "Haemosexuality," 87.
[41] The mystical ingestion of the communion wafer was a weekly, when not daily, feature of my Irish Catholic upbringing.
[42] Riordan, "Haemosexuality," 88.

170   THE BIBLE AFTER DELEUZE

the body into a triumphant action . . . in this depth beneath the fissured surface," of engendering "a glorious body"—more precisely, a glorious "Body without Organs" (*The Logic of Sense*, 88).[43] This transformation is an anxious, agonizing process. The bloody BwO laid in the tomb is conscious of "larvae and loathsome worms" beginning to infest it (Deleuze and Guattari, *Anti-Oedipus*, 13). But something else is also moving. "The Body without Organs is not God," as we saw previously. "Quite the contrary," in fact. Nevertheless, "the energy that sweeps through it is divine" (13). Or, to say the same thing,

> "The plane of immanence includes both the virtual and its actualization
> simultaneously" (Deleuze and Parnet, *Dialogues II*, 149).

the energy that sweeps through it is virtual.

A word of explanation is in order here. On our way to the tomb with the women ("[they] brought spices, so that they might go and anoint him"—Mark 16:1), we detoured through the garden—not the garden in which the Fourth Gospel situates the tomb (John 19:41–42; 20:15), but the primeval garden (Gen 2:8–17) in which the Bible situates us all. There Eve and Adam are presented with the forbidden fruit (2:15–17; 3:1–5), a moment massively pregnant with virtuality. They both partake of the beguiling fruit (3:6),

> "The actual falls from the plane [of immanence] like a fruit" (Deleuze and
> Parnet, *Dialogues II*, 150).

and from that particular actualization of this singular virtuality—incorporeally mythic in its conception but immeasurably consequential in its effects—an entire world unfolds, preeminently a Christian world in which Adam and Eve's "original sin" also marks the origins of human history. Also contained, however, within the virtual moment in which Eve and Adam are presented with the fruit is an altogether different actualization: they refuse the fruit, resist the temptation. An alternative world then unfolds, one in which there is no "fall" or "original sin" or ever has been. Not our world, then.

At this point, Deleuze, whose paraphrase of Leibniz I have been paraphrasing, observes, "Between the two worlds there exists a relation other than one of contradiction" (*The Fold*, 59),[44] for a nonsinning

---

[43] This is the earliest appearance of the BwO in Deleuze's writings, as we noted earlier.

[44] Leibniz is a philosopher to whom Deleuze returned repeatedly, admiringly elaborating his thought even while thoroughly detheologizing it.

SEX (A THOUSAND TINY SEXES, A TRILLION TINY JESUSES)   171

Adam[45] is neither an inherently contradictory nor impossible notion. Such an Adam, however, would be situated "neither [in] the same garden, nor the same primeval world"; "bifurcation" would have occurred (61). Deleuze is much taken with Leibniz's name for the perplexing relation between two nonconvergent worlds: incompossibility (*Inkompossibilität*).

Where or what is God in all of this? For Leibniz, God is the supreme being who presides over the possible, who chooses between the infinity of incompossible possible worlds, and, being God, chooses only "the best" (Deleuze, *The Fold*, 60). One day, however, not long after Leibniz's death, this God himself died. The effects of his demise were felt early in philosophy (Nietzsche, in particular, presenting us with a world, with multiple worlds, that flow from the simple roll of a dice) (67) and eventually in literature, preeminently, for Deleuze, in Borges's short story "The Garden of Forking Paths,"[46]

> "On [the] question of the game of repetition and difference . . . , no one has gone further than Borges, throughout [this] astonishing work" (Deleuze, *Difference and Repetition*, 116).

effectively Borges's "reply to Leibniz" (Deleuze, *Cinema 2*, 131), "a baroque labyrinth whose infinite series converge or diverge, . . . embracing all possibilities" (Deleuze, *The Fold*, 62).

Within the labyrinth book of Ts'ui Pên around and in which Borges's story circles, a stranger arrives unexpectedly at Fang's door; in one possible past the stranger is Fang's enemy, in another his friend, and so the encounter might result in the death of one, or neither, of them—and so on through an interminable series of possible permutations.[47] "The line . . . forks and keeps on forking" (Deleuze, *Cinema 2*, 131),

> "A more frightening labyrinth than a circular labyrinth is a labyrinth in a straight line" (Deleuze and Parnet, *L'Abécédaire*, n.p.).

passing through innumerable incompossible presents. In the Garden of Forking Paths, unlike the Garden of Eden, incompossible worlds actualize

---

[45] Eve does not feature prominently in Leibniz's speculations, nor in Deleuze's following him.

[46] Jorge Luis Borges, "The Garden of Forking Paths," trans. Helen Temple and Ruthven Todd, in his *Ficciones* (New York: Grove Press, 1962), 89–101.

[47] Borges, "The Garden of Forking Paths," 98–100.

172 THE BIBLE AFTER DELEUZE

promiscuously, diverge infinitely. Virtuality displaces divinity, in short, rendering God redundant or "dead." As we noted earlier, when actualization of the virtual amounts to counteractualization of the present, such actualization qualifies as queer. The virtual dead God, then, is a revivified divine force ripe with queer potential.

And so we are returned to Queer Mark's not-quite-empty tomb, which is the tomb both of Jesus and of God in this narrative. For God is already dead, or might as well be, in the closing scenes of the Markan drama. God was last heard from in the transfiguration episode (9:7); since then God has gone ominously silent, inaudibility compounding invisibility. So one-sided does Jesus' conversation with God feel in that other Garden of Forking Paths, Gethsemane—so like an anguished plea projected into the void (14:33–36)— that a subsequent redactor of Mark (whether the writer we call Luke or a subsequent copyist) anxiously inserted in the tale an unequivocal sign that the distraught prayer has not dropped into an indifferent abyss: "Then an angel from heaven appeared to him, strengthening him" (Luke 22:43). And in the Markan crucifixion scene,

> "... the brute meat, and the screaming mouth" (Deleuze, *Francis Bacon*, 53).

the dying Jesus apparently feels the absence of God so acutely as to cause him to scream aloud in abject misery, "My God, my God, why have you forsaken me?" (15:34). Or, to put it more succinctly, "The BwO howls" (Deleuze and Guattari, *A Thousand Plateaus*, 159). The bloody BwO is suspended on its cross,

> "A cry suspended between life and death, an intense feeling of transition, ... pure, naked intensity stripped of all shape and form" (Deleuze and Guattari, *Anti-Oedipus*, 18).

stretched between two countervailing forces, "the surfaces of stratification," on the one (nailed) hand, that paralyze and delimit it, and "the plane of [immanence]," on the other, "in which it unfurls and opens to experimentation" (Deleuze and Guattari, *A Thousand Plateaus*, 159).

Second, God is dying or already dead, becoming more and other than he was, than they were, in the closing scenes of the Markan narrative, because a confluence of details unique to it conspire to desupernaturalize it as it hastens

SEX (A THOUSAND TINY SEXES, A TRILLION TINY JESUSES)   173

toward its precipitous (non)ending. The long path that leads to the tomb in Mark passes through, or threads, the natural and the supernatural in intricate twists and turns that create "a zone of indiscernibility or undecidability" (Deleuze, *Francis Bacon*, 20) between them.

Most obviously, no resurrected body is displayed in Mark. Moreover, the character stationed in the empty tomb to announce to the women that the crucified corpse they have come to anoint "is not here" (16:6) is oddly ordinary. He might be an angel; then again, he might not. The narrative describes him as a *neaniskos*, a "young man" (16:5). The only other character labeled a *neaniskos* in Mark was the unnamed Jesus-follower who fled naked from Gethsemane on the night of Jesus' arrest (14:51–52), opening up the possibility that they are one and the same *neaniskos*.[48] In other words, the young man who fled in shame has rallied sufficiently to "follow at a distance," like Peter (14:54), but all the way to Golgotha, unlike Peter; consequently, like the female witnesses, he has seen the place "where the body was [eventually] laid" (15:47); and he has arrived at the tomb ahead of the women. What the women, and the wider audience, are hearing, then, in 16:6–7, on this elaboration of the plot, is (merely) the young man's theological construal of the enigmatic datum of the empty tomb: "He has been raised [*ēgerthē*]" (16:6). A path forks and forks again within the narrative universe, causing it to split into multiple incompossible worlds, some of which we explore later.

God is dying, already dead, or re-created so as to become unrecognizable in the climactic scenes in Queer Mark because its author makes absolutely no attempt to prevent the narrative universe he has fashioned from fissuring in this way,

> "A cry . . . makes an incorporeal, intensive, non-discursive, pathic
> Universe suddenly appear, and as a result other Universes, . . . other
> machinic bifurcations are brought about. . . . The most elaborate narra-
> tives, myths, and icons always return us to this point of chaosmic see-
> sawing" (Guattari, *Chaosmosis*, 95–96).

massive cracks extending outward, opening up canyons, chasms as the tale ends. In having the woman "[flee] from the tomb, terrified and amazed,"

---

[48] A conjecture that first surfaced in the scholarly imagination (specifically, that of Albert Vanhoye, Robin Scroggs, Detlev Dormeyer, and John Dominic Crossan) in the early 1970s.

174   THE BIBLE AFTER DELEUZE

> "People ask, So what is this BwO?—But you're already on it, . . . running
> like a lunatic" (Deleuze and Guattari, *A Thousand Plateaus*, 150).

and "[say] nothing to anyone" (*oudeni ouden eipan*) of what they have seen
or heard (16:8), the author undercuts his own authority utterly, telling us
obliquely that none of what he has just reported could actually have filtered
down to him, and thereby inviting us to multiply the fissures, to cause the
possible and incompossible worlds alike to proliferate.

At least we now know why the tomb is empty—or seems to be, at any rate. It
is because the queer, disabled Markan Messiah has succeeded in creating for
himself an extraordinarily effective Body without Organs. In consequence,
he has ceased to be a body as commonly understood, as ordinarily experienced, a normal, or normative, human organism, becoming instead an egg

> "The Body without Organs is an egg: it is crisscrossed with axes and
> thresholds, . . . traversed by gradients marking the transitions and the
> becomings, the destinations of the subject developing along these par-
> ticular vectors. Nothing here is representational; rather, it is all life and
> lived experience" (Deleuze and Guattari, *Anti-Oedipus*, 19).[49]

> "The BwO is the egg. But the egg is not regressive; on the contrary it is
> perfectly contemporary, you always carry it with you as your own milieu
> of experimentation" (Deleuze and Guattari, *A Thousand Plateaus*, 164).

in which "flows in all directions," unfettered intensities, and as yet "unformed . . . matters" circulate incessantly (40). The tomb itself has become that
egg. And the tomb as egg—a figure of paradox: ending as beginning, ceasing
as becoming—is now the glorious Body without Organs of the queer Markan
Messiah.

The Tomb with a Thousand Exits

To say the same thing differently, Queer Mark's empty tomb, at once void
and infinitely full, has become a virtual portal to multiple worlds. This tomb

---

[49] Translation lightly modified. Deleuze and Guattari merge the BwO with the Dogon egg (*Anti-
Oedipus*, 19, 154, 158, 281; *A Thousand Plateaus*, 149, 153, 164–65; cf. Deleuze, *Difference and
Repetition*, 249–52), the World Egg associated with the cosmology of the Dogon people of Mali, West
Africa (as well as other geographically dispersed cosmologies).

SEX (A THOUSAND TINY SEXES, A TRILLION TINY JESUSES) 175

has one entrance ("Who will roll away the stone for us from the entrance [lit. 'door,' *ek tēs thyras*] to the tomb?"—16:3) but innumerable exits, each one opening onto a different world that is also a different time. For although the two announcements made by the *neaniskos* in the tomb are spatial indexes ("He is not *here* [*hōde*]. See *the place* [*ho topos*] where they laid him"; "But go, tell his disciples and Peter that *he is going before you* [*proagei hymas*] to Galilee; *there* [*ekei*] you will see him, just as he told you"—16:6–7; cf. 14:28), "it is not space but time which forks" (Deleuze, *Cinema 2*, 49), in general but most especially in the tomb. If time forks wildly within this particular tomb, womb, or egg, it is because of how the path to the tomb has been constructed, as we have seen. Where, then, does the path, do the paths, from the tomb lead? To what worlds, when, and populated by whom?

The most proximate worlds are those that have us exiting the tomb only to be faced once again with its entrance. In one of these worlds, the supernatural has reasserted itself sternly, the mysterious young man morphing into a terrifying angel, with a newly transcendent God glowering over his shoulder: "And behold there was a mighty earthquake, for an angel of the Lord, descending from heaven, rolled back the stone and sat on it. His appearance was like lightning and his raiment white as snow. And for terror of him the guards trembled and became like dead men" (Matt 28:2–4). Ostensibly, the angel has seemed to open the tomb; in effect, however, he has closed it, rendered passage into it and through it, and consequent metamorphosis, redundant. The world that then transpires unfolds on this side of the tomb, not on the far side of it, and begins as a markedly unqueered world,

"There are, in fact, several ways of botching the BwO: either one fails to produce it, or one produces it more or less, but nothing is produced on it, intensities do not pass or are blocked" (Deleuze and Guattari, *A Thousand Plateaus*, 161).

displaying an imperial, despotic, hypermasculine Jesus being worshiped, first by submissive women ("And they took hold of his feet and worshiped him"— 28:9) and then by submissive men (28:17), and demanding absolute obedience from every other human subject ("All authority in heaven and on earth has been given to me. Go, therefore, and make disciples of all the nations ..., teaching them to observe all that I have commanded you"—28:18–20).

A world equally proximate to Queer Mark's unfolds rather differently. We are permitted to enter the tomb, as are the women, where we encounter a

176   THE BIBLE AFTER DELEUZE

queer couple, "two men" (*andres duo*) dressed in "dazzling" outfits (*en esthēti astraptousē*—Luke 24:4), who intone in chorus their announcement that the Body without Organs "is not here" (24:5), a message we might rephrase in terms we considered earlier: "You never reach the Body without Organs, you can't reach it, you are forever attaining it, it is a limit" (Deleuze and Guattari, *A Thousand Plateaus*, 150).

The intractable elusiveness of the BwO is also the theme of the scene that follows. The risen BwO is now reembodied but hidden even from former associates: "Now on that same day two of [his disciples] were journeying to a village . . . called Emmaus and discussing with each other everything that had happened. And it came to pass that . . . Jesus himself drew near and journeyed with them, but their eyes were blocked from recognizing him [*ekratounto tou mē epignōnai auton*]" (Luke 24:13–16). It is not that the risen BwO now cuts a dazzling figure, like the couple in the tomb; the BwO looks perfectly ordinary, in fact,

"To become imperceptible . . . . A clandestine passenger on a motionless voyage" (Deleuze and Guattari, *A Thousand Plateaus*, 197).

just another stranger who has journeyed (*paroikeis*) to Jerusalem for Passover. But it is now unutterably more than the "I" that it was, which is what sets it outside the segmenting, stratifying space of identification and identity: "It is not 'my' Body without Organs," this altogether strange, thoroughly queer stranger might say to their two companions (having already said it to us earlier in this chapter); "instead the 'me' is on [the BwO], or what remains of me, . . . changing in form, crossing thresholds" (161).

It is only when the three sit at table that evening and the BwO performs the ritual gesture that symbolically reenacts the bloody events that enabled his transition to BwO in the first place—"he took bread, blessed and broke it, and gave it to them" (Luke 24:30; cf. 22:19)—that the two disciples finally see the BwO for what it is: "Then their eyes were opened and they recognized him" (24:31). In that same moment, however, the BwO becomes "invisible to them" (*autos aphantos egeneto ap' autōn*—24:31). More precisely, the BwO becomes "imperceptible" in the Deleuzian sense, which is to say unrepresentable.[50] And the now invisible BwO declares inaudibly to its awed devotees: "I have cracked the wall of the tomb, crawled out of the egg as an

---

[50] "Becoming-imperceptible" (*devenir-imperceptible*), for Deleuze, is escaping "all the objective [and objectifying] determinations which fix us, put us into a grille, identify us and make us

SEX (A THOUSAND TINY SEXES, A TRILLION TINY JESUSES)   177

ineffably glorious yet altogether mundane Body without Organs. Your eyes are now of no use to you, for they merely render back to you the face of the familiar, the image of the known, the absence of the queer. My unrepresentable body is now in constant transition, perpetual transformation, never again to be arrested, never again to be territorialized"[51]—all impossible, of course, except in principle, precisely as impossible as the Deleuzoguattarian conception of the queer as incessant counteractualization, which is why one never attains the BwO completely.

As though to illustrate the point, the risen BwO itself in the very next scene, the final scene of this narrative, seems to falter, to lose its nerve, begging its disoriented disciples: " 'Look at my hands and feet; see that it is I myself! Touch me and see; for a ghost [*pneuma*] does not have flesh and bones as you see that I have. . . . Have you anything here to eat?' They gave him a piece of broiled fish, and he took it and ate it in their presence" (Luke 24:39–43). The BwO appears to disavow its recently attained imperceptibility, to insist that it is a human organism like any other—an eminently identifiable one, what is more—momentarily forgetting all that it taught its disciples when it previously moved among them, namely, that the organism, enslaved by self-interest, shackled by custom, in thrall to hierarchy (e.g., 6:6–10, 20–36; 11:37–44; 13:11–17; 14:7–14; 16:19–31; 18:9–14, 18–25), "is not life" but rather "what imprisons life" (Deleuze, *Francis Bacon*, 45).

In yet another world, more distant from Queer Mark's, that begins to dawn on the other side of the tomb,

> "To be present at the dawn of the world . . . . To find one's zone of indiscernibility" (Deleuze and Guattari, *A Thousand Plateaus*, 280).

> "Just as day was dawning, Jesus stood on the beach; but the disciples did not know it was Jesus" (John 21:4).

the narrative fades out with a queer love triangle: " 'Simon, son of John, do you love me more than these men?' . . . 'Yes, Lord, you know I love you.' . . . He said to him a second time, 'Simon, . . . do you love me?' . . . 'Yes, Lord, you know I love you.' He said to him a third time, 'Simon, do you love me?'

---

recogniz[able]" (Deleuze and Parnet, *Dialogues II*, 45). Becoming-imperceptible thus aligns with the outermost edge of the anti-identitarian pole of queer sensibility.

[51] (Very) loose paraphrase of some sentences from Deleuze and Guattari, *A Thousand Plateaus*, 171.

178   THE BIBLE AFTER DELEUZE

Peter was upset [*elypēthē*]. . . . 'Lord, you know everything; you know I love you.' . . . Peter . . . saw the disciple whom Jesus loved following them, the one who had leaned on [Jesus'] chest. . . . 'Lord, what about this man?'" (John 21:15–21).

This is all promisingly different from a command by an imperial Christ to his subordinates to bring every nation under his sway. What might not happen sexually in a world whose dawning moments stage this scene? Indeed, the narrative's closing statement (actually an opening statement) is, "And there are also many other things that Jesus did; if every one of them were written down, I suppose the world itself could not contain the books that would be written" (21:25). Or, alternatively, "And there are also countless other acts contained virtually within the risen Body without Organs; if all of them were actualized, no book could enclose all the worlds that would unfold." No book could encompass them because of their profusion, but also because of the incompossiblity of so many of them.[52]

In one Queer Mark satellite world, for example, we exit the tomb only to discover that the tomb has disappeared, that it has, in fact, never existed— not historically, anyway, Queer Mark having hewn it from imaginary rock (cf. 15:46).[53] To encounter the Body without Organs we would then have to retrace our steps to the cross where it still hangs, writ(h)ing its all-but-wordless, asignifying, affective anthem; but it would be a bloody, not a glorious, BwO.

In still other worlds that have diverged less dramatically from Queer Mark's, Mary Magdalene achieves voice, her flight from the tomb in Queer Mark

"The line of flight is a deterritorialization. . . . One only discovers worlds through a long, broken flight" (Deleuze and Parnet, *Dialogues II*, 36).

---

[52] Incompossibility, for Deleuze, denotes absolute as opposed to relative divergence. For relatively divergent worlds, one can "retrace one's path [from the point of divergence] and find a point of convergence" (Deleuze, *Difference and Repetition*, 123). This would be the case, arguably, for the divergent Matthean and Lukan resurrection narratives that find their mutual point of convergence outside the Markan tomb, which is where this particular path forked. The next example I provide in the main text—that of a world in which the Markan tomb itself has been erased—would seem to be an example of absolute divergence. But the line between absolute and relative divergence is often blurred; consequently, deciding which worlds are incompossible and which are not is frequently an imprecise exercise.

[53] That the empty tomb was a Markan creation (particularly since Paul seems to know nothing of it: see esp. 1 Cor 15:3–8) is a relatively common scholarly argument.

SEX (A THOUSAND TINY SEXES, A TRILLION TINY JESUSES) 179

becoming a Deleuzian line of flight. She bursts into the Johannine resurrection scene, but finds no release there,

> "What is it which tells us that, on a line of flight, we will not rediscover everything we were fleeing?" (Deleuze and Parnet, *Dialogues II*, 38).

being passed over for the Beloved Disciple and even the bumbling Peter (John 20:17). From there, undeterred, she eventually makes her way into the *Gospel of Mary*, and discloses in its poignant climactic scene (9:3–9) that she, in that world at least, was herself the Beloved Disciple,

> "A man and a woman are flows. All the becomings which there are in making love, all the sexes, the *n* sexes in the single one" (Deleuze and Parnet, *Dialogues II*, 47).[54]

the one whom Jesus secretly loved more than any of his male disciples.

The Polyamorous Body without Sexual Organs

And in yet another world, as we already saw, a secret world, Jesus seems to have a nocturnal sexual tryst with a nameless young man who, like that other young man (but perhaps it is the same one) who follows Jesus to Gethsemane (Mark 14:51–52), wears a linen cloth over his naked body.[55] The question of whether the Secret Mark fragments are authentically ancient or a modern forgery has no bearing on the question of whether Secret Mark contours a world that is absolutely divergent, or only relatively divergent, from Queer Mark's world. Secret Mark's young-man-loving (homo)sexually active Jesus might be said to be a plausible actualization of certain palpable virtualities in Queer Mark's homosocial Jesus.

But that counteractualization of the norm-anchoring Jesus of the orthodox Christian tradition, however significant, would be but a tentative first step on the path for a millisexual Jesus who, on the far side of the Markan tomb, would have embarked on his own interminable line of flight, now forever intent on eluding the normalizing clutches of the hordes of self-proclaimed

---

[54] Translation lightly modified.
[55] See p. 157.

180 THE BIBLE AFTER DELEUZE

followers who would "come out to restrain him" (Mark 3:21). For a sexual line of flight is not a case of actualizing "one or even two sexes," as we have seen again and again, but "*n* sexes," so that "making love is . . . becoming as a hundred thousand" (Deleuze and Guattari, *Anti-Oedipus*, 296). What body would be equal to such lovemaking? Not a body conceived as sexed in the standard mode. That is why the organs that the Body without Organs is without—even, or especially, the glorified, and glorious, Body without Organs—are first and foremost sexual organs.

4

RACE (Jesus and the white faciality machine)

How best to theorize race and, thereby, racism? Race has commonly been conceived in the humanities and social sciences as *representation* and hence as *construction*. Race is a matter, not *of* matter, but of representation. Race is a linguistic construct, a cultural construct, an ideological construct, and, as such, not ontologically "real." That concept of race is rooted philosophically in Kantian and Hegelian categories, as we shall see. Here I trace the concept's passage through, alongside, and beyond poststructuralist theory, the para- and post-poststructuralist swerves constituting ambitious attempts to think race differently, to reinstate the material, especially corporeal, dimensions of race that representationalist-constructivist construals of it elide—not with the purpose of further reifying race, however, but rather of rendering it yet more fluid. More especially, I trace the passage, the flow, of race, variously conceived, through the semiotically supersaturated figure of Jesus of Nazareth.

To restate the foregoing more concretely, poststructuralist discourse on race passes most conspicuously through the 1985 collection, *"Race," Writing, and Difference*,[1] and the wider work of three of its most illustrious contributors: Edward Said, Gayatri Chakravorty Spivak, and Homi

[1] Henry Louis Gates Jr., ed., "'Race,' Writing, and Difference," *Critical Inquiry* 12, no. 1 (1985), a thematic issue of the journal that, together with response articles that appeared in a subsequent issue, was published as a book under the same title by the University of Chicago Press the following year. The collection was by no means a univocal manifesto by a team of self-identified poststructuralists. Its editor, however, chose to characterize "the gesture in which the contributors [were] collectively engaged" in Derridean and Foucauldian terms: "to deconstruct . . . the ideas of difference inscribed in the trope of race" and "to explicate discourse itself in order to reveal the hidden relations of power and knowledge inherent in popular and academic usages of 'race'" ("Editor's Introduction: Writing 'Race' and the Difference It Makes," *Critical Inquiry* 12, no. 1 [1985]: 6). Additionally, the collection's title was designed to echo Derrida's *Writing and Difference* (trans. Alan Bass [Chicago: University of Chicago Press, 1978]), while its final essay (its last word, if you will) was Derrida's "Racism's Last Word" (290–99). Reflecting retrospectively on the collection, Gates acknowledged the catalytic role

The Bible after Deleuze. Stephen D. Moore, Oxford University Press. © Oxford University Press 2023.
DOI: 10.1093/oso/9780197581254.003.0005

182 THE BIBLE AFTER DELEUZE

Bhabha. Arguably, however, the most radical analysis of race and racism to have emerged out of, or to the side of, poststructuralist theory is the "Year Zero: Faciality" chapter of Deleuze and Guattari's *A Thousand Plateaus* (167–91)—a chapter that, as it happens, assigns central significance to Jesus as the retroactive linchpin of the "faciality machine" that produces white maleness as Christian universalism. And whereas race and racism for Said, Spivak, and Bhabha are matters of representation, Deleuze and Guattari's analysis of whiteness is (as we would expect by now) resolutely nonrepresentational. What this means, why it matters, and how it enables us to ponder anew the intersections of empire, whiteness, and Christianity (not least the Christian testament that white Christendom claims as its charter document) are the issues this chapter ultimately addresses. Some framing reflections are, however, first in order.

Part I: The *Matter* of Race

White Light

How Whiteness Was Made

Jesus and whiteness? The tale most often told about that troubled relationship is a subplot in a more sweeping saga. Construction of the hierarchical binary opposition that is the modern Eurorooted ideology of race—an opposition in which the term in the upper tier is incandescently white—began in earnest in the eighteenth century by people who were beginning to identify fundamentally as white, and it coalesced fully in the nineteenth. The systematic European exploration and colonization of the Americas, Africa, and the extra-European world in general was both the catalyst for, and the context of, the cultural construction of whiteness, which is to say that it was also intimately bound up with the transatlantic slave trade. This account of the invention of whiteness, which long antedates the field of whiteness studies, is now closely associated with the field. Jun Mian Chen, surveying several decades of historical scholarship on whiteness, summarizes its enabling assumptions as follows:

his personal relationship with Derrida had played in its emergence ("Reading 'Race,' Writing, and Difference," *PMLA* 123, no. 5 [2008]: 1535–36).

RACE (JESUS AND THE WHITE FACIALITY MACHINE)   183

White and black racial identities are constructed simultaneously. . . . The thought process [undergirding this co-constitution] would look something like this: *If I am not that (black), then I am this (white).* This thought process established a self-Other dialectic, where the negative representation of the Other simultaneously and positively represents the self, and vice versa. Hence, whiteness co-emerged with the concept of blackness; yet, whiteness is the invisible while blackness is that which is visible.[2]

The terms "dialectic" and "representation" are highly significant here, as we shall see.

The Way, the Truth, and ... White?

Meanwhile, tidily folded into this metanarrative is another in which the pre-eminent religiocultural product of the European enterprise that was the creation and consolidation of white racial identity was a racially white Jesus, a (re)transfiguration of the Eastern Mediterranean Jewish Jesus(es) refracted in the pages of the New Testament. As the nineteenth century, in particular, unfolded and European colonialism began to reach the apex of its ascent, and the European Jesus correspondingly began to tower over the entire planet, depictions of Jesus as not just light-skinned, but as light-haired and light-eyed additionally, began to proliferate.

More subtle dynamics are also read into this process, different critics articulating the complexities of the white Jesus's relationship to the concept of racial whiteness that birthed him. Especially notable is Richard Dyer's articulation of them in *White*, a seminal text for whiteness studies in the cultural studies mode.[3] For Dyer, white Christians have long found Jesus's body good to think with when it comes their own bodies. Jesus's transcending of his own flesh through his passion and resurrection, his ascent from darkness to light, becomes emblematic of the white Christian's culturally implanted sense of being *in* a body while not being *of* it. While nonwhite people are reducible to their bodiliness and hence to their race, white people are not. Like Jesus, with

---

[2] Jun Mian Chen, "The Contentious Field of Whiteness Studies," *Journal for Social Thought* 2, no. 1 (2017): 16.

[3] Richard Dyer, *White*, 20th ann. ed. (New York: Routledge, [1997] 2017).

184   THE BIBLE AFTER DELEUZE

Jesus, they transcend the dark fleshliness of subhuman existence and ascend with him toward the light,

"[We] will be caught up in the clouds ... to meet the Lord in the air"
(1 Thess 4:17).

their own light skin pigmentation mirroring Jesus's imagined whiteness and serving as a visible marker of their racial invisibility. And the mechanism continues to operate even in contexts in which Jesus has floated out of view, non-Christian and post-Christian whites benefiting equally with Christian whites from the privilege of white invisibility.[4]

Dark Matter, I

An Unhappy Hegelian

The sweeping origin story in two acts just recounted—a tale of how the white race was born, coupled with a tale of how the Christian savior was re-born as white—is good as far as it goes. Arguably, however, it is an overly white tale informed by certain assumptions that are thoroughly white, far removed from the lived experiences of Black or brown bodies. That, in any case, is what Frantz Fanon, in particular, provokes the present white author to think—not that Fanon talks about Jesus and whiteness per se.[5] But in *Black Skin, White Masks*, his first book, published in 1952,[6] we find Fanon wrestling autobiographically, autotheoretically, and affectively with race and racism in ways that challenge us to rethink the dialectical and representational underpinnings of that origin story.[7]

The Fanon of *Black Skin, White Masks* analyzes race and racism out of a Hegelian framework, broadly speaking; but he is not an altogether happy Hegelian, which is what confers contemporary theoretical relevance on his

---

[4] My very loose paraphrase of Dyer, *White*, 14–18, 27–28, 118.

[5] Although Fanon does talk briefly, and scathingly, about colonial Christianity and whiteness in *The Wretched of the Earth*, trans. Constance Farrington (New York: Grove Press, [1961] 1963), 42.

[6] Frantz Fanon, *Black Skin, White Masks*, trans. Charles Lam Markmann (London: Pluto Press, [1952] 2008).

[7] Note that Dyer's focus, in particular, is representationist throughout: "This book is a study of the representation of white people in white Western culture. . . . My focus is representation" (*White*, xxxiii).

RACE (JESUS AND THE WHITE FACIALITY MACHINE) 185

reflections. Hegel's first appearance in *Black Skin, White Masks* is already arresting. Hegel's celebrated exposition of the master-slave dialectic in *The Phenomenology of Spirit* is exquisitely abstract.[8] Neither the master nor the slave is explicitly racialized or ethnicized; each is a barely embodied mind, a philosophical self-consciousness, in the Hegelian mold. What Hegel elides, Fanon discloses with matter-of-fact casualness. Lining up his principal resources for analyzing "the conception of the world held by the man of color," Fanon remarks, "Since the black man is a former slave [*un ancien esclave*], we will turn to Hegel too."[9]

Factual Blackness

The Hegelian dialectic flows into *Black Skin, White Masks* primarily through Jean-Paul Sartre. Fanon quotes Sartre's dialectical formula of anti-Semitism: "It is the anti-Semite who *makes* the Jew."[10] Fanon's formula of white-on-black racism is no less dialectical: "*It is the racist who creates his inferior.*"[11] Yet there is a crucial ontological difference, for Fanon, between Sartre's constructed Jew and what Fanon feels himself to be—what, indeed, he is never allowed to forget that he is. "The Jew can be unknown in his Jewishness," Fanon reflects. Circumstances permitting, "he can sometimes go unnoticed."[12]

In other words, and extrapolating from Fanon's observation, Jews—most often Ashkenazi Jews as distinct from Sephardic or Mizrahi Jews—can pass in white gentile society, if they choose, convincingly donning the white cloak

---

[8] Georg Wilhelm Friedrich Hegel, *The Phenomenology of Spirit*, ed. and trans. Terry Pinkard, Cambridge Hegel Translations (New York: Cambridge University Press, [1807] 2018), 113–16.

[9] Fanon, *Black Skin, White Masks*, 44. Admittedly, "the slave" of Hegel's discourse is, in German, *der Knecht* not *der Sklave*, and the former is more accurately translated "the servant" or "the bondsman," as has often been argued. Even with *Knecht*, however, Hegel's philosophical allegory about how individual consciousness is constituted through a process of reciprocal recognition between self and other has to navigate the tortuous complexities thrown up by the unequal social positions of the master and the servant. Had the *Knecht* been a *Sklave*, the allegory would likely have imploded completely. Tellingly, the slaveholding master, as Fanon conceives of him, "differs basically from the master described by Hegel." For the former, "the consciousness of the slave" is an irrelevance; "what he wants from the slave is not recognition but work" (*Black Skin, White Masks*, 172 n. 8).

[10] Jean-Paul Sartre, *Anti-Semite and Jew: An Exploration of the Etiology of Hate*, trans. George J. Becker (New York: Grove Press, [1946] 1960), 69, emphasis in original, quoted in Fanon, *Black Skin, White Masks*, 69.

[11] Fanon, *Black Skin, White Masks*, 69, emphasis in original. Elsewhere Fanon writes: "It is the white man who creates the Negro," adding: "But it is the Negro who creates negritude" (*A Dying Colonialism*, trans. Haakon Chevalier [New York: Grove Press, (1959), 1965], 47).

[12] Fanon, *Black Skin, White Masks*, 87.

186 THE BIBLE AFTER DELEUZE

of racial invisibility. Fanon's dark skin, in contrast, does not permit him to perform that vanishing trick: "I am given no chance. I am overdetermined from without. I am the slave not of the 'idea' that others have of me but of my own appearance."[13] "The Fact of Blackness" (as the chapter in which these reflections occur is titled)[14] stubbornly resists, indeed renders nonsensical, a dialectical or representational theory of race. Fanon's factual blackness,[15] on Fanon's own account, tethers him tightly to his body, does not allow him to float free of it, necessitating instead a materialist theory of race. This becomes fully apparent in Fanon's subsequent, anguished quarrel with Hegel and Sartre.

But first, Jesus is raising his hand, eager to enter the debate. What Fanon has to say about Jews passing as white resonates mightily with much in this particular Jew's improbably long life.

Jesus in Jackboots

A Whiter Shade of Pale

Jesus's gentilization long anteceded Jesus's whitening. Jesus's gentilization has its ancient roots in the dejudaization of the Jewish movement he inaugurated. Jesus could not become white, however, until whiteness coalesced as a racial category and physical marker. Jesus's incremental whitening is most graphically visible in the history of European Christian art. Returning to Richard Dyer, I find myself transfixed with him before Giovanni Bellini's *Madonna and Child with John the Baptist and St. Elizabeth* (see Figure 1).

In the foreground of this sumptuous painting, a porcelain-pale nude infant Jesus solemnly raises his chubby right hand in blessing. He appears to be uncircumcised. He sits in the lap of his mother. She too is light-skinned, although her hand extended protectively across her child's torso reveals her to be a shade darker than him. Darker still is Elizabeth, Mary's relative (*syngenis*—Luke 1:36), who stands behind her left shoulder gazing down upon the infant. Darkest of all, however, deep bronze, is John the Baptist, Elizabeth's son, who stands behind Mary's right shoulder and also gazes down

---

[13] Fanon, *Black Skin, White Masks*, 87.

[14] In English, anyway. The chapter's title in French is "L'Expérience vécue du noir" (The Lived Experience of the Black Man).

[15] Or "lived experience" of blackness.

Figure 1 Giovanni Bellini and Workshop, *Madonna and Child with John the Baptist and St. Elizabeth* (1490–1500)

upon the child, his expression rapt, his attitude worshipful. Dyer remarks, "Historically speaking, all these people are Jews, but Christ and Mary are enlightened, saved Jews, that is, Christians, whereas John and Elizabeth, key witnesses to the coming of Christianity, are nonetheless pre-Christian, perhaps even unsaved."[16] Jesus is visibly lightening, whitening before our own wondering gaze in this iconic painting, his pale skin combining with his uncircumcised penis to proclaim his distance from the despised race whom he has been sent to redeem.

But the whitening of the Christ child has only just begun. Bellini's Jesus and Mary look positively saturnine when set beside those of William-Adolphe Bouguereau's *The Virgin of the Lilies* (see Figure 2).

Four centuries of European imperial expansion have elapsed since Bellini's Madonna and child. The Christ child fetishized, repeatedly reincarnated,

---

[16] Dyer, *White*, 67.

Figure 2 William-Adolphe Bouguereau, *The Virgin of the Lilies (La Vierge au lys)*, 1899

in the Madonna-and-child paintings of Bouguereau,[17] one of the most acclaimed and successful artists of his era, has advanced from pale to pallid; he is almost as melanin-starved as it is possible for a human child to be. And his hair, merely light brown in Bellini's rendition of him, has become bleach blonde. With terrifying precocity, he gazes directly at the viewer, his

---

[17] One of those paintings, *The Virgin, Jesus and Saint John the Baptist* (1881), reprises the Bellini technique of juxtaposing a light-skinned Jesus with a dark-skinned Baptist, both children in this rendition, Jesus elevated above John, John's hands clasped worshipfully as he looks up at him.

RACE (JESUS AND THE WHITE FACIALITY MACHINE)   189

unnerving stare accentuated by his mother's modestly downcast eyes, while both of his toddler arms are raised imperiously over a world he was born to rule.

The Apotheosis of Whiteness

Bouguereau's blindingly white Christ child, the iconic product of a white-identified ultra-imperial culture, provides the most spectacular aesthetic example of the phenomenon to which Fanon refers, that of "the Jew [becoming] unknown in his Jewishness."[18] This Jew, this Jesus, is not simply *passing* as white; he is *surpassing* the white race itself, becoming the very apotheosis of whiteness. Entailed in this elevation is the absolute erasure of Jesus's Jewishness. Jesus is assimilated without remainder to the dominant culture, made its very symbol, which is also to say that he is separated definitively from the longest-persecuted ethnic minority in European history. The Jewish peasant troublemaker crushed contemptuously under the heel of one empire is reborn as the incandescent emblem of another empire. Every last drop of Jewishness has been leached from his pellucid white body, presaging the fate threatening all Jews within the white, imperial, anti-Semitic social body of fin de siècle Europe.

For what might such a child, grown to adulthood, become? What but a National Socialist Jesus, of course? Tellingly, the first chapter of Susannah Heschel's *The Aryan Jesus*, her already classic chronicle of the maturation within the Third Reich of this jackbooted savior, is titled "Draining Jesus of Jewishness."[19] But what remains, racially speaking, of a Jesus thus drained? A translucent, all but invisible husk that is so light (in both senses of the word), so little weighed down by bodily particularity as to seem to float free from the crass category of race altogether

"Against the white background . . . the crucified Christ-turned-kite-machine" (Deleuze and Guattari, *A Thousand Plateaus*, 178).

---

[18] Fanon, *Black Skin, White Masks*, 87.
[19] Susannah Heschel, *The Aryan Jesus: Christian Theologians and the Bible in Nazi Germany* (Princeton, NJ: Princeton University Press, 2008), 26–66.

190 THE BIBLE AFTER DELEUZE

even while reaping inestimable racial privileges from the condition to which it clings so lightly? Or is the white Jesus no less tightly tethered to the body than a Black or brown Jesus would be? It is time to return to Fanon.

Dark Matter, II

Fanon's Fury

At the end of a long autobiographical sequence in which Fanon recounts his successive attempts to redeem his blackness from white racism ("Every hand was a losing hand for me"),[20] he writes, "And, when I tried, on the level of . . . intellectual activity, to reclaim my negritude [*négritude*], it was snatched away from me."[21] Specifically, it was snatched away by Sartre, who in Hegelian-Marxist tones had declared:

> Negritude appears as the minor term of a dialectical progression: The theoretical and practical assertion of the supremacy of the white man is its thesis; the position of negritude as an antithetical value is the moment of negativity. But this negative moment is insufficient by itself, and the Negroes who employ it know this very well; they know that it is intended to prepare the synthesis or realization of the human in a society without races.[22]

Fanon confesses that on reading those words, "I felt that I been robbed of my last chance." An apparent "friend of the colored peoples," in arguing the transitory inadequacy of the negritude movement, was showing himself incapable of knowing—corporeally, viscerally—that negritude acquired its value "from an almost substantive absoluteness."[23] Sartre's dialectic, writes Fanon, "drives me out of myself. . . . Black consciousness is immanent in its own eyes. I am not a potentiality of something, I am wholly what I am. I do not have to look for the universal. . . . My Negro consciousness does not hold itself out as a lack. It *is*."[24]

---

[20] Fanon, *Black Skin, White Masks*, 101.

[21] Fanon, *Black Skin, White Masks*, 101.

[22] Jean-Paul Sartre, "Orphée Noir," preface to *Anthologie de la nouvelle poésie nègre et malgache* (Paris: Presses Universitaires de France, 1948), xl–xli, quoted in Fanon, *Black Skin, White Masks*, 101–2.

[23] Fanon, *Black Skin, White Masks*, 102.

[24] Fanon, *Black Skin, White Masks*, 103.

RACE (JESUS AND THE WHITE FACIALITY MACHINE)   191

These words, written in France almost seventy years ago, in the shadow of existentialism and before the ascent of structuralism, might well serve as a summative epigraph for Arun Saldanha's post-poststructuralist introduction to the collection *Deleuze and Race*. Saldanha observes, "The philosophical impetus for overcoming racism has for decades been derived from the legacies of Kant and Hegel."[25]

Parenthetically, one might note the jaw-dropping irony at play here. Shawn Kelley begins his own book, *Racializing Jesus*, by reminding us of certain of the more atrocious pronouncements that Kant, Hegel, and other paragons of Enlightened rationality made about what we now call people of color—Kant, for example, opining, "[Native] Americans and Blacks are lower in their mental capacities than all other races," and again: "This fellow was quite black from head to foot, a clear proof that what he said was stupid"; and Hegel pronouncing, "Want of self-control distinguishes the character of the Negroes. This condition is capable of no development or Culture. . . . The only essential connection between the Negroes and the Europeans is slavery. . . . We may conclude slavery to have been the occasion of the increase in human feeling among the Negroes."[26]

Saldanha continues, "Today's most sophisticated theorisations of racism continue . . . a fundamentally Euro-American programme of retrieving a cosmopolitanism above the ostensibly inconsequential phenotypical differences Europeans have, for centuries, called race. Are phenotypical differences really inconsequential? The idealist metaphysics of the Enlightenment presupposes a *de jure* equality of the human species."[27]

What could be more rational, more humane? Yet the Kantian-Hegelian paradigm founds universalism upon representationalism and dialecticism, and, as Fanon contended, the body, not least the black body, goes missing in such a theory of race. While Fanon was passionately insisting on his ontologically immanent blackness, "while I was shouting that, in the paroxysm of my being and my fury," Sartre was calmly insisting that Fanon's blackness "was only a minor term" in the dialectical march to what we would now call the postracial society.[28] Stripped of his flesh, Fanon's "feet could no longer feel

[25] Arun Saldanha, "Introduction: Bastard and Mixed-Blood Are the True Names of Race," in *Deleuze and Race*, ed. Arun Saldanha and Jason Michael Adams, Deleuze Connections (Edinburgh: Edinburgh University Press, 2013), 6.

[26] Quoted in Shawn Kelley, *Racializing Jesus: Race, Ideology and the Formation of Modern Biblical Scholarship* (New York: Routledge, 2002), 2.

[27] Saldanha, "Introduction," 6–7.

[28] Fanon, *Black Skin, White Masks*, 105–6. In these pages, I am cutting a narrow path through an immense terrain. Complexification of the issues might begin with Victor Anderson's *Beyond Ontological*

192 THE BIBLE AFTER DELEUZE

the touch of the ground."[29] Sartre had forgotten, or simply had never known, "that the Negro suffers in his body quite differently from the white man."[30] On the anguished testimony of this singular Black thinker, then,

"All this whiteness that burns me" (Fanon, *Black Skins, White Masks*, 86).

dialecticism and, by extension, representationalism are wholly insufficient for taking the measure of white-on-black racism.

Du Bois's Cave

W. E. B. Du Bois, in his own classic writings on blackness and whiteness, makes the same point even more powerfully. What blackness signifies, for Du Bois, is indelibly inscribed in Black bodies—not as genetic destiny, however, but as cultural memory: "a common history," "a common disaster," "one long memory," "the social heritage of slavery."[31] Du Bois's further reflections on "the badge of color"[32] that a common history has carved into Black bodies lead to what is, in effect, a searing recasting of Plato's allegory of the cave. Impressing on those who have never experienced in their own bodies "the full psychological meaning of caste segregation" is, for Du Bois, a challenging, indeed impossible, task:

It is as though one, looking out from a dark cave . . . sees the world passing and speaks to it; speaks courteously and persuasively, showing them how these entombed souls are hindered in their natural movement, expression, and development; and how their loosening from prison would be a matter not simply of courtesy, sympathy, and help to them, but aid to all the world. One talks on evenly and logically in this way, but notices that the passing throng does not even turn its head, or if it does, glances curiously and walks on. It gradually penetrates the minds of the prisoners that the people

Blackness: An Essay on African American Religious and Cultural Criticism (New York: Continuum, 1995). Anderson, for his part, does not mention Fanon.

[29] Fanon, *Black Skin, White Masks*, 106.
[30] Fanon, *Black Skin, White Masks*, 106.
[31] W. E. B. Du Bois, *Dusk of Dawn: An Essay toward an Autobiography of a Race Concept*, The Oxford W. E. B. Du Bois (New York: Oxford University Press, [1940] 2007), 59.
[32] Du Bois, *Dusk of Dawn*, 59.

RACE (JESUS AND THE WHITE FACIALITY MACHINE)   193

passing do not hear; that some thick sheet of invisible but horribly tangible plate glass is between them and the world. They get excited; they talk louder; they gesticulate. Some of the passing world stop in curiosity. . . . They still either do not hear at all, or hear but dimly, and even what they hear, they do not understand. Then the people within may become hysterical. They may scream and hurl themselves against the barriers, hardly realizing in their bewilderment that they are screaming in a vacuum unheard. . . . They may even, here and there, break through in blood and disfigurement, and find themselves faced by a horrified, implacable, and quite overwhelming mob of people frightened for their own very existence.[33]

Whereas in Plato's allegory it is those inside the cave who are unable to apprehend the real, in Du Bois's allegory it is those outside the cave who are unable to apprehend it. Du Bois graphically illustrates why it is that, as Spivak would say, "the subaltern cannot speak"—speak, that is, so as to be heard by non-subalterns.[34] Du Bois's "thick sheet of invisible but horribly tangible plate glass" is, as he subsequently implies, a discourse of representation employed even by well-meaning white allies that is simultaneously a discourse of misrepresentation: "Not being . . . among the entombed or capable of sharing their inner thought and experience, this outside leadership will continually misinterpret and compromise and complicate matters, even with the best of will."[35]

Cone's Black Christ

What of Jesus, himself once among the entombed? How can he be *kept* in the tomb, in the cave, prevented from wafting out of it like a disembodied vapor, white as light in his insubstantial effulgent risenness,

"I was traveling to Damascus . . . , when at midday . . . I saw a light from heaven, brighter than the sun, shining around me" (Acts 26:12–13).

---

[33] Du Bois, *Dusk of Dawn*, 66. Du Bois's cave allegory forms the climax of the chapter titled "The Concept of Race."
[34] Gayatri Chakravorty Spivak, "Can the Subaltern Speak?," in *Can the Subaltern Speak? Reflections on the History of an Idea*, ed. Rosalind C. Morris (New York: Columbia University Press, 2010), esp. 62–63.
[35] Du Bois, *Dusk of Dawn*, 67.

194   THE BIBLE AFTER DELEUZE

claimed as one of their own—as the quintessence, indeed, of who and what they are—by the "horrified, implacable, and quite overwhelming mob of [white] people [who are] frightened for their own very existence"[36] when confronted with impassioned Black demands for justice issuing from contemporary tombs and prisons, both literal and metaphorical?

Arguably, there is only one way to keep Jesus among the entombed, and James Cone, the progenitor of Black theology, long ago hit on it and memorably articulated it in his first book, *Black Theology and Black Power*. "Whether whites want to hear it or not, *Christ is black, baby*," Cone exuberantly proclaimed.[37] Even if the Jesus of history was *not* Black (and Cone was not claiming that he was), the Christ of faith *is* Black—*must* be Black, indeed. If he is to be, to incarnate, "where the oppressed are," then "his present manifestation must be the very essence of blackness."[38]

And that melanin boost would not have amounted to a major metamorphosis, a Mount of Transfiguration moment, for the historical Jesus anyway, born as he was into a dirt-poor family on the bottommost rungs of the socioeconomic ladder; into a colonized people who, additionally, were a frequently despised ethnic group; and, because of his subversive activities on behalf of his class, the hyperexploited social underclass, was subjected to the excruciating form of execution that, most often in his world, was reserved for slaves: death on the cross, an instrument of utter pain and abject humiliation that, in Cone's later work, morphs into the lynching tree.[39]

Race, for Cone as for Du Bois before him, is, apparently, the inalienably felt fact, the primal affective fact,

> "As I face Africa I ask myself: what is it between us that constitutes a tie which I can feel better than I can explain?" (Du Bois, *Dusk of Dawn*, 59).

of being in a body that is the crudely fabricated product of a common history: in the case of Black bodies, a crushing history of absolute "discrimination and insult."[40] We should not be surprised, therefore, to encounter in Cone's inaugural book a statement about the central conviction animating

[36] Du Bois, *Dusk of Dawn*, 66.
[37] James H. Cone, *Black Theology and Black Power*, 50th ann. ed. (Maryknoll, NY: Orbis Books, [1969] 2018), 77, emphasis in original. This claim, variously expressed and differently argued, runs as a leitmotif through many of Cone's books.
[38] Cone, *Black Theology and Black Power*, 78.
[39] James H. Cone, *The Cross and the Lynching Tree* (Maryknoll, NY: Orbis Books, 2011).
[40] Du Bois, *Dusk of Dawn*, 59.

RACE (JESUS AND THE WHITE FACIALITY MACHINE)   195

his work that would be equally at home in Fanon's *Black Skin, White Masks* as a repudiation of dialecticism and representationalism: "This work further seeks to be revolutionary in that 'The fact that I am Black is my ultimate reality.' My identity with *blackness*, and what it means for millions living in a white world, controls the investigation. It is impossible for me to surrender this basic reality for a 'higher, more universal' reality."[41]

Is Race Structured Like a Language?

Generally speaking, Fanon's, Du Bois's, and Cone's pronouncements on race run counter to the "classic" tenets of poststructuralism, whether in its originary French articulations[42] or its Anglo-American and other appropriations, prompting the question: Are classic poststructuralisms adequate to the task of analyzing race/ethnicity and deconstructing racism? And if not, why not?

Rigorously Arbitrary Racial Signifiers

On the face of it, after all, the structural linguistics of Ferdinand de Saussure, the headwaters of structuralism and poststructuralism alike,[43] provide an immensely illuminating resource for analyzing race. If race is culturally constructed (so the argument might unfold), then it is constructed, structured, like a language,[44] language being the semiotic system par excellence, the universal paradigm of meaning-making, for structuralists and poststructuralists alike.[45] For Saussure, it will be recalled, the linguistic sign

[41] Cone, *Black Theology and Black Power*, 37.

[42] Such as Foucault's body-discursivism, which we pondered earlier on pp. 112–113.

[43] A sweeping assertion, I realize, but I see most of the French thinkers customarily clustered under the poststructuralism umbrella (Derrida, Lacan, Kristeva, later Barthes, even Foucault) as engaged in radicalizing retoolings of one dimension or other of Saussure's philosophy of language.

[44] With apologies to Jacques Lacan: "The unconscious is structured like a language," in *The Seminar of Jacques Lacan, Book XI: The Four Fundamental Concepts of Psychoanalysis*, ed. Jacques-Alain Miller, trans. Alan Sheridan (New York: Norton, [1964] 1998), 20.

[45] As Saussure himself phrased it, "Linguistics can become the master-pattern for all branches of semiology although language is only one particular semiological system." Ferdinand de Saussure, *Course in General Linguistics*, ed. Charles Bally and Albert Sechehaye with Albert Riedlinger, trans. Wade Baskin (New York: McGraw-Hill, [1915] 1986), 68. Race does crop up in the *Course* (mainly in its opening chapter, "A Glance at the History of Linguistics"), but not racism. Others, however, have analyzed racism with the resources Saussure provided. Particularly notable among such attempts was Stuart Hall's "Race, the Floating Signifier," a lecture delivered at Goldsmiths' College, University of London in 1996 and widely disseminated ever since as a video recording, most recently through

196 THE BIBLE AFTER DELEUZE

has two components, the signifier (*significant*), which is the material or sensory component of the sign as apprehended by the mind (Saussure's own example being the sound-image *tree*); and, inextricably entwined with the signifier, the signified (*signifié*), which is the conceptual component of the sign (in the case of *tree*, that of a tall perennial plant with an elongated single stem or trunk and lateral branches).[46] In race considered as a language, the signifiers would be differences in skin pigmentation visually apprehended or "read" as words ("black," "white," etc.), while the signifieds would be the concepts attaching to those signifiers (relatively innocuous concepts such as "blackness" and "whiteness," but, in the case of racism, additional toxic concepts such as "inferiority"

> "... the internalization—or, better, the epidermalization—of this inferiority" (Fanon, *Black Skin, White Masks*, 4).

and "superiority").

For Saussure, moreover—and most importantly for this thought experiment—"the bond between the signifier and the signified is arbitrary."[47] There is no necessary or ontological link between the concept of a tree and the sound that, say, English speakers use to represent it, since speakers of other languages use altogether different sounds for it. Few assertions are more common in critical discourse on race, meanwhile, than that race is an arbitrary construct. To cull a single but typical example, Gates insists in his introduction to *"Race," Writing, and Difference*, "Race is the ultimate trope of difference because it is so very arbitrary in its application. The biological criteria used to determine 'difference' in sex simply do not hold when applied to 'race.'"[48]

Let's unpack the arbitrariness attribute of race considered as a "language." The signifiers, the sound-images, of the language that is race are arbitrary indeed. Most "white" people are not quite white; many of us, for example,

---

streaming services. The central argument of the lecture was "that *race works like a language*" (from the transcript, 8, emphasis in original: https://www.mediaed.org/transcripts/Stuart-Hall-Race-the-Floating-Signifier-Transcript.pdf). An earlier version of the lecture was delivered at Harvard University in 1994 and published posthumously under the title "Race—The Sliding Signifier," in Stuart Hall, *The Fateful Triangle: Race, Ethnicity, Nation*, ed. Kobena Mercer, The W. E. B. Du Bois Lectures (Cambridge, MA: Harvard University Press, 2017), 31–79.

[46] Saussure, *Course in General Linguistics*, 65–67.
[47] Saussure, *Course in General Linguistics*, 67; see further 113.
[48] Gates, "Editor's Introduction," 5.

RACE (JESUS AND THE WHITE FACIALITY MACHINE)   197

are more pink than white, and some of us (not usually the pinker specimens) work so assiduously to acquire deep tans as to become darker than many "black" people, most of whom are brown, yet are conventionally distinguished from other people more usually designated "brown"; and all "nonwhites" collectively are "people of color" (including people formerly labeled "red" and "yellow" by "whites," many of the formerly "yellow" people being whiter than most "whites"), as though white were not a color, which, scientifically speaking, it is not, but neither is black; and neither "white" nor "black" people are white or black anyway in the absolute sense.[49] In short, racial signifiers are a morass of contradiction, a quagmire of incoherence.

How, then, does race function on the linguistic model? The answer is simple: Race is a differential system.[50] The racial signifier "white" is intelligible not because of what it *is* but only because of what it *is not*—not "black," in particular, which term, reciprocally, is readable only because it is not "white," and neither "white" nor "black" are "brown," "red," or "yellow" either (to shade from the racial into the racist), and vice versa.

The Transcendental Racial Signified

Conspicuously absent thus far from our Saussurean account of race is the issue of hierarchy. How do we explain the historical elevation of one racial signifier, "white," above all the other racial signifiers in the system? Here we might have recourse to Derrida's concept of the transcendental signified—in this case a concept of racial whiteness that would exceed the differential process that simultaneously enables and imprisons it, that would ascend above that process to center and control it, the entire modern history of European

---

[49] Hall writes autobiographically about the simultaneous artificiality and colossal consequentiality of the "black"/"white" polarity in his childhood context: "In practice, race was a sliding signifier in Jamaica. The social slippage—the sliding of the signifier—was extensive, constitutive of social life itself. There were wide skin colour variations even within the same family, as was the case in my own. Jamaican society gossiped, monitored intensely and speculated riotously about this perpetual, confusing fluidity of the body. When I was a child it's what Jamaica *was*." Stuart Hall with Bill Schwarz, *Familiar Stranger: A Life between Two Islands* (Durham, NC: Duke University Press, 2017), 101–2.

[50] "*In the language itself, there are only differences*" (Saussure, *Course in General Linguistics*, 118, emphasis in original). See further 118 ("*Arbitrary* and *differential* are two correlative qualities") and 120–22.

198 THE BIBLE AFTER DELEUZE

culture thus bespeaking the "exigent, powerful, systematic, and irrepressible desire for such a signified."[51]

The ultra-whitened Jesus of colonial-imperial Europe, whose sun-starved features we earlier contemplated with concern, would be the divine personification of this particular transcendental signified. This mythological northern European deity would constitute the consummate representation of whiteness as a racial concept, its ultimate signified. Where, then, would the signifier of whiteness be found? On and in the skin of each and every "white" person, an innumerable multitude of signifiers for this altogether singular signified? Not quite. Saussure's signifier is not simply material, not purely physical. It is, indeed, barely less conceptual, hardly less abstract, than Saussure's signified.[52] "Signifier," for Saussure, is a synonym for "sound-image" (*image acoustique*), and the latter "is not the material sound, a purely physical thing, but the psychological imprint of the sound, the impression that it makes on our senses. . . . If I happen to call it 'material,' it is only in that sense."[53]

All of which is to say that although Kant is never named in Saussure's *Course*, Kant is nonetheless everywhere present in the *Course*. As we noted earlier, Saussure's signifier and signified are each creatures of the *phenomenon*, in Kant's technical sense of the term, material reality as empirically apprehended by the senses. Altogether absent from Saussure's philosophy of language (as ghostly as the Kant who presides over its pages) is the material as such—the stubbornly solid tree, say, that one should carefully circumvent (as Saussure himself does, metaphorically speaking) and not walk into—which is to say Kant's *Ding an sich*, the thing in itself that Kant terms the *noumenon* and declares unknowable.[54] Within the language model of race as conceived, or as conceivable, in classic structuralist and even poststructuralist terms, which is to say representationally, that *noumenon*, that unknowable *Ding an sich*, would be the body of the racial subject.[55]

---

[51] The quoted words are from Jacques Derrida, *Of Grammatology*, trans. Gayatri Chakravorty Spivak, 40th ann. ed. (Baltimore: Johns Hopkins University Press, [1967] 2016), 53, who, however, is not writing specifically about race in this instance.

[52] "Both parts of the sign [that is, signifier no less than signified] are psychological" (Saussure, *Course in General Linguistics*, 15).

[53] Saussure, *Course in General Linguistics*, 66. Cf. 6: "Everything in language is basically psychological, including its material and mechanical manifestations." And again: "[Sound] is only the instrument of thought; by itself, it has no existence" (8).

[54] See pp. 117–118 earlier.

[55] Hall's concept of race, for instance, is representational, as he makes explicit, appealing to Foucault to articulate this facet of his argument ("Race, the Floating Signifier," 10; also see his *The*

RACE (JESUS AND THE WHITE FACIALITY MACHINE) 199

The consequence of consigning the body—or, more specifically, bodiliness in its lived immanence—to the outside, the unknowable beyond, in a philosophical or semiotic system in which the representable marks the threshold of the knowable, the articulable, and the incorporable (pun intended), is that language becomes a closed and constricting structure that replicates sameness by regulating difference, and sets limits to thought and hence to action—in this case, a radical rethinking of what it means to live as a singular body among a multiplicity of bodies, and a radical reordering of that embodied reality. The agony of being imprisoned, entombed, within the conventional discourse on race—even in its most benign or "emancipatory" manifestations—has been articulated with particular power by Du Bois and Fanon, as we heard. Their searing statements should give pause to any white analyst of race,

"I walk on white nails" (Fanon, *Black Skin, White Masks*, 95).

including the present writer. I venture, nonetheless, in what follows to dance into the minefield (fools rush in where bomb disposal technicians fear to tread), equipped only with the tools that Deleuze and Guattari (two other well-meaning white people) devised for conceptually dismantling the prison house of representation as it pertains to race. I will also be looking to locate Jesus in that structure and, if possible (in good action-thriller style), to break him out of it.

Part II: Race and Face

Assembling Race

How is race made? How does it operate? What forces drive it? For Deleuze and Guattari, race and racism alike are products of the "abstract machine of

---

Fateful Triangle, 46–47). But Hall is not oblivious to the mechanism of exclusion operative within the languagelike model of race: "There is always a certain sliding of meaning, always a margin . . . , always something about race left unsaid, always someone [who is] a constitutive outside, whose very existence the identity of race depends on, and which is absolutely destined to return from its expelled and abjected position outside the signifying field to trouble the dreams of those who are comfortable inside" ("Race, the Floating Signifier," 8; cf. *The Fateful Triangle*, 73).

200   THE BIBLE AFTER DELEUZE

faciality [*visagéité*]" (*A Thousand Plateaus*, 168), more on which later.[56] We begin at a more fundamental level: "Abstract machines operate within concrete assemblages" (510),[57]

> "The abstract machine is like the cause of the concrete assemblages that execute its relations" (Deleuze, *Foucault*, 37).

and as such race and racism are fabricated within assemblages.[58] What, again, is an assemblage (*agencement*) in the Deleuzoguattarian sense? Previously, we have pondered partial answers to this question. Let us descend into the details.

Inside the Assemblage

"On a first, horizontal, axis," it may be recalled, "an assemblage comprises two segments, one of content, the other of expression" (Deleuze and Guattari, *A Thousand Plateaus*, 88). Counterintuitively, "content" in this case is not merely mental or immaterial; in other words, content is "not a signified" (91, 140) in the Saussurean sense of the term. For Deleuze and Guattari, language, the social, and the political interpenetrate too inextricably for that. Indeed, the assemblage's content component "is a machinic assemblage *of bodies*," an "intermingling" of bodies interacting (88), somatically but also affectively: "all the attractions and repulsions, sympathies and antipathies, alterations, amalgamations, penetrations, and expansions that affect bodies of all kinds in their relations to one another" (90), bodies both human and nonhuman, organic and inorganic. A *prison* is a concrete example of such content pondered elsewhere by Deleuze (*Foucault*, 31–33).[59] Content in this

---

[56] The neologism *visagéité* is rendered less elegantly as "faceity" or "faceicity" in English translations of some of Deleuze's solo works that employ the term.

[57] As Guattari explains elsewhere, the term "abstract machine" is an antonym for "abstract universal" (*The Machinic Unconscious*, 12). Its sphere of operations is the immanent rather than the transcendent, and the virtual rather than the actual.

[58] A theme Jasbir Puar has explored brilliantly in relation to U.S. "war-on-terror" Islamophobia; see her "Queer Times, Queer Assemblages," *Social Text* 23, nos. 3–4 (2005): 121–39, together with her *Terrorist Assemblages: Homonationalism in Queer Times*, Next Wave: New Directions in Women's Studies (Durham, NC: Duke University Press, 2007). Also important are Alexander G. Weheliye, *Habeas Viscus: Racializing Assemblages, Biopolitics, and Black Feminist Theories of the Human* (Durham, NC: Duke University Press, 2014), and Aisha M. Beliso-De Jesús, *Electric Santería: Racial and Sexual Assemblages of Transnational Religion* (New York: Columbia University Press, 2015).

[59] An example highly relevant to the problem of systemic racism, as it happens.

instance would be the physical structure of the prison itself, in all its intricate constricting functionality, but also its human occupants, beginning with the prisoners who are its raison d'être.

But content is only one component of any such mechanism, any such assemblage, which always works like a loom. "The woof of bodies," we are told, is nonoperational, nonproductive without "the warp of the expressed" (Deleuze and Guattari, *A Thousand Plateaus*, 86). Expression may be defined as "a collective assemblage of enunciation, of acts and statements, of incorporeal transformations attributed to bodies" (88).[60] In the case of the prison, a mechanism for "acting on bodies" (Deleuze, *Foucault*, 32), the word "prisoner" does not simply refer to the concept of an incarcerated person, the way a Saussurean signifier would refer to its signified, but the word is embedded primarily and pragmatically in a series of speech acts and appellations that effect incorporeal transformations in the subject upon which they are pronounced: "suspect"; "defendant"; "Your Honor, the members of the jury find the defendant guilty"; "I hereby sentence you to seven years of imprisonment"; "felon"; "inmate," and so on. Expression passes into content through order-words, which, as we saw, are not restricted to direct commands but encompass the ubiquitous, ordinarily implicit imperatives that structure every facet of social existence (Deleuze and Guattari, *A Thousand Plateaus*, 75–85). In passing into content, expression reaches into, and flows through, bodies, which is to say that the relationship of expression to content is always one of power.

For Deleuze and Guattari, "expression" and "content" replace, displace, "signifier" and "signified." Where might Saussurean linguistic theory fit into their assemblage theory? Entirely in the second horizontal axis of the machine, it would seem (they imply as much in *A Thousand Plateaus*, 111–12), the axis they name the collective assemblage of enunciation. Missing from Saussurean linguistic representationalism, then, is the machinic assemblage of bodies, which is to say, bodies qua bodies, not least human bodies—bodies expressively enfleshed in human language, language ineradicably rooted in human flesh.

Extrapolating from Deleuze and Guattari, we might say that the incessant shuttling, weaving motion (expression becoming content, content generating further expression) that produces the social category of

---

[60] That, however, is merely an ad hoc definition of "expression" in the Deleuzoguattarian sense. We explored the concept in more detail earlier (pp. 85–98).

202   THE BIBLE AFTER DELEUZE

"race" admits of no mental concept of "blackness," "whiteness," or any racial-color-whatsoever-ness that floats free of bodies. It admits of no racial signified, in short, and hence of no representational theory of race. The necessary complement of the mental concept of "blackness" in a representational theory would be the relevant racial signifiers: physical skin tones in combination with the word "black" and its racial, when not racist, synonyms—*arbitrary* signifiers, as we saw earlier, that engender meaning only through differential interaction with other arbitrary signifiers ("white," "brown," and so on). As we also saw, the actual bodies of the human subjects thus differentiated and identified recede, in a representational theory of race, behind the socially charged signifiers that flicker across their surfaces so to render the bodies unknowable in themselves, in their immanent, lived materiality.

The resulting paradox is particularly stark in Stuart Hall's influential articulation of representational race theory, which beckons to us once more. At one point in "Race, the Floating Signifier," Hall (himself of Black Jamaican descent, as indicated earlier) inquires, "What trail through history is more literally marked by blood and violence [than that of race]?" and as evidence he adduces "the genocide of the Middle Passage, the horrors of plantation servitude, and the hanging tree."[61] But what *is* race ultimately, for Hall? "A signifier, a discourse, yes, that is my argument."[62] To appeal to the body to counter this argument, Hall contends, is to transform the body into "the ultimate transcendental signifier," as though it were "the marker beyond which all arguments will stop, all language will cease, all discourse will fall away."[63] But what if the body were already immanently ingrained in all language, indissociable from all discourse, first and foremost the language, the discourse, of race?

Immanent corporeality is germane to Deleuze and Guattari's materialist theory of race, which we have yet to consider as such. We have been using their assemblage theory to reflect on race; but it is within their concept of the "faciality machine," which they define as "the social production of face" (*A Thousand Plateaus*, 181) and which we wheel in below, that their own theory of race finds expression. Moreover, all our reflection on and application of assemblage theory thus far has been staged upon the *horizontal axis* of the assemblage, made up, as we saw, of the machinic assemblage of

---

[61] Hall, "Race, the Floating Signifier," 9; see also his *The Fateful Triangle*, 44–45.
[62] Hall, "Race, the Floating Signifier," 9.
[63] Hall, "Race, the Floating Signifier," 15.

bodies in incessant interaction with the collective assemblage of enunciation. That horizontal axis, however, is transected by a *vertical axis*. When an assemblage slides down the vertical axis, so to speak, it is "territorialized" or "reterritorialized"—captured, locked in, immobilized; but when it ascends the vertical axis, it acquires "cutting edges of deterritorialization, which carry it away" (88).

Disassembling the Crucifixion

The carrying away, the lines of flight, we consider in the latter stretch of this chapter. First, however, note how Jesus's trial(s) and execution as narrated in the four canonical gospels graphically illustrate the horizontal axis of an assemblage of power. On the level of expression, speech acts, order-words, and appellations effecting incorporeal transformations abound: "All of them condemned him as deserving death" (Mark 14:64; cf. Matt 26:66); "They shouted all the more, 'Crucify him!' So Pilate . . . handed him over to be crucified" (Mark 15:13–14; cf. Matt 27:22–26; Luke 23:20–24; John 19:13–16); "And they began saluting him, 'Hail, King of the Jews!'" (Mark 15:18; cf. Matt 27:29; John 19:2–3); "The inscription of the charge against him read, 'The King of the Jews'" (Mark 15:26; cf. Matt 27:37; Luke 23:38; John 19:19–22); "Now the centurion who stood facing him said, 'Truly this man was God's Son!'" (Mark 15:39; cf. Matt 27:54), and other examples too numerous to list. On the level of content, meanwhile, these potent identity-conferring and body-modifying expressions lock together, cog to wheel, with a machinic assemblage of bodies—human, nonhuman, and inhuman: a captive body become a surface for punitive inscriptions;

> "The needles of the machine write the sentence on the body of the condemned . . . at the same time as they inflict their torture upon him"
> (Deleuze and Guattari, *Kafka*, 43).

one or more flogging implements to remove strips of flesh from that body; a crown of thorns to be pressed ceremoniously into its skull; an instrument of execution composed of an upright post with a transverse bar to which the body may be nailed—an excruciating subassemblage nested within the larger assemblage that Christian piety has named

204   THE BIBLE AFTER DELEUZE

> **"It is a machinic assemblage of bodies, of actions and passions"** (Deleuze
> and Guattari, *A Thousand Plateaus*, 88).

the passion of Jesus Christ.

In contemporary terms, that inhumanely inflicted passion

> **"The black hole of Christ and the passion of Christ"** (Deleuze,
> "A Thousand Plateaus I, Lecture 4," n.p.).

would be a horrific racist act.[64] Key here is the titular inscription above the cross labeling the brutalized victim "The King of the Jews." Neither Mark, Matthew, nor John[65] leave any doubt that the title is an epithet dripping with derision. The title features prominently in the jocular ritual of humiliation that "the soldiers of the governor" (Matt 27:27) stage with the Jewish captive,[66] one that also entails the crown of thorns (Matt 27:29; Mark 15:17; John 19:2, 5), a purple robe (Matt 27:28–29; Mark 15:17; John 19:1–2, 5), mock obeisance (Matt 27:29–31; Mark 15:18–20; cf. Luke 23:11; John 19:3), spitting (Matt 27:30; Mark 15:19), and beating (Matt 27:30; Mark 15:19; John 19:3). Within this collective assemblage of vicious enunciation and machinic assemblage of acting-reacting, affect-suffused bodies, the titular inscription over the cross turns continuously like a cog to transmit a visceral message, one expressed in "a material and affective language," as Deleuze might say, "one that resembles cries [cf. Mark 15:34, 37 and pars.] rather than the discourse of the concept" (*Essays Critical and Clinical*, 144). And the message thereby cranked out? *Accept your inferior place in the world that has been given to* us *to rule—or accept the crushing consequences of refusing our rule.* James Cone's juxtaposing of the Roman cross and the white supremacist

---

[64] A fact notably neglected in critical scholarship on the passion narratives, even of the past fifty years. The rule-proving exception is Wongi Park's *The Politics of Race and Ethnicity in Matthew's Passion Narrative* (New York: Palgrave Macmillan, 2019), which culminates with an extended "ethnoracial reading" of Matt 26–27 (107–47).

[65] Luke glosses over certain of the shaming aspects of Jesus' ordeal, as has often been noted, including several of the elements that, in the other three passion narratives, work in shame-accentuating synergy with the titular inscription (note the paucity of Lukan references in the lists that follow).

[66] Assuming that the implied ethnic composition of "the entire cohort" (*holēn tēn speiran*—nominally around six hundred soldiers) gathered around Jesus (Matt 27:27; cf. Mark 15:16) is predominantly, even if not exclusively, gentile. On the ethnic demographics of Roman legionaries, auxiliaries, and allied armies within the first-century Jewish homeland, see Christopher B. Zeichmann, *The Roman Army and the New Testament* (Lanham, MD: Lexington Books / Fortress Academic, 2018), 1–22 passim, and on Matt 27:27–31 specifically, see 72–74.

RACE (JESUS AND THE WHITE FACIALITY MACHINE)   205

lynching tree again comes to mind: "Lynching was the white community's way of forcibly reminding blacks of their inferiority and powerlessness."[67]

Of course, the white Christians doing the lynching would not have seen the lynching tree as a cross, nor the Black body suspended from it as the body of their Christ. Their Christ had long ceased being Black, had long passed over into whiteness, was now passing so convincingly that they would never have thought to think that he might have once been Black or as good as Black.[68] An extraordinary transfiguration all told, far more miraculous than Jesus's gospel transfigurations.

Fanon's Train Ride with Jesus

The gulf over which the as-good-as-Black Jesus has passed gapes open every time white-on-black racism rears its hideous head, which is to say that it is an unhealing wound of immeasurable magnitude. In what is surely the most famous, and is certainly the most searing, scene in *Black Skin, White Masks*, Fanon is minding his own business on a train, searching for an empty seat, perhaps, when he is abruptly transformed into an object of terror by a white child: "'Look, a Negro!' It was an external stimulus that flicked over me as I passed by. . . . 'Mama, see the Negro! I'm frightened!'"[69] Suddenly assailed from all sides by the white gaze, Fanon's "corporal schema crumbled, its place taken by a racial epidermal schema. . . . I was responsible at the same time for my body, for my race, for my ancestors."[70]

Switch to the as-good-as-Black Jesus in his own hour of trial: "They kept coming up to him, saying 'Hail, King of the Jews!' and striking him on the face" (John 19:3). This Jewish victim casually humiliated by gentile soldiers,[71] forced to accept responsibility for his circumcised body, for the entire collective history of his regularly despised,[72] repeatedly conquered race, has, as

---

[67] Cone, *The Cross and the Lynching Tree*, 7.

[68] For a critical survey of the complex, at times contentious, scholarly debate on whether or to what extent Jews in general were commonly considered to be Black in Europe from the Middle Ages through the nineteenth century, and even beyond, see Ran HaCohen, "The 'Jewish Blackness' Thesis Revisited," *Religions* 9, no. 7 (2018): 1–9: https://doi.org/10.3390/rel9070222.

[69] Fanon, *Black Skin, White Masks*, 84.

[70] Fanon, *Black Skin, White Masks*, 84.

[71] See p. 204 n. 66 for the necessary qualification.

[72] For a concise and erudite survey of the ongoing scholarly debate on whether common gentile attitudes toward Jews in the Roman world amounted to proto-racism or nascent anti-Semitism, see Erich S. Gruen, "Judaism in the Diaspora," in *Early Judaism and Its Modern Interpreters*, ed. Matthias Henze and Rodney A. Werline, 2nd ed. (Atlanta: SBL Press, 2020), 82–84. Even if they did not, many

206   THE BIBLE AFTER DELEUZE

Fanon says of himself in the train incident, been "woven ... out of a thousand details, anecdotes, stories."[73] In Fanon's case, these narrative threads, into which are knotted jagged imagistic fragments, are woven forcibly, cruelly, casually through his flesh while he is speared, squirming, on the collective white gaze. They include "tom-toms, cannibalism, intellectual deficiency, fetishism, racial defects, slave-ships, and above all else, above all: 'Sho' good eatin.'"[74] The histories and fantasies sewn into the Black-become-white Jesus's skin also include consumption of human flesh (*Hoc est corpus meum*), fetishism (crucifixion, to be precise), and slave-ships (Jesus having transitioned, however, from being potential cargo for a slave-ship—"[he] emptied himself, taking the form of a slave [*morphēn doulou labōn*]" [Phil 2:7]—to being a slave-ship figurehead).

If Jesus is also on the train with Fanon, however, as he surely is (this is mid-twentieth-century France, after all, still predominantly and vigorously Roman Catholic), he is not there as yet another racial bogeyman ("Look, Mama, a Jew! I'm frightened!"), huddled shoulder-to-shoulder with Fanon. Rather, Jesus has shed his ethnic otherness like a ragged overcoat and become the whitest person on the train. Long before now he has become Bouguereau's pellucid-white Christ child. This is the flesh in which he has been reincarnated. It is, indeed, this imperious Christ child who, quivering on his queenly mother's lap, points a little white digit at the sole Black body in the carriage: "Mama, see the Negro! I'm frightened!"

What is "race" in this scene? Arun Saldanha, reflecting on the incident, pushes back against the classic poststructuralist tendency to construe race in such a context as an affair of words. Like other Deleuzians, Saldanha singles out Judith Butler as the quintessential exponent of poststructuralist body-constructivism.[75] Saldanha conjectures that such theorists might contend

---

ancient sources, as Gruen documents, leave no doubt that Jewish Sabbath observance, abstention from pork, and, above all, circumcision were frequent fodder for gentile mockery, parody, ridicule, and derisive amusement in general. See further Martin Goodman, *Rome and Jerusalem: The Clash of Ancient Civilizations* (New York: Alfred A. Knopf, 2007), 366–76.

[73] Fanon, *Black Skin, White Masks*, 84.

[74] Fanon, *Black Skin, White Masks*, 84–85. "Sho' good eatin'" is a free paraphrastic rendering of "*Y a bon banania*" (see Frantz Fanon, *Peau noire, masques blancs* [Paris: Éditions du Seuil, 1952], 90; the phrase also occurs on 27, 42 n. 12, 150, and 186). Banania is a popular chocolate drink of Nicaraguan origins and also the name of the French company that began to distribute it in 1912. From 1915 through 2005 the company's logo sported a grinning Black man uttering the words "Y'a bon banania," a pidgin French expression whose closest English equivalent would be "Me like banania."

[75] "Signification produces as an *effect* of its own procedure the very body that it ... claims to discover." Judith Butler, *Bodies That Matter: On the Discursive Limits of "Sex"* (New York: Routledge,

that "Fanon is 'interpellated' as black subject by the use of racist *language*, while the boy reproduces himself as white," both subjects being equally "produced by discourse."[76] In effect, Saldanha's retort is that bodies, far from vanishing endlessly over the event horizon of language, are instead the sine qua non of language. To begin with, "the statement '*Tiens, un nègre*' requires a larynx" and the bodily "proximity of a Negro."[77] But the scene in the train carriage entails far more than that, which is where Saldanha has recourse to the Deleuzoguattarian concept of the assemblage. Rejecting the neo-Kantian affirmation that "language (or culture at large) is a screen which *mediates* between consciousness and the obscure matter of the body," Saldanha states:

> There is no mediation, only a pair of eyes, an exclamation, and a little index finger connecting to a body with darker skin, in a train of paler bodies. There are the memories of exploration and slavery, carried around by bodies which were brought up with them and subsequently charge situations like this. There is moreover [Fanon's] wry smile, panic, bitterness, shame, and disgust.[78] Finally, there are seats, compartments, tickets, windows, the winter temperature outside, and the snow-covered *paysage* gliding by. Race is a whole event.[79]

In the case of Jesus, race is an epochal event spanning millennia, entailing innumerable pairs of eyes, ringed at first around his cross, then, eventually, fixated on his image, his countless images,

> **"All the resources of the Christ-face..."** (Deleuze and Guattari,
> *A Thousand Plateaus*, 178).

displayed in chapels, in basilicas, in art museums, in Christian homes, in children's Bibles (little index fingers pointing animatedly at them, capacious imaginations connecting with his body, now become unambiguously white);

1993), 30, quoted in Arun Saldanha, "Reontologising Race: The Machinic Geography of Phenotype," *Environment and Planning D: Society and Space* 24 (2006): 12.

[76] Saldanha, "Reontologising Race," 11, emphasis in original.
[77] Saldanha, "Reontologising Race," 12.
[78] Affects activate within assemblages, as we have already seen—are, indeed, inseparable from assemblages (Deleuze and Guattari, *A Thousand Plateaus*, 90, 399)—and within certain assemblages, not least racial assemblages, affects function like projectiles or weapons (400).
[79] Saldanha, "Reontologising Race," 12, emphasis in original.

208   THE BIBLE AFTER DELEUZE

> **"Using the face of Christ to produce every kind of facial unit and every degree of deviance" (178).**

entailing atrocious enterprises of exploration and enslavement carried out in his name (enterprises that turned him several shades whiter, as we saw earlier, shading our eyes from the glare); the pews, the hymnals, the heated sermons, the tepid temperature outside the stained-glass windows, all of Christian history slowly gliding by, the entire inconceivably complex event of Jesus's race, an immense assemblage of sociocultural and religiopolitical power.

But the train has finally arrived at our stop. Let us alight.

Facing Race

What a Horror!

The chapter (or, more properly, plateau) of *A Thousand Plateaus* titled "Year Zero: Faciality" is an exercise in radical defamiliarization, of rendering alien what is most intimately familiar in order to subject it to critical inspection. In effect, it is as though Deleuze and Guattari are extraterrestrial visitors to our planet, in shock from their initial encounter with the human species:

> *The face, what a horror.* It is naturally a lunar landscape, with its pores, planes, matts, bright colors, whiteness, and holes: there is no need for a close-up to make it inhuman; it is naturally a close-up, and naturally inhuman, a monstrous hood.[80] Necessarily so because it is produced by a machine and in order to meet the requirements of the special apparatus of power that triggers the machine. (*A Thousand Plateaus*, 190, emphasis in original)

The occurrence of the word "whiteness" (as opposed to "blackness," say) in their narration of the horror

> **"The face is a horror story"** (*A Thousand Plateaus*, 168).

---

[80] See further Deleuze, *Cinema 1*, 99–100, which extends these reflections on the facial close-up, ascribing "a nudity [to] the face much greater than that of the body, an inhumanity much greater than that of animals."

RACE (JESUS AND THE WHITE FACIALITY MACHINE)   209

is not adventitious. The particular face on which Deleuze and Guattari are fixated is the consummate product of "the white wall / black hole system" that, in turn, is "the abstract machine of faciality," the virtual mechanism that operates unceasingly to turn out acceptable faces that "conform in advance to a dominant reality" (167–68).

Guattari's Face

But let's back up. The best way into "Year Zero: Faciality," arguably, is through the "Signifying Faciality, Diagrammatic Faciality" chapter of Guattari's solo work *The Machinic Unconscious*, released a year before *A Thousand Plateaus*.[81] "Modern intersubjectivity," Guattari contends, "is . . . primarily founded upon a vacuous faciality [*visagéité*], a blind face-to-face between two absent gazes" (*The Machinic Unconscious*, 79). The function of the face in modern societies is to stabilize "normal" signification—indeed, to signify normality itself (78, 84, 93). "During the course of a day," muses Guattari, "I travel from one faciality to another" (81). This slipping on and slipping off of predetermined faces is conducted in a social context in which prefabricated faces of all kinds circulate endlessly: "The 'a priori' [face] of the doctor, the robotic face of the 'insane' or the police" (81), the "made-up" face of the "attractive" woman (94), "the face of 'our President' on TV" (90)—in short, "social, mass-mediated faciality" in general (86),

> "The mass media . . . are machines for reproduction" (Deleuze and
> Guattari, *A Thousand Plateaus*, 345).

which exceeds the face proper; for so acutely regulated by the "sensitive slab" that is the face are all aspects of physical and personal self-representation as to produce a facialization of the entire body (Guattari, *The Machinic Unconscious*, 94).[82] It all amounts to a "general flattening of

---

[81] The other Guattari book in which faciality features prominently is *Schizoanalytic Cartographies* (see esp. 247-52), occasionally conjoining with Christianity in it: see, e.g., 64, which speaks of "the incorporeal faciality of Christ . . . travers[ing] spaces before they have unfolded"; or 144, which styles certain faciality traits as "facialitarian" (*visagéitaire*), capable of "catalyz[ing] a cultural effusion without any precise limits, as was the case . . . with the face of Christ Pantocrator, which began literally to haunt the multiple horizons of Christianity." More on Christ Pantocrator later.

[82] A mundane illustration: "Clothes are a facialization of the body." Deleuze, "A Thousand Plateaus I, Lecture 6," n.p.

210   THE BIBLE AFTER DELEUZE

the world . . . onto a signifying screen" (92), which is also "the wall of the signifier" (102).

But because signification is always threatening "to leak" (Guattari, *The Machinic Unconscious*, 78), to reveal that its center is "everywhere and nowhere," as "primitive," "insane," "infantile," or "poetic" signification tirelessly testifies, the faciality machine needs not just a planet-sized "signifying screen" to operate but also an accompanying "black hole"

> "[The] face inscribed on the white wall, flowing toward the black hole" (Deleuze, "A Thousand Plateaus I, Lecture 4," n.p.).

to serve simultaneously as "a vanishing point and a centralizing point" for signification (Guattari, *The Machinic Unconscious*, 86–87). "Facialized signification cannot allow any matter of expression to escape that would allow it to leak" (78), hence the black hole. As Guattari had concisely put it a few years earlier while visiting Deleuze's seminar, "The face is . . . a center of gravity in the form of a black hole around which everything is organized" (Deleuze, "A Thousand Plateaus I, Lecture 6," n.p.).

Yet it is also "primarily through its facial substance that language escapes itself, fleeing in all directions" (Guattari, *The Machinic Unconscious*, 84). Even black holes emit particles (91). Such emissions may be hazardous, for "the empty eye of power ostracizes a faciality which 'does not return to it'" (95). "Sexual choice," for instance, will need "to be posted clearly on the face" when one is under the inquisitorial gaze of the empty eye; "not only must it be immediately understood that one is dealing with a man, a woman, even a homosexual, but moreover with which kind of man, woman, or homosexual" (97). To fall or fail before the gaze of power is to present a "deviant faciality"

> "A face functions as a kind of oscillograph establishing what is allowed and what is forbidden. There are always standard deviations around which a face oscillates. You can smile but not too much because if it turns into a grimace, you must be mad, delinquent . . . or whatever" (Deleuze, "A Thousand Plateaus I, Lecture 6," n.p.).

and to risk triggering an "entire machinery of correction and recuperation" (Guattari, *The Machinic Unconscious*, 95–96).

Did Jesus Invent the Face?

What of *racial* deviant facialities? Guattari does gesture to "a universal racism that has become inherent to white capitalistic faciality" (*The Machinic Unconscious*, 90), but it is only in his collaboration with Deleuze that this theme comes to the fore. The wall of the signifier now becomes a "white wall," as we already saw, but the white wall in turn becomes a white face, "a chalk face" in which the eyes form black holes (Deleuze and Guattari, *A Thousand Plateaus*, 167). "The face is a politics" (181), the white face most of all. For "the face is not a universal," Deleuze and Guattari contend (176), in an implicit critique of Levinas, for whom the face is a universal summons to ethical responsibility.[83] Certain social formations, certain assemblages of power, "require the production of a face," but "others do not" (175, 180).[84] In one far-flung social formation, through one multi-tributaried history, the facility machine has achieved the pinnacle of its development. The white wall / black hole system "is White Man himself," as is implied in what has already been said, "with his broad white cheeks and the black holes of his eyes" (176)

But to the extent that the face in question is that of "the White Man as Christian universal" (Deleuze and Guattari, *A Thousand Plateaus*, 182), the face is also that of Christ himself (176). Deleuze and Guattari's next leap is one that any self-respecting biblical scholar will find absurdly naïve. If it is possible to assign the faciality machine a date of birth, or at least of construction, Deleuze and Guattari conjecture, that year would be "the year zero of Christ" (182). Jesus Christ "invented the facialization of the entire body and spread it everywhere" (176). Yes, quite ridiculous—except that what Deleuze and Guattari are unapologetically laying at the dusty, nail-perforated feet

---

[83] See further Gavin Rae, "The Political Significance of the Face: Deleuze's Critique of Levinas," *Critical Horizons* 17, nos. 3–4 (2016): 279–303.

[84] Elsewhere Deleuze recapitulates the thought processes that led to this conclusion: "Félix was working on black holes.... I was working, rather, on a white wall.... We had not brought the two ideas together, but we noticed that each was tending of its own accord towards the other.... For black holes on a white wall are in fact a face, a broad face with white cheeks.... Now it no longer seems like a face, it is rather the assemblage or the abstract machine which is to produce the face. Suddenly the problem bounces back and it is political: what are the societies, the civilizations which need to make this machine work, that is, to produce, to 'overcode' the whole body and head with a face, and to what end?" (Deleuze and Parnet, *Dialogues II*, 17–18). Guattari's thesis, articulated in Deleuze's seminar, on why the transition from tribal and agrarian societies to capitalist societies entailed an unprecedented investment in the face: "The 'natural,' ancestral, territorial references have collapsed. So the decoded lines of society, desire's lines of flight, throw themselves at the available hooks and holds. They race towards the abyss, towards nothing. We have to reconstitute artificial points of reterritorialization, which will be faces, couple relations, identities, . . . nationalities, you name it" (Deleuze, "A Thousand Plateaus I, Lecture 4," n.p.).

212 THE BIBLE AFTER DELEUZE

of the historical Jesus is his time-transported future self (the authors of "Year Zero: Faciality" are, after all, alien visitors from another planet, as we observed earlier), the imperial Jesus whom the peasant Jesus is doomed to become through a series of monstrous mutations, receiving massive booster shots, first, from the irruption of imperial Christendom in late antiquity; then, from the European "discovery," colonization, and Christianization of the Majority World that commenced in the early modern period; and, finally, from the toxic coalescence of "scientific racism" in the nineteenth century.

Iconic Whiteness

Might we nevertheless assign the white Jesus a more plausible date of birth than "year zero"?[85] The earliest extant version of the Christ Pantocrator icon, a sixth-century encaustic-painted wood panel in Saint Catherine's Monastery at the foot of Mount Sinai / Jebel Musa (see Figure 3), might be as good an imprecise point of origin as any, although produced more than a millennium before whiteness began to crystallize fully as a racial identity marker.

From the icon a consummately imperial Christ—he is, after all, *pantakratōr*, "Ruler of All," and the imperial Christendom of which he is the eternal emblem is taking off splendidly—stares somberly at the viewer. His right hand is raised in blessing while his left hand grips an ornate gospel book. He is golden-haloed, dark-haired, and full-bearded. And he is fair-complexioned (more on which shortly). This white-skinned, physically arresting figure is among the earliest extant Jesus-images whom modern persons, whether Christian or not, would automatically identify *as* Jesus.[86]

Michel Quenot writes intriguingly of Byzantine iconography in general, and the Christ Pantocrator genre in particular: "As the visual center of the body, the face dominates everything else [in the image]."[87] The entire body becomes facialized,

---

[85] Even the historical Jesus cannot plausibly be said to have been born that year, as New Testament scholars will be lining up to insist, most assigning his birth instead to 6–4 BCE.

[86] On the genesis of this Christ-type, and the clean-shaven, short-haired, boyish representations that both preceded and competed with it, see Joan E. Taylor, *What Did Jesus Look Like?* (New York: Bloomsbury T&T Clark, 2018), 69–108, 123–38 passim.

[87] Michel Quenot, *The Icon: Window on the Kingdom*, trans. anon. (Crestwood, NY: St. Vladimir's Seminary Press, 1991), 93.

RACE (JESUS AND THE WHITE FACIALITY MACHINE) 213

Figure 3 The oldest known icon of Christ Pantocrator, a sixth-century encaustic painting on wood from Saint Catherine's Monastery, Sinai Peninsula, Egypt

"Those icons . . . are centered upon a mystic, almost sacramental, faciality" (Guattari, "Existential Affects," 171 n. 20).

as Deleuze and Guattari might say (*A Thousand Plateaus*, 170). "Certain assemblages of power [*pouvoir*] require the production of a face," as they also say (175) and as we already saw. Imperial Christendom was—and arguably still is—a monumental, epochal example of such an assemblage, or mega-assemblage, of power. Quenot continues, "Greeks called a slave *aprosopos*,

214   THE BIBLE AFTER DELEUZE

i.e., he who has no face. So, by assuming the features of a human face, God restored to us a face in His own image, chained as we were like slaves without faces—*aprosopos*—because of sin."[88]

In Quenot's gloss on the incarnation, God does not become *flesh* so much as God becomes *face*. One could, of course, argue that the face God restores to human beings is merely the face human beings bestowed on God in the first place, God returning the loan. In the Sinai Christ icon, that face borrowed by God, and rendered divine on its return (infinite interest thereby being paid on the loan), is an embryonic *white* face. Not that the face is of northern European stock, needless to say; most likely it was painted by a Constantinoplean artist within the immediate orbit of Emperor Justinian I. Yet, as Maximos Constas attests from close firsthand observation, the face is "mostly ivory in tone," and "the modeling of the forehead is executed with white highlights, along with small white lines around the eyes, hatched in with a fine brush."[89] This is a Jesus who will pass comfortably as white—once white becomes a legible racial identity marker, that is.

Among Deleuze's solo writings, the face features most prominently in his first film book, *Cinema 1*, and much of what he has to say there about what he terms "the reflective face" (*le visage réflexif*) applies mutatis mutandis to Christ Pantocrator. The formal features of this faciality type make it the ultimate machine-face. It is, simultaneously, a "receptive immobile surface" and a "receptive plate of inscription" (*Cinema 1*, 87). It is "a petrified face," in short (90). But why is it a reflective face? Both because it reflects without absorbing the gaze brought to bear on it, its impassivity not admitting penetration, and because it has an occluded relationship to thought (*réflexion*/reflection in its other sense). Ordinarily, there are two sorts of questions that can be put to a face, muses Deleuze: "What are you thinking about?" and "What are you feeling?" (88). Both questions rebound from the Christ Pantocrator face. This is a face so devoid of interiority as to render such questions irrelevant in advance.

That is not to say, however, that thought as such is irrelevant to this face. Deleuze declares with regard to the cinematic faces he deems "reflective" (Christ Pantocrator would, of course, be an iconic example of this facial

---

[88] Quenot, *The Icon*, 93. Quenot is assumedly referring to Theophilus's Greek paraphrase of Justinian's Latin *Institutes* 3.18, which declares that slaves are *aprosōpoi*: without face, without personhood, faceless nonpersons.

[89] Maximos Constas, *The Art of Seeing: Paradox and Perception in Orthodox Iconography*, Contemporary Christian Thought 25 (Alhambra, CA: Sebastian Press, 2014), 48.

RACE (JESUS AND THE WHITE FACIALITY MACHINE)   215

genre, no pun intended):[90] "We are before a reflective face as long as the features remain grouped under the domination of a thought which is fixed or terrible, . . . immutable . . . , in a way eternal" (Deleuze, *Cinema 1*, 89–90). And again: "The reflective face expresses a pure Quality, that is to say a 'something' common to several objects of different kinds" (90). In the case that concerns us, that of the Sinai Christ Pantocrator, that Quality—terrible, immutable, eternal—is Sovereignty, and prominent among the "several objects of different kinds" assembled within its territory

> "The assemblage is fundamentally territorial" (Deluze and Guattari,
> *A Thousand Plateaus*, 323).

would be a lowborn Jewish peasant become All-Sovereign Ruler and Judge; and a gospel collection (he clutches an opulent gospel book, as we saw) whose own meandering passage from the outer margins of the empire to the inner sanctum of the imperial palace is no less improbable.[91] Where does the face's whiteness fit into this all-encompassing assemblage of power?

To the reflective face, Deleuze opposes "the intensive face" (*le visage intensif*, intensity in the special Deleuzian sense being intimately interwoven with affect, sensation, and becoming, as we have seen). "From the stone to the scream," as he puts it (*Cinema 1*, 89). "We find ourselves before an intensive face each time that the traits break free from the outline, begin to work on their own account, and form an autonomous series which tends toward a limit or crosses a threshold" (89). The intensive face is a would-be escaping face, intent on pursuing a line of flight from the faciality machine itself. Within the petrified reflective face that is the Sinai Christ Pantocrator, an intensive face is pressing against, attempting to flow through, the bars. For, famously, the Sinai Christ is a Janus-faced Jesus, his asymmetrical face split down the middle, a vulnerably relational, affectively vibrant face on one side, and a divine imperial judge on the other side, the latter a "dark counterpart" to the former, as Constas puts it, "a ponderous Titan, aloof to all relation."[92]

---

[90] Ironically, however, *icon* is an important technical term in *Cinema 1*. It designates affect "as expressed by a face, or a facial equivalent" (217).

[91] Although Justinian I, the Byzantine emperor over whose reign the Sinai Christ's right hand is likely raised in blessing, appears himself to also have been of peasant stock, as was his predecessor Justin I, the Sinai Christ's symbiotic relations with the emperor thus exceeding that Christ's regal garb and aspect.

[92] Constas, *The Art of Seeing*, 51.

216   THE BIBLE AFTER DELEUZE

The dark counterpart, however, is really a white counterpart, a God become (white) man whose devotees will eventually weaponize his whiteness by elevating and fetishizing their own whiteness, bowing down before it, worshiping it, all the while deceiving themselves and those whom they are colonizing and Christianizing that that apotheosized whiteness is a transcendent divine being, namely, their white God. Within the Sinai Christ icon, the attempt of the counterimperial intensive face to escape from the imperial reflective face never ends

> "And we look at his face and we see that he no longer has one. The traits
> of faciality have freed themselves from the face's domination" (Deleuze,
> "A Thousand Plateaus I, Lecture 6," n.p.).

and forever fails, the intensive face being continually captured by the reflective face, being constantly sucked back into the black hole of its imperious impassivity, but only to draw anew further lines of flight from it in an endless recursive loop. The double-faced Sinai Pantocrator icon thus tells proleptically and compactly the history of Christianity as a history of incessant becoming and recurrent capture—which, in a Deleuzian framework,

> "Becomings are something quite distinct from history. . . . They trans-
> mute and reappear in different, unexpected forms in the lines of flight of
> some social field" (Deleuze, *Negotiations*, 152–53).

is no history at all.[93]

How the White Faciality Machine Operates

All this to say, among other things, that the White Jesus did not descend fully formed to earth, or that "he invented the facialization of the entire body and spread it everywhere,"

> "Christ invented the face" (Deleuze and Parnet, *Dialogues II*, 45).

---

[93] See pp. 14–19 earlier.

contrary to what Deleuze and Guattari assert (*A Thousand Plateaus*, 176).[94] Indeed, the historical Jesus himself is not a little startled and confused by the snow-skinned, blond-haired, blue-eyed figure whom Deleuze and Guattari have caused to materialize in his presence. The gaze that the White Jesus casts over the brown-skinned Mediterranean Jewish peasant is one of cold dismissal. This White Jesus, assembled over many centuries, is the incarnation, not of the transcendent God of Israel, but of the abstract machine of faciality; and "at every moment, the machine rejects faces that do not conform, or seem suspicious" (177). The machine is programed to compute normalities, to detect deviances (177–78). And if the standard face in relation to which the machine is calibrated is white, then the first divergence-types will be racial: black, brown, yellow, red (178). And because the calibrating face is male and "rational" in addition to being white, other divergences will also be inscribed on the wall and sucked into the hole. The white face, retroactively apotheosized as the White Jesus, "moves across all of space," which is to say "the entire screen" (292), at precisely the same rate as the imperial armies of soldiers, merchants, and missionaries, producing divergent and deviant subjects everywhere it goes, strapping them into the "dualism machines" that are plugged into the faciality machine,

> "We would have a more flexible and precise hinge between power assemblages and faciality if we managed to show how and why the face has a fundamental rapport with binary choices. . . . The face instigates dichotomies in every direction. You're a man or you're a woman, you're rich or you're poor. Look at your face! You're a woman. Why do you dress like a man?" (Deleuze, "A Thousand Plateaus I, Lecture 6," n.p.).

---

[94] In one of Deleuze's as yet unpublished seminars, a more nuanced position comes to expression: "In this matter of the face, . . . Christ had a fundamental role from the pictorial point of view, from the plastic point of view. . . . With Christ appears a completely different type of face" (Deleuze, "A Thousand Plateaus V, Lecture 6," n.p.). There have been at least three attempts to relate Deleuzoguattarian faciality to the face(s) of Jesus: see Janell Watson, "The Face of Christ: Deleuze and Guattari on the Politics of Word and Image," *The Bible and Critical Theory* 1, no. 2 (2005): doi: 10.2104/bc050004; Petra Carlsson, "The Christ under Reconstruction: From the Face to the Celestial Machine," *Svensk Teologisk Kvartalstidskrift* 3 (2018): 49—59; and Sharon Jacob, "Face-ing the Nations: Becoming a Majority Empire of God—Reterritorialization, Language, and Imperial Racism in Revelation 7:9-17," in *Critical Theory and Early Christianity*, ed. Matthew G. Whitlock, Studies in Ancient Religion and Culture (Sheffield, UK: Equinox, 2022), 184—210.

218   THE BIBLE AFTER DELEUZE

the white face ceaselessly "reproducing itself" as "the principal term in the oppositions" produced by these binary machines (Deleuze and Guattari, *A Thousand Plateaus*, 292).

That is not to say, however, that the imperious white male machine-face, the mechanized White Jesus–face, automatically transforms Black and brown male subjects; female subjects and sexually nonconforming subjects of any color; and nonhuman animal subjects into Others. Deleuze and Guattari's theory of race is nondialectical, as noted earlier,[95] meaning that it does not conceive of the racist (1) constructing the racial Other; (2) as being reciprocally co-constructed in the process ("Because you are black, I am white"); and (3) as simultaneously banishing the racial Other into a conceptual Outside that is securely walled off from the elite enclave of the racially "superior." Fanon, we recall, was profoundly uncomfortable in the dark Outside space created by dialectical analysis of the white racism under which he suffered, his feet "no longer feel[ing] the touch of the ground,"[96] even while being reassured by Sartre that this antithetical zero-gravity space was merely a waiting room, a place to prepare for "the synthesis or realization of the human in a society without races."[97]

Fanon might be uncomfortable on other grounds with Deleuze and Guattari's theory of race and racism, but it is not a theory that allows racial or racist signifiers to float free of the bodies they name; instead it latches onto the faces and facialized bodies that subtend those signifiers.[98] Neither does their theory contain racial Others or an absolute Outside. For white racists (so they argue), "there is no exterior, there are no people on the outside. There are only people who should be like us and whose crime it is not to be" (*A Thousand Plateaus*, 178). In place of a single line of partition between an absolute Inside and an absolute Outside, Deleuze and Guattari posit multiple dividing lines, multiple gradations of divergence and deviance. "Racism operates by the determination of degrees of deviance in relation to the White Man face," most often "tolerating them ... under given conditions, in a given ghetto," say, but sometimes "propagat[ing] waves of sameness until those who resist identification have been wiped out," erased from the wall of acceptable significations and the concomitant sphere of acceptable facialities (178).

---

[95] Deleuze would later describe *A Thousand Plateaus* as "resolutely anti-Hegelian" (*Two Regimes of Madness*, 309).

[96] Fanon, *Black Skin, White Masks*, 106.

[97] Fanon, *Black Skin, White Masks*, 102.

[98] Extrapolating from Deleuze and Guattari, *A Thousand Plateaus*, 179–80.

RACE (JESUS AND THE WHITE FACIALITY MACHINE)   219

"Nothing can escape the universal white power of the normal face," Guattari had declared earlier in Deleuze's seminar (Deleuze, "A Thousand Plateaus I, Lecture 6," n.p.)—a little too precipitately, as we will discover. For much of Christian history, that universalizing, whitening, normalizing power has been emblematized and legitimized by the fabricated white face of Jesus Christ. What becomes of the global megamachine of white faciality with the ascent of secularism in much of the Global North, Jesus beginning to leach his divine power, to fade into near invisibility (now becoming the embodiment of white invisibility), in certain societies over which he formerly towered, omnipresent and omnipotent? Neither Deleuze nor Guattari address that question explicitly, but Guattari provides an implicit answer to it when he remarks in passing on the effacement of "God's own son" in the operations of the white global faciality machine (*The Machinic Unconscious*, 90).[99] For the machine continues to turn over—indeed, to produce more prodigiously than ever—even when Jesus has been entombed invisibly within it or has ascended to invisibility from its surface. The machine's central engine is now a non-center, an "empty faciality . . . which, having its center everywhere and nowhere, remains unlocalizable within space-time coordinates" (93). Although omnipresently godlike, it no longer has any truck with transcendence. There is, indeed, no longer any need "for a transcendent center of power," power now being entirely "immanent" instead, "operating through normalization" (Deleuze and Guattari, *A Thousand Plateaus*, 129–30).

Defacing Race

Launch the Probe-Heads!

Is that the ultimate untranscendable reality then, the world only becoming "human, rational, and universal" through "calibrated facial formulas" (Guattari, *The Machinic Unconscious*, 93) that maintain an essential relation, sometimes overt, more often covert, to whiteness? Deleuze and Guattari's irrepressible utopianism[100] precludes them from prostrating before the empty,

---

[99] Guattari also observes in an interview he and Deleuze conducted, "What has become outdated in the Church is its ideology [read: theology], not its organization of power" (Deleuze, *Desert Islands*, 271). That is why "the face of Christ . . . hasn't stopped haunting Western capitalistic subjectivity" as the ostensibly absent fulcrum of its "facialitarian" system (Guattari, *Schizoanalytic Cartographies*, 250).

[100] Deleuze and Guattari ascribe considerable positive political valence to utopianism in *What Is Philosophy?*, 99–100.

220 THE BIBLE AFTER DELEUZE

omnipresent eye of the faciality machine. But because the faciality machine produces the human in its predominant contemporary form—most of all in media-saturated, and hence facial-image-suffused, "advanced" societies (*become this face, these faces; slip them on, feel with them, interface with others through them; find your identity in them*)[101]

> "You don't so much have a face as slide into one" (Deleuze and Guattari, *A Thousand Plateaus*, 177).

—to dismantle the face, to break though the white wall, to climb out of the black hole, means discovering "a nonhuman life [yet] to be created" (191). To that end, "probe-heads" (*têtes chercheuses*) need to be sent out, "cutting edges of deterritorialization" capable of catalyzing "strange new becomings" (190–91).[102]

All exquisitely vague, to be sure. At the very least, however, extrapolating for present contexts, what Deleuze and Guattari's radical ruminations on the prodigious productivity of the white faciality megamachine invite are acknowledgment that the passage to a "postracial society" (that much-maligned utopian concept) is more arduous even than we had supposed, that such a social transformation is entirely chimerical so long as we remain strapped into the machine, mesmerized by its flickering white wall and voracious black hole. What faciality theory conjures up, indeed, beyond the white wall and outside the black hole is less a postracial society than a postfacial society.[103] And it is in quest of such a counterreality

> "How to unmake the face, by liberating in ourselves the questing heads [*têtes chercheuses*] which trace the lines of becoming?" (Deleuze and Parnet, *Dialogues II*, 45–46).

---

[101] Elsewhere—and long before the advent of *Face*book—Guattari writes of the soporific effect of contemporary visual culture: "What is emitted . . . is not simply a discourse, but intensities of all kinds, constellations of . . . faciality, crystallizations of affects" (*Chaosophy*, 264).

[102] Cf. Guattari, *The Machinic Unconscious*, 192: ". . . probe heads or guiding devices [*têtes chercheuses*] of active deterritorialization that untie their passage from the nodes of faciality." The "guiding device" or "seeking device" connotation of *têtes chercheuses* evokes missiles dispatched to destroy specified targets. After the *têtes chercheuses* have accomplished their mission, "there are no more concentrically organized strata, no more black holes around which lines coil to form borders, no more walls to which dichotomies, binarities, and bipolar values cling" (Deleuze and Guattari, *A Thousand Plateaus*, 190). In Deleuze and Parnet, *Dialogues II*, 46, *têtes chercheuses* is rendered more neutrally as "questing heads," also relevant, as we shall see in a moment.

[103] The difference between postracial and postfacial emerges at the conclusion of this chapter.

RACE (JESUS AND THE WHITE FACIALITY MACHINE)   221

that Deleuze and Guattari (once again in their alien observer role) would have us launch probe-heads like escape pods from the inconceivably vast white faciality machine (it spans several continents and throws deep shadows over several others), seeking "the establishment of another human world" in nonhuman space (Guattari, *The Machinic Unconscious*, 105).

The Faceless Jesus and the Solar-Faced Jesus

What resources, if any, might the teachings of Jesus provide for postfacial social experimentation—not the teachings of the White Jesus, that ultimate product of the white faciality machine, but those of the pre-white Jesus as refracted in the gospels (those two bodies of teaching admittedly being one and the same body of teaching pressed through different text processors)? None to speak of, Deleuze and Guattari seem to suppose. "How hard it is to break through the wall of the signifier," they muse. "Many people have tried since Christ, beginning with Christ. But Christ himself botched the crossing, the jump, he *bounced* off the wall" (*A Thousand Plateaus*, 187, emphasis in original). Ultimately, Christ did bounce, becoming white himself as he struck the imperious, the imperial, white wall

"On the white wall . . . the signifier inscribes its characters, which are not information but orders" (Deleuze, "A Thousand Plateaus I, Lecture 6," n.p.).

and falling back to earth as "the White Man as Christian Universal" (Deleuze and Guattari, *A Thousand Plateaus*, 182), which is how Deleuze and Guattari see him no matter how often they spin him around and examine him.[104] But let's replay Jesus's leap in slow motion, at least as the New Testament gospels dramatize it.

How prominent, how protuberant, is the face—Jesus's face or anyone's face—in the gospels? The simple answer is that the face is utterly effaced in them. Even Jesus's own face is mentioned mainly to be slapped and spat on: "Then they spat in his face [*prosōpon*] and struck him, and some slapped

---

[104] In one of his seminars, Deleuze even charges Christ with inventing subjectivity, the corollary of faciality: "A phenomenon that was invented by Christ: subjectivity" ("A Thousand Plateaus I, Lecture 4," n.p.).

222   THE BIBLE AFTER DELEUZE

him" (Matt 26:67; see also John 18:22; 19:3, together with Mark 15:19 in which Jesus's face is merely an implicit object of abuse). At the opposite pole from the debased face is the exalted face: "The appearance of [Jesus's] face [*prosōpon*] change[s]" on the mountain of transfiguration, according to Luke (9:29), it "[shines] like the sun," according to Matthew (17:2); but we are never told in any of the Synoptic Gospels what that face changed *from*. The face—Jesus's face or anyone's face—is never described, even minimally, in any of the canonical gospels, as we noted earlier.[105]

That datum might have been interesting to Deleuze and Guattari. They write of an unspecified "regime of signs," one of several,[106] whose nexus is the face of the despot-god who is its absolute ruler. Through his administrative and religious apparatus, the despot-god "brandishes his solar face that is his entire body" and his subjects are coerced or enticed to bow down before it (*A Thousand Plateaus*, 115). Deleuze and Guattari are not writing explicitly about the Roman imperial cult, but they might as well be. They also write, "The face or body of the despot or god has something like a counterbody: the body of the tortured, or better, of the excluded." And "the one who is tortured is fundamentally one who loses his or her face" (115–16). They are not writing explicitly about the gospel Jesus(es), but they might as well be. That Jesus, those Jesuses, live their entire literary lives as though they have already lost their face, marching facelessly page after page toward the cruciform torture instrument whose imperious summons calls their incorporeal counterbodies into being.

The risen Christ of Revelation's inaugural vision loses that facelessness, assumes a solar face ("his face [*opsis*] was like the sun shining with full force"—1:16) that is also a despotic face. The eyes "like a flame of fire" (1:16) that glow in it will later reappear on the face of the "King of kings and Lord of lords" (19:16; cf. 17:14; 1 Tim 6:15) who will "strike down the nations" with the "sharp sword" he unsheathes from his throat (Rev 19:15; cf. 1:16; 2:12)

"The apocalyptic Christ (the man with the sword between his teeth) . . . "

(Deleuze, *Essays Critical and Clinical*, 50).

---

[105] See pp. 125–127.

[106] They write of it in a plateau whose title, indeed, is "587 B.C–A.D. 70: On Several Regimes of Signs." What they have to say about the Jerusalem temple, and the Jewish God, is a topic for another time. Roland Boer has written incisively about it; see his "Between the Goat's Arse and the Face of God: Deleuze and Guattari and Marx and the Bible," *Journal for the Study of the Old Testament* 37, no. 3 (2013): 295–318.

RACE (JESUS AND THE WHITE FACIALITY MACHINE) 223

and "will rule them with a rod of iron" (19:15; cf. 12:5). This face might indeed be said to already be speeding toward post-Constantinian Christendom and the fabled monastery at the foot of Mount Sinai to reincarnate itself in the imperial icon of Christ Pantocrator (that whey-faced Despot of despots) that had recently taken up residence there,[107] if it were not for one intriguing complicating factor.

The Christ of Revelation's initial vision has hair "white as wool [*erion*]" and his feet are "like burnished bronze refined as in a furnace [*homoioi chalkolibanō hōs en kaminō pepyrōmenēs*]" (1:14–15), details that legions of interpreters of African descent have taken to refer to Afro-textured hair and dark skin.[108] Within Africa and the African diaspora, the Rastafari have been especially notable for their strategic deployment of these verses to counter the Eurocentric erasure of dark-skinned people from biblical history, and the whitening of Jesus in particular. More generally, many Black Christian communities worldwide, often emboldened by the verses, have installed visual depictions of a dark-skinned Jesus in their places of worship or other communal spaces. Having had to pass as white for centuries, Revelation's Jesus is now able to come out as Black, thanks to the faciality machine's color selection switch. As Deleuze and Guattari remark in a different connection, "the wall could just as well be black, and the hole white" (*A Thousand Plateaus*, 169).

The Probe-Head on the Road to Emmaus

Meanwhile, back in the gospels, Jesus's face is undergoing other significant transformations. Once the Lukan Jesus exits his tomb, his previously undescribed, nonrepresented face—already a barely facialized face—appears to dissolve altogether. Two of his disciples are traveling "to a village called Emmaus" when "Jesus himself" approaches and accompanies them, "but their eyes were prevented from identifying him [*hoi de ophthalmoi autōn ekratounto tou mē epignōnai auton*]." He asks what they are conversing about, receiving the perplexed reply, "Are you the only stranger sojourning

[107] In gold coins (*solidi*) minted by Emperor Justinian II in 692–95 CE, Christ Pantocrator makes his first numismatic appearance, the inscription on the coins identifying him as *IhS Cristos R[ex re]gnantium*, "Jesus Christ King of kings." See further Constas, *The Art of Seeing*, 45, 89.

[108] See further Brian K. Blount, "Revelation," in *True to Our Native Land: An African American New Testament Commentary*, ed. Brian K. Blount et al. (Minneapolis: Fortress Press, 2007), 526–27; Jeffrey O. G. Ogbar, *Black Power: Radical Politics and African American Identity* (Baltimore, MD: Johns Hopkins University Press, 2004), 155.

224 THE BIBLE AFTER DELEUZE

[*su monos paroikeis*] in Jerusalem who does not know the things that have occurred there...?" (Luke 24:13–18). For his trek with the two disciples, Jesus has apparently unscrewed and slipped off his individually machined face

"Nothing is less personal than the face" (Deleuze and Parnet, *Dialogues II*, 21).

and borrowed an unidentifiable face, "becom[ing] imperceptible," as Deleuze and Guattari might say, "becom[ing] clandestine, ... by strange true becomings that get past the wall and get out of the black hole" (*A Thousand Plateaus*, 171). The two disciples do not yet know that they are traveling with a probe-head, that "a real that is yet to come" (142) is emerging, hatching, before their sightless eyes.

And when the probe-head chooses the moment to reveal itself, the revelation does not simply consist in slipping back on its familiar face. It is as a head connected to a body, not a disincarnated face floating free of a body, bobbing above it like a transcendent balloon, that the probe-head discloses itself; for it now knows that "the face is produced only when the head ceases to be a part of the body, ... when it ceases to have a multidimensional polyvocal corporeal code" (Deleuze and Guattari, *A Thousand Plateaus*, 170).[109] And so it is through bodily acts that the defacialized probe-head now reveals itself to its befuddled disciples: "When he was at table with them, he took bread, blessed and broke it, and gave it to them (Luke 24:30; cf. 9:16; 22:19). Their climactic recognition of the probe-head, however, coincides with the probe-head once again manifesting itself as imperceptibility:

"... both the face and its effacement" (Deleuze, *Cinema 1*, 100).

"Then their eyes were opened and they recognized him; and he vanished from their sight [*kai autos aphantos egeneto ap' autōn*]" (24:31).

"Certain assemblages of power require the production of a face, others do not," as we have seen more than once already (Deleuze and Guattari, *A Thousand Plateaus*, 175). For now, this assemblage of power materializing

---

[109] To the regime of signs whose fulcrum is the face (consummately, contemporary global capitalism), Deleuze and Guattari contrast a "so-called primitive," implicitly tribal, regime in which "there is no reduction to faciality as the sole substance of expression," but rather "a pluralism or polyvocality of forms of expression" in which "corporeality, gesturality, rhythm, dance, and rite coexist heterogeneously with the vocal form" (Deleuze and Guattari, *A Thousand Plateaus*, 117).

RACE (JESUS AND THE WHITE FACIALITY MACHINE)   225

before the astonished disciples does not. All too soon, however, it will. As the disciples hurry back to Jerusalem (Luke 24:33), they have simultaneously and unknowingly set foot on the royal road leading to Constantinople, imperial Christendom, the Sinai Christ Pantocrator, the full reinstatement of the despotic solar face, and, ultimately, the embryonic white face.

But the text's own signposts, were the disciples not too ecstatic to heed them, would send them in another direction to a different destination. The defacialized probe-head that, minutes before, had become altogether imperceptible the moment they properly apprehended it,

> "After the face, we come to an invisible becoming" (Guattari, *Molecular Revolution*, 162).

had earlier appeared to them as a *paroikoumenos* when they first encountered it. Recall again their wondering words to it: "Are you the only one *paroikeis* in Jerusalem who does not know the things that have occurred there . . . ?" (Luke 24:18). Why not allow the verb *paroikeo* its "full biblical weight" here,[110] that ponderous bulk deriving from Hebrews 11:9 ("By faith, [Abraham] sojourned as a foreigner [*parōkēsan . . . hōs allotrian*] in a promised land, dwelling in tents"; cf. 11:13) together with Acts 7:6, 29; 13:17; Ephesians 2:19; and 1 Peter 2:11,[111] all echoing related Septuagintal sojournings, such as Genesis 17:8; 20:1; 21:34; 23:4; 26:3; Exodus 6:4; 12:40; and Leviticus 18:3?[112] What precisely would that combined mass squeeze from Luke 24:18? Contemporary relevance, perhaps.

For what the disciples have constructed, it seems, from their encounter with the mysterious but mundane figure on the road is a foreign-born migrant who is entirely incognizant of local conditions, but whose presence, as such, is a provocation, an invitation, to radical hospitality, which is what the disciples end up extending to the *paroikoumenos*: "Stay [*meinon*] with us," they insist (24:29). The longer we ponder this scene, indeed, the more this probe-head—or, more aptly in this instance, questing head[113]—merges with

---

[110] We wouldn't be the first to do so; see, for example, Andrew Arterbury, *Entertaining Angels: Early Christian Hospitality in Its Mediterranean Setting*, New Testament Monographs 8 (Sheffield: Sheffield Phoenix Press, 2005), 135–52; Adelbert Denaux, "Stranger on Earth and Divine Guest: Human and Divine Hospitality in the Gospel of Luke and the Book of Acts," in *Strangers and Pilgrims on Earth: Essays in Honor of Abraham van de Beek*, ed. Eduardus van der Borght and Paul van Geest (Leiden, The Netherlands: Brill, 2012), 92–95.

[111] Also see Philo, *On the Cherubim* 108, 119–21; *On the Confusion of Tongues* 76–82.

[112] The *paroikeo-paroikos-paroikia* Greek cluster rendering the *gêr-tôšāḇ* Hebrew cluster.

[113] An alternative translation for *tête chercheuse*, as noted earlier.

226   THE BIBLE AFTER DELEUZE

contemporary migrants, refugees, and asylum seekers. In the process, the questing head begins to appear ever less white even as the unfolding narrative reveals it to be ever more divine. The questing head is not a direct progenitor, then, of the imperial Christ who is the apotheosis of whiteness. That blindingly white Christ, were he to materialize on the Emmaus road, would not recognize himself in the postfacial features of the questing head, nor could he, being a human, all-too-human deity. Nailed to the cross? Rather, the imperial Christ has been "pinned to the white wall and stuffed in the black hole" (Deleuze and Guattari, *A Thousand Plateaus*, 181), a death altogether more resistant to resurrection.

The Parable of the Thousand Tiny Races

What else might any of this have to do with race? To see that, we need to cut into the parallel lane, that along which the Gospel of Matthew is cruising. Is Jesus's face equally effaced in this narrative? Yes and no. Its author evinces an incipient addiction to apocalypticism. The face of his hero on the mountain of transfiguration is apocalyptically irradiated (17:2; cf. Dan 10:6; 12:3; *1 Enoch* 38:4; *2 Enoch* 1:5; *Apocalypse of Zephaniah* 6:11; Rev 1:16; 10:1), less the face of the Son in that moment than the face of the Sun. This Jesus's death is accompanied by an apocalyptic earthquake (Matt 27:51; cf. *1 Enoch* 1:6–7; *Assumption of Moses* 10:3–4; Rev 6:12; 8:5; 11:13, 19; 16:18) and a mass emergence of the dead from their tombs (Matt 27:52–53; cf. Dan 12:2; Rev. 20:4). Later, at Jesus's own tomb, there is a second earthquake as an apocalyptic angel, whose appearance is "like lightning," descends from heaven and rolls back the stone (Matt 28:2). Following these fireworks, we should expect Jesus to erupt from the tomb like a solar flare as a grand finale. He does not, however, which is what makes Matthew's resurrection narrative interesting. Somehow Matthew holds the risen face in, hides it inside the hood of his hero's head,

> "The head is included in the body, but the face is not. . . . The face is produced only when the head ceases to be a part of the body. . . . What accomplishes this is . . . the abstract machine producing faciality" (Deleuze and Guattari, *A Thousand Plateaus*, 170).

even when he has the hero receive imperial obeisance ("And they . . . took hold of his feet and worshiped him"—28:9; see also 28:17a) and make imperial pronouncements ("All authority on heaven and on earth has been given to me. Go therefore and make disciples of all nations, . . . teaching them to obey everything that I have commanded you"—28:18–20).

The Matthean audience has already been told what has happened—more precisely, what *will* happen—to the risen Jesus's missing face. In an earlier scene in the narrative, but one set in the dimly distant future, the risen Jesus returns, resplendent in imperial majesty: "When the Son of Man comes in his glory, and all the angels with him, then he will sit on the throne of his glory. And all the nations will be gathered before him . . ." (Matt 25:31–32). What he tells the innumerable multitude assembled before him in awe and trepidation is that he is now a body without a face, a body with a dismantled or defacialized face,

> "Undo the face, unravel the face . . ." (Deleuze and Parnet, *Dialogues II*, 23).

that they should not expect to behold *a* face atop his risen body. His is now a multiple face, a face proliferating in a multiplicity without end, delocalized from his individual body and relocalized unceasingly, disseminated through history and throughout the world. It is a face that has been reunited not with *a* body, but with *bodies*; for this body no less than this face is now no longer one.

All of this is implicit in the familiar unfolding dialogue of the parable, the enigmatic invitation of the Emperor (*ho basileus*), "Come . . . , inherit the empire [*tēn . . . basileian*] prepared for you, . . . for I was hungry and you gave me food," etc., eliciting the invitees' puzzled response, "Lord, when was it that we saw you hungry and gave you food, or thirsty and gave you something to drink? And when was it that we saw you an alien [*xenos*] and welcomed you, or naked and gave you clothing? And when was it that we saw you sick or in prison and visited you?" to which the Emperor responds in turn, "Truly I tell you, inasmuch as you did it to one of the least of these my brothers [*heni toutōn tōn adelphōn mou tōn elachistōn*], you did it to me" (25:34–40).[114] No less than in the case of the migrant person encountered on the road to

---

[114] Ulrich Luz was able to report more than two decades ago that the "universal" interpretation of "the least of these"—that which construes them as the marginalized in general, irrespective of religious affiliation (as opposed to needy Christians or, more narrowly still, afflicted Christian missionaries)—was by then the most widely accepted scholarly interpretation, a situation that, if anything, seems to be even more true today. See Ulrich Luz, *Das Evangelium nach Matthäus (Mt 18–25)*,

228   THE BIBLE AFTER DELEUZE

Emmaus, this face, these faces, in this Last Judgment scene are dark faces, for the most part

> "People keep on being sunk in black holes, pinioned on a white wall. This is what being identified, labelled . . . is" (Deleuze and Parnet, *Dialogues II*, 18).

—or would be in "our" world, anyway (and this epic parable unfolds at the end of our world as we know it). And so we are returned once more to James Cone's prophetic proclamation: not that Jesus *was* Black, but that Jesus *is* Black, always and already.

It might be objected that such a blackening of Jesus, even a risen and returned Jesus, would not throw a wrench in the works of the faciality machine, that the machine would simply shrug its mechanical shoulders, switch the WHITE JESUS setting in its calibration unit to the BLACK JESUS setting,

> "The wall could just as well be black, and the hole white" (Deleuze and Guattari, *A Thousand Plateaus*, 169).

and proceed to churn out standardized faces at precisely the same prodigious rate as before, the only difference being that all the faces would now be graded and stamped in accordance with their degree of deviation from the black face. To argue this, however, would be to misapprehend the faciality machine's raison d'être. Once again: "Certain assemblages of power require the production of a face, others do not" (175). White culture has been one such assemblage of power, easily the most notable of the past five hundred years, and the white faciality machine, with its calibration unit locked to the image of a white Jesus, has existed to serve and maintain that mega-assemblage.[115] Arguably, neither the Gospel of Matthew nor the Gospel of Luke, when read more closely than they generally have been in white culture, are optimally equipped to function as operating manuals

---

Evangelisch-Katholischer Kommentar zum Neuen Testament (Zürich: Benziger Verlag, 1997), 521–25.

[115] Become a MAGA-assemblage in the recent history of the United States, which is the topic of my final chapter.

RACE (JESUS AND THE WHITE FACIALITY MACHINE)   229

> "What are the societies, the civilizations which need to make this ma-
> chine work . . . ?" (Deleuze and Parnet, *Dialogues II*, 18).

for such a machine. Lines in these texts that look like they were custom written for such a manual (all the hyper-hierarchical, proto-imperial, and proto-racist lines) are rendered nonsensical by other lines that intersect with them (lines of the kind we have been considering).

The white faciality machine runs on a binary code, as we noted earlier . As Deleuze and Guattari explain, "the machine constitutes a facial unit, an elementary face in biunivocal relation with another" (*A Thousand Plateaus*, 177): white face / black face, white face / brown face, white male face / white female face, white male face / black female face, and so on through the entire chain of possible permutations, which is also a chain of possible deviations from the white (male) face standard. If the binary mechanism were to stall and grind to a halt, what would become of race as we moderns tend to conceive of it? Deleuze and Guattari do not address this question directly, but they do write in a related register:

> Everything is political, but every politics is simultaneously a *macropolitics* and a *micropolitics*. Take aggregates of the perception or feeling type: their molar organization, their rigid segmentarity, does not preclude the existence of an entire world of unconscious micropercepts,[116] unconscious affects, fine segmentations that . . . are distributed and operate differently. . . . If we consider the great binary aggregates, such as the sexes or classes [but also, we might add, the races], it is evident that they also cross over into molecular assemblages of a different nature. . . . For the two sexes imply a multiplicity of molecular combinations . . . : a thousand tiny sexes. (213)

But why not *a thousand tiny races* in addition, as Arun Saldanha has proposed?[117]

Returning to the Matthean Jesus's panoramic, but problematic, parable of the Sheep and the Goats, we discover that the thousand tiny races erupt out of it—unexpectedly so, since the parable bristles with macropolitical

---

[116] See p. 139 n. 60 earlier on percepts.

[117] Saldanha, "Reontologising Race," 20–23. The sensibilities Saldanha brings to his rethinking of race are shaped by Deleuze and Guattari, as noted earlier. Rick Dolphijn and Iris van der Tuin also reapply the thousand tiny sexes concept to race; see their "A Thousand Tiny Intersections: Linguisticism, Feminism, Racism and Deleuzian Becomings," in *Deleuze and Race*, ed. Saldanha and Adams, 129–43.

230   THE BIBLE AFTER DELEUZE

protuberances: The "Son of Man" returning in numinous splendor, hailed as *basileus* (king, emperor), seated on "his glorious throne," attended by the angelic host, with "all the nations . . . gathered before him" for judgment (Matt 25:31–32, 34a, 40a). Great binary aggregates, rigid segmentarity, are also much in evidence: "He will separate [*aphorisei*] people one from another as a shepherd separates the sheep from the goats, and he will put the sheep at his right hand and the goats at the left" (25:32–33).

But every macropolitics is simultaneously a micropolitics of molecular assemblages. As we have already witnessed, in awed astonishment, the Emperor's body, even as he speaks—through his speech, indeed—is incorporeally transformed, becoming a thousand, a million, and eventually, as the centuries flit by, a trillion sub-bodies ("I was hungry . . . , I was thirsty . . . , I was an alien . . . , I was naked . . . , I was sick . . . , I was in prison"—25:35–36; cf. 25:42–43), each sub-body, incalculably numerous, needing to enter into assemblage with still other bodies so as to cross the threshold from starvation to satiety, from alienness to acceptance, from incarceration to liberation,

"If the face is a politics, dismantling the face is also a politics involving real becomings" (Deleuze and Guattari, *A Thousand Plateaus*, 188).

and so on. Within the world in which we now apprehend the parable, poverty, migration, and incarceration are racially imbued issues—as, for that matter, are homelessness ("I was naked / insufficiently clothed" [*gymnos*]) and pandemic-induced illness ("I was sick/diseased" [*ēsthenēsa*]). What might the multiplicity of molecular combinations operating in and between bodies, as invoked by the parable, realize, or release, in racial terms?

Nonbinary proliferations is the answer implicit in the question, virtual profusions, an open-ended multiplication of the potentialities for being racially embodied, and racially embedded, in the world. For race is not always, or not only, a mechanism of containment, an implement of oppression, as Saldanha insists: "The molecular energies of race can be sensed . . . and harnessed to crumble the systemic violence currently keeping bodies in place. Hoping for, striving for a thousand tiny races is . . . immersing oneself in nature's lines of flight."[118] Those thousand tiny races are stirring, are hatching, in the parable formerly known as the Sheep and the Goats. The

---

[118] Saldanha, "Reontologising Race," 23. He continues, "This politics is . . . not mystical or anarchistic, it is pragmatic. . . . It is first of all empirical: understand what race is, know its potentialities, try to sense them hiding around you, find out what is keeping them from becoming actual."

RACE (JESUS AND THE WHITE FACIALITY MACHINE)   231

proto–White Christian Universal Male who is the seemingly omnipotent Emperor, to whom "all authority in heaven and on earth has [ostensibly] been given" (Matt 28:18), is making a self-dismantling pronouncement about his own body, effecting an incorporeal self-transformation right before our disbelieving eyes, *not* declaring that all the other bodies populating the parable (malnourished or starving bodies, lacking safe drinking water; migrant and "undocumented" bodies; homeless bodies; bodies ill without access to medical resources; incarcerated bodies) exist in "degrees of deviance in relation to [it]" (Deleuze and Guattari, *A Thousand Plateaus*, 178), but rather declaring that all those other bodies commingle with his own body (now leaking imperiality at an alarming rate), are inseparably spliced with it,

> ". . . no more concentrically organized strata, no more black holes around which lines coil to form borders, no more walls to which dichotomies, binaries, and bipolar values cling" (190).

that "the particles of the other" (178), of all the others, intermix promiscuously with his own particles. This is the "interkingdom" (242) over which this curiously unimperial Emperor now presides ("To you has been given to know the mysteries of the interkingdom of heaven"—Matt 13:11), which his parabolically performative words are bringing into being. Within this interkingdom, "there are as many sexes as there are terms in symbiosis" (242). And as many races, too.

And the Emperor's incipiently white face is splitting (whether with anguish or joy is impossible to tell) as he delivers his self-dismantling address to the *ethnē*. "Before him all the *ethnē* [are] gathered" (Matt 25:32), as we recall. But who or what are these *ethnē*? They are the nations, they are the peoples.[119] They are also the races,[120] even if not yet the thousand tiny races. These *ethnē* still "keep bodies in place" (to echo Saldanha's phrase),[121] separated, segmented on the ethnoracial grid (although not nearly as

---

[119] As many commentators have remarked, the "universal judgment" theme of the parable makes it unlikely that *ta ethnē* here carries the restricted sense of "the gentiles."

[120] Wongi Park in his *Race and Ethnicity in Matthew's Passion Narrative* (see n. 64 earlier) uses the terms "race" and "ethnicity" "interchangeably and in combination" (3). Erich S. Gruen in his *Ethnicity in the Ancient World—Did It Matter?* (Berlin: Walter de Gruyter, 2020) also opts to employ the term "ethnicity" "loosely, unfettered by a precise denotation. . . . First, it can carry the broad and indistinct meaning of a communal self-perception. And second, it can refer to a sense of collective identity in which the predominant element is ancestry or kinship, essentially equivalent to the normal understanding of 'race' " (4).

[121] Saldanha, "Reontologising Race," 23.

232 THE BIBLE AFTER DELEUZE

rigorously as the white *ethnos* will eventually segregate and police them). But the Emperor's face is splitting, not unlike that of the Sinai Christ Pantocrator, his direct descendant; the latter's face also pulls in two conflicting directions, as we saw earlier, threatening to tear apart altogether. And as the Emperor's pre-prototypical white face rips open allowing a thousand tiny races to spill forth from it,[122] the white faciality machine disintegrates along with it. "Yes, the face has a great future," Deleuze and Guattari announce with satisfaction, as though they themselves were beholding the eschatological spectacle—"but only if it is destroyed, dismantled," they hastily add (*A Thousand Plateaus*, 171).

---

[122] Brazilian culture provides a partial preview of the spectacle. Sharon A. Stanley writes, "It has become virtually cliché to comment upon Brazil's dizzying variety of colour terms. Famously, in an open-ended 1976 survey . . . , respondents chose 134 distinct colour terms to describe themselves, including such creative terms as *sapecada* (burnished red), *paraíba* (like the colour of *marupa* wood), and *morena-cor-de-canela* (cinnamon-hued brunette). . . . This baroque colour vocabulary has sometimes been taken to indicate that 'race' simply does not function as a socially significant category in Brazilian life. . . . Yet careful study of how Brazilians use racial and colour categories reveals that bipolar (black vs. white) racial categories *do* function in everyday Brazilian discourse— alongside dozens of colour categories" ("Stuart Hall against Stuart Hall," *Contexto Internacional* 41, no. 2 [2019]: 452–53). All this would admit of easy translation into Deleuzoguattarese: Lines of flight and acts of capture, deterritorializations and reterritorializations, molecular revolutions and microfascisms—and emerging always out of the melee the anguished question, "What can be done to prevent the theme of a race from turning into a racism . . . ?" (*A Thousand Plateaus*, 379).

5

POLITICS (beastly boasts, apocalyptic affects)

It was not the best of times to begin with. Indeed, this unforeseen time, this time of Trump, seemed already, for many of us, to be the worst of times. That was before COVID-19, that time of plague. Here in the United States, Trump time and plague time looped around each other in a helical spiral that mimicked the structure of the virus itself: "The coronavirus fusion peptide forms a short helix and a loop."[1] Curling around both of these times in turn, enfolding them in its sinuous embrace, was the book of Revelation. What pulled COVID-19, with Trump clinging onto it, into Revelation's eschatological coils? Multiple factors, as we shall see, not least the term "plague" itself.

A plague summons forth plague diaries and plague journals,[2] and a (chronologically reshuffled) plague journal makes up much of what follows. What mainly follows, however, is a simultaneous journal of life under an autocrat in a democratic nation—an unexpected, but only-to-be-expected, autocrat, a Beast from the abyss beneath every democracy,

> "He opened the shaft of the bottomless abyss, and from the shaft rose smoke like that of a great furnace, and the sun and the air were darkened with it" (Rev 9:2).

an abyss easier to uncover than reseal.

---

[1] Fang Li, "Structure, Function, and Evolution of Coronavirus Proteins," *Annual Review of Virology* 3 (2016): 237.

[2] The genre-establishing anglophone examples being *The Diary of Samuel Pepys* (1660–69) and Daniel Defoe's *A Journal of the Plague Year* (1722, but set in 1665), both products of the Great Plague of London.

The Bible after Deleuze. Stephen D. Moore, Oxford University Press. © Oxford University Press 2023.
DOI: 10.1093/oso/9780197581254.003.0006

234 THE BIBLE AFTER DELEUZE

Reign of the Beast, Day 1226 / Plague Journal, May 29, 2020

Our text today is, or might well be, Revelation 15:1: "And I saw another sign in heaven, great and marvellous, seven angels having the seven last plagues; for in them is filled up the wrath of God" (KJV). John of Revelation, surgically masked and gloved, lifts the localized plagues of Egypt from the book of Exodus (7:1—15:21) and, assisted by a team of angels in celestial hazmat suits, grows them hyperbolically, horribly, in his biological warfare lab, transmuting them into global plagues (as in Rev 9:18, for instance: "By these three plagues [*plēgai*] a third of humankind was killed"; see also 9:20; 15:1, 6, 8; 16:9, 21).

What do Revelation's plagues have to do with COVID-19? Everything or nothing, depending on whom you read. And there is much to read, a sanity-destabilizing quantity of material. On this day of May 29, 2020, feeding "COVID-19 book of Revelation" into the Google search engine causes it to spit out almost forty million results, most of them interpretations of the virus as one or other of Revelation's eschatological plagues. This is what Revelation is for, this is what Revelation does. This is the default function of this disaster-voracious book in a time of global crisis. Specifically, for hundreds of millions of Christians worldwide, Revelation is subsuming the infra-agential activity of submicroscopic suborganisms under the supra-agential activity of a yet more invisible and yet more inscrutable divine being, thereby transforming a time of pandemic into a time of plague.

President Trump seems to have contracted the plague term himself of late, calling COVID-19 a plague more than once, most (melo)dramatically and most apocalyptically in a tweet of May 3, 2020: "And then came a Plague, a great and powerful Plague, and the World was never to be the same again! But America rose from this death and destruction, always remembering its many lost souls, and the lost souls all over the World, and became greater than ever before!" What role, precisely, might the term "plague" be playing in Trump's virulent white nationalist post-ideology? Something to ponder in future journal entries.

Unmethodological Prelude

My own presumption is not that the COVID-19 pandemic is prophesied in the book of Revelation; my presumption, rather, is that Revelation possesses multiple convenient sockets into which the pandemic and the Trump presidency alike may be plugged so as to illuminate both phenomena. To approach Revelation thus, to circle and peer into it in this way, is to "ask what it functions with" in current religiopolitical contexts of reception, "in connection with what other things it does or does not transmit intensities," and "in which other multiplicities its own are inserted and metamorphosed" (Deleuze and Guattari, *A Thousand Plateaus*, 4). "Intensity" is a concept inextricably entangled with "affect" for Deleuze and Guattari, as we saw previously, so much so as to function as a synonym for it much of the time,

> "Lived experience is 'intensive': *I feel*.... 'I feel' means that something is happening in me, I am experiencing an intensity.... The body is crossing a threshold of intensity" (Deleuze, *Desert Islands*, 238).

and affect looms large in this chapter.

Like any work of literature, Revelation is "a little machine" (Deleuze and Guattari, *A Thousand Plateaus*, 4), but it is immensely more powerful than most other literary machines, not least in its affective capacities. To understand what this little machine does, what it is capable of doing, is to determine which other machines it "can be plugged into" so as to operate optimally (4). These other machines have assumed an astonishing variety of forms through the centuries: textual and nontextual, discursive and nondiscursive, human and nonhuman, organic and nonorganic. They have ranged from the book of Daniel to the Roman imperial cult, from the medieval papacy to the bubonic plague, and from the Trump presidency to the novel coronavirus pandemic, to cull only a small sample of the often enormous machines that have interlocked intricately in the seething "mechanosphere"

> "Every abstract machine is linked to other abstract machines, not only because they are inseparably political, economic, scientific, artistic, ecological, cosmic—perceptive, affective, active, thinking, physical, and semiotic—but because their various types are as intertwined as their operations are convergent. Mechanosphere" (Deleuze and Guattari, *A Thousand Plateaus*, 514).

in which Revelation has lived intensively, moved incessantly, and had its being in always becoming more and other than it was meant to be.

236 THE BIBLE AFTER DELEUZE

The standard critical-scholarly approach to Revelation is a depth hermeneutic, a vertical mineshaft, whose two supporting struts are intentionalism and representationalism. Employing the formidable historical-critical
tools developed during the Enlightenment and its aftermath, scholars have
bored down through two millenia of presentist and futurist interpretations
of Revelation and carved out a capacious cavern that is at once the interior
of John of Patmos's skull, a space in which presumed *authorial intentions* flit
about, begging to be netted and described, and John of Patmos's social world
whose inhabitants and institutions are assumed to be *represented* in his symbolic visions, which as such demand decoding.

This depth hermeneutic has been immensely productive and indispen-
sably valuable. But the mine has long been all but exhausted, commen-
taries on Revelation saying less and less that is new at ever greater length
as the decades roll by. Contextual hermeneuts of various stripes—feminists,
womanists, (other) liberationists, queer, postcolonial, and decolonial critics,
along with ecocritics—do read Revelation in ways that effectively, and at
times affectively, plug its (re)constructed context of production into their
lived contexts of reception. Such readings regularly critique what these critics
take to be Revelation's representations, such as its representation of imperial
Rome as a promiscuous woman sorely in need of sexual shaming and violent
eradicating (Rev 14:8; 17:1–18; 18:3, 9; 19:2).[3]

What if, without surrendering the political edge of such readings, representation itself, rather than specific representations, were the object of critique, or set to the side at least? What rereadings of Revelation might that
make possible? What previously unnoticed doors

"There in heaven a door stood open" (Rev 4:1).

might it open?

Reading Revelation representationally is a less than elegant exercise, after
all, at least when focused through a Deleuzian lens. The critic approaches
the skittish book laden down with "the four iron collars of representation"—
identity, opposition, analogy, and resemblance (Deleuze, *Difference and
Repetition*, 262)—and attempts to herd the book into its assigned corral in
a larger conceptual enclosure containing, not only "a field of representation

---

[3] Much of my own previous work on Revelation falls comfortably into this category. My purpose
here is not to repudiate such work but rather to augment and extend it.

POLITICS (BEASTLY BOASTS, APOCALYPTIC AFFECTS)   237

(the book)," but also "a field of reality (the world)," and "a field of subjectivity (the author)" (Deleuze and Guattari, *A Thousand Plateaus*, 23). Revelation, in such a reading, is—can only be—its author's representation of his world to his audience.

But the book is far too fast, too fluid,

> **"Something leaps from the book, making contact with a pure outside"**
> **(Deleuze, *Desert Islands*, 256).**

for such clumsy containment. It is an assemblage of simultaneous material, semiotic, and social flows (Deleuze and Guattari, *A Thousand Plateaus*, 22–23). It is at once "a collective assemblage of enunciation" and "a machinic assemblage of desire, one inside the other and both plugged into an immense outside" (23), an outside that neither begins nor ends in the first-century Roman province of Asia. If it begins anywhere, it begins, and always anew, in the moment in which we currently find ourselves.

Loosening representation's iron-collar hold on our readings of Revelation would enable us, while still working out of a critical paradigm, to relate its visions to consequential contemporary phenomena like the crisis of US democracy or the COVID-19 pandemic, not by reading for relations of re-semblance, analogy, or identity between these ancient visions and current persons or events (Donald J. Trump, say, craving adulation above all, resembling the Beast of Revelation that demands the worship of all), but rather by reading the persons or events as though they were intricately folded into the visions, coextensive with and co-implicated in them (Trump and the Beast commingling, each passing into and flowing through the other)

> **"There is a pure plane of immanence ... upon which unformed elements**
> **and materials dance ... and ... enter into this or that individuated as-**
> **semblage depending on their connections, their relations of movement.**
> **A fixed plane of life upon which everything stirs, slows down or acceler-**
> **ates" (Deleuze and Guattari, *A Thousand Plateaus*, 255).**

in a continuous plane of instantaneous interconnection.

How might such a reading strategy be related to pop-evangelical, apocalyptic expositions of "Bible prophecy," that derided other of critical biblical scholarship? More than any previous US president, Trump provided a blimp-sized target for such expositions, some of them tongue in cheek, many more

238　THE BIBLE AFTER DELEUZE

of them deadly serious. In almost all of them, Trump was identified as the Beast, Revelation's ultimate image for the absolute despot (13:1–18). More precisely, the Beast *represented* the Donald in such expositions, the Beast having always, with inhuman patience, been waiting in the wings of history, apparently, to represent this US president above all US presidents, popes, dictators, or sundry other dignitaries and despots—all of which is to say that the "prophecy news watch" approach to Revelation is an allegorical enterprise through and through, each use-worn vision in the ancient book finally finding its corresponding person or event in the contemporary sociopolitical and geopolitical milieu.

The reign-of-the-Beast journal and the plague journal that make up the bulk of the present chapter seek, together with the chapter's post-Beast postscript, to relate the Beast to Trump (more precisely, to unleash the Beast against Trump) nonallegorically, in a nonrepresentational reading strategy, impelled by the nonrepresentational turn in theory and its "constant war on frozen states."[4] In the case of Revelation, the frozen state would be a fossilized Beast, the Beast excavated by historical critics of Revelation, most of whom never tire of telling each other and anyone else who will listen that the Beast was—and, indeed, still is—the emperor Nero,[5] and as such a metonym for imperial Rome. Nonrepresentational theory would reanimate this mummified Beast, would cause all fourteen of its eyes (cf. Rev 13:1; 17:3, 7, 9) to snap open abruptly and alarmingly.

Reconceived nonrepresentationally, Revelation's Beast would not, of course, simply reawaken, return to life, as a representation of Donald J. Trump, squeezing into Trump's navy-blue shoulder-padded jacket, clipping on his too-long Republican-red tie, curiously running its newly acquired fingers through his wispy orange hair (combover? toupee?). One might, indeed, be tempted to imagine the opposite—that Trump is instead a representation of the Beast, in the sense that this particular US president is, or was ("The

---

[4] Nigel Thrift's phrase; see his *Non-Representational Theory: Space, Politics, Affect*, International Library of Sociology (New York: Routledge, 2008), 5. Deleuzian philosophy has been an important catalyst for the nonrepresentational turn. Large claims have been made for this turn; for example: "Non-representational theory is now widely considered to be the successor of postmodern theory, the logical development of poststructuralist thought, and the most notable intellectual force behind the turn away from cognition, symbolic meaning, and textuality." Phillip Vannini, "Non-Representational Methodologies: An Introduction," in *Non-Representational Methodologies: Re-Envisioning Research*, ed. Phillip Vannini, Routledge Advances in Research Methods (New York: Routledge, 2015), 2.

[5] A conclusion reached by applying the principles of ancient gematria/isopsephy to Rev 13:18 ("Let anyone with understanding calculate the number of the beast, for it is the number of a person. Its number is six hundred sixty-six"), using Hebrew as the code language.

POLITICS (BEASTLY BOASTS, APOCALYPTIC AFFECTS)   239

Beast that you saw was, and is not"—Rev 17:8), but the latest in a long line of autocrats or would-be autocrats who have re-presented the Beast, made it present once again, by stepping into the role scripted for it in Revelation, thereby embodying and enacting it anew. But because Revelation's Beast thus reanimated, plugged into Donald J. Trump (into a secret socket beneath his Brioni jackets), became more and other than it was before, was irreducibly different from all previous actualizations of the Beast, it cannot simply be regarded as an original that preexisted the Trumpian Beast in a primal sense, a Platonic original of which the forty-fifth US president was merely a late copy. And so the concept of representation is of little use for apprehending the operative mechanism, the engine, of the Trump-Beast assemblage.

I am ascribing more nonrepresentational potency to Revelation here than Deleuze himself does. In "Nietzsche and Saint Paul, Lawrence and John of Patmos,"[6] the 1978 essay on Revelation that Deleuze coauthored with Fanny Deleuze,[7] Revelation is seen as being thoroughly in thrall to the allegorical and hence to the representational (Deleuze, *Essays Critical and Clinical*, 42, 48–52). Here the Deleuzes are (unwittingly?) marching in lockstep with an entire army of Revelation interpreters, both precritical and critical, extending from Joachim of Fiore to John Nelson Darby and on down to Wilhelm Bousset, Henry Barclay Swete, and other architects of the historical-critical interpretation of every vision, every verse, of Revelation. For allegorical exposition by any other name is also what historical critics of Revelation do and have always done (notwithstanding the fact that medieval and early modern allegorical deciphering of the book was the constitutive other for emergent historical criticism of it), interpreting chimerical character χ as representing ancient political power A (Rome and its emperors, say); bizarre detail ρ as representing ancient historical event B (the death of Nero, say); surreal visionary sequence σ as representing ancient socioreligious institution C (the Roman imperial cult, say), and so on meticulously and often ingeniously.

The Deleuzes, too, read Revelation as allegory. They see the four horses that famously gallop forth in Revelation 6:1–8, for example, as inanimate allegorical animals. Each horse "is nothing but a beast of burden to which one says 'Come!' and what it bears are abstractions"—Conquest, War, Famine,

---

[6] For a rare critical engagement with this essay, see Mary Bryden, "Nietzsche's Arrow: Deleuze on D. H. Lawrence's *Apocalypse*," in *Deleuze and Religion*, ed. Mary Bryden (New York: Routledge, 2001), 101–14.

[7] Formerly Denise Paul Grandjouan, Deleuze's life partner. Of her influence on his thought, he once wrote, "Her ideas always seized me from behind, coming from far away in another direction, so that we crossed all the more like the signals from two lamps" (Deleuze and Parnet, *Dialogues II*, 10).

240   THE BIBLE AFTER DELEUZE

and Death—whereas the horses could have been assemblage animals instead, a "lived symbiosis" of human and nonhuman elements (Deleuze, *Essays Critical and Clinical*, 47). But why can't the Four Horsemen of the Apocalypse (as tradition has dubbed them) be that as well or instead? The Deleuzes have already described Revelation as "a great machinery" (44), and within every great machine are many lesser machines, and (which is to say the same thing) many lesser assemblages also.[8] The most interesting facet of the Deleuzes' reading of Revelation, for me, is not what they say it is but what they say it is not, because often that *is not* seems, to me, to be precisely what it is—or, rather, what it does.

The term conscripted to do the philosophical heavy lifting in this essay is *symbol*—not a term otherwise accorded central importance in any of Deleuze's solo or joint works, so far as I am aware. It is borrowed from D. H. Lawrence. "Nietzsche and Saint Paul, Lawrence and John of Patmos" was written as a preface to Fanny Deleuze's French translation of Lawrence's *Apocalypse*.[9] For Lawrence, the pagan cosmos is a palpable presence in Revelation, but only so that its author can "finish it off," as the Deleuzes put it, "bring about its hallucinatory destruction"; and that cosmos is, for Lawrence, in its essence, "the locus of great vital symbols and living connections, the more-than-personal life" (Deleuze, *Essays Critical and Clinical*, 45). The Deleuzes follow the Lawrencian line that John of Revelation undertakes a systematic suppression of the cosmos, thus understood, including the displacement of symbols with allegories. In the final pages of the essay (48–52), many of the most recognizable Deleuzian themes are packed into the symbol concept, and done so in a prolonged burst of the familiar Deleuzian style, flaring up fully for the first time in the essay.

What, then, is the Lawrencian-Deleuzian symbol (*symbole*) that Revelation allegedly represses? It is "a concrete cosmic force [or power, capacity, or potential: *puissance*]" (Deleuze, *Essays Critical and Clinical*, 48). The symbolic in this sense is also the sexual (in the expanded Deleuzian sense):[10] "They amount to the same thing . . .—the life of forces or flows [*la vie des forces ou des flux*]" (51). As opposed to the static or fixed "allegorical idea," the symbol is processual, "a dynamic process, . . . an ever increasing becoming-conscious"

---

[8] Not that the term "assemblage" [*agencement*] features explicitly in the essay, although it might have. The assemblage concept figures prominently in Deleuze and Guattari's *Kafka*, published three years earlier.

[9] D. H. Lawrence, *Apocalypse: Traduction nouvelle de l'anglais par Fanny Deleuze* (Paris: Minuit, [1978] 1993).

[10] We explored that expanded sense in pp. 150–155 earlier.

POLITICS (BEASTLY BOASTS, APOCALYPTIC AFFECTS)   241

(48). The symbol is even methodological. It is "a method of the Affect [*une méthode d'Affect*], intensive, a cumulative intensity, which merely marks the threshold of a sensation, the awakening of a state of consciousness" (48). And the symbol is nonrepresentational. "The symbol means nothing, and has neither to be explained nor interpreted, as opposed to [the] allegory" (48). The symbol *acts*, which is why it does not need to mean. It is immediate, immanent, and immersive—"the thought of flows, in contrast to the intellectual and linear process of allegorical thought" (49). And so on.

The sole symbol the Deleuzes seem to locate in Revelation is the scroll of 5:1—but only while it remains unopened: "Then I saw in the right hand of the one seated on the throne a scroll [*biblion*] written on the inside and on the back, sealed [*katesphragismenon*] with seven seals."[11] As opposed to a "linear allegorical chain," the sealed scroll is a "mysterious point" that causes everything to "whirl about [it]"—"And I saw a mighty angel proclaiming with a loud voice, 'Who is worthy to open the scroll and break its seals?' And no one in heaven or on earth or under the earth was able to open the scroll or to look into it" (Rev 5:2–3)—"until it produces that intense state out of which the solution, the decision, emerges" (Deleuze, *Essays Critical and Clinical*, 48–49): "Do not weep! See, the Lion of the tribe of Judah, the Root of David, has conquered, so that he can open the scroll and its seven seals" (Rev 5:5).

Could it not, however, be argued, that the entire book of Revelation has, throughout its improbably long history, functioned precisely as a sealed scroll, a sealed book,[12] and hence as a symbol in the sense we have been considering? "The symbol is a maelstrom," write the Deleuzes; "it makes us whirl about [it]" (*Essays Critical and Clinical*, 49). "It is a *rotative thought*, in which a group of images turn ever more quickly around a mysterious point" (48; see also 134). Why not conceive of Revelation's sense-overloading visions ("the symbol evokes and unites all the ... senses" [49]) as an image group of exactly this sort? These visions, these images, spin ever more perplexingly around a mysterious point until they induce an "intense state" out of which "the solution, the decision, emerges" (49)—but always provisionally. For the images never stop turning and the mysterious point never stops shifting, never

---

[11] They do not explain why the sealed scroll "perhaps retain[s] its power [*puissance*] as a symbol" (Deleuze, *Essays Critical and Clinical*, 49). In what follows, I attempt to fill in the blank using certain of the statements that have led up to it.

[12] As though John had politely ignored the angelic injunction of 22:10: "And [the angel] said to me, 'Do not seal up the words of the prophecy of this book [*tou bibliou toutou*]'" (cf. Dan 12:4, 9).

242   THE BIBLE AFTER DELEUZE

ceases becoming. It never freezes fully in "the flow-thought" (*la pensée des flux* [49]) that the book as symbol never stops generating.

To frame the foregoing differently, Revelation might be said to open itself up to a mode of actualization altogether different from the neoallegorical mode that has predominated in critical scholarship on the book, an actualization attuned not to temporally remote persons and events but to presently emerging, action-impelling affects, sensations, and emotions—an actualization that does not attempt to reify (and thereby neutralize) Revelation's symbols through meaning-fixing pronouncements

> "Everything stops dead for a moment, everything freezes in place—and then the whole process [begins] all over again" (Deleuze and Guattari, *Anti-Oedipus*, 7).

but seeks to flow with the symbols instead, to be carried along in their current, to see where else we might be borne by means of them, in which as yet unthought territories we might land, and in which other arrangements of power we might thereby be equipped to intervene.[13]

All of which brings us back to Revelation's Beast and its most recent return to the US political stage. In order, however, to relate Revelation to the Trump phenomenon, including the former president's political manipulation of the COVID-19 crisis, we must first put the question to Trump that we earlier put to Revelation. That question (also a Deleuzian one) is a question not of identity but of function, not of hermeneutics but of pragmatics, not *who* was Donald Trump but *what* was Donald Trump? What manner of machine was "the Donald," and what did this machine do? What, for that matter, does it still do (Trump having long since bloated to become Trumpism)? "Pragmatics is a politics of language" (Deleuze and Guattari, *A Thousand Plateaus*, 82), and never more than when the object of analysis is a populist politician.

---

[13] Catherine Keller arrives at a related beginning(-again) point for her own recent reading of Revelation, although by way of different theoretical backroads: "*Facing Apocalypse* suggests first of all that there will be in our time no *honest* escape from the notion of apocalypse, and therefore from the question of its meaning. For whatever happens socially, politically, pandemically, and economically, global warming is sure to keep the metaforce charged. Not . . . because predictions of an ancient text are finally 'coming true'. . . . Truth is not something fixed in advance. . . . It does not transcend its context of tangled relations, but it may transform their meaning" (*Facing Apocalypse: Climate, Democracy, and Other Last Chances* [Maryknoll, NY: Orbis Books, 2021], xv). Keller's neologism "metaforce" carries a charge similar to the Lawrencian-Deleuzian concept of symbol: "The metaphor of apocalypse—really, metaphor is too weak a notion, why not call it *metaforce*—has been playing itself out for a couple of millenia" (xiii).

The "What is Trump?" question has already been pondered by Brian Massumi, one of many theorists and scholars of affect who have analyzed Trump and Trumpism, drawn like moths to an orange flame.[14] Acute attunement to the movements of affect is essential to the task of analyzing political power after ideology,[15] and Trump epitomizes post-ideological politics, as we shall see. In what follows, and through my two symbiotically interleaved journals, I construct a bricolage (cf. Deleuze and Guattari, *Anti-Oedipus*, 7) that begins with Massumi's affective analysis of the Trump phenomenon; extends to further pertinent reflection by other affect theorists, much of it also on Trump; and gradually braids in the COVID-19 pandemic, all the while interfacing with Revelation in aleatory fashion as points of connection present themselves—as they inevitably do; for this is precisely the kind of literary machine that Revelation is and always has been. Deleuze and Guattari will also accompany us on the adventure, interjecting as they feel moved, although mainly saving themselves for the post-Beast postscript.

Tweets from the Bottomless Abyss

Reign of the Beast, Day 1,547

Four questions perplex me on Day 1,547 (also known as April 14, 2020), but, really, they are one question: What is Revelation's Beast? What does the Beast do? What is Donald Trump? What does Donald Trump do? The Beast embodies empire, as it always has, that empire forever reconfiguring, perpetually mutating. The Beast possesses, perennially, "power and [a] throne and

---

[14] Prominent members of this group have included (in addition to Massumi) Ben Anderson, Lauren Berlant, William Connolly, Lawrence Grossberg, Jasbir Puar, and Donovan Schaefer. See Ben Anderson, "'We Will Win Again. We Will Win a Lot': The Affective Styles of Donald Trump," *Society and Space* (February 28, 2017): https://www.societyandspace.org/articles/we-will-win-again-we-will-win-a-lot-the-affective-styles-of-donald-trump; Lauren Berlant, "Trump, or Political Emotions," *New Inquiry* (August 5, 2016): https://thenewinquiry.com/trump-or-politi cal-emotions/; Lauren Berlant, "Big Man," *Social Text* (January 19, 2017): https://socialtextjournal. org/big-man/; William E. Connolly, *Aspirational Fascism: The Struggle for Multifaceted Democracy under Trumpism*, Forerunners: Ideas First (Minneapolis: University of Minnesota Press, 2017); Lawrence Grossberg, *Under the Cover of Chaos: Trump and the Battle for the American Right* (London: Pluto Press, 2018); Jasbir Puar, "Postscript: Homonationalism in Trump Times," in her *Terrorist Assemblages: Homonationalism in Queer Times*, 10th ann. exp. ed. (Durham, NC: Duke University Press, 2017), 223–41; and Donovan O. Schaefer, "Whiteness and Civilization: Shame, Race, and the Rhetoric of Donald Trump," *Communication and Critical/Cultural Studies* 17, no. 1 (2019): 1–18.

[15] Grossberg leaves us in no doubt about that; see *Under the Cover of Chaos*, 10–11, 91–111.

244 THE BIBLE AFTER DELEUZE

great authority" (Rev 13:2). Or, in the incumbent Beast's own words: "Well, I have the ultimate authority. The president of the United States has the authority to do [fumbling pause] what the president has the authority to do, which is very powerful. . . . If somebody's the president of the United States the authority is total, and that's the way it's gotta be. . . . Total. It's total."[16]

The empire that the current Beast embodies, the ultimate source of its totalizing power, exceeds the nation for which the Beast is so solicitous ("We gotta put America first!"), overflows its borders immeasurably. That empire is global capitalism. But "embodies" is not the best term here; it is too static a descriptor for what the Beast is, for what it does, in relation to the chaotic, hydraulic megamachine that is global capitalism,

"Capitalism . . . has no exterior limit, but only an interior limit that is capital itself" (Deleuze and Guattari, *Anti-Oedipus*, 230–31).

an inconceivably colossal, infinitely fluid, incessantly restless, "so-called stateless, monetary mass" that circulates everywhere and encircles everything, "constituting a de facto supranational power" (Deleuze and Guattari, *A Thousand Plateaus*, 453). Vast and also voracious. But the Beast does not interpose its own considerable bulk between the omnivorous megamachine and its most vulnerable victims. The Beast loves walls, loves barriers, but is not itself a rampart of this sort. The Beast is "not a bulwark against the excesses of capitalism" but rather "an opening of the floodgates."[17] The Beast is itself, indeed, both the open floodgate and what flows through the floodgate. Far from taking a stand against capitalism's excesses, the Beast "flows with them"[18] and becomes them, identifying itself utterly with unfettered immoderation. The Beast is the very "personification of capital."[19]

"A personification is an expression of nonhuman forces,"[20] not least when that personification is a Beast and when what it personifies is capital.

---

[16] "Donald Trump: 'When Somebody Is President of the United States, the Authority Is Total'—Video," *The Guardian*, April 14, 2020: https://www.theguardian.com/us-news/video/2020/apr/14/donald-trump-when-somebody-is-president-of-the-united-states-the-authority-is-total-video.

[17] Brian Massumi, "Affect, Power, Violence—The Political Is Not Personal: Brad Evans Interviews Brian Massumi," *Los Angeles Review of Books* (November 13, 2017): https://lareviewofbooks.org/article/histories-of-violence-affect-power-violence-the-political-is-not-personal/. This interview includes Massumi's extended reflections on Trump.

[18] Massumi, "Affect, Power, Violence," n.p.

[19] Massumi, "Affect, Power, Violence," n.p.

[20] Brian Massumi, *99 Theses on the Revaluation of Value: A Postcapitalist Manifesto* (Minneapolis: University of Minnesota Press, 2018), 77. Massumi is reflecting further on Trump here.

POLITICS (BEASTLY BOASTS, APOCALYPTIC AFFECTS)   245

Universal human values are not the engine of global capitalism, to state the obvious. "The market is the only thing that is universal in capitalism" (Deleuze and Guattari, *What Is Philosophy?*, 106). Like capitalism itself, the Beast has, with spectacular success, "made a habit of feeding on the contradictions it gives rise to, on the crises it provokes, on the anxieties it engenders" (Deleuze and Guattari, *Anti-Oedipus*, 151). Like capitalism too, the Beast has long "ceased doubting itself," knowing that "no one has ever died from contradictions," not even billionaire populist politicians. "And the more it breaks down, . . . the better it works" (151). If capitalism is indeed "the end of history" (153), the glacially slow apocalypse, then the Beast is (for now, anyway) the (im)perfect personification of that improbably prolonged eschatological moment.

The Beast has ascended "from the bottomless abyss" (Rev 11:7),[21] but it is not only from the abyss that the Beast has ascended. Revelation 13:1 reads, "And I saw a Beast rising out of the sea." What is this sea that it should birth such a Beast?[22] This Beast is equipped with "a mouth," we also read, and that mouth *laloun megala*, "is speaking boastful things" (13:5; cf. Dan 7:8, 11, 20). More literally, and more aptly for the current Beast, that mouth is "talking big." "I play to people's fantasies," the Beast long ago confessed. "People may not always think big themselves, but they can still get very excited by those who do. That's why a little hyperbole never hurts. People want to believe that something is the biggest and the greatest and the most spectacular."[23]

The Beast's incessant bragging is awash in inconsistency, as we already observed. Its mouth utters "one thing one day, something else the next. The center does not hold. There is no center. There is just an eddy of bluster on the roiling seas of social media."[24] This then is the sea, these then are the seas, out of which the Beast has emerged. The particular sectors of social media that are

---

[21] The idea of infinite depth is implied in the Greek term *abyssos* (David E. Aune, *Revelation 6–16*, Word Biblical Commentary 52B [Nashville: Thomas Nelson, 1998], 525–26; Craig R. Koester, *Revelation: A New Translation with Introduction and Commentary*, The Anchor Yale Bible [New Haven, CT: Yale University Press, 2014], 456–57]), which is used seven times in Revelation, twice with reference to the Beast (11:7; 17:8). NRSV renders *abyssos* as "bottomless pit."

[22] And what manner of sea life is it? Already in 1989 Guattari could write, "Just as monstrous and mutant algae invade the lagoon of Venice, . . . men like Donald Trump are permitted to proliferate freely, like another species of algae, taking over entire districts of New York and Atlantic City; he 'redevelops' by raising rents, thereby driving out tens of thousands of poor families, most of whom are condemned to homelessness, becoming the equivalent of the dead fish of environmental ecology" (*The Three Ecologies*, 43).

[23] Donald J. Trump with Tony Schwartz, *Trump: The Art of the Deal* (New York: Ballantine Books, 1987), 58.

[24] Massumi, "Affect, Power, Violence," n.p.

the Beast's habitat "[breed] dark, degrading, and dehumanizing discourse"; they "[breed] vitriol and violence; in short [they breed] Donald Trump."[25] The Beast's obsession with Twitter, in particular, is legendary. Indeed, its "life-form" appears to be "inseparable from [Twitter]." The Beast "receives with a shudder waves of social and political static," and spews them "back out with a Twitter spasm, in a self-perpetuating cycle."[26] All of which is to say that the Beast and its Twitter account form a particularly potent affective assemblage, one consummately "capable of plugging into desire, of effectively taking charge of desire" (Deleuze and Guattari, *A Thousand Plateaus*, 166).

Whose desire, precisely, is a question for future journal musings. For Jasbir Puar is correct when she states that "the jolt of Trump is not that he revealed something heretofore unknown, but that he has accelerated and vastly expanded [it]."[27] The abyss out of which the Beast has crawled is capacious, indeed bottomless, because all the most abysmal aspects of US history are contained within its dismal depths.

Reign of the Beast, Day 1,816

The unthinkable has happened. The Beast's vocal cords have been forcibly removed. On this day of January 8, 2021, Twitter has permanently suspended

"...so that he would deceive the nations no more" (Rev 20:3).

the Beast's account.[28] Henceforth, all seven of the Beast's mouths (cf. Rev 13:1; 17:3, 7, 9) will continue to move as they always have, spouting boasts, spewing lies, and spitting racist slurs, but the Beast's followers will no longer be able to hear the words of the Beast. Its mouths will move ever more frantically, but now silently.

---

[25] Brian L. Ott, "The Age of Twitter: Donald J. Trump and the Politics of Debasement," *Critical Studies in Media Communication* 34, no. 1 (2017): 62.

[26] Massumi, "Affect, Power, Violence," n.p.

[27] Puar, "Homonationalism in Trump Times," 224.

[28] The Beast had been banned indefinitely from Facebook and Instagram the previous day.

POLITICS (BEASTLY BOASTS, APOCALYPTIC AFFECTS)   247

Post-Beast Interjection, June 1, 2021

It makes no difference. Although the Beast is still all but mute(d)—and not even mute on its throne but mute without a throne—the Beast still reigns with "power . . . and great authority" (Rev 13:2b). The Beast is still worshiped by its followers ("They worshiped the Beast"—13:4a), and those followers still intone, "Who is like the Beast, and who can fight against it?" (13:4b). And they are still fighting for it.

Reign of the Beast, Day 980

The Beast roars and the nation listens—rapt, enthused, disgusted, or amused. Endless boasts and tweets from the bottomless abyss. But blasphemies too. For the mouth that the media have bestowed on the Beast doesn't only talk big, it also talks blasphemously: "The Beast was given a mouth uttering boasts and blasphemies [*kai blasphēmias*]" (Rev 13:5). Against what does the Beast blaspheme? The Beast blasphemes against the egalitarian values that incrementally, painfully, over many generations, had established a foothold, or at least a toehold, in large sectors of the Beast's nation, values venerated, held sacred, in those sectors. Adorning the Beast's multiple, self-contradictory heads, indeed, are "names of blasphemy" (Rev 13:1, KJV): *racist, white supremacist, xenophobe, misogynist, sexual predator, homophobe, climate denier. . . .* As Massumi has noted, the Beast relishes "trading in cartoonish exaggerations" of political incorrectness, "refracted through the distorting prism of a white hypermasculinity bloated to absurd dimensions."[29] The Beast does not care that it is a cartoon rendition of itself. As Berlant has remarked, the Beast "is unafraid of being a cartoon because cartoon characters never die, they keep going long after mere humans would be destroyed."[30]

Although the Beast breathes out noxious ideologies, polluting vapors from the bottomless abyss,

> "There is no ideology, there are only organizations of power" (Deleuze, *Desert Islands*, 264).

---

[29] Massumi "Affect, Power, Violence," n.p.
[30] Berlant, "Trump, or Political Emotions," n.p.

248 THE BIBLE AFTER DELEUZE

the Beast is not, at base, an ideological animal. Although ideology still flourishes in the kingdom of the Beast, "often in the most virulent of forms," it is now merely "one mode of power in a larger field that is not defined, overall, by ideology."[31] The appearance of coherence necessary for political ideology is discarded in the post-ideological epoch, which Massumi sees as already emerging in the presidency of Ronald Reagan, who was "an idiocy musically coupled with an incoherence."[32] With the rise of the Beast, however, even the musicality has fallen, with a discordant jangle, into the abyss.

Yet the Beast's inarticulate incoherence is essential to its mesmerizing power. Revelation 13:3 reads, "One of [the Beast's] heads seemed to have received a death-blow, but its mortal wound [*hē plēgē tou thanatou autou*] had been healed." Spectacular inability on the part of any human head to sound "presidential"—except briefly when reading (robotically) from a teleprompter—or even to utter two successive well-formed sentences would, prior to the rise of the Beast, indeed have been a mortal wound, a deadly affliction, for the owner of the said head had he or she aspired to occupy the Oval Office. With a perpetually bandaged head and a mouth ever ready to spill over with absurdities,

> "... a certain mode of terror, which can entail a maximum of clownishness as well as grotesqueness" (Deleuze, *Desert Islands*, 108).

the Beast is the apocalyptic antitype of the traditional presidential statesman.

"In amazement," nonetheless, "the entire earth follow[s] the Beast" (Rev 13:3)—on Twitter, on Facebook, on Instagram, and on every news media outlet. Indeed, "all the inhabitants of the earth ... worship [the Beast]" (13:8; cf. 13:4, 12)—or at least the indefatigably self-exalting Beast assumes that they should. That was why the Beast was momentarily taken aback when, on September 25, 2018, a wave of laughter erupted from the floor of the United Nations General Assembly Hall in response to the Beast's casual boast that the achievements of its administration already exceeded those of any other

---

[31] Brian Massumi, *Parables for the Virtual: Movement, Affect, Sensation*, Post-Contemporary Interventions (Durham, NC: Duke University Press, 2002), 42. Massumi was not, of course, referencing Trump in this statement, but the Trump presidency might be regarded as the full flowering of post-ideological politics. As democratic socialist Bernie Sanders correctly observed, "Donald Trump is a guy who has absolutely no ideology. . . . His goal, his only goal is to win. . . . He will say or do anything to do that" (*RealClearPolitics*, April 9, 2020: https://www.realclearpolitics.com/video/2020/04/09/).

[32] Massumi, *Parables for the Virtual*, 41.

POLITICS (BEASTLY BOASTS, APOCALYPTIC AFFECTS) 249

in the history of its nation. Although the Beast is fervently loathed by legions of its US subjects, surprisingly little in the US political or cultural arenas had prepared it for this spontaneous show of collective derision. Massumi writes of Reagan, "What is astonishing is that Reagan wasn't laughed and jeered [at]."[33] Oh, but he was, just not, or not so much, in the United States. Symptomatic of the general derision directed toward Reagan in much of the rest of the world were his weekly appearances throughout his second term as a grotesque life-sized puppet on *Spitting Image*, the viciously satirical, and vastly popular, BBC show. Reagan was a figure of savage fun in Britain and beyond because he seemed to so many to be a vacuous imbecile, a ham actor of his own plastic persona.

With the Beast it's a little different. It has provided rich fodder for satire on a weekly, when not daily, basis ("More than any other president in the history of our country—not even close," the Beast itself might interject), and has indeed been lampooned mercilessly, most famously on *Saturday Night Live*. But the Beast flirts so consistently with self-caricature as to render caricature by others redundant. The Beast is a hyperbolic simulacrum of itself. The Beast is "the image of the Beast" (Rev 13:14–15; 14:9, 11; 15:2; 16:2; 19:20; 20:4), and that image is always teetering on the edge of excess—or plunging recklessly over that precipice. The Beast is always about to "go to destruction" (17:8, 11)—before bandaging its horrible head wound yet again and rising from the ruins of its own misrule.

Reign of the Beast, Day 1,385

The drunken spectacle of "Babylon the great, mother of whores and of earth's abominations" (Rev 17:4–6) has been insufficiently recognized by scholars of Revelation as an ancient political cartoon,

"Everything leads to laughter. . . . Everything is political" (Deleuze and Guattari, *Kafka*, 42).

---

[33] Massumi, *Parables for the Virtual*, 40.

250 THE BIBLE AFTER DELEUZE

a savage satire, a comedic send-up of imperial Rome. Still less has the Beast from the bottomless abyss been recognized as such.[34] Plug Donald J. Trump into Revelation's Beast machine, however, and gigantic gales of canned laughter (recorded in the UN General Assembly Hall) resound through the universe as he performs his abysmal stand-up schtick: "I was watching the other night the great Lou Dobbs [Fox television personality], and he said . . . , 'Trump is a great president.' *(Anticipatory chuckles.)* Then he said, 'Trump is the greatest president since Ronald Reagan.' Then he said . . . , 'No, no, Trump is an even better president than Ronald Reagan!' *(Whoops and whistles.)* And now he's got me down as the greatest president in the history of our country, including George Washington and Abraham Lincoln!'"[35] *(General unconstrained laughter.)*

Reign of the Beast, Day 1,551 / Plague Journal, April 18, 2020

The (Sea) Beast's knee-slapping stand-up routine is further enlivened by the entrance of the hilariously humorless Second Beast: "Then I saw another beast that rose up out of the earth . . ." (Rev 13:11). Who plays straight-man Land Beast to President Trump's Sea Beast? Why, Vice President Pence, of course. The function of the Land Beast, however, also known as "the False Prophet" (16:13; 19:20; 20:10), is not to cause "the earth and its inhabitants" to laugh at the First Beast so much as to "worship the First Beast" (13:12), and to paraphrase articulately the First Beast's inarticulate ramblings "so that the image of the Beast could even speak" (13:15).[36]

Vice President Pence's Land Beast role was never more obvious than during the daily White House Coronavirus Task Force press briefings, which began in March 2020 and continued for six weeks, one part bizarre reality show

---

[34] Both lacks have, however, recently been remedied by Sarah Emanuel; see her *Humor, Resistance, and Jewish Cultural Persistence in the Book of Revelation: Roasting Rome* (Cambridge: Cambridge University Press, 2020), 126–66.

[35] Verbatim from a Trump rally in Lexington, Kentucky: November 4, 2019, https://www.media matters.org/lou-dobbs/donald-trump-brags-about-lou-dobbs-declaring-him-greatest-president-history-our-country.

[36] *Post-Beast footnote:* The False Prophet is lamblike ("it had two horns like a lamb"—Rev 13:11), docile in relation to the Sea Beast. Ultimately, however, the False Prophet did not prove docile or deceitful enough for the Sea Beast, declining to conspire with it in overturning the results of the 2020 presidential election. The Sea Beast turned savagely on the Land Beast in consequence (lambs should not consort with predators); and when the Beast's army invaded the Capitol on January 6, 2021, chants of "Hang Mike Pence!" echoed through the building and a makeshift scaffold was erected outside it.

POLITICS (BEASTLY BOASTS, APOCALYPTIC AFFECTS)   251

(Trump repeatedly touting the television ratings of the briefings on Twitter as "through the roof"—"Monday Night Football, Bachelor Finale type numbers")[37] and two parts surreal reelection rally ("Going to win. We're going to close it out. . . . Look at us: We had the greatest economy in the history of the world. . . . We had the highest stock market in history, by far. And I'm honored by the fact that it has started to go up very substantially. That's because the market is smart. . . . And they're viewing it like we've done a good job. . . . We've done a fantastic job. We're the talk of other nations").[38] And the Land Beast's function in this unreal spectacle? The Trump reinvented in VP Pence's unctuous utterances (the object of his obsequious effusions all the while hovering by his shoulder) was a pillar of wisdom, a beacon of guidance, and a fountain of compassion for his virus-beleaguered people: "Thank you, Mr. President. This day should be an inspiration to every American . . . thanks to your leadership. . . . Mr. President, from early on, you took decisive action. . . . Mr. President, you have forged a seamless partnership with every state and every territory in this country to put the health of our nation first."[39]

We should not be surprised; we should rather be *amazed*. For with uncanny aptness, Revelation declares "amazement" to be the primary affect engendered by the First Beast (as in: First Lady, First Family, First Beast): "In amazement the entire earth followed the Beast" (literally, "And the entire earth was amazed after the Beast" [*kai ethaumasthē holē hē gē opisō tou thēriou*]—13:3). This amazement, like the Beast's multiple heads, is able to face in two directions at once. It is the awed, true-believer wonder of those for whom the Beast is indeed the most amazing president in the history of the United States ("In the history of the world, even," the Beast adds). Simultaneously, it is the drop-jawed, disbelieving astonishment of those who are still regularly stunned by what comes out of the Beast's mouth. And awful things do come out of it: "And I saw three foul spirits like frogs coming from the mouth of the Dragon, from the mouth of the Beast, and from the mouth of the False Prophet" (Rev 16:13).

---

[37] Donald J. Trump, Twitter posts, April 8–10, 2020: http://twitter.com/realDonaldTrump.

[38] Sample remarks culled from the White House Coronavirus Task Force Press Briefing of April 18, 2020: https://www.whitehouse.gov/briefings-statements/remarks-president-trump-members-coro navirus-task-force-press-briefing-2/.

[39] Representative remarks taken from the White House Coronavirus Task Force Press Briefing of March 13, 2020: https://theconservativetreehouse.com/2020/03/13/transcript-of-coronavirus-task-force-press-conference/.

252 THE BIBLE AFTER DELEUZE

Reign of the Beast, Day 1,517 / Plague Journal, March 15, 2020

The COVID-19 crisis is, of course, proving definitive for the Beast, revealing more than any previous event what the Beast "was and is not" (Rev 17:8, 11). The Beast's name will now forever be linked with the novel coronavirus, the virus that takes its name from its crownlike structure. With impeccable logic, therefore, when the Beast is first described in Revelation, it is said to have multiple "crowns" (*diadēmata*) on its horns. Uncharacteristically, the current Beast does not relish this regal adornment. It has tried repeatedly to shrug it off, indeed, shaking its many heads vigorously, each one voicing its own disavowal of the novel coronavirus ("It's one person coming in from China. We have it totally under control"; "It will go away in April with the heat"; "Within a couple of days it's going to be down to close to zero"; "It's going to disappear. One day—it's like a miracle [conjuring hand gesture]—it will disappear"), but to no avail. The Beast is stuck to it and stuck with it. The Beast may not (yet) have the virus, but the virus has the Beast by the horns.

Reign of the Beast, Day 1,560 / Plague Journal, April 27, 2020

The novel coronavirus early infected the contemporary reception of Revelation, as we saw, mutating into an apocalyptic event as it passed into the book and coursed through its pages. How precisely did the virus affect, or infect, the Beast? Particularly pertinent here is Revelation 16:10, the fifth of the seven eschatological plagues "pour[ed] out upon the earth" (16:1), as it is the plague that touches the Beast most directly: "The fifth angel poured out his vial [*phialē*][40] upon the throne of the Beast, and its kingdom was plunged into darkness" (16:10). The throne of the Beast, the seat and source of its globe-encircling power, is, first and foremost, the economy it inherited, and this economy is what the coronavirus plague has paralyzed.

The kingdom that was plunged into darkness by the plague was an eschatological kingdom, the capitalist utopia toward which all human history had

---

[40] Resurrecting the KJV's translation of *phialē* as "vial" throughout Revelation (see also 15:7; 16:1–4, 8, 12, 17; 17:1; 21:9, together with 5:8). The term "vial," which, as it happens, derives from *phialē*, seems particularly apt in the current context, evoking for the contemporary ear—most of all the contemporary Trumpian ear acutely attuned to conspiracy theories—a divine laboratory in heaven where deadly chemical agents are concocted.

been tending, at least as the Beast sees it. "I built the greatest economy in the history of the world," the Beast boasted at the Coronavirus Task Force press briefing today, April 27, 2020.[41] "No one [could] buy or sell" in that utopia "who did not have the mark . . . of the Beast" (Rev 13:17), for they all owed their prosperity to the Beast. But the plague came and the economy died.

As the personification of capital, the Beast is affectively equipped to feel wrenching loss, searing grief, only at capital's demise. In the Task Force press briefings, it doesn't even pretend to be affected by the virus's horrifically escalating death toll. On the rare occasions it mentions that toll, already exacted or still impending, individual lives tended to be rolled into the impersonal abstraction "death" and the delivery tends to be flat and emotionless: "And there will be a lotta death, unfortunately, but a lot less death than if this wasn't done [the Beast's 'China ban'], but there will be death."[42] As Lauren Berlant has observed in a different context, "[Affective] flatness is different than lack. It is not only a subtraction, but a form of performance, a style of showing up."[43]

Who or what was showing up in the Beast's flat death prediction, its flatline performance? What other monster was performing on that occasion in addition to the "corpse-green horse [*hippos chlōros*] [whose] rider's name was Death" and who had been "given authority over a fourth of the earth to kill with . . . pestilence" (Rev 6:7–8)? The many-tentacled monster of systemic racism, perhaps? Even as the Beast was pronouncing its "lotta death" sentence, African American communities were, at grotesquely disproportionate rates, bearing the brunt of the COVID-19 death toll across the United States.

Larval Fascisms, Insect Apocalypses

Reign of the Beast, Day 1,310

What, then, is the Trump machine, the Beast machine? Having now reigned 1,310 days, what has it shown itself to be? It is a mouth, mainly ("The Beast was given a mouth . . ."—Rev 13:5), an organic mouth that is

---

[41] From the transcript: https://www.democraticunderground.com/10021335936.

[42] "There Will Be a Lot of Death': Trump Warning as COVID-19 Cases in US Pass 300,000," *The Guardian*: April 5, 2020, https://www.theguardian.com/world/video/2020/apr/05/there-will-be-a-lot-of-death-trump-warning-as-covid-19-cases-in-us-pass-300000-video.

[43] Lauren Berlant, "Affective Assemblages: Entanglements and Ruptures—An Interview with Lauren Berlant," *Atlantis* 38, no. 2 (2017): 16.

254 THE BIBLE AFTER DELEUZE

also an electronic mouth. This mouth brags constantly ("speaking boastful things"—13:5) and lies continually. Through its fabrications, astonishing in their profusion, it produces its own habitat, one in which it is an object of worship for its followers: "They worshiped the Beast, saying, 'Who is like the Beast . . . ?'" (13:4). The Beast nods its seven heads sagely, and retweets approvingly ("Thank you for the very nice words. . . . Wow!"), an effusion by an especially devout follower declaring the Beast to be "the King of Israel" and "the second coming of God."[44] This same day, August 21, 2019, the Beast has announced on the north lawn of the White House, while looking up to heaven,

> "The despot or god brandishes [his] solar face" (Deleuze and Guattari, *A Thousand Plateaus*, 115).

"I am the Chosen One."[45]

The Beast is also a political paradox of the first order. On the one hand, the Beast uniquely embodies the telos of democracy, the election to the most powerful political office on the planet of someone who might as well have been plucked at random from the *demos*, the people, milling in the street (Wall Street, anyway, if not yet Main Street), so spectacularly unqualified is he to assume the immensely consequential responsibilities of that office. On the other hand, the Beast's election and the nature of its reign emblematize, not just the crisis of democracy, but, incrementally and seemingly inexorably, its final failure,

> "Democratic States are so bound up with, and compromised by, dictatorial States that the defense of human rights must necessarily take up the internal criticism of every democracy" (Deleuze and Guattari, *What Is Philosophy?*, 106).

the erosion of its values and institutions,

> "Democratic, dictatorial, totalitarian . . .".

---

[44] Donald J. Trump, Twitter post, August 21, 2019: http://twitter.com/realDonaldTrump.

[45] Kevin Breuninger, "'I Am the Chosen One,' Trump Proclaims as He Defends Trade War with China," *CNBC*, August 21, 2019: https://www.cnbc.com/2019/08/21/i-am-the-chosen-one-trump-proclaims-as-he-defends-china-trade-war.html.

POLITICS (BEASTLY BOASTS, APOCALYPTIC AFFECTS)   255

its potential slippage back into the bottomless abyss where the Beast has its lair and out of which every cruel, capricious, or deranged despot in history had crawled—until democracy stepped in, ostensibly to put an end to dynastic games of chance that could put a monster, a moron, or a moronic monster on the throne.

The totalitarian tendencies of democracy that Deleuze and Guattari wrote about more than thirty years ago have been inflamed immeasurably and made luridly visible by the utterances and actions of the Beast. Democracy is never an achieved state; it is only ever a process, a "becoming-democratic" that is not a "State of law" (*What Is Philosophy?*, 113), much less a State of Law and Order of the sort venerated by the Beast.[46] The conundrum for the *democratic process* (as we customarily and appropriately term it) is that "democracies are majorities, but a becoming is by its nature that which always eludes the majority" (108). Meanwhile within the United States, as democracy labors to actualize its virtuality,

"The actual is not what we are but, rather, what we . . . are in the process of becoming" (112).

Europeanization continues to masquerade as democracy. "Europeanization does not constitute a becoming," however, but is "merely the history of capitalism, which prevents the becoming of subjected peoples" (108). The white-nationalist Beast, itself the veritable personification of capitalism-as-Europeanization, simply shrugs and yawns.

Reign of the Beast, Day 1,289 / Plague Journal, July 31, 2019

What is the reason for the Beast's amazing success? What is the Beast, exactly, for its followers? What does it enable them to be and to do? And how is that being and doing affected, infected, by COVID-19?

Trumpism is itself an infection. Consider the Beast at its most iconic, towering above the throng at a rally, whipping it into a frenzy. As Michael Richardson notes, "Crowds are affective formations . . . , particularly susceptible to contagion, the leaping of affect from body to body,"[47] and a Trump

---

[46] Law and Order is a prominent theme of the post-Beast postscript with which this chapter ends.

[47] Michael Richardson, "The Disgust of Donald Trump," *Continuum* 31, no. 6 (2017): 752.

256   THE BIBLE AFTER DELEUZE

rally is a superspreader event for such affective contagion. The Trump rally is also a particularly arresting example of what Lauren Berlant has termed "an intimate public,"[48] an "affect world" in which "matters of survival" are urgently at stake. "You do not need to audition for membership in [an intimate public]. Minimally, you need just to perform audition, to listen," and to open yourself unreservedly to the "visceral impact" of that highly charged space.[49]

This is not to imply that the intimate-public participants in a Trump rally have no active role to play in the performance. For it is not the Beast that roars at the rally, but rather the crowd that is an active extension of the Beast, forming with it a machinic assemblage of interreacting bodies (Deleuze and Guattari, *A Thousand Plateaus*, 88). And what does the becoming-Beastly crowd

> **"A becoming-animal always involves a pack, a band, a population, a peopling, in short, a multiplicity" (239).**

roar? "Incantations of containment and control":[50] "Build that wall!" "Lock her up!" "Send her back!"[51]

As it happens, an impressively high wall bisects the final two chapters of Revelation. The book's climactic vision is set in a divinely designed gated community,

> **"All relatively healthy readers of the Apocalypse will feel they are already in the lake of sulfur" (Deleuze, *Essays Critical and Clinical*, 46).**

a heavenly walled enclave. The celestial city that descends to earth in this culminating vision is surrounded by a high wall ("It has a great, high wall"—Rev

---

[48] Lauren Berlant, *Cruel Optimism* (Durham, NC: Duke University Press, 2011), 226.

[49] Berlant, *Cruel Optimism*, 226.

[50] Richardson, "The Disgust of Donald Trump," 752.

[51] Hillary Clinton has been the most frequent target of the Trump rally "Lock her up!" chant. In July 2019, Democratic congresswoman Ilhan Omar, an outspoken Trump critic and a US citizen who had come to the country as a child refugee from Somalia, became the target of the "Send her back!" chant. A "Send them back!" chant also flourished briefly during this period, three other Democratic congresswomen of color, Alexandria Ocasio-Cortez, Ayanna Pressley, and Rashida Tlaib, all born in the United States, being grouped with Omar as its target. Trump had earlier tweeted, "So interesting to see 'Progressive' Democrat Congresswomen, who originally came from countries whose governments are a complete and total catastrophe, the worst, most corrupt and inept anywhere in the world (if they even have a functioning government at all), now loudly and viciously telling the people of the United States, the greatest and most powerful Nation on earth, how our government is to be run. Why don't they go back and help fix the totally broken and crime infested places from which they came?" Donald J. Trump, Twitter post, July 14, 2019: http://twitter.com/realDonaldTrump.

21:12), "one hundred forty-four cubits" high (21:17), to be precise, which translates to around two hundred sixteen feet,

"The New Jerusalem . . . is an architectural terror" (46).

a height far exceeding even the Beast's most ambitious dreams for its own wall: "I will build a great wall, and nobody builds walls better than me, believe me. . . . I will build a great, great wall." Like the Beast's wall, designed to exclude anathematized ethnic others ("You wouldn't believe how bad these people are. These aren't people. These are animals"),[52] the heavenly city's wall is also designed to shut out undesirables,

"There is a great resemblance between the New Jerusalem and the future that we are now being promised" (45).

including animalized others: "Outside are the dogs [*hoi kynes*][53] and sorcerers and fornicators . . . " (Rev 22:15).

Plugging the Revelation machine into the Trump machine causes the latter to light up but it also causes the former to malfunction. Circuits are scrambled, components melt into each other. Within the Revelation-Trump megamachine, God is no longer the only builder of a wall; the Beast becomes obsessed with building its own wall, and would love nothing better than to build it to an ungodly height. But this usurpation is part of a larger disintegration. Pre-Trump Revelation constructed God's empire as rigidly regulated by purity codes. Before Trump, the God-ordained symbolic lines of separation in Revelation ran obsessively between the pure and the polluted, the unmixed and the hybrid (e.g., 3:4–5; 7:14b; 14:4–5; 19:8, 14; 21:27; 22:14–15). The pre-Trump Beast, its proxies, and its entire empire, in contrast, were a seething morass of cultic impurity and cultural hybridity (e.g., 2:14, 20–21; 17:4–5; 18:2).[54] But when the Revelation machine is plugged into the Trump

---

[52] Gregory Korte and Alan Gomez, "Trump Ramps Up Rhetoric on Undocumented Immigrants," *USA Today*, May 17, 2018: https://www.usatoday.com/story/news/politics/2018/05/16/trump-imm igrants-animals-mexico-democrats-sanctuary-cities/617252002/.

[53] A term some scholars of Revelation have interpreted as denoting sexual deviants. For examples and discussion, see Eric A. Thomas, "The Futures Outside: Apocalyptic Epilogue Unveiled as Africana Queer Prologue," in *Sexual Disorientations: Queer Temporalities, Affects, Theologies*, ed. Kent L. Brintnall, Joseph A. Marchal, and Stephen D. Moore, Transdisciplinary Theological Colloquia (New York: Fordham University Press, 2018), 94–97.

[54] The first scholars of Revelation to recognize the extent of its preoccupation with purity were David Frankfurter, "Jews or Not? Reconstructing the 'Other' in Rev 2:9 and 3:9," *Harvard Theological*

258 THE BIBLE AFTER DELEUZE

machine, the separatist imperative ("Come out of her, my people"—18:4) passes into the Beast like an immense electric charge, and the Beast itself becomes an uncompromising custodian of purity.

For as Richardson perceives, "Walls and bans are not simply policies of exclusion, but of purity."[55] Their function is to "harden the lines"[56] between one culture conceived as preeminent, privileged, and pristine—in a word, as *white* ("I saw a great white throne"—Rev 20:11)—and other cultures conceived as inferior, polluted, and defiling. "Why are we having all these people from shithole countries come here?" rages the Beast.[57] In short, the purpose of the Beast's wall and its bans is to "[prevent] transmission that might . . . infect the homeland."[58]

Richardson's use of epidemiological metaphors for Trumpism here and elsewhere in his pre-COVID-19 article acquires added significance from the pandemic. Richardson sums up the Trumpist white-nationalist mindset as follows: "If the economy is sick, if communities are sick, if life is just *different* now, then it must be because some impurity has crossed over. All too often, this is an impurity embodied by the other who looks, speaks or acts differently."[59] In the transformed social world ushered in by COVID-19—a world in which life is undeniably different, in which communities and economies are desperately ill—the Beast has instinctively seized on the virus as a potent metaphor—or, better, a potent *metaforce*[60]—for the cultural crisis, the existential threat, that undocumented immigrants, migrants, asylum seekers, and refugees

> "Degrees of deviance in relation to the White-Man face . . . People who should be like us and whose crime it is not to be" (Deleuze and Guattari, *A Thousand Plateaus*, 178).

Review 94, no. 4 (2001): esp. 410–12; and John W. Marshall, *Parables of War: Reading John's Jewish Apocalypse* (Waterloo, ON: Wilfred Laurier University Press, 2001), esp. 155–62.

[55] Richardson, "The Disgust of Donald Trump," 747.

[56] Richardson, "The Disgust of Donald Trump," 748.

[57] Leighton Akio Woodhouse, "Trump's 'Shithole Countries' Remark Is at the Center of a Lawsuit to Reinstate Protections for Immigrants," *The Intercept*, June 28, 2018: https://theintercept.com/2018/06/28/trump-tps-shithole-countries-lawsuit/. Trump's former attorney Michael Cohen also testified that Trump once asked him if "could name a country run by a black person that wasn't a 'shithole.'" From Cohen's testimony to the Committee on Oversight and Reform of the U.S. House of Representatives, February 27, 2019: https://www.theguardian.com/us-news/2019/feb/27/full-text-michael-cohen-statement-to-congress.

[58] Richardson, "The Disgust of Donald Trump," 748.

[59] Richardson, "The Disgust of Donald Trump," 751.

[60] See n. 13 earlier.

POLITICS (BEASTLY BOASTS, APOCALYPTIC AFFECTS)   259

embody in its xenophobic demagoguery.

Reign of the Beast, Day 1,533 / Plague Journal, March 31, 2020

In an Oval Office address to the nation on March 11, 2020, the Beast described COVID-19 as the "foreign virus." By now, just a few weeks later, the Beast is repeatedly referring to the pandemic as "the plague." Both characterizations of COVID-19 appear to be intimately interlinked in the Beastly psyche. Pre-COVID-19 and for the prepresidential Beast, Ebola was the plague. Attempting to stoke (white) hysteria during the West African Ebola outbreak of 2014 to 2016, the Beast grimly warned that unless the United States banned flights from the region, "the plague will start and spread inside our 'borders'"[61] (scare quotes around "borders" regarded as too porous to protect against contamination). And when President Obama sent a military force to Liberia to build healthcare facilities there and train medical personnel, the Beast exclaimed, "Why are we sending . . . soldiers into Ebola infested areas of Africa! Bring the plague back to U.S.?"[62]

Reign of the Beast, Day 1,556 / Plague Journal, April 23, 2020

"Outside are the dogs," Revelation's Christ declares of the book's eschatological wall (22:15).[63] "Outside are the vermin," the Beast might declare of its own desired wall. "Infest," "infested," and "infestation" have, for the Beast, always been ready terms of contempt when speaking about people of color. Democrats "want illegal immigrants . . . to pour into and infest our Country."[64] The predominantly African American Baltimore district of Congressman Elijah Cummings "is a disgusting, rat and rodent infested mess,"[65] as is the Atlanta district of African American civil rights icon and congressman John

---

[61] Quoted in John J. Pitney Jr., *Un-American: The Fake Patriotism of Donald J. Trump* (Lanham, MD: Rowman and Littlefield, 2020), 62.

[62] Quoted in Pitney, *Un-American*, 62.

[63] Taking Jesus to be the speaker of Rev 22:14–15 (cf. 22:12–13, 16).

[64] Quoted in Pitney, *Un-American*, 62–63.

[65] Quoted in Pitney, *Un-American*, 63.

260   THE BIBLE AFTER DELEUZE

Lewis.[66] Sanctuary cities that harbor undocumented immigrants are "crime-infested" and "breeding" sites.[67] And too much else of that ilk to list.

Deleuze's insectile trope "larval fascism" (*Essays Critical and Clinical*, 4) is especially apt here. For the Beast's infestation image amounts not just to an animalization of the racial other,[68] but to a verminization of the racial other.[69] And vermin are carriers of plague. This is a particularly virulent example of what Gerald V. O'Brien has termed "the organism metaphor,"[70] a means "for denigrating vulnerable populations" that feeds on visceral revulsion at the possibility of one's physical or social body being invaded by aliens, parasites, germs, or other creatures of nightmare. The organism metaphor, deployed against immigrants and migrants of color, together with other "foreign bodies," exploits this primal horror rhetorically.

The perceived infestation of the vermin causes worshipers of the Beast to "gnaw their tongues in agony" and "curse God" because of their imagined "pains and sores,"

"Delirium is a disease, the disease par excellence, whenever it erects a race it claims is pure" (Deleuze, *Essays Critical and Clinical*, 4).

as Revelation reports when the fifth plague-bowl (a bowl of vermin?) is "poured out," the one poured directly "upon the throne of the Beast"

---

[66] Doug Criss, "Atlanta Hasn't Forgotten That Trump Called It 'Crime Infested' and in 'Horrible Shape,'" *CNN*, January 9, 2018: https://edition.cnn.com/2018/01/08/politics/trump-atlanta-trnd/index.html.

[67] Z. Byron Wolf, "Trump Blasts 'Breeding' in Sanctuary Cities. That's a Racist Term," *CNN*, April 24, 2018: https://www.cnn.com/2018/04/18/politics/donald-trump-immigrants-california/index.html.

[68] Congressman Cummings's district is a place where "no human being would want to live." Earlier, an underresourced area of Chicago through which Trump was being driven elicited the comment "that only the blacks could live like this" (Michael Cohen's testimony to the Committee on Oversight and Reform of the US House of Representatives, February 27, 2019: https://www.theguardian.com/us-news/2019/feb/27/full-text-michael-cohen-statement-to-congress).

[69] We are no longer on the train with Frantz Fanon and the finger-pointing white child (see pp. 205–208 earlier); we are now on the train with Audre Lorde, herself still a child. Audre's mother has hastily seated her next to a white woman on the Christmas-crowded New York City subway train to Harlem. The woman's mouth "twitches" as she glares at the five-year-old girl. "Her gaze drops down, pulling mine with it. Her leather-gloved hand plucks at the line where my new blue snowpants and her sleek fur coat meet. She jerks her coat closer to her. I look. I do not see whatever terrible thing she is seeing on the seat between us—probably a roach. But she has communicated her horror to me. . . . And suddenly I realize there is nothing crawling up the seat between us; it is me she doesn't want her coat to touch" (Audre Lorde, *Sister Outsider: Essays and Speeches* [Berkeley, CA: Crossing Press, 1984], 147).

[70] Gerald V. O'Brien, *Contagion and the National Body: The Organism Metaphor in American Thought* (New York: Routledge, 2018), 2 (although without reference to Trump or his infestation trope).

POLITICS (BEASTLY BOASTS, APOCALYPTIC AFFECTS)   261

(16:10–11). The intolerable sensation of the vermin skittering across its flesh, entering the orifices of its body, the unbearable feeling of being invaded, of being contaminated, causes the Beast to descend into madness on national television, climbing naked into its tanning bed while clutching a bottle of disinfectant and a syringe:

> So, supposedly we hit the body with a tremendous, whether it's ultraviolet or just a very powerful light. . . . And then I said supposing you brought the light inside the body, which you can do either through the skin or in some other way. . . . Sounds interesting, right? And then I see the disinfectant, where it knocks it out in one minute. And is there a way we can do something like that by injection inside or almost a cleaning because you see it gets in the lungs and does a tremendous number on the lungs, so it would be interesting to check that so that you're going to have to use medical doctors with [*sic*], but it sounds interesting to me.[71]

The "mortal wound" (Rev 13:3, 12), finally, from which no politician in a democratic society could possibly recover? "It'll heal," mutters the Beast impatiently, climbing out of the tanning bed and swabbing its bleeding head with a towel. "It always does."

Reign of the Beast, Day 1,607 / Plague Journal, June 13, 2020

The Beast is a creature of disgust, not only in the sense that its words and actions disgust innumerable people in its own kingdom and around the world, but in the sense that it is driven by disgust. It is disgusted by the leakiness, the porousness, the messiness of bodies—the national body but also the human body, specifically the *female* human body, the Beast infamously declaring of Republican presidential debate moderator Megyn Kelly, "There was blood coming out of her eyes, blood coming out of her wherever,"[72] and of Hillary Clinton taking a bathroom break during a Democratic presidential debate, "I know where she went, it's disgusting, I don't want to talk

---

[71] From the White House Coronavirus Task Force Press Briefing of April 23, 2020: https://www.rev.com/blog/transcripts/donald-trump-coronavirus-press-conference-transcript-april-23.

[72] Ironically, this was Trump's subsequent characterization of the following statement made to him by Kelly in the debate: "You've called women you don't like fat pigs, dogs, slobs, and disgusting animals."

262   THE BIBLE AFTER DELEUZE

about it. No, it's too disgusting. Don't say it, it's disgusting, let's not talk," a pleonastic outburst of gynophobic revulsion that also plugs magnetically into Revelation. For Hillary Rodham Clinton, even before she became the Democratic nominee for president of the United States, was, in the right-wing evangelical imagination, a leading candidate for the "Great Whore" role in Revelation (17:1; 19:2; cf. 17:5); and the Beast is scripted to "loathe the Whore" and demean her absolutely and obliteratively (17:16). "Such a nasty woman!"[73]

The national body with its no less leaky borders is equally an object of re-vulsion and anxiety for the Beast, eliciting reflexive gestures of sealing up, shutting out, and warding off. The unsettlingly open national body is per-ceived by the Beast as vulnerable to infecting infestations, to swarms of sub-human vermin pouring into it like a plague. Measures designed to turn back the influx of immigrants, migrants, and refugees of color ("my beautiful wall," "my Muslim ban") have, more recently, been supplemented by measures designed to turn back the influx of viral infection by excluding those whom the Beast has branded the virus's most noxious carriers ("my China ban").

The two primary meanings of "plague," literal and metaphorical, thereby merge in the Beast's visceral rhetoric of revulsion. The virus ("I call it the invisible enemy")[74] becomes in that rhetoric a metaphor for undocu-mented border crossers (whom the Beast apparently considered labeling "enemy combatants" at one time).[75] More precisely, the migrant plague is metamorphosed

> "Metamorphosis is the contrary of metaphor. There is no longer any proper sense or figurative sense. . . . Instead, it is now a question of a be-coming, . . . the crossing of a barrier" (Deleuze and Guattari, *Kafka*, 22).

into the virus plague within the belly of the Beast ("I have a gut, and my gut tells me more sometimes than anybody else's brain can ever tell me")[76] and

---

[73] Trump's putdown of Clinton, uttered with deliberate audibility during the final presidential de-bate of 2016 as she criticized his policy on Social Security.

[74] A Trump refrain during the White House Coronavirus Task Force press briefings.

[75] So Anon, *A Warning* (New York: Hachette, 2019), 42: "If we said these illegals were a national security threat, Trump reasoned, then the administration had an excuse to keep all of them out of the country." The anonymous author of this whistle-blowing book credibly claimed to be an official in the Trump administration.

[76] Sarah Zhang, "Trump's Most Trusted Adviser Is His Own Gut," *The Atlantic*, January 13, 2019: https://www.theatlantic.com/politics/archive/2019/01/trump-follows-his-gut/580084/.

POLITICS (BEASTLY BOASTS, APOCALYPTIC AFFECTS)   263

transmitted, thus transmuted, from the Beast's mouth, without ever having passed through the Beast's conscious mind.

What is transmitted through that mouth—the "mouth given to" the Beast (Rev 13:5)—is *infection*; for the Beast's disgust is highly contagious, a pandemic in itself. Trump's fervent followers open themselves up to their leader's disgust, allow themselves to be infected by it,

> "Interests can be deceived, . . . but not desire. . . . No, the masses were not deceived, they desired fascism, and that is what has to be explained" (Deleuze and Guattari, *Anti-Oedipus*, 257).

and flood him with their own disgust in turn, in a continuous politico-epidemiological loop. The followers *feel with* the leader, and while so many nonfollowers are disgusted *by* him, the followers are disgusted *with* him,[77] channeling their revulsion through his, and feeling it flow back into them in an ecstatic process of circulation

> "There is a circuit of states that forms a mutual becoming, in . . . a necessarily multiple or collective assemblage" (Deleuze and Guattari, *Kafka*, 22).

that is the lifeblood of the national body they crave, fantasized as a pellucidly white, entirely decontaminated body. That is why Trumpism is a secular religion of purification and why the Beast is an addictive object of worship for its most ardent followers: "And they worshiped the Beast saying, 'Who is like the Beast . . . ?'" (Rev 13:4). To which the Beast continually replies, implicitly but occasionally explicitly, "There's nobody like me. Nobody."[78]

---

[77] Richardson, "The Disgust of Donald Trump," 753.
[78] Donald J. Trump, *Crippled America: How to Make America Great Again* (New York: Simon & Schuster, 2015), 74.

264   THE BIBLE AFTER DELEUZE

Horrible Hope

Reign of the Beast, Day 1,532 / Plague Journal, March 30, 2020

Hope in a time of emerging autocracy? Optimism in a time of proliferating plague? The Beast may be regarded as a consummate object of what Lauren Berlant has termed *cruel optimism*—so much so, indeed, that her 2011 book of that title reads at times like a secular prophecy of the rise and reign of the Beast.[79] As she explains, "A relation of cruel optimism exists when something you desire is actually an obstacle to your flourishing. It might involve . . . a kind of love; it might be a fantasy of the good life, or a political project." Such optimism becomes cruel "when the object that draws your attachment actively impedes the aim that brought you to it initially."[80]

In the case of the Beast and its followers, that the latter were drawn to the former in the first place, that they so fervently invest their hope in its cult, is an enigma to those who do not bear "the mark . . . of the Beast" (Rev 13:17). "By what criterion," muses Massumi, "is there an identity or sameness between a billionaire born into wealth and privilege and a middle American in the Rust Belt with the fear of God in them about falling into poverty (if they are not already in it)?"[81] As Massumi also recognizes, however, it is not identification as representational mimesis that fuels the Trump machine but identification as affective immersion. His followers do not identify with him so much as submerge themselves in what flows through him—in "capitalism's

---

[79] The US president when the book was published was, of course, Barack Obama, and although Berlant only devotes a single paragraph to his presidency, he is a felt presence in much of the remainder of the book. She writes of "the election of Barack Obama as the President of the emotional infrastructure of the United States as well as its governing and administrative ones," and asks, "What is the effect of Obama's optimization of political optimism against the political depression of the historically disappointed, especially given the President's limited sovereignty as a transformative agent in ordinary life? . . . Splitting off political optimism from the way things are can sustain many kinds of the cruelest optimism" (*Cruel Optimism*, 228).

[80] Berlant, *Cruel Optimism*, 1.

[81] Massumi, "Affect, Power, Violence," n.p. Even the apparent physical resemblance of the Beast to many of its devotees is an illusion, Carleigh Morgan argues: "Trump looks as fit as the average American," but the corporeal resemblance is mere "hallucination." Trump's body is "the product of a lifestyle of luxurious, conspicuous excess. . . . He has never been in the position of foregoing diabetes medication due to rising medication prices; has never had to settle for junk food while living in an economically depressed food desert littered with high fat, high salt, edible detritus; he does not know what it is like to stitch up his own lacerated hand because the thought of incurring several thousand dollars in Emergency Room bills might provoke yet another psychic and physical trauma. . . . He is a fake body attached to a simulated image." Carleigh Morgan, "Trump: Image without Body," *Furtherfield* (May 18, 2017): https://www.furtherfield.org/trump-image-without-body/.

deregulated overspilling of the norms," in "'politically incorrect' excess over regulated norms of behavior,"[82] in a fantasized "exceptionalism" experienced as a continuous consolidation of their own exemplary Americanness over against all non-Americans everywhere and all "un-American" Americans at home: liberals, progressives, and their "fake news" / mainstream media mouthpieces; the "deep state" establishment; immigrant "job-stealers"; "entitled" African Americans, and on down the ever-expanding list.[83]

The hope invested in the Beast feels, for many of its followers, like a desperate hope, a last hope. Berlant's words, written before the rise of the Beast, are again apt: "Cruel optimism is the condition of maintaining an attachment to a significantly problematic object, [such] that the loss of the promising object . . . itself will defeat the capacity to have any hope about anything."[84] But incapacity to have any hope about anything, ever again, is no less a life-or-death issue for Beast loathers, and it hinges no less than for Beast lovers on the Beast's ultimate victory or defeat. For the legions of those within the United States for whom Trump is an abomination, "the significantly problematic object" might be the dream that he be defeated in the 2020 presidential election—significantly problematic because Trump, whatever outrages he utters, whatever injustices he enacts, can never be pronounced politically dead, his many "mortal wounds," all apparent "death-blows," somehow being "healed" (Rev 13:3, 12) over and again,

"[The Apocalypse] is the book of Zombies" (Deleuze, *Essays Critical and Clinical*, 37).

as his election as president in the first place already demonstrated. And so devastating might be "the loss of the promising object"—someone else, anyone else, in the White House—as to defeat utterly thereafter the capacity of Beast loathers "to have any hope about anything," politically speaking. Optimism on either side of the political divide in this instance seems equally cruel.

What happens when we plug the book of Revelation into "the emotional infrastructure"[85] of cruel optimism? What does Revelation, thus connected,

[82] Cf. Berlant, "Trump, or Political Emotions," n.p.: "You watch him calculating, yet not seeming to care about the consequences of what he says, and you listen to his supporters enjoying the feel of his freedom."
[83] Massumi, "Affect, Power, Violence," n.p.
[84] Berlant, *Cruel Optimism*, 24.
[85] Berlant, *Cruel Optimism*, 228.

266   THE BIBLE AFTER DELEUZE

have to say about hope? Nothing whatsoever, to the extent that neither the Greek verb nor noun for "hope" (*elpizō, elpis*) make an explicit appearance in it. Revelation is utterly without hope in this sense. Implicitly, however, Revelation is animated by a hope so audacious as to be all but delusional. Translated into the fraught political terms of the 2020 US presidential election, Revelation's hope is that the incumbent Beast, the one with "a mouth like a lion" (Rev 13:2), would be thoroughly defeated—and defeated, what is more, not just by another white, cisgender, heterosexual male, but by a brown-skinned challenger (with skin "like burnished bronze [*homoioi chalkolibanō*]"—1:15)[86] who is also a trans man (dressed "with a golden sash across his [female] breasts [*pros tois mastois*]"—1:13),[87] and whose answer to the stock grade-school question, "What animal would you most like to be?" would not be the answer favored by cisgender boys, "I'd like to be a *lion!*" but the altogether queerer answer, "I'd like to be a *lamb!*" (thinking to behold yet another would-be lion in the heavenly throne room, the author of Revelation is surprised, perhaps even shocked, to see a lamb instead—5:5–6). "It is better to live one day as a lion than one hundred years as a sheep," is the Beast's scornful response.[88]

Donald Trump losing the presidency to a trans man of color (even if any such person were running)? Impossible? Undoubtedly. Apocalyptic hope, however, does not trade in the possible but in the virtual. "The possible is opposed to the real," writes Deleuze. "By contrast, the virtual is not . . . ; it possesses a full reality by itself" (*Difference and Repetition*, 211).[89] The reality of the virtual is particularly evident in the work of art, including the literary work, which, of course, is what Revelation is. Appropriating Deleuze and Guattari's reflections on art, we might say that Revelation "incorporates" virtuality and thereby creates "a universe" for it in which it may possess "a life" (*What Is Philosophy?*, 177). More precisely, Revelation creates "a bloc

[86] And hair like "wool" (*erion*). These anatomical details in Revelation's head-to-toe description of the risen Jesus (1:12–16) have long been of interest to people of African descent, as we noted earlier (p. 223).

[87] These queer breasts featured unapologetically in the Latin Vulgate and early English translations of the Greek New Testament (Wycliffe, Tyndale, Douay-Rheims, Bishops' Bible, Authorized Version), but were quietly heteronormalized as a manly chest in twentieth-century English translations. See further Jesse Rainbow, "Male *mastoi* in Revelation 1.13," *Journal for the Study of the New Testament* 30 (2007): 249–53; Stephen D. Moore, *Untold Tales from the Book of Revelation: Sex and Gender, Empire and Ecology*, Resources for Biblical Study 79 (Atlanta: Scholars Press, 2014), 149–53.

[88] Unacknowledged Mussolini quotation in Donald J. Trump, Twitter post, February 28, 2016: http://twitter.com/realDonaldTrump.

[89] For the full elaboration of this notion, see Deleuze, *Difference and Repetition*, 208–14, and for a differently formulated version, see his *Bergsonism*, 94–103.

POLITICS (BEASTLY BOASTS, APOCALYPTIC AFFECTS)   267

of sensations" (167, 176), a fluid, ever-mobile body of affects, which actualize themselves in communities of readers and liturgical audiences. More specifically still, Revelation "confides to the ear of the future the persistent sensations that embody . . . constantly renewed suffering" (see Rev 2:10, 13; 6:9; 7:14; 13:15; 17:6; 18:24; 20:4) and summon forth ever-reiterated "protestations"

"How long, O Lord . . . ?" (Rev 6:10).

and ever-resumed "struggle" (176–77).

All of which is to say that apocalyptic hope is less an attainable hope, plausibly possible, umbilically linked to the question "Can it happen?" than a virtual hope, umbilically linked (and at times um-biblically linked) to the question "Can it be imagined?" and operating through affects to produce effects that are experienced as real. One generation's unimaginable, moreover ("A black man as US president? Right. Why not give him an African name for good measure?"), becomes a subsequent generation's actuality,

"It is our ignorance of the virtual that makes us believe in . . . negation"
(Deleuze, *Desert Islands*, 43).

hope holding the virtual door open in the face of patent impossibility.

But there is also another side to hope in Revelation, a side altogether less buoyant, weighed down by something more akin to hopelessness. And it is this obverse of Revelation's double-sided version of hope that connects our multisocketed machine-book once again with the COVID-19 pandemic. Leading ecocritic of Revelation, Barbara R. Rossing, reports in the preface to the paperback edition of her academic bestseller *The Rapture Exposed*—whose subtitle, not coincidentally, is *The Message of Hope in the Book of Revelation*—that on the day the original edition was released she was asked on *ABC World News Tonight* "to say in seven seconds why [she] consider[s] *Left Behind* theology so dangerous," to which she replied, "God is coming to heal the world, not to kill millions of people."[90] This is Rossing's antidispensationalist counterreading of Revelation, her construal of its

---

[90] Barbara R. Rossing, *The Rapture Exposed: The Message of Hope in the Book of Revelation*, 2nd ed. (New York: Basic Books, 2007), vii, referring to Tim LaHaye and Jerry B. Jenkins, *Left Behind: A Novel of the Earth's Last Days* (Wheaton, IL: Tyndale House, 1995).

268 THE BIBLE AFTER DELEUZE

"message of hope." Arguably, however, Revelation's message of hope is more incoherent than Rossing recognizes or acknowledges, better expressed as two disjointed statements rather than one unified statement: *God is coming to heal the world. God is coming to kill millions of people.* For millions of nameless people do die in Revelation due to the relentless succession of shock-and-awe strikes originating in the heavenly throne room become war room, and unleashed against the earth and its inhabitants (e.g., 6:3–4, 7–8; 9:13–19; 14:20; 19:11–21; 20:7–9).[91]

These two disjointed statements, wheeling around each other in mid-heaven (cf. Rev 19:17)

"A *rotative thought,* in which a group of images turn ever more quickly
around a mysterious point . . ." (Deleuze, *Essays Critical and Clinical,* 48).

and failing to conjugate, might be said to constitute a message of horrible hope appropriately fitted to our time of plague. For hope, even when it survives, is a shrunken emotion in such a time. Hope in a time of plague is itself infected by horror, not least the horror, the hideousness, of systemic racism, as we noted earlier, Americans of color, most of all Black Americans, dying from COVID-19 at rates disproportionate to white Americans.

On this day of March 30, 2020, day 1,532 of the Beast's reign, horrible hope, its racial underbelly decorously concealed, has incarnated itself in the benign person of Dr. Deborah Birx, become "America's doctor" by now, together with Anthony Fauci, due to their highly visible roles on the White House Coronavirus Task Force. Positively beaming with earnestness, Dr. Birx has announced to the nation, "If we do things together well, almost perfectly, we could get in the range of a hundred thousand to two hundred thousand fatalities."[92] This is hopeless

---

[91] Rossing argues that the disasters are directed, not at the earth, but rather at the Romans who exploit the earth; see Rev 11:18, together with her "Alas for Earth! Lament and Resistance in Revelation 12," in *The Earth Story in the New Testament,* ed. Norman C. Habel and Vicki Balabanski (Cleveland: Pilgrim Press, 2002), 180–92, and her "For the Healing of the World: Reading Revelation Ecologically," in *From Every People and Nation: The Book of Revelation in Intercultural Perspective,* ed. David Rhoads (Minneapolis: Fortress Press, 2005), 170, 172–75. She does not, however, adequately address the problem of collateral damage—loss of life, both human and nonhuman—which, like so much else in Revelation, is colossal in scale.

[92] *Post-Beast footnote*: The United States passed the 100,000 mark on May 27, 2020, less than two months after Dr. Birx's prediction. On June 11, 2021, as I write this footnote, the recorded U.S. death toll stands at 598,744. The death rate in the United States has slowed dramatically in recent months due to the Biden administration's aggressive vaccination initiative. Worldwide, however, more people have already died of COVID-19 in 2021 than in all of 2020, which is to say that the racial

POLITICS (BEASTLY BOASTS, APOCALYPTIC AFFECTS)   269

hope.[93] This is hope in a time of apocalypse, and it is consonant with hope in *the* Apocalypse. For Revelation is not entirely without hope, as we have seen, but its hoped-for surcease from suffering lies on the other side of mass death on such a scale as to render that hope utterly horrible—so horrible as to silence altogether, seemingly, any utterance of the word "hope" in the book.

Reign of the Beast, Day 1,571 / Plague Journal, May 8, 2020

"Death, death, this is the only judgment" (Deleuze, *Essays Critical and Clinical*, 51). In the midst of the pandemic and its daily spectacle of mass death, the Beast has now stood up and boasted that it had stood in the breach on the day of judgment and beat back the worst of the plague, not permitting it to vent the full measure of its wrath

> "... seven angels with seven plagues, which are the last, for with them the wrath of God is ended" (Rev 15:1).

upon the American people. "In every way the best economy in the history of the world," the Beast began its monologue yet again. But the Beast had shut down the eschatological economy, because if it hadn't been willing to sacrifice what it most loved, "we would have lost two million, two and a half million, maybe more than that, people," whereas now the losses amounted only to "two Yankee Stadiums of people" (blue-state stadiums packed with people who likely were not there to cheer for the Beast, anyway).[94]

Earlier the Beast claimed to have saved the entire nation, if not the entire planet, from nuclear annihilation, declaring with reference to North

---

inequity-revealing elements and necropolitical ramifications of the pandemic are becoming ever more apparent globally.

[93] It does not fit easily into the taxonomy of hope with which Ben Anderson's pre-COVID-19 book, *Encountering Affect: Capacities, Apparatuses, Conditions* (Farnham, UK: Ashgate, 2014), begins (1–5). For Anderson, hope as affect may be "an *object-target*," as "in the example of consumer confidence"; it may be "a *bodily capacity*," as in the case of a rescue of trapped miners; and it may be "a *collective condition*" as it was "at Obama's inauguration" (although we might equally say, as it is at a Trump rally). Dr. Birx's prediction seems in its data-and-model-driven aspect to participate in the first kind of hope; in its visceral life-or-death aspect to participate in the second kind; and in its "we're all in this together" aspect to participate in the third kind—while also eluding or exceeding all three categories.

[94] *Fox & Friends* interview with President Trump, May 8, 2020: https://factba.se/transcript/donald-trump-interview-fox-and-friends-may-8-2020.

270 THE BIBLE AFTER DELEUZE

Korea: "Look, if I wasn't elected, you would right now—maybe the world—would be over."[95] The Beast, then, is what holds the apocalypse at bay. Yet the Beast is also what is precipitating the apocalypse, at least in the United States, the apocalypse of democracy, its incremental self-dismemberment, its slow-motion fall back into the despotic, and chaotic, abyss.

For what, after all, is the Beast? What would we actually behold if, like John of Revelation, we were empowered to ascend, if not to the heavenly throne room (4:1–2), then at least to the Oval Office, to hover outside its bulletproof windows and observe its current occupant, long after his courtiers have been dismissed for the evening, typing furiously into his cell phone? Deleuze and Guattari said it best many decades ago: "A huge, pudgy, bloated boy working one of his little desiring-machines, after having hooked it up to a vast technical social machine—which . . . is what even the very young child does" (*Anti-Oedipus*, 7).

Post-Beast Postscript

Post-Beast postscript? That, at any rate, is what I had optimistically imagined, prior to the 2020 US presidential election, that this postelection afterword would be titled. Either the Beast would have triumphed or the Beast would have been defeated. I naively failed to fathom the fact that *the fact*, as formerly understood (*Did he win? Did he lose?*), had undergone transformation, even mutation, during the Beast's reign,

> "The angel said to me, 'Why are you so amazed?'" (Rev 17:7).

the Beast daily feeding the pre-Beastly (already changing but still familiar) concept of factuality into its monstrous media machine, from which the fact emerged, altogether retooled, as—what? Several singular things, as we shall see.

But first a scene-setting counterfact. At the time of writing, more than seven months after the election, a significant majority of the Republican electorate still believes that the Beast won the contest and is thus the true US

---

[95] Daniel Smith, "Briefing or Rally? Trump Shifts to Campaign Mode as He Rails against the Media," *The Guardian*, April 18, 2020: https://www.theguardian.com/us-news/2020/apr/18/donald-trump-press-briefing-rally-campaign-media.

POLITICS (BEASTLY BOASTS, APOCALYPTIC AFFECTS)   271

president; and all but a small handful of Republican lawmakers either act like they also believe that fraught counterfact

> **"These are united in yielding their power and authority to the Beast" (Rev 17:13).**

or do actually believe it.

An Incompossible Victory

Donald J. Trump *lost* the 2020 US presidential election, "but his opposite," a Donald J. Trump who *won* that same election, "is neither impossible nor inherently contradictory" (Deleuze, *The Fold*, 59).[96] Between the two worlds—the world in which Trump lost, on the one hand, and the world in which he won, on the other—"there exists a relation other than one of contradiction" (59). A reelected Trump is not an *impossibility*, in other words, but only an *incompossibility* (a concept we already circled, probed, and prodded in a previous chapter).[97] "Compossible means 'being possible with,'" specifically, "with the world that exists." Donald J. Trump *could* have been reelected, actually *was* reelected—"yes, provided that there was another world." This two-term President Trump "belongs to another world," one that "is incompossible with the existing world" (Deleuze, "Leibniz," Lecture 1, n.p.). Such incompossibility marks a "divergence in the series," an inability to "belong to the same world" ("Leibniz," Lecture 2, n.p.). Or does it?

Leibniz, whom Deleuze has been encapsulating, and whom he dubs "the first theoretician of alogical incompatibilities" (*The Logic of Sense*, 171), would not think that Trump the Winner and Trump the Loser could coexist in the same world. Neither would the anti-Trump and anti-Trumpism US political establishment, channeled and amplified by the liberal and progressive media: for them, the Trumpist claim that Biden did not actually win the election is an alogical incompatibility, or, as they prefer to say, *the Big Lie*—a term originally coined by Adolf Hitler, as it happens,[98] and which has now been

---

[96] Converting Deleuze's statements on Leibniz's Adam into statements on Trump. Much conversion of this kind takes place in the following pages.

[97] See pp. 170–171.

[98] In one of *Mein Kampf*'s many anti-Semitic diatribes: "But it remained for the Jews, with their unqualified capacity for falsehood, and their fighting comrades, the Marxists, to impute responsibility for [Germany's defeat in World War I] to the man who alone had shown a superhuman will and

272 THE BIBLE AFTER DELEUZE

seized by the Beast itself—"The Fraudulent Presidential Election of 2020 will be, from this day forth, known as THE BIG LIE!"[99]—the term passing from Hitler's raised, *Sieg-Heiling* hand to the Beast's outstretched claw through the Beast's critics.

For critics of the Beast, then, its claim that it was the true winner of the 2020 presidential election is the Big Lie. For the Beast itself, contrariwise, the claim that its opponent won the election is the Big Lie. How can two immensely consequential but wholly incompossible Big Lies possibly coexist in the real world, even the world of realpolitik? Because the Beast does not employ a rationalist, Leibnizian calculus of possibility and reality; rather, the Beast deploys an affective, Deleuzian calculus

"Gilles Deleuze looks extremely nauseated."[100]

of virtuality and actuality.

It's all devastatingly simple, really. Virtually, the Beast was the victor in the 2020 presidential election. The Beast and its followers have collectively coopted that raw, roiling virtuality. They have created a jagged bifurcation, an unseemly divergence, in the previously orderly, serial US presidential succession. For Leibniz (a near-contemporary of the framers of the US Constitution) and the rationalist mindset he emblematizes, "bifurcations and divergences of series are genuine borders between incompossible worlds" (Deleuze, *The Fold*, 81). For Deleuze, in contrast, as for many of the thinkers he most admires (some of them philosophers, others literary artists), "bifurcations, divergences, incompossibilities . . . belong to the same motley world" (81). With the "unfurling of divergent series in the same world, comes the irruption of incompossibilities on the same stage, where Sextus will rape *and* not rape Lucretia, where Caesar crosses *and* does not

energy," General Erich Ludendorff, himself a virulent anti-Semite. Hitler continues (and in a vein that eerily, if crudely, anticipates the affective force of the Trumpist Big Lie): "All of this was inspired by the principle—which is quite true within itself—that in the Big Lie [*in der Größe der Lüge*] there is always a certain force of credibility; because the broad masses of a nation are always more easily corrupted in the deeper strata of their emotional nature than consciously or voluntarily; and thus in the primitive simplicity of their minds they more readily fall victims to the big lie than the small lie." Adolf Hitler, *Mein Kampf*, trans. James Murphy (London: Hurst and Blackett, 1939), vol. 1, 134.

[99] A statement posted on May 3, 2021, by Trump's Save America PAC: https://www.donaldjtrump.com/news/statement-by-donald-j-trump-45th-president-of-the-united-states-of-america-05.03.21.

[100] Transcriber's interjection in Deleuze, "Spinoza's Concept of *Affect*," n.p. Deleuze is discoursing on people in power "who can only construct their power [*pouvoir*] on the sadness of others," who "can only reign over slaves."

POLITICS (BEASTLY BOASTS, APOCALYPTIC AFFECTS)   273

cross the Rubicon" (82). And where Donald J. Trump loses *and* wins the 2020 presidential election.

Posttruth Trumpist politics have amounted, among other things, to a forceful demonstration "that incompossibles belong to the same world, that incompossible worlds belong to the same universe" (Deleuze, *Cinema 2*, 131). "The form of the true," which, in the political sphere in particular, has repeatedly had to be hauled out of the mud, washed clean, and sequestered once again "in the eternal or in what imitates the eternal," has been displaced by "the power of the false [*la puissance du faux*]" (130–31), a mud-creature

"And I saw a Beast rising out of the sea" (Rev 13:1).

whose capacity for innovation and production/fabrication far exceeds that of truth. "It is a power of the false which replaces and supersedes the form of the true, because it poses the simultaneity of incompossible presents"—*Joseph R. Biden Jr. is the forty-sixth president of the United States; Donald J. Trump is the forty-sixth president of the United States*—"or the coexistence of not-necessarily true pasts"— *Biden defeated Trump; Trump defeated Biden; Biden only appeared to win; Trump only seemed to lose (Cinema 2, 131).*[101] But why is the Trumpist calculus of virtuality and actuality also an *affective* one, as I affirmed earlier?

An Affective Counterfact

A year before the election, and not with reference to the election, Brian Massumi perfectly named what the election aftermath has been. Massumi remarked, "It is often said that we are in a post-fact world. I think that where we are in is the realm of the affective fact."[102] The realm of the affective fact,

---

[101] Deleuze himself, not having a Beast to wrestle with, leans positively into the power of the false, placing it under a Nietzschean banner: "It is Nietzsche, who, under the name of 'will to power,' substitutes the power of the false for the form of the true, and resolves the crisis of truth . . . in favour of the false and its artistic, creative power" (*Cinema 2*, 131).

[102] Brian Massumi with Jacob Ferrington, Alina Hechler, and Jannell Parsons, "Affect and Immediation: An Interview with Brian Massumi," *disClosure: A Journal of Social Theory* 28 (2019): https://doi.org/10.13023/disclosure.28.09. Massumi's affective fact concept long predates this interview. It can be traced at least as far back as a 2005 conference paper Massumi wrote, which morphed into "The Future Birth of the Affective Fact: The Political Ontology of Threat," his contribution to *The Affect Theory Reader*, (ed. Melissa Gregg and Gregory J. Seigworth [Durham, NC: Duke University Press, 2010], 52–70), which migrated into his *Ontopower: War, Powers, and the State of Perception* (Durham, NC: Duke University Press, 2015), becoming its final chapter (189–205). I can't help feeling, however, that the affective fact concept has been circling restlessly all this time in search

274   THE BIBLE AFTER DELEUZE

one might add, has consummately been the realm of the Beast. And nowhere has this been *felt* more than in the wake of the election. Massumi continues, "An affective fact is the felt imperative of an event that did not take place, except through the feeling of the *potential* that it *might* [have taken place]."[103] Once felt, an affective fact cannot be unfelt. When an affective fact does not have recourse to the indicative mood and the declarative statement (*The election was stolen from Trump; he actually won it*), it has recourse to the conditional mood and the modal verbs *might* or *could*. Again and again during the (still-unfolding) postelection saga, Trump voters asked by roving reporters whether they believed, even in the absence of hard evidence, that widespread election fraud occurred, have doggedly replied, "It *might* have" or "It *could* have."

The affective fact of a second Trump triumph never left the domain of virtuality, never crossed the threshold of actuality. But it did not need to in order to be fully felt, in order to feel utterly persuasive, far more compelling than matter-of-fact fact. Deleuze again: "The virtual is not opposed to the real; it possesses a full reality by itself" (*Difference and Repetition*, 211). And the affective is intimately enfolded in the virtual's seductive embrace (*Cinema 2*, 83).

The affective fact has matter-of-fact effects. At the time of writing, Republican lawmakers have introduced 389 bills in forty-eight US states designed to restrict voting rights—specifically, the voting rights of the communities of color that were instrumental in pushing Biden over the finish line, the Beast snarling at his heels. Officially, this wall of legislation, engineered by the technicians of the white faciality machine, is designed to "restore confidence" in an electoral system that, in the matter-of-fact sphere, enabled a secure, fair election, but, in the affective-fact sphere, spawned a corrupt, fraudulent election. Massumi's preelection question assumes unprecedented relevance in the postelection context: "How could the nonexistence of what has not happened

"The Beast that you saw was, and is not" (Rev 17:8).

of the optimal political phenomenon to swoop in on and bury its incisive analytic teeth in, and that phenomenon has turned out to be the Big Lie controversy.

[103] Massumi, "Affect and Immediation," n.p.

POLITICS (BEASTLY BOASTS, APOCALYPTIC AFFECTS)   275

be *more* real than what is now observably over and done with?"[104] How, indeed, but through the virtual, reality-generating power of the affective counterfact.

The Order-Word Become Flesh

Let's back up. In the realm of matter-of-fact fact, the dull but "decent" candidate defeated the seldom dull, indefatigably indecent candidate. In the realm of affective fact, meanwhile, that defeat was a mirage, a sham, a fraud. The Beast itself had preemptively, and repeatedly, declared its defeat an impossibility during the long run-up to the day of battle: "The only way we're going to lose this election is if the election is rigged." The Beast reiterated the message on the night of the battle: "This is a fraud on the American public.... We did win this election."[105] And during the protracted aftermath of the battle, the reality-conjuring words rose in unison from the throats of Beast-followers throughout the land (*won ... rigged ... fraud ... stolen*), a mass-incantation mingling with the Beast's own outraged conjuration of its stolen victory.

The anti-Beast political establishment, meanwhile, together with the Beast-critical media, tirelessly insisted that the "We won, stop the steal!" incantation was "the Big Lie." It could only be that in matter-of-fact land. But in affective-fact land, the incantation was the faithful's proclamation of covered-up Truth, of veiled Truth, which is to say of *apocalyptic* Truth, apocalypse being, both etymologically and theologically, an unveiling, an uncovering

> "Jesus Christ's uncovering [*Apokalypsis Iēsou Christou*], which God
> granted him to display to his slaves" (Rev 1:1).

of what has been concealed. Within the neo-apocalyptic realm of election conspiracy theory, the Beast is fully and finally itself in a way it could never be in the White House. Its throne, its reign, is now solely virtual,

---

[104] Massumi, *Ontopower*, 189.
[105] And so on at considerable length: "Donald Trump 2020 Election Night Speech Transcript," November 4, 2020: https://www.rev.com/blog/transcripts/donald-trump-2020-election-night-spe ech-transcript.

276 THE BIBLE AFTER DELEUZE

> "It operates in a virtuality that is already real without yet being actual (the diabolical powers of the future that for the moment are only brushing up against the door)" (Deleuze and Guattari, *Kafka*, 48).

which is to say, altogether affective. But that does not mean that the Beast is now no longer effective.

For the magical incantation was also an *order-word* in the Deleuzoguattarian sense of the term, and not only the "Stop the steal!" part of it but the "We won!" part as well. "Order-words [*mots d'ordre*] do not concern commands only," Deleuze and Guattari remind us (*A Thousand Plateaus*, 79). Every verbal production of whatever kind is replete with implicit presuppositions, unspoken expectations, that connect, whether directly or circuitously, to social obligations. "Questions, promises, are order-words" (79). So are declarations of election victories; they too effect "incorporeal transformations" (80–81), as do all order-words. A US senator is transformed into a US president-elect, say. Or a first-term president is transformed into a second-term president-elect—less by a single speech act, however, than by what Deleuze and Guattari call a "mass media act" (81).

Incorporeal transformations can occur only within collective assemblages of enunciation: statements, expressions, sign regimes, semiotic machines (*A Thousand Plateaus*, 83, 88). Outside of the authorizing assemblage, anyone can, say (to modify Deleuze and Guattari's own example), shout in the street, "I am the president of the United States!" but their announcement will be heard only as "an act of puerility or insanity" (82). As we may recall, collective assemblages of enunciation are themselves inextricably interconnected with "machinic assemblages of bodies, of actions and passions, an intermingling of bodies reacting to one another" (88)[106]—such as on the afternoon of January 6, 2021, for example, when the ragtag army of the dethroned Beast, summoned by it

> "Then I saw the Beast and [its army] gathered to make war" (Rev 19:19).

and sent forth to do battle, invaded and overran the Capitol, seat of the US Congress in Washington, DC,

> "They marched up ... and surrounded the camp of the saints" (Rev 20:9).

---

[106] See pp. 132 and 200–201 earlier.

POLITICS (BEASTLY BOASTS, APOCALYPTIC AFFECTS)   277

and clashed with its sorely outnumbered security personnel in a melee of intermingling bodies, of sacrilegious actions and violent passions, all interspersed with fervent, furious, incorporeally transformative statements declaring that their leader, the one who had sent them into battle, was the second-term president-elect of the United States, a hidden apocalyptic reality imminently about to be unveiled.

The banners carried by the insurgents on that day included the white Trumpnationalist standard, "JESUS IS MY SAVIOR. TRUMP IS MY PRESIDENT."[107] Trump is no longer president in matter-of-fact land, only in affective-fact land, which has had the effect of causing the Jesus-Trump parallel proclaimed in the slogan to become a parity. Trump's two-term presidential status is no less dependent on faith, on feeling, on affective facticity than Jesus' savior status.

(Horrified, the Lamb finds itself pressed up against the Beast in the midst of the rioting Capitol mob, the Beast's fourteen baleful eyes glaring menacingly into the Lamb's seven vulnerable eyes.)

The Trump-Jesus affective symbiosis was proleptically displayed on an electronic highway billboard

". . . make an image for the Beast" (Rev 13:14).

activated on Interstate 170 near St. Louis, Missouri, on November 1, 2018. The billboard featured an image of Trump in full rally mode, right hand upraised as if in blessing. The top right-hand corner of the billboard displayed an American flag superimposed upon a cross, with the legend "Make the Gospel Great Again." Beneath Trump's image, in outsized letters, white on red, were the words, " 'The Word Became Flesh . . .'—John 1:14."

But it was really the Order-Word that became flesh in the presidency of Donald J. Trump. Or even the Law-and-Order-Word. And the iconic enactment of that enfleshment entailed another Beast-Bible coupling, the most memorable of its reign.

On June 1, 2020, exactly one week after white police officer Derek Chauvin's public execution by slow suffocation of African American petty

---

[107] A common Trumpist slogan that has been underremarked, even in the Trump-critical media. At the time of writing, the slogan is apparently still available not only on banners and flags but also on lawn signs, bumper stickers, caps, T-shirts, tank tops, sweatshirts, hoodies, spandex leggings, mugs, spiral notebooks, and pens. Also available since Biden took up residence in the White House: "Jesus is my Savior. Trump is *still* my President."

278   THE BIBLE AFTER DELEUZE

crime suspect George Floyd had precipitated an unprecedented wave of (mostly peaceful) demonstrations across the United States and around the world, the Beast delivered a singular speech in the White House Rose Garden. The speech implicitly addressed the question, what Matters more than Black Lives being casually snuffed out

"Their dead bodies will lie in the street" (Rev 11:8).

by white racist police officers? And the answer the speech explicitly gave to its unarticulated driving question was: *Law and Order*. Indeed, the address, delivered by a speaker declaring himself to be "your President of Law and Order,"[108] amounted to a veritable ode to Law and Order: "One Law and Order and that is what it is. One Law, we have one beautiful Law."[109]

But the Beast's incorporeal self-transformation into the President of Law and Order required a theatrical second act. On completing its speech, the Beast set off at a brisk pace, headed for St. John's Episcopal Church in Lafayette Square, a five-minute walk from the White House. The Beast was flanked by a phalanx of Secret Service agents, and its entourage also consisted of seventeen senior administration officials and advisers, including the secretary of defense, the chairman of the Joint Chiefs of Staff, and the attorney general. Approximately fifteen minutes before the Beast began its Rose Garden speech, hundreds of police officers in riot gear, including a mounted contingent, had descended on a large crowd in Lafayette Square and surrounding streets peacefully protesting police brutality. As the Beast began its address ("My fellow Americans, my first and highest duty as president is to defend our great country and the American people . . ."), CS gas, pepper ball rounds, stinger ball grenades, white smoke grenades, and batons were being used to clear a path to the church for the Beast's postspeech performance.

On arriving at the church, the Beast did not enter it nor did it deliver any formal remarks. The Beast was handed a Bible,[110] which it held aloft,

---

[108] On the 2015–16 campaign trail, Trump had styled himself "the candidate of Law and Order."
[109] "Donald Trump Speech Transcript, June 1": https://www.rev.com/blog/transcripts/donald-trump-speech-transcript-june-1-trump-may-deploy-us-military-to-cities. (The capitals are my own addition to the transcript, but they were implicit in the oration.)
[110] By daughter Ivanka Trump, who, as senior adviser to the president, was a member of the official entourage, and had borne the Bible to the church in a $1,540 Max Mara handbag. What emerged from the designer handbag, however, was likely not the senior adviser's own Bible. It was an altogether generic Bible, dark-covered, featureless, old and tired-looking, as though it had led a life of neglect in a drawer or on the bottom shelf of some seldom-visited bookcase. The Beast glanced quizzically at the Bible's spine (*Holy Bible: Revised Standard Version* . . . Hmm) before displaying it briefly in front of its belly and then hoisting it in the air.

POLITICS (BEASTLY BOASTS, APOCALYPTIC AFFECTS)   279

unopened. The Beast scowled, the camera shutters clicked. Arguably, it amounted to the most iconic presidential Bible-moment in US history. But what did it mean?

That might not be the right question to put to this singular piece of political street theater. Deleuze and Guattari enable us to frame it in terms other than presumed intended meanings and corollary acts of interpretation designed to lift the lid off this brazen Bible-brandisher and peer inside its mind. The Beast itself declared its distance from the object in its hand. When asked by a reporter, "Is that your Bible?" the Beast replied, "It's *a* Bible." The Beast did not need to be in a personal relationship with the Book in order for the Book to do what it was doing. The Beast did not need to know what the Book says, much less where it says it. The Beast did not even need to believe what the Book says. What, then, was the Book doing through its Beast?

The Book "communicates," the Book "informs,"

> **"Communication is no better a concept than information" (Deleuze and Guattari, *A Thousand Plateaus*, 78).**

but in a highly qualified sense, one that does not require that the Beast read from it or even open it. "Information is a set of imperatives, slogans, directions—order-words. When you are informed, you are told what you are supposed to believe" (Deleuze, *Two Regimes of Madness*, 320). The Beast's mute elevation of the Book was an informative act of precisely this sort.

Deleuze's next statement is even more relevant to the machinic assemblage within which the Beast's authoritarian street theater was enacted. That assemblage included, not only a Beast, a Bible, a church, and an elite company of Beast-followers (a four-star general, members of cabinet, an attorney general, other senior officials, a glamorous senior adviser), but also an inner protective circle of Secret Service agents and an outer protective circle of police in riot gear,

> **"Who but the police and armed forces that coexist with democracies can control and manage poverty . . . ? What social democracy has not given the order to fire when the poor come out of their territory or ghetto?"**
> **(Deleuze and Guattari, *What Is Philosophy?*, 107).**

helmeted, shielded, body-armored, laden down with crowd-suppressing weaponry. Deleuze continues, "Police declarations are appropriately called

280 THE BIBLE AFTER DELEUZE

communiqués. Information is communicated to us, they tell us what we are supposed to be ready to, or have to, or be held to believe. And not even believe, but pretend like we believe. We are not asked to believe but to behave as if we did" (*Two Regimes of Madness*, 320–21). The Book held aloft by a Beast ringed about by armed minions became a police communiqué of this kind. What the Book actually says, what counterstatements might ameliorate its hyperauthoritarian statements, what love-and-serve commands might cancel out its exterminate-and-subjugate commands, was irrelevant to its functioning in this particular moment. The Beast's Book became the Order-Word of God, the Law-and-Order-Word of the God of Law and Order.

But the Beast's stern, silent Bible moment was not the only political mime show of its presidency. The other notable performance of this kind finally brings us back to the pandemic. On October 5, 2020, while the nation watched, a lone masked man—tall, portly, navy blue–suited, orange-haired—ascended the exterior South Portico steps of the White House. Arriving on the balcony, the figure faced the cameras and dramatically removed his mask. It was the Beast! It stood silently—and awkwardly—on the balcony for several minutes before going inside maskless, breathing contagion on its staff. (What to do with one's hands when one is posing for photographs not with a smile but with a scowl? How to avoid looking like a surly schoolboy? The Beast fidgets with its jacket buttons. It attempts a show of dominance. Double thumbs up! Yes! Next a thirty-second faux military salute. That went well! A second salute.) Such was the Beast's triumphant return to the White House following its weekend treatment for COVID-19 at the Walter Reed National Military Medical Center. Once again, a "mortal wound had been healed" (Rev 13:3, 12).

The mask was the crucial Beast accessory in this White House assemblage tableau, just as the Bible had been the crucial accessory in the church assemblage tableau. But whereas the Bible had been pulled like a magician's rabbit out of a designer handbag and solemnly displayed, the mask had been whipped off and impatiently stuffed into a jacket pocket. In other words, whereas the Bible had been an object to be affirmed, the mask was an object to be renounced.

Yet, the mask removal, no less than the Bible elevation, sounded a resounding (if equally soundless) order-word. In and through the Beast's silent self-unmasking, its followers were being told, not so much what they were supposed to believe, as what they were supposed to do. They were being told, not so much to believe, as "to behave as if [they] did" (Deleuze, *Two Regimes*

POLITICS (BEASTLY BOASTS, APOCALYPTIC AFFECTS)   281

of Madness, 320–21). They were being told to go maskless, like their Beast and as a token of their loyalty to it, whether or not they themselves believed they were putting themselves, their loved ones, and their communities at risk by doing so. The mask was the mark of this Beast,

> "It causes all, both small and great, both rich and poor, both slave and free, to be marked" (Rev 13:16).

or, rather, the *absence* of the mask was that mark. Refusal of the mask was the mark of loyalty to the Beast, of obedience to the order-word it embodied through its own renunciation of the mask.[111]

At least 209,881 people had died of COVID-19 in the United States when the Beast theatrically ripped its mask off

> "The question was not how to elude the order-word but how to elude the death sentence it envelop[ed]" (Deleuze and Guattari, *A Thousand Plateaus*, 110).

in its self-scripted Return-of-the-Beast performance. By the time the Beast left office on January 20, 2021, that number had risen to 401,820. "Let anyone with understanding calculate the number of the Beast," Revelation urges (13:18). The number of the Beast, its true number, the real measure of its casual malevolence, is the indeterminable number of people who would not have died of the pandemic had the Beast behaved responsibly in relation to it. "I could stand in the middle of Fifth Avenue and shoot somebody, and I wouldn't lose any voters," the Beast famously boasted during its 2016 election campaign. "It's like, incredible." What if the number of people mowed down by the Beast on Fifth Avenue ran in the tens, even the hundreds, of thousands? And if it didn't lose any voters as a result but added them instead? More incredible still, but that is essentially what happened. At least 11,231,326 more people voted for the Beast in 2020 than had voted for it in 2016. That particular Beast number, not the puny 666,

---

[111] Of course, the mask admits of more than one reading in relation to Revelation. For legions of evangelical renouncers of the mask, the mask itself is the mark of the Beast. "Mask" is only one letter removed from "mark," after all, and what clearer reference to commercial mask mandates could possibly be imagined than Revelation 13:17: "No one can buy or sell who does not have the mark . . . of the Beast"? At the time of writing, tens of millions of impassioned views on this question, together with the companion question of whether the COVID-19 vaccine is instead the mark of the Beast, swirl and spiral through the internet.

282 THE BIBLE AFTER DELEUZE

> "Groups and individuals contain microfascisms just waiting to crystal-
> lize" (Deleuze and Guattari, *A Thousand Plateaus*, 9–10).

is surely the most terrifying Beast number of all.

For the Beast is not, and never was, one; rather, the Beast is, and always has been, many. Donald J. Trump is but the roaring mouthpiece

> "Its mouth was like a lion's mouth" (Rev 13:2).

of this Beastly multiplicity, its avatar, its incarnation as (Order-)Word. Does this multiplicity itself have a name? It has numerous names, but its principal name

> "... the name of the Beast or the number of its name" (Rev 13:17).

is the white faciality megamachine, the same apparatus whose ponderous bulk, tortuous machinations, and terrifying productivity

> "This is the signifying despotic face and the multiplication proper to it,
> its proliferation.... The despot or his representatives are everywhere"
> (Deleuze and Guattari, *A Thousand Plateaus*, 183).

we pondered in the previous chapter.

Worse, to be a Beast, or a Beast avatar, means that one doesn't simply slink away. No matter if you are a one-term president twice impeached (mortal wound, mortal wound . . .). To be a Beast is to refuse the shame that is rightly yours. To be a Beast is to refuse to remain in the bottomless abyss to which you have justly been returned (there to labor eternally on improving your golf swing). To be a Beast is to crawl out of the abyss instead

> "The Beast ... was and is not and is to come" (Rev 17:8).

and threaten a second run.

A Beastly second term, not just in affective-fact land but in matter-of-fact land? You will know, future reader, what did and did not come to pass and in which realm of reality. At the time of writing, in any case, the affective apocalyptic reality of Beastly virtuality burns like the bottomless abyss itself, smoke rising from it as if from "a great furnace" (Rev 9:2), the same furnace

POLITICS (BEASTLY BOASTS, APOCALYPTIC AFFECTS) 283

that powers the highly antiquated white faciality machine. On this day of June 6, 2021, online acolytes of the Beast, those who dwell in the deepest, darkest caverns of its domain, are feasting frenziedly on the tantalizing scrap of hope it has fed them—that it will be reinstated in the White House this August, an incompossible three years before the next presidential election.[112] At present, too, and not just in the subterranean conspiracy-caverns but all across the land, the Beast is the runaway frontrunner to become the Republican nominee for president, should it decide to run again in 2024. Just last night, indeed, the Beast delivered an hour-and-a-half oration, punctuated by standing ovations, at a Republican convention in North Carolina that sounded unnervingly like the inaugural stump speech of a 2024 run.

And beneath the familiar Beastly stump-shtick, suffused with lies, laced with racist remarks,[113] another voice, a colder, more calculating voice,

"The Dragon . . . had given its authority to the Beast" (Rev 13:4).

could be heard muttering to itself in a language the Beast did not know that it knew:

> The collective assemblage is always like the murmur from which I take my proper name, the constellation of voices, concordant or not, from which I draw my voice. I always depend on a molecular assemblage of enunciation that is not given in my conscious mind, any more than it depends solely on my apparent social determinations, which combine many heterogeneous regimes of signs. Speaking in tongues . . . to bring this assemblage of the unconscious to the light of day, to select the whispering voices, to gather the tribes and secret idioms from which I extract something I call my Self. *I* is an order-word. (Deleuze and Guattari, *A Thousand Plateaus*, 84)

---

[112] Polls reveal that, even above ground, almost a third of the Republican electorate shares this expectation of an imminent Beastly second coming. The myth of Trump *redivivus* is a distant eerie echo of the myth of Nero *redivivus* that scholars of Revelation have long seen lurking behind 13:3, 12, 14: the popular ancient anticipation that Nero, ostensibly dead and gone, would return to reclaim his throne and wreak revenge on his enemies. Back in the present, the Beast is about to kick off what is widely dubbed a "revenge tour"—a series of rallies aimed to unseat the pitiful handful of elected Republicans who have dared to publicly question the Beast's authority or impugn its veracity.

[113] "Donald Trump Speech Transcript at North Carolina GOP Convention Dinner, June 5 [2021]": https://www.rev.com/blog/transcripts/donald-trump-speech-transcript-at-north-carolina-gop-convention-dinner-june-5.

284 THE BIBLE AFTER DELEUZE

Did the order-word incarnate hold aloft the Book of Order-Words in his oration, just as he had in his mute minute of testimony outside St. John's Episcopal Church on June 1, 2020?[114] He did not need to. In the minds of the Beast's white, Christian followers, *the Book is with the Beast* even when not visibly clutched by the Beast. The Book and the Beast form an assemblage of power fueled by desire, the Beast's absolute desire for absolute power. All of which is to say, with Deleuze, that in its most grotesque mutations, "it is Christianity [itself] that becomes the Antichrist" (*Essays Critical and Clinical*, 38).

[114] See p. 278 earlier.

Index

For the benefit of digital users, indexed terms that span two pages (e.g., 52–53) may, on occasion, appear on only one of those pages.

Acts of Paul and Thecla, 126–27
Affect theory
  biblical-scholarly appropriations of, 34n.61
  and Body without Organs, 101
  and Brian Massumi, 35–36, 48n.86
  cultural lens of, 36n.67
  and Donald Trump, 243
  and Gilles Deleuze, 7–9, 34–37
  and Félix Guattari, 47
  origins of term, 8n.18
  See also Ahmed, Sara; Berlant, Lauren; Cvetkovich, Ann; Sedgwick, Eve Kosofsky, Tomkins, Silvan
Agamben, Giorgio, 7
Ahmed, Sara, 35–36, 47n.83
Aichele, George, 10n.23, 158n.27
Alayón, Tito Mitjans, 149n.9
Alexamenos graffito, 123–24
Anderson, Ben, 243n.14, 269n.93
Artaud, Antonin, 49n.87, 99–100, 104n.101, 107n.102
Arterbury, Andrew, 225n.110
Assemblage
  and affect, 28, 76–77, 200–1, 207n.78
  Bible as, 75–77, 81, 104–7, 109
  and Body without Organs, 98–99
  book as, 27–29, 30
  conceptual origins of, 24–25
  definition/description of, 26, 96, 200–1, 202–3
  and desire, 25, 29–30, 70, 245–46
  and desiring-machine, 25n.49
  and Donald Trump, 279–80, 283–84
  and faciality, 211, 213–14, 224–25, 228

horses in, 76–77, 239–40
  and passion narratives, 203–5
  and plane of immanence, 26–27
  and power, 70
  race and racism as fabricated within, 199–200, 201–5, 206–8, 228, 230
  and Synoptic Gospels, 130–33, 141–42, 203–5
  as translation of *agencement*, 29n.56
  See also Deleuze, Gilles; Guattari, Félix; John, Gospel of; Luke, Gospel of; Mark, Gospel of; Matthew, Gospel of; Revelation, book of
Auerbach, Erich, 125
Aune, David E., 245n.21

Badiou, Alain, 7
Barthes, Roland, 31–32, 66, 89–90, 195n.43
Beckman, Frida, 146n.2, 154n.21
Beliso-De Jesús, Aisha M., 200n.58
Bellini, Giovanni, 186–87
Bergson, Henri, 35
Berlant, Lauren, 35–36, 253, 265–66
  on Barack Obama, 264n.79
  on cruel optimism, 264, 265
  on Donald Trump, 243n.14, 247, 265n.82
  on intimate publics, 255–56
Bersani, Leo, 147n.4, 153n.20
Bhabha, Homi K., 181–82
Biden, Joseph R., Jr., 268–69n.92, 271–72, 273, 274, 277n.107
Birx, Deborah, 268–69
Black, Fiona C., 34n.61
Blount, Brian K., 223n.108

286 INDEX

Body without Organs, 24, 27, 162–63
  and affect, 38–39, 100–1
  and assemblage, 98–99, 165
  bloody, 169–70, 172, 178
  botched, 175
  conceptual origins of, 99–100
  as cosmic egg, 106, 174, 176–77
  as desire, 166–67
  and disability studies, 164n.33
  as the earth, 101, 103
  as glorious, 169–70, 178
  how to make a, 107–8, 165
  as limit of the social, 102, 163
  as nonnormative, 163
  as plane of consistency, 107, 165
  and plane of immanence, 53, 104, 165
  as quasi-divine, 104, 105–10
  as queer counteractualization, 176–77
  and representation, 100–1
  and sexuality, 166–67
  and sexual organs, 100, 179–80
  unattainability of, 107, 165, 175–76
  See also Deleuze, Gilles; Guattari,
    Félix; Jesus; Luke, Gospel of; Mark,
    Gospel of
Boer, Roland, 222n.106
Bogue, Ronald, 155n.22
Borges, Jorge Luis, 171–72
Bouguereau, William-Adolphe, 187–
  89, 206
Bousset, Wilhelm, 239
Bray, Karen, 24n.47, 34n.61, 36n.67
Breed, Brennan W., 10n.23
Brintnall, Kent L., 257n.53
Brown, Peter, 113n.9
Bryden, Mary, 239n.6
Buchanan, Ian, 24n.47
Butler, Judith, 100
  on the body, 119–20, 121
  Deleuzian critique of, 120, 146–47, 206–7
  and gender performativity, 113–15, 120
  and Michel Foucault, 119
  Kantianism of, 117, 119
  on representation, 126n.49
  representationalism of, 119n.29

Callon, Callie, 125n.48
Chen, Jun Mian, 182–83

Cicero, 164–65n.34
Clement of Alexandria, 157n.24
Clinton, Hillary, 256n.51, 261–62
Clough, Patricia Ticeneto, 8n.16
Colebrook, Claire, 158n.27
Cone, James H., 195
  on blackness of Christ, 194, 228
  on cross as lynching tree, 194, 204–5
  on lived experience of
    blackness, 194–95
Connolly, William, 243n.14
Constas, Maximos, 214
Conway, Colleen M., 114–15
Cross, D. J. S., 36n.71
Cvetkovich, Ann, 35–36, 37–38n.72

Darby, John Nelson, 239
Davis, Nick, 146n.2
Dean, Tim, 147n.4
Defoe, Daniel, 233n.2
Deleuze, Fanny (Denise Paul
  Grandjouan), 239–42
Deleuze, Gilles
  and affect, 7–9, 21–23, 34–51, 76–77,
    141, 144, 200–1, 204–5, 207n.78, 215,
    234–35, 240–41
  on animals, 74–75, 76–77, 80, 143–45,
    239–40, 256
  on the Antichrist, 284
  and Antonin Artaud, 99–100, 104n.101,
    107n.102
  on assemblages, 24–30, 70, 96, 98–99,
    101–2, 132–33, 200–1, 215, 237,
    239–40, 283
  and Baruch Spinoza, 34–51, 100
  on beatitude, 49–50
  on becoming, 13–19, 73–75, 151–52,
    216, 255, 262
  on becoming-imperceptible, 176–77n.50
  on the Bible, 2
  biblical-scholarly engagements with,
    10n.23, 24n.47, 104n.101, 158n.27,
    218n.95, 223n.107
  on the body, 37–38, 39n.75, 40, 42–43,
    50–51, 100n.96, 133, 141, 142–43
  on Body without Organs, 24, 27, 38–39,
    53, 98–102, 107–8, 163, 165, 166–67,
    169–70, 172, 174, 175

and Brian Massumi, 8, 35–37, 47–51
on capitalism, 244–45
on deconstruction, 30–32
on democracy, 254–55, 279
on desiring-machines, 24–25, 147–48, 155, 161, 270
on desire, 25, 29–30, 69–72, 147–48, 152–53, 154–55, 166–67, 245–46
on D. H. Lawrence, 240–41
on difference, 33
and Emmanuel Levinas, 211
on emotion, 50–51
on the event, 33, 88–90
on expression, 85–98, 200–1
on faciality, 181–82, 199–200, 202–3, 208–9, 210, 211–12, 211n.83, 213–15, 216–18, 219–20, 221–22, 224–25, 226, 227, 228, 229, 230, 231–32, 282
on fascism, 260, 263, 282
on flux, 33, 73–75, 240–41
on the fold, 45–46
on Friedrich Nietzsche, 273n.101
and God, 102–4
on Gottfried Wilhelm Leibniz, 170–71, 271–73
and Guy Hocquenghem, 152–54
and hermeneutics, 20–21, 73–75, 85–98
on history and historiography, 14–19, 216
on identity, 150–52, 228
on incompossibility, 170–72, 178n.52, 271, 272–73
on incorporeal transformations, 81, 83–85, 133–34, 201
on incorporeals, 81n.54, 123, 127–29, 132–33
influence of, 7–8, 9–10
on intensity, 235
on interiority, 20–21, 30
on interpretation, 12, 13, 20–21
on interpretosis, 3, 20–21
and Jacques Derrida, 5–6, 30–32
on Jerusalem temple, 222n.106
on Jesus, 20n.39, 211–12, 216–18, 221, 222
on Jorge Luis Borges, 171–72
on judgment of God, 102–3
and language, 31–33, 79, 97–98, 242

and liberation, 14–15, 18–19, 84–85, 92
on life, 109, 177
on lines of flight, 26–27, 70, 71, 102–3, 107, 178–79
on literary characters, 22–23
and literature, 19
Lobster God of, 104–10
and Louis Hjelmslev, 93–94
and Marxism, 147
as metaphysician, 1, 139
and Michel Foucault, 4–5, 15–16, 58, 59, 67–72, 119n.29, 146–47
on micropolitics, 18–19, 68, 69, 96, 153, 229
on mysticism, 44–45, 49
and the nonhuman, 7–8, 24, 25, 29–30, 40, 94n.80, 108–9, 143–45, 155, 162–63
on order-words, 79–80, 91–92, 201, 276, 279, 280–81, 283
on a people to come, 96–98, 106
as philosopher of immanence, 20, 34
on plane of consistency, 13n.25, 29
on plane of immanence, 13–14, 29, 45–46, 70, 103–4, 170, 237
and Platonism, 81n.54, 124–25
and postracial society, 220
and poststructuralism, 6, 30–34
and post-poststructuralism, 32–33, 191
on power, 39, 68–69
on power of the false, 273
on probe-heads, 220–21
and queer theory, 120, 146–55
on race and racism, 181–82, 199–200, 209n.81, 217–18, 258, 260
and representation, 7–8, 12, 46, 94, 122, 124–25, 138–40, 236–37, 239, 240–41
on resistance, 71–72
on Revelation (book of), 239–42, 256, 257, 265
on rhizome, 71, 108–9, 162
and schizoanalysis, 161n.31
on sensation, 21–22
on sense, 127–28
and sexual identity, 148, 149–53, 217, 229, 231
on sexuality, 152–53, 162, 166–67, 179–80

288 INDEX

Deleuze, Gilles (*cont.*)
  and Sigmund Freud, 147–48
  on simulacra, 124–25
  on the social, 71–72, 88
  on societies of control, 29
  and speech act theory, 84n.55
  and Stoic philosophy, 81n.54,
    84n.55, 123
  on the strata, 101–3, 107–8, 165
  and structuralism, 4–5
  on symbol, 240–42
  and transcendence, 20–21
  on theology, 1–2, 103
  and utopianism, 219–20
  and virtuality, 1n.1, 4n.3, 14, 68, 129–
    30, 158–59, 266–67, 274, 276
  on war machine, 30–31
  on zone of indistinction, 22–23, 43–44,
    74–75, 141, 172–73
  See also Guattari, Félix; Parnet, Claire
Denaux, Adelbert, 225n.110
Derrida, Jacques, 7, 11, 30–32, 58–59, 117,
    181–82n.1, 195n.43
  on Gilles Deleuze, 5–6
  Gilles Deleuze on, 30–31
  and race, 181–82n.1, 197–98
Desiring-machines, 24–25, 147–48, 155,
    161, 270
  See also Deleuze, Gilles; Guattari, Félix
Dinkler, Michal Beth, 34n.61
Disability studies
  Body without Organs and, 164n.33
  Deleuzoguattarian schizoanalysis as,
    161n.31
  and gospels, 116, 131, 160–61, 164,
    169–70, 174
Dolphijn, Rick, 229n.117
Dosse, François, 35n.64, 69n.36
Du Bois, W. E. B., 194, 195, 199
  blackness as affective fact for, 194–95
  blackness as cultural memory
    for, 192
  cave allegory of, 192–93
Dyer, Richard, 183–84, 184n.7, 186–87

Edelman, Lee, 146–47, 148, 153n.20
Emanuel, Sarah, 250n.34
Ewald, François, 70n.37

Faciality, 181–82, 199–200
  defamiliarized, 208
  defined, 202–3
  and God, 212–14
  and normativity, 209–10, 219
  and probe-heads, 219–21
  and racism, 217–18, 229
  as white wall/black hole, 209, 210–11,
    223, 228, 231
  See also Deleuze, Gilles; Guattari,
    Félix; Jesus
Fanon, Frantz, 194–95
  and dialectical race theory, 185–86,
    190, 191–92
  on Jews, 185–86, 189
  on lived experience of blackness, 185–
    86, 190, 191–92, 218
  and negritude, 185n.11, 190
  and white child on train, 205–7
Ferrari, Gloria, 112
Foucault, Michel, 99, 150n.13, 195n.43
  on the author, 60
  and biblical scholarship, 60–64, 86n.59,
    113–15, 120–21
  on the body, 112–13, 119, 120–21
  on Gilles Deleuze, 4–5
  Gilles Deleuze's critique of, 69–72
  on discourse, 58–60, 65–66, 118
  on freedom, 15
  on hermeneutics, 87–88
  and intertextuality, 65–66
  Kantianism of, 117, 118–19
  on power, 67–69
  representationalism of, 119
  on sexology, 149
  on structuralism and poststructuralism,
    5
  text theory of, 64–66
Frank, Adam, 8
Frankfurter, David, 257–58n.54
Freud, Sigmund, 148

Gates, Henry Louis, Jr., 181–82, 196
Glancy, Jennifer A., 120–22
Goodman, Martin, 205–6n.72
Gospel of Mary, 179
Graybill, Rhiannon, 24n.47
Gregg, Melissa, 7–8, 273–74n.102

Grossberg, Lawrence, 243nn.14–15
Gruen, Erich S., 205–6n.72, 231n.120
Guattari, Félix
  on affect, 46–47, 139–40, 220n.102
  on contemporary culture, 220n.102
  on desire, 155
  on Donald Trump, 245n.22
  on face of Christ, 209n.81, 219n.100
  on faciality, 209–10, 219, 225
  on gender/sexual identity, 210
  on genesis of faciality, 212n.86
  on icons, 213
  on Jesus and faciality, 219
  on Louis Hjelmslev, 93
  machine concept of, 21
  and Marxism, 21n.42, 147
  on postmodernism, 32–34n.60
  on probe-heads, 220n.102
  as queer ally and activist, 150n.13
  on racism, 211, 219
  on representation, 139–40
  schizoanalytic method of, 161n.31
  on structuralism and poststructuralism,
    32–34n.60
  on virtuality, 139–40
  See also assemblage; Body without
    Organs; Deleuze, Gilles; desiring-
    machines; faciality; incorporeal
    transformations; line of flight; order-
    words; plane of consistency; plane of
    immanence; rhizome; virtuality

Hall, Stuart, 232n.122
  autobiographical reflections on race,
    197n.49
  on race as structured like a language,
    195–96n.45, 198–99n.55, 202
Hegel, Georg Wilhelm Friedrich, 184–86, 191
  and Deleuze, 218n.95
Hickey-Moody, Anna, 146n.2
Hitler, Adolf, 271–72
Hjelmslev, Louis, 93–94
Hocquenghem, Guy
  and antisocial thesis in queer theory,
    146–47, 153–54
  Gilles Deleuze on, 153–54
  on sexual desire, 152–53
Hoke, Jimmy, 34n.61

Incorporeal transformations
  in and through biblical texts, 81–
    85, 133–38
  and Donald Trump, 278
  in judicial system, 201
  Synoptic Gospels as products of, 111n.1
  See also Deleuze, Gilles; Guattari, Félix
Irenaeus, 124n.45

Jacob, Sharon, 217n.94
James, William, 50–51
Jaquet, Chantal, 54n.100
Jenkins, Jerry B., 267n.90
Jeong, Dong Hyeon, 16n.32, 24n.47,
    162n.32
Jerome, 160n.30
Jesus
  as apotheosis of whiteness, 189, 198,
    206, 216, 217–18, 225–26
  as Black, 194, 205–6, 223, 227–
    29, 265–67
  as body of judgment, 142, 143
  as body of justice, 142–43
  as Christ Pantocrator, 212–16, 223,
    224–25, 231–32
  as Composite Christ, 142–43
  as cosmic egg, 174, 176–77
  as crucified Body without Organs, 163–
    69, 172
  as disabled, 160–61, 164, 174
  as haemosexual, 166–69
  as imperceptible, 176–77, 224, 225
  incorporeal blood of, 169
  incorporeal bodies of, 129, 136–38,
    141–42, 222
  as linchpin of white faciality machine,
    181–82, 211–12, 216–17, 219, 228
  in microhistory, 16–18
  as millisexual, 179–80
  as National Socialist, 189–90
  and the near-naked youth, 157, 179
  and the nonhuman, 130–32
  as probe-head, 223–26, 227–28, 229–32
  and problem of representation, 123–27
  queer counteractualization of, 179–80
  queer counterfamily of, 159–60, 168
  as racial assemblage, 207–8
  as risen Body without Organs, 169–80

290 INDEX

Jesus (*cont.*)
    thousand tiny races of, 229–32
    on the train with Fanon, 205–8
    as trans man, 265–67
    as trillion and tiny, 167
    as unrepresentable, 176–77
    as victim of horrific racist act, 204–6
    virtuality of, 178
    See also John, Gospel of; Luke, Gospel
        of; Mark, Gospel of; Revelation,
        book of; Paul, apostle; Romans,
        Letter to the
Joachim of Fiore, 239
John, Gospel of, 90–91, 170
    assemblages in, 203–5
    body in, 122
    Body without Organs in, 178
    face of Jesus in, 221–22
    incorporeal transformations in, 203
    Mary Magdalene in, 178–79
    microhistorical Jesus in, 16–17
    mythic author of, 90–91
    queer love triangle in, 177–78
    virtuality in, 178
    See also Jesus
John, Helen C., 84–85
Justaert, Kristien, 14n.27
Justinian I, 214, 215n.92
Justinian II, 223n.107

Kant, Immanuel, 116–19, 181, 191, 198
Keller, Catherine, 242n.13, 258n.60
Kelley, Shawn, 191
Koester, Craig R., 245n.21
Koosed, Jennifer L., 34n.61
Kotrosits, Maia, 34n.61
Krafft-Ebing, Richard von, 149–50
Kristeva, Julia, 31–32, 66, 195n.43

Lacan, Jacques, 11, 31–32, 146–47, 195nn.43–44
LaHaye, Tim, 267n.90
Lawrence, D. H., 240–41
Lawrence, Louise J., 116
Leibniz, Gottfried Wilhelm, 159n.29, 170–
    71, 271–73
Levinas, Emmanuel, 211
Leys, Ruth, 34n.62
Li, Fang, 233n.1

Line of flight, 26–27, 97, 102–3, 107–8,
    150–51, 203
    definition of, 70, 71
    of Markan Jesus, 179–80
    of Mary Magdalene, 178–79
    primacy of, 107
    and race, 230–31
    See also Deleuze, Gilles; Guattari, Félix
Lorde, Audre, 148–49, 260n.69
Luke, Gospel of, 12, 172
    assemblages in, 132, 203–5
    Body without Organs in, 175–77
    Emmaus encounter in, 176–77, 223–26
    incorporeal transformations in and
        through, 133–38, 203
    Jesus's face in, 221–22, 223–25
    Jesus's masculinity in, 115
    Jesus as probe-head in, 223–26
    Last Supper in, 136
    Mary of Nazareth in, 134–35
    and the nonhuman, 131–32
    passion narrative of, 204n.65
    and physiognomy, 125
    resurrection in, 136–38, 175–77
    See also Jesus
Luther, Martin, 94–95

Marchal, Joseph A., 257n.53
Mark, Gospel of, 12, 91
    assemblages in, 132, 163, 203–5
    becoming-child in, 163–64
    Body without Organs in, 163–80
    call of first disciples in, 159–60
    corporal vernacular of, 120–21
    death of God in, 172, 173–74
    descriptive minimalism in, 127, 221–22
    disabled Jesus in, 160–61, 164, 169–
        70, 174
    empty tomb in, 169–80
    flight of naked young man in, 173
    Gerasene demoniac in, 140–41, 156–57
    Gethsemane scene in, 158–59, 172
    God as virtuality in, 158–59, 169–70
    God's Empire in, 159, 161–65
    haemosexuality in, 168–69
    incorporeal transformations in and
        through, 133–34, 203
    Jerome on, 160n.30

INDEX   291

Last Supper in, 166–69
Mary Magdalene in, 178–79
and millisexuality, 156–57, 179–80
and the nonhuman, 130–32
Papias on, 157n.23
passion narrative of, 166–67, 172
queering, 156–80
vegetal parables of, 161–63
See also Jesus; Secret Gospel of Mark
Marshall, John W., 257–58n.54
Martin, Dale B., 114n.11
Mary Magdalene, 178–79
Mary of Nazareth, 134–35, 186–89
Massumi, Brian
    on affect/emotion distinction, 35–
        36, 47–51
    on affective facts, 273–74
    on Baruch Spinoza, 35, 47–50
    on Donald Trump, 243, 244–46, 247–
        48, 264–65
    on expression, 85–88, 89–90, 93, 96–97
    and Gilles Deleuze, 8, 35–37, 47–
        51, 150–51
    on Ronald Reagan, 248–49
    See also affect theory
Matthew, Gospel of, 12
    assemblages in, 132, 203–5, 230
    descriptive minimalism in, 126–
        27, 221–22
    imperial Jesus in, 175, 226–27, 229–30
    incorporeal transformations in and
        through, 133–34, 203, 230–31
    Jesus as probe-head in, 229–32
    mythic author of, 90–91
    and the nonhuman, 131–32
    parable of sheep and goats in, 226–32
    resurrection in, 175, 226–27
    solar Jesus in, 226
    thousand tiny races in, 229–32
    See also Jesus
McLean, Bradley H., 10n.23, 104n.101
Mesters, Carlos, 85n.57
Morgan, Carleigh, 264n.81
Muñoz, José Esteban, 158
Murphy, David J., 72–73

Nealon, Jeffrey, 20
Negri, Antonio, 16

Nietzsche, Friedrich, 39n.75, 48–49nn.86–
    87, 103n.98, 171, 273n.101
Nigianni, Chrysanthi, 120, 146n.2

Obama, Barack, 259, 264n.79, 267
O'Brien, Gerald V., 260
O'Donnell, Aislinn, 154
Ogbar, Jeffrey O. G., 223n.108
Order-words, 201
    Bible as book of, 77–81, 91–92, 105–6
    and Donald Trump, 276–81, 283–84
    See also Deleuze, Gilles; Guattari, Félix
O'Rourke, Michael, 146n.2
Ott, Brian L., 245–46

Park, Wongi, 204n.64, 231n.120
Parnet, Claire, 19, 26
    See also Deleuze, Gilles
Parsons, Mikeal C., 125n.48
Paul, apostle, 23, 65
    through a Deleuzoguattarian
        lens, 92–96
    as Foucauldian author, 61–63
    on the risen body, 137–38
    See also Romans, Letter to the
Pepys, Samuel, 233n.2
Philo of Alexandria, 225n.111
Plane of consistency, 13n.25, 104, 107
    See also Deleuze, Gilles; Guattari,
        Félix
Plane of immanence, 13–14, 29
    and assemblage, 70
    and Body without Organs, 53, 104,
        169–70, 172
    as "God-word," 103–4
    as plane of life, 237
    and Spinoza's single substance, 45–46,
        51, 53, 103–4
    See also Deleuze, Gilles; Guattari, Félix
Plato, 124–25, 192–93
Puar, Jasbir K., 146n.2, 164n.33, 200n.58,
    243n.14, 246

Queer theory, 11, 96, 112, 151–52
    anti-identitarianism of, 148
    antisocial thesis in, 146–47,
        153n.20, 156–57
    Deleuzian turn in, 120, 146–47, 155

292 INDEX

Queer theory (*cont.*)
  See also Butler, Judith; Edelman, Lee;
    Foucault, Michel; Hocquenghem,
    Guy; Muñoz, José Esteban; Sedgwick,
    Eve Kosofsky
Quenot, Michel, 212–14

Rae, Gavin, 211n.83
Rainbow, Jesse, 266n.87
Rawson, A. Paige, 24n.47
Reagan, Ronald, 248–49
Redell, Petra Carlsson, 119n.29, 217n.94
Reed, Conor Tomás, 148–49
Representation, 7–8, 12, 46, 94, 119
  and aesthetic artifacts, 139–40
  and biblical bodies, 116, 122, 123–27,
    138–40, 145
  four iron collars of, 124, 236–37
  race theorized as, 181–82, 183, 184n.7,
    191–92, 198, 201–2
  and Revelation, 236–39
  See also Deleuze, Gilles; Guattari, Félix
Revelation, book of,
  abyss in, 245, 282–83
  and affect, 234–35, 242, 251, 253, 255–
    56, 263, 265–66
  allegorical and neoallegorical
    interpretations of, 239–41, 242
  amazement in, 251
  as assemblage, 237
  assemblages in, 239–40, 256
  Babylon in, 236, 261–62
  Beast(s) of, 233, 237–39, 243–84
  blasphemy in, 247
  comedy in, 249–50
  contextual hermeneutics and, 236
  and COVID-19, 233–35, 237, 242–43,
    252–53, 255–70, 280–82
  D. H. Lawrence on, 240
  and Donald Trump, 233–35, 237–
    39, 242–84
  and Exodus (book of), 234
  False Prophet in, 250–51
  Four Horsemen of Apocalypse in, 239–
    40, 253
  Gilles Deleuze and Fanny Deleuze on,
    239–42, 256, 257, 265
  hope in, 265–69

  Jesus as Black in, 223
  Jesus's full body reveal in, 126, 222–
    23, 265–67
  Jesus as trans in, 265–66
  Jesus as white in, 222–23
  as machine, 234–35, 243, 257–
    58, 267–68
  mark of the Beast in, 252–53, 280–81
  mass-death in, 267–69
  metaforce in, 242n.13, 258
  and Mike Pence, 250–51
  mortal wound in, 248, 261, 265,
    280, 282
  New Jerusalem in, 256–57, 259–60
  nonrepresentational reading of, 236–39
  number of the Beast in, 238n.5, 281–82
  plagues in, 234, 252–53, 260–61, 269
  and pop-apocalypticism, 237–38
  purity in, 257–58
  sealed scroll in, 241–42
  and sensation, 266–67
  and virtuality, 266–67
  See also Jesus
Rhizome, 71, 108–9, 162
  See also Deleuze, Gilles; Guattari, Félix
Richardson, Michael, 255–56, 258, 263
Riordan, Gretchen, 168–69
Romans, Letter to the, 94–96
  See also Jesus; Paul, apostle
Rossing, Barbara R., 267–68
Ruffolo, David V., 146n.2

Said, Edward W., 119n.29, 181–82
Saldanha, Arun, 191, 206–7, 229, 230–32
Sanders, Bernie, 248n.31
Sartre, Jean-Paul, 185–86, 190, 191–
    92, 218
Saussure, Ferdinand de, 59, 93–94
  Kantianism of, 117–18, 198
  and race, 195–98
Schaefer, Donovan O., 243n.14
Schleiermacher, Friedrich, 86–87
Secret Gospel of Mark, 157, 179
Sedgwick, Eve Kosofsky, 8, 35–36, 120
Seigworth, Gregory J., 7–8, 36n.71,
    273–74n.102
Sherwood, Yvonne, 6–7
Shildrick, Margrit, 164n.33

INDEX 293

Smith, Morton, 157
Spinoza, Baruch, 100
  on affect, 34–51, 52–54
  on *affectio*, 40–41
  on *affectus*, 37–41, 53
  on the Bible, 51–54
  on God, 45, 52
Spivak, Gayatri Chakravorty, 181–82, 193
Stanley, Sharon A., 232n.122
Storr, Merl, 120, 146n.2
Swete, Henry Barclay, 239

Taylor, Joan E., 212n.87
Thomas, Eric A., 257n.53
Thrift, Nigel, 238n.4
Tomkins, Silvan, 8, 35–36
Trump, Donald J., 233–35, 237–39, 242–84
Tuhkanen, Mikko, 158n.27

Valerius Maximus, 164–65n.34
Van der Tuin, Iris, 229n.117
Van Gogh, Vincent, 44
Vannini, Phillip, 238n.4
Virtuality, 1n.1, 4n.3, 14
  and affect, 274
  and Body without Organs, 169–70

and divinity, 171–72
and the event, 89n.68
in Garden of Eden, 170
and incorporeality, 129–30
and Johannine Jesus, 178
and literature, 139–40
and queerness, 158, 171–72, 179
and race, 230–31
and Revelation (book of), 266–67
and Trumpism, 272–73, 274–76, 282–83
See also Deleuze, Gilles; Guattari, Félix

Walker, Rachel Loewen, 146n.2
Waller, Alexis G., 157–58n.25
Watson, Janell, 217n.94
Weheliye, Alexander G., 200n.58
West, Gerald O., 84–85
Whitlock, Matthew G., 10n.23, 104n.101
Whiteness studies, 182–84
Wilson, Brittany E., 115
Wittig, Monique, 100

Zeichmann, Christopher B., 204n.66
Žižek, Slavoj, 7